D1595529

# Why Sports Morally Matter

When we accept that advertisers and sponsors dictate athletic schedules, that success in sport is measured by revenue, that athletes' loyalty lies with their commercial agents instead of their teams and that game rules exist to be tested and broken in the pursuit of a win, what does our regard for sport say about the moral and political well-being of our society?

*Why Sports Morally Matter* is a deeply critical examination of pressing ethical issues in sports – and in society as a whole. Exploring the historical context of modern ethical America, William J. Morgan argues that the current state of sport is a powerful indictment of our wealth-riven society and hyper-individualistic way of life.

Taking on critics from all sides of the political debate, Morgan makes the case that, despite the negating effect of free market values, sports still possess important features that encourage social, moral and political values crucial to the flourishing of a democratic polity. It is this potential to transform society and the individual that makes sports a key battleground in the struggle for the moral soul of contemporary America.

*Why Sports Morally Matter* represents an important contribution to the ongoing debate about the role of sports in society. For students and researchers working in sport studies, philosophy, cultural studies, and for anyone who cares seriously about sports, this is an essential text.

**William J. Morgan** is Professor in Sport and Exercise Humanities and Cultural Studies at the Ohio State University, Columbus. He has written widely on the ethics and philosophy of sport, on social and political philosophy and on critical social theory. He is the author of *Leftist Theories of Sport* and former editor of the *Journal of the Philosophy of Sport*.

## Routledge Critical Studies in Sport

*Series editors Jennifer Hargreaves and Ian McDonald*
University of Brighton

The Routledge Critical Studies in Sport series aims to lead the way in developing the multi-disciplinary field of Sport Studies by producing books that are interrogative, interventionist and innovative. By providing theoretically sophisticated and empirically grounded texts, the series will make sense of the changes and challenges facing sport globally. The series aspires to maintain the commitment and promise of the critical paradigm by contributing to a more inclusive and less exploitative culture of sport.

# Why Sports Morally Matter

William J. Morgan

Routledge
Taylor & Francis Group

NEW YORK AND LONDON

175
M84w

First published 2006
by Routledge
270 Madison Ave, New York, NY 10016

Simultaneously published in the UK
by Routledge
2 Park Square, Milton Park, Abingdon, Oxon OX14 4RN

*Routledge is an imprint of the Taylor & Francis Group, an informa business*

© 2006 William J. Morgan

Typeset in Goudy by
HWA Text and Data Management, Tunbridge Wells
Printed and bound in Great Britain by
MPG Books Ltd, Bodmin

*Library of Congress Cataloging-in-Publication Data*
Morgan, William John, 1948–
   Why sports morally matter / William J. Morgan.
      p.   cm. –   (Routledge critical studies in sport)
   Includes bibliographical references and index.
   1. Sports–Moral and ethical aspects–United States. 2. Sports–United
States–Sociological aspects. I. Title. II. Series.
GV706.3.M67 2006
175–dc22                                                        2005036481

*British Library Cataloguing in Publication Data*
A catalogue record for this book is available from the British Library

ISBN10: 0–415–35773–X (hbk)
ISBN10: 0–415–35774–8 (pbk)
ISBN10: 0–203–00373–X (ebk)

ISBN13: 978– 0–415–35773–9 (hbk)
ISBN13: 978– 0–415–35774–6 (pbk)
ISBN13: 978– 0–203–00373–2 (ebk)

For Susan, Jennifer, and Melanie

# Contents

# Series editors' preface

It is often said that the most useful exchanges at academic conferences take place outside of the formal program of plenary speakers and PowerPoint presentations. In what is widely known as 'networking', an unfortunate term imported from the business world, it is in the informal social gatherings tucked away in the spaces around the conference venue that the most productive discussions are usually held. This was certainly the case at the North American Society for the Sociology of Sport conference in Tucson, Arizona in 2004. Not that this conference was lacking in engaging and interesting papers, but it was during discussions over lunch and coffee that we met William Morgan and came to know about a book he was writing on morality and sports. As a term, morality has tended to be claimed as the preserve of the political right and sport romantics. Morgan contests any such associations, provoking us to challenge our own complacent acceptance of dominant discourses. And as Morgan spoke passionately and persuasively about his latest project, to catalogue and analyse the decline of morality in American life which is writ large in contemporary American sports, and to insist on the importance of moral considerations in sporting matters today, it was immediately clear that this was the kind of text that needed to be included in the Routledge Critical Studies in Sport series.

*Why Sports Morally Matter* draws on philosophical discourse to offer an immanent critique of contemporary American sports. Morgan offers an innovative analysis since it raises ethical and social issues about sport in the context of a social-historical account of the Progressive movement and its heirs. As such it is not simply an argument concerning the philosophy of sport, but more importantly for us as series editors, the political philosophy of sports. Thus, *Why Sports Morally Matter* is not a nostalgic yearning for a mythical era of a moral sport, still less is it a conservative rant at the apparent decline of ethical considerations. Rather, it stands as an important contribution to criticism from the left of the corruptive effects of extending the sphere of markets too far into the sphere of (sporting) culture. However, building on his criticism of the left's disdain for the popular appeal of sport, most fully articulated in *Leftist Theories of Sport*, Morgan constructs a defense of the ethical power and richness of sport as a social practice. Unlike many leftist commentators, Morgan is not dismissive of the social obsession with sport, indeed he comments that "there is no reason to bemoan Americans' enthusiasm for sports especially at their best, since such enthusiasm is not only fully justified but a possible harbinger of good things to come". In the best tradition of social criticism, *Why Sports Morally Matter* outlines the redemptive power of contemporary sports.

Whether one agrees or disagrees with Morgan's analysis and prognosis is a matter of great consequence for the critical sociology of sport irrespective of which country the reader comes from. While focused on American sports, Morgan's thesis transcends its geographical specificity. *Why Sports Morally Matter* poses key questions for our time and reflects the rationale of the Routledge Critical Studies of Sport series. The guiding philosophy for the series can be summarized as:

- Interrogative: challenging common sense ideas and exposing relations of power in the world of sport.
- Interventionist: highlighting the relationship between theory and practice and providing arguments and analyses of topical and polemical issues
- Innovative: seeking to develop new areas of research, and stimulating new ways of thinking about and studying sport.

A key aspect of the series is to make sense of the changes and controversial developments that are transforming the ways in which sport is experienced and understood. Many of the old ideas about sport embracing 'noble' and 'educational' values, offering disadvantaged peoples 'a way out', bringing nations closer together, or creating healthy bodies seem increasingly to lack credibility. In particular, there are widespread concerns that economic and political forces are becoming too influential and are distorting the role and place of sport in societies across the world. William Morgan, one of the most highly respected authors in the field of sports philosophy, directly addresses all of these issues. *Why Sports Morally Matter* is a compelling polemic that demands to be read and accounted for by anyone seriously interested in the problems and potential of modern sport.

Jennifer Hargreaves and Ian McDonald
(University of Brighton)

# Preface

In his path-breaking book *After Virtue* (1984), Alaisdair MacIntyre famously claimed that every moral theory and scheme of moral beliefs presupposes a sociology. Many of his contemporary moral theorists took issue with his claim, insisting instead that our deepest moral problems arise independently of our social circumstances rather than sensibly extending his claim to read that every morality presupposes not only a sociology but a history and psychology as well. Their objection is a testament to their own obtuseness rather than an indictment of MacIntyre's claim. For it seems as plain as day that both our moral difficulties and their possible resolution are intimately bound up with our social and historical circumstances, with the kinds of lives they render possible and incline us to live. Fortunately, there are encouraging signs of late that contemporary moral theorists are finally – if slowly – coming around to accept such a socially and historically embedded view of the moral life.

However, the more important point I seek to press here, a point I feature as the central argument of my book, is that the present sociology that informs morality in contemporary America imperils the moral life, indeed, makes it difficult for people even to think in moral terms. And I argue that this story of the decline of moral life is writ large in contemporary American sports. Sports in this case, I argue further, are no mere reflection of larger society's growing indifference to moral considerations but, in part because of their prominent standing in contemporary society, both a conspicuous exemplification of such moral callousness and an important sign of things to come. As such, the attack on the moral life waged within their precincts is a high-stakes one that we can ill afford to ignore – if only because the stories that we Americans tell about ourselves would lose much of their resonance, their capacity to unite and move us, if moral considerations no longer figured in them.

The impetus to write this book came in part from students enrolled in my sport ethics classes during the last few years, in particular from a noticeable coarsening of their attitude regarding moral considerations of sports. At first, I found their resistance to moral treatments of sports merely curious, but I soon came to regard it as deeply troubling. In particular, what grabbed my attention was their almost visceral rejection of any claim that one should adhere at least to some subset of rules when participating in sports because of considerations of fair play or of basic human decency owed to others. This recalcitrance to accord one's peers in sports practically any moral standing was especially worrying to me: my ethics class, as I was acutely aware, was the only class that most of them would take in their undergraduate programs and would touch on these matters, and because it wasn't so very long ago that many of my students found these very same claims persuasive, not just intellectually persuasive but practically persuasive. In other words, these previous students were prepared not only to believe that there is something morally crass about breaking rules to advance one's own self-interests but to act on such moral considerations. Of course, I would be the last to claim that our class discussions of moral issues directly transferred over to their actual sporting lives, but that was the clear impression most of them gave me.

No matter how much I prodded my more recent students, however, and forcefully pressed them to consider how they or their offspring would like it if they were similarly treated as mere instruments of someone else's egoistic desires (which is what self-interested rule breaking and rule bending come down to), I continued to run into a brick wall. Just as I thought I was losing my grip – a worry that, having recently reached middle-age, I didn't need reinforced by obstreperous students – I alighted on the idea of using case-studies to illuminate the arguments discussed in class. I reasoned that because the students were probably less disposed to abstract-sounding arguments regarding the moral rectitude of rule following than I, reared as they were, as I was not, on a steady diet of vivid visual images furnished by the likes of MTV, video games, and computers, fortifying these arguments with dramatic real-life examples of exemplary athletic moral conduct would get them over the hump, would help them to see firsthand the importance of leading a morally reflective athletic life.

In this regard, one of the first examples of morally upstanding sporting conduct I came across, which continues to be one of my favorites, concerned a 1967 German international tennis championship between Hungarian player Istvan Gulyas and his Czech opponent, Kukal. The closely contested match had come down to the fifth and final deciding set with the score tied. With the match still undecided, Kukal suddenly collapsed on court with a severe cramp. Gulyas immediately came to his aid and helped him to his feet, but after a short rest, Kukal was still hampered by the cramp and unable to play. At this point, strict enforcement of the rules would dictate that Gulyas be declared the winner by forfeit. Undaunted by this technicality, Gulyas petitioned the umpire to defer his decision and to call for a doctor. The umpire agreed, and after receiving medical attention, Kukal was not only able to resume play but went on to win the match.

Moved as I was by Gulyas's unselfish example, by his display of moral respect for both his opponent and the game itself, I was sure that my students would find his conduct morally uplifting as well. I could not have been more wrong. Most of them came to class with their minds already made up that Gulyas had done the wrong thing and that he had not only impugned the authority of the umpire but undermined the integrity of the match as well. Stunned, I asked them why they were judging Gulyas so harshly, reminding them, as is my custom, that I only wanted to hear their reasons, not their unadorned opinions, their gut feelings of approval or disapproval.

The first objection raised was reasonable enough: a student argued that Gulyas was the more superbly conditioned of the two athletes, as evidenced by the fact that his opponent suffered a cramp as a result of Gulyas's blistering play. Hence, the student validly concluded, Gulyas should have accepted the victory with no questions asked. As we turned this claim over in class, though, it became apparent that it rested on a dubious empirical assumption. The fact was, as other students duly noted, we cannot at all be sure Kukal came down with the cramp because he was less fit, as cramps can happen even to the most fit of people, including those who pay scrupulous attention to their fluid intake. Besides, it was further noted, Kukal was an elite professional tennis player, and any suggestion that he was less conditioned than his counterparts seemed suspicious on its face, especially in the absence of any corroborating evidence. At this point, I could tell by the looks on my students' faces that they concurred.

Satisfied that we were making some headway in defending Gulyas's conduct, I was not prepared for what happened next. A student shot up her hand and blurted out that Gulyas should be morally rebuked for his actions because he had deliberately broken a rule. "What rule was that," I asked in amazement. The student quickly replied, "The rule governing the length of time allowed players to recover from injuries or traumas suffered on the court." "But," I retorted, "he consulted the relevant game authority, the umpire, who was evidently persuaded that it was in the best interest of the game and all concerned that, if at all possible, the match be continued." However, the student remained undaunted, and she was not alone as the students squirming uncomfortably in their chairs made all too clear to me. I then threw out the claim that the time rule in question was surely not a very important rule of tennis and that it certainly did not qualify as one of its constitutive rules that must, no matter the circumstance, always be observed. Again, the student in question remained adamant in her view that Gulyas had done something wrong, and now just about all the students in class were nodding their heads in agreement.

Frustrated, but still determined, I offered what I thought was my strongest rebuttal: isn't it a rather striking contradiction that most of you were quick to reprimand Gulyas for breaking a rule but that in our previous discussions of the morality of rule observance, just about the whole lot of you were just as quick to say there was nothing really wrong with breaking a rule as long as you didn't get caught (and the problem with getting caught was not a moral one requiring appropriate moral redress but a bonehead, strategic one requiring those caught to fess up to their own stupidity in being found out). To this, the students replied, as they had before when we discussed these matters, that it was the job of the referees to ensure that those who break rules are caught and punished, which, they therefore concluded, this time invalidly, relieved them of any moral responsibility for complying with the rules. When I replied this was more a cop out, an excuse to further their own self-interests, than a defensible justification of rule breaking, their eyes glassed over. They were not in the least convinced and were increasingly skeptical of every word I uttered in Gulyas's defense.

To say the least, the first time that this happened in class, I was taken aback, not to mention dispirited. I was taken aback because, to reiterate, I never dreamed that my students would react this way; I was dispirited because my idea to use examples to stir their reflective juices was an obvious and resounding failure and because I could not fathom why they were put off rather than inspired by Gulyas's example.

However, when I started getting much the same reasons and answers in semester after semester, my disappointment turned into hard-boiled cynicism. Contributing to my growing cynicism was my gradual realization that what was happening in class was that the moral examples I was bringing into class were falling on deaf ears for the same reason that the moral arguments I earlier and successfully interjected into our class discussions had fallen of late on deaf ears: the students were simply not morally engaging with them. To be sure, they were just as polite, bright, and studious as their predecessors, but what had changed was their willingness or capacity (or both) to consider sports from a moral angle. So, instead of considering the effects of their actions on others and on the game itself or, what is the same thing, reversing roles and putting themselves in someone else's shoes, they were playing a cost–benefit language game in which the objective was to further their own preferences and desires. This explains their otherwise contradictory regard for the rules in the aforementioned discussion. For what removes the contradiction of claiming one has no moral responsibility to abide by the rules and condemning someone for breaking them is the calculus of self-interest. That is, what the students were really saying is that rules should be viewed and treated as egoistic devices, which means that we should follow them when it is in our self-interest to do so and break them when it is not. Gulyas's failing, then, was not so much that he broke a rule but that he did so for the wrong reason. Because the students' only apparent vocabulary for evaluating actions in sports was in terms of their positive (benefits) or negative (costs) affect on the aims and desires of the individuals who play them, Gulyas's strategic misuse of the rules was mistakenly branded as a moral failure. This brings us back exactly to where we started: the students' unwillingness or incapacity to view sports from a moral vantage point.

Of course, it occurred to me that my students' supposed resistance to moral considerations in sporting matters or, to put the same point otherwise, their conflation of egoistic calculation and moral reflection was not really resistance at all but a consequence of my own shortcomings as a teacher, my inability to get them to think morally. However, the more I thought about it, the more I was convinced that something much larger and more important was going on here than my evident failings as a teacher. For I had to admit that my students' reticence to take up sports morally was, as far as I could tell, equally true of their adult counterparts, which takes in practically the entire world of sports: those who play, finance, govern, and watch them, as well as those who report and comment on them in the media. In all these cases, moral considerations of sports were clearly and regularly trumped by considerations of athletic success and failure narrowly construed as winning and losing.

It was also clear to me that what was happening morally inside sports was also happening morally outside them in the larger social world. It was not for nothing, after all, that Christopher Lasch in his wide-ranging critique of contemporary American culture dubbed it the *culture of narcissism*, which, so as not to leave any doubt about his unsparing assessment of the American scene, doubled as the title of his book. Narcissism on this scale, it hardly needs to be said, is not especially a cultural brew favorable to a moral life. It was also not for nothing, however, that Lasch's indictment of narcissistic America pointed us back to sports, which he fingered as one of the contributing causal forces. However, if sports were on Lasch's account part of the moral problem, they were also, interestingly enough, on his same account, part of the solution. For in spite of their obvious moral shortcomings, he insisted that there was something morally ennobling about sports (among other things, their adherence to clear standards of excellence and conduct), which offered hope, he thought, not only for their eventual moral rehabilitation but as well for the moral rehabilitation of America itself. Of course, what seems so striking about these claims today, written as they were some quarter of a century ago, is how incongruous they appear to everything that is presently going on in sports.

So, thus it was that my student's resistance to moral considerations of sports provoked me to further reflection, which, in turn, led me to write this book. In particular, they prompted the following series of tantalizing questions all bound up with one another in more or less complicated ways: why is it, exactly, that we Americans find it difficult even to contemplate sports in moral terms? Why does Lasch's hopeful moral reading of them today seem at best quaint and at worse wishful if not self-deluded thinking? What causal forces are responsible for this apparent demoralization of sports and American society? Which way do the causal vectors run: from sports to society or vice versa or in both directions? Finally, and in a somewhat different vein, when did sports and America lose their moral soul – from their very institutionalization in American life in the middle and later parts of the nineteenth century, as many critics claim, or sometime in the latter part of the twentieth century, as Lasch and other critics claim?

My intent in this book, then, is to try to give some clear and illuminating answers to these important questions. In the course of doing so, I try as well to give credence to the hope expressed in my title: that sports morally matter as much now and perhaps even more than they did in the important Progressive period of American history, which is the main and recurrent theme of the chapters to come.

# Acknowledgments

I thank first my undergraduate students, whose recalcitrance even to think about sports in moral terms – something that I discuss in greater detail in the Preface – got me to thinking about why. Second, I thank the graduate students in a seminar I conducted last year, in which I first tried out some of the central ideas discussed in this book. I learned a lot from both these groups of students, and they helped to shape the book into the form in which it now appears.

My knowledge of and interest in the Progressive movement and its treatment of sport is owed to Mark Dyerson's fine book, *Making the American Team: Sport, Culture and the Olympic Experience*. It was from reading Dyerson's book that I first learned how important sports were to Progressive-minded reformers and how sophisticated an understanding of sports many of them had. I am indebted to Dyerson also for sending me copies of articles from *Outing* and other journals of that ilk containing many of the writings of Progressives on sports, articles that I could not locate in my own university library.

I would be remiss if I did not thank as well my wonderful colleagues at Ohio State University, Mel Adelman and Sarah Fields, both of whom encouraged my interest in this project and were willing to discuss my ideas with me. They also created a stimulating intellectual environment in which to think and write about sports in a serious and critical vein.

I further acknowledge Samantha Grant, editor of Sports Studies books at Routledge, and her editorial assistant, Kate Manson, for their encouragement and help along the way. Samantha is the best editor I or anyone else could hope for, always enthusiastic and never too busy to respond to my queries, even the inane ones. Kate is also a delight to work with and has kept me fully informed about what I needed to do at each stage of the publication of this book.

Finally, I thank the editors of the Routledge Critical Studies in Sport series, Jennifer Hargreaves and Ian McDonald. My main contact has been with Ian, who convinced me that my book was a good fit for the series and has been supportive of this project from the get-go. However, I thank *both* for seeing fit to put my book in their first-rate series.

Of course, I am obliged to say at this point, as all authors are, that I am fully responsible for the ideas that appear here and, therefore, for any errors or less-than-stellar arguments evident in the text. So, I am entirely to blame for whatever is wrong with this book. I only wish I could say the same for whatever the book's strengths might be – that is, that I am wholly responsible for them as well – but that would be a lie and thus an especially bad way to start a book that focuses on ethics and claims to be interested in the moral failings of modern sports and how they might be rectified.

# Introduction

Imagine a society racked by a huge and growing gulf between the rich and poor. The gulf is so deep and wide that neither of these groups shares anything in common with the other anymore, which means that the social and political divisions of this society are as pronounced as those of its economics. A society so constituted, of course, would have little reason to encourage other-regarding sentiments or actions (or both), as it can point to no common good to orient its actions in this manner. This would explain, among other things, why its affluent members would not in the least be disposed politically to let themselves be taxed to support the growing underclass of the poor or to be coaxed morally, by their few remaining responsible – and therefore marginalized – members and intellectual minions to pay their employees a "living wage" so that they might enjoy a decent standard of living. In a very real sense, then, this is a society in name only, because the weak associational ties that hold it together have no real binding political or moral force. If anything, these ties leave individuals dangling to fend for themselves, so much so that any egalitarian complaint that these free-floating individuals at very least should be treated fairly (i.e., begin their solipsistic pursuits of the good life from the same starting line) would likely be dismissed as mere radical twaddle.

Now, the reason why we contemporary Americans have no difficulty in conjuring up such a disturbingly fractured social order is that it is a fairly accurate description of our own highly fractured, egocentrically riven society. What is more, the image of such a society could also easily double as a more-than-passable description of American society at the turn of the twentieth century, similarly plagued by a great and ever-growing disparity between the rich and poor.[1] The fact that a large and complex country such as ours has experienced economic inequality on this scale before is not especially remarkable, particularly because the causal forces responsible for each differed in important respects. However, what is truly remarkable, I think, is the widely divergent way in which we contemporary Americans have so far responded to this crisis as compared to our forebears. For our earlier peers, or at least for a goodly number of them, looked morally askance at this skewed distribution of wealth and set in motion a social movement called *Progressivism* to remedy it, a movement that, among other things, argued that the market must be morally reined in and that a new relationship between the individual and society must be forged so that private aspirations no longer take precedence over common, public ones.

And sports figured mightily in their moral equation, because Progressivist thought that sports offered what William James called a "moral equivalent of war" (i.e., a form of life that could produce the strong ties that a people feel when they are at war but one absent the destructive tendencies and consequences of martial conflicts). In particular, sports' dedication to the ideal of fair play and its inculcation of "team spirit" were regarded by many Americans of this time as just the right moral antidote to cure the atomistic ills of an overly commercialized society.

By contrast, we modern-day Americans have responded to these inequalities in financial and political fortune with nothing stronger than a yawn. That is in part because we act as if little can be done to ameliorate such inequalities (e.g., to undo the great concentration of wealth in a few hands) save by offering tax breaks to those who already possess large chunks of this wealth in the vain hope (on my more cynical days I would say on the not-so-vain political calculation that slighting the poor is not likely to cause any significant political damage to those doing the slighting) that somehow this will improve the unenviable lot of the poor.

In fact, these days about the only thing that we Americans are urged to do to help our fellow citizens is to shop until we drop: to indulge our private preferences in the market rather than to exercise moral constraint over them for some larger, more noble cause – what is popularly (and sarcastically) called "market" patriotism. And if anyone were to venture the idea (as William James once did) that sport is a moral equivalent of war – one especially promising moral way to curb our narcissistic appetites and establish some meaningful bond with our fellow citizens – they would be widely ridiculed for their naiveté, if not stupidity. Indeed, for most modern Americans, sports are considered just another commodity to be consumed, simply an extension of the vast entertainment industry and so a big part of the problem rather than a part of the solution.

What accounts for these striking differences in responses to the economic and moral dilemmas Americans at the turn of the twentieth century and present day Americans both faced? More particularly, why are we contemporary Americans so averse to moral calls for the redistribution of wealth and leery of any form of patriotism save, apparently, military displays of chauvinism or consumer demonstrations of our willingness to buy yet more to safeguard the economic prosperity of our country? And, of particular note for my purposes, what explains not just our present lowered moral expectations for sports but our seeming inability even to entertain the idea that sports might be moral vehicles that serve larger moral purposes? In other words, how did we get from the view that sport is a moral cure for the inegalitarian tendencies that ail us to the present view that sport is itself nothing more than an inegalitarian tendency, a way to get ahead at the expense of others, or a way to escape our problems, to forget that we live in a society marred by these great inequalities?

These are the sorts of questions I try to answer in this book. In doing so – in examining both the moral successes and failings of sports – I would like to think I am making some contribution to the social criticism of larger America and its major sports. Further, in pitching my inquiry in this way, I would also like to think that I am making some contribution to a distinguished American Leftist tradition of critical thought in and outside of sports. My reason for thinking so is because I agree wholeheartedly with Rorty that it is to the Left that we need to turn for moral counsel on how to improve the lot of our fellow citizens and (for me) on how to make sports morally better than they presently are as part of this grander effort to reinvigorate America morally.[2] That is because the Right seems to think that even to mention the moral and social problems that presently beset our country and its representative sports is in bad taste, to even concede, for example, that the poor are faring badly these days or that women continue to be barred from playing certain sports or are discriminated against in many of the sports in which they have recently won the right to engage. We need look no further than the Right's immediate, knee-jerk retort of "class warfare" to any suggestion that all is not well in the heartland for confirmation of Rorty's point. For the cranky cry of class warfare is for the Right merely a conversation stopper, a rhetorical device designed to prevent us from thinking, let alone thinking critically. What is especially contemptible about the Right's use of this rhetorical strategy is that its intended effect of putting the poor and humiliated out of our mind is itself, of course, the genuine item, the real way in which class warfare is waged in our country.

Having said all this, however, does not absolve the Left of any blame for our present moral predicament, notwithstanding its single-handed willingness to fight the good fight. On the contrary, I think one of the reasons why we contemporary Americans have lost our zeal for moral reform in and outside of sports can be laid at the Left's feet. I have specifically in mind here two important groups of Leftist critics of sport: those for whom money is the principal source of the degradation of sports today and those for whom sadism – the humiliation of identity groups (e.g., groups marked by their race, ethnicity, sexual identity, and the like) – is the main source of their corruption.[3]

However, first a few words about what these two groups of critics got right in their respective critiques of sports. To begin with the economically oriented critics of American sports, whose numbers and influence have waned significantly in the last three or four decades: we owe them a great debt of gratitude for calling our attention to the tawdry economic infrastructure of present-day sports. For it is at this economic level, of course, that many of the problems of modern sports can be traced and not (as in the case of larger society) in the actual immiseration of the producers and the athletes (at least in professional sports), many of whom have become wealthy beyond their dreams, but in the economic control and makeover of the game itself. These critics, then, have done yeoman service in showing how sports have ceded more and more of their soul to the whims of the market and to those who do its bidding. I believe that they are not only correct about this but that money remains the most serious moral scourge that sports face in our times. So, I shall have considerably more to say about the pernicious role that money plays in sports in the chapters that follow.

Likewise, we owe a great debt of gratitude to the critics of sadism in sports as well. Here I again share Rorty's view that such critics (for him in the larger sphere of American society and for me in the more particular sphere of North American sports) deserve our praise for making previously socially acceptable forms of sadism (e.g., race baiting and gay bashing) socially unacceptable, especially to educated Americans.[4] True, much work still remains to be done in American society and perhaps even more work in sports. Despite the enormous success of people of color on their playing fields and the recent inroads that women have made in gaining access to them, sports continue to serve up hurtful stereotypes of the so-called natural black athlete. Such stereotypes are invidiously played off against both "hardworking" white athletes and alleged superior white "intellectualism" and continue to question both the sexual identity of women (not to mention gender-bending male athletes) who engage in sports and the athletic standing of the sports they play.[5]

What each group has achieved in these areas is no small accomplishment. Nonetheless, each in their own way has also put obstacles in the way of the moral reform of sports. In the case of the first group, the main obstacle has to do with their stubborn insistence that any genuinely critical talk about the role of money in sports must take its point of departure from Marxist theory in one form or another. This has been unfortunate in at least two important respects: first, in spreading the specious idea that the only way to get a critical handle on the havoc that money has wreaked in sports is to frame it in a Marx-like vocabulary and, second, that the only way to undo the harm that money has done in sports is to do away with markets themselves (i.e., to eschew piecemeal reform in favor of full-blown revolution).

I believe they are wrong – and grievously so – on both counts. To begin with, I have no doubt that we can readily understand the many and insidious ways in which money has perverted sports without recourse to the arcana of Marxist theory; such authors as Andrew Zimbalist, in his fine book *Unpaid Professionals: Commercialism and Conflict in Big-Time College Sports*, have managed to do just that.[6] That is, such critics have ably exposed the economic chicanery that goes on in elite sports in a vocabulary that is less daunting and abstruse than any Marxist analysis of sport I am aware of. Further, in the aftermath of 1989, which marked the beginning of the end of Marxist-Leninist governments throughout Eastern Europe, any call for a Marxist revolution of bourgeois societies and sports is only likely to elicit detached bemusement rather than revolutionary fervor.[7] That is because such notions as nationalizing the means of production, the dictatorship of the proletariat, and – closer to home – sports without markets no longer possess any critical traction. They only serve to remind us of the still-fresh failures of these pre-1989 regimes and of the still-fresh failures of Marxist critics of sports to figure out how to stanch the flow of money into sports, let alone figure out why these bourgeois pastimes captured the fancy of their favored working class. Finally, there is the no less trifling matter of their failure to see that sadism would not cease either in or out of sports once societies opted for a planned economy over a market economy, that economic determinism only takes us so far in explaining why some people get their kicks out of humiliating especially vulnerable groups.

In the case of the critics of sadism in sports, they have rendered the moral reform of sports more difficult by not paying enough attention to money. That is, as they have become more sophisticated in plying their craft of what is variously called the "politics of difference" or what others such as Charles Taylor (more aptly) call the "politics of recognition"[8] to their critique of sports, they have almost had nothing to say about the political economy of sports. As a result, the increasing economic exploitation of sports has for the most part fallen off their sadist-calibrated radar screens. This at a time when economic inequality is not only rife in American sports and in larger American society as well but is greater than it has ever been in any other period of the history of the republic. Further, by fixing their critical gaze on the humiliation of identity groups in sports and letting the co-optation of sports by the market go mainly unremarked, the sadistic consequences of such market co-optation have also largely escaped their critical notice.

I am thinking here, for one, of the clever but morally contemptible strategy used mainly by male athletic directors in intercollegiate sports to derail the noble intentions of Title IX legislation to increase opportunities for women in these sports. That strategy involved cutting men's so-called nonrevenue sports rather than increasing the number of women involved in sports, which had the double effect not only of shielding that sacred cow of men's sports – football – from having to share any of the financial burden (it also helped to divert attention away from the fact that most big-time college sports programs lose rather than make money) but of pitting the cash-strafed, often badly treated men's "minor" sports against the equally cash-strafed, often badly treated women's sports. This conveniently – but, of course, wrongly – rendered women's sports programs the scapegoat and thus an easy mark against whom disgruntled, angry male athletes could direct their pent-up sadistic rage.

However, both these groups of critics share one further thing in common that, I believe, skews their moral counsel and lessens the force of their criticisms. That thing has to do with what makes for good social criticism, for spinning out accounts that carry the maximum critical wallop as determined by whether they actually move people to take such criticism seriously and do something about it.

Of course, what constitutes effective social criticism is, to say the least, a large and vexing issue. Boiled down to its essentials, however, I think it is fair to say that such criticism depends crucially on two features. First, of course, is a conviction not to take things on face value: to settle either for authoritarian declarations by well-heeled, silver-tongued ideologues that all is right by sports and the world or complacent, less canned, common-sense-wrapped assertions of the same. In other words, social critics who do their jobs well are debunkers, writers insistent on "telling it like it is" and letting the chips fall where they may regardless of the consequences.

However, a feature of social criticism no less important is getting people to sit up straight and take one's criticisms to heart, at least enough to heart to act on them. This approach requires giving people some hope, some credible belief that what they want to act on is worth acting on: to put it bluntly, that there is good reason to believe that they can make a difference, that there is a good chance that what they want to change can be changed for the better.

From what little has been said thus far, why social criticism is such a delicate exercise is easy to see, because debunking beliefs and giving people hope often work at cross-purposes to one another. For if one carries the debunking bit too far, the effect is to dash people's hope. By the same token, if one carries the hope bit too far, the danger is that we might all end up romantic dimwits, ready to endure the harshest oppression or put up with the worst sorts of corruption in the vainglorious hope that tomorrow will bring a new and better day merely because it is another day.

The dangers of hypercriticism and excessive romanticism, of course, bear directly on my present project: my effort to explore the legacy of the Progressive conception of sports as a moral model for the criticism and reform of contemporary sports. For as Delbanco astutely notes, "[T]he future is always at stake in how we understand the past."[9] Consider his example of the complex issue of race in America. One could tell a true story about America, he says, that has as its main theme "the poisonous idea of race," a story that runs from Jefferson's odious claim that the Orangutan prefers "black women over those of his own species" to W. E. Du Bois's century-later encounter in a natural history museum of "a series of skeletons arranged from a little monkey to a tall well-developed white man, with a Negro barely outranking a chimpanzee."[10] However, Delbanco hastens to add that one could tell an equally true story about race in America in which moral struggle and uplift rather than moral debauchery are the central themes, a story that features America's effort to honor the principle of "inalienable" rights that Jefferson first articulated and included in the Declaration of Independence, and that such people as Dubois devoted most of their waking hours to defending and expanding.[11] Delbanco's point is simple but telling: that both stories should be told, that one should not be allowed to suppress or replace the other.

The point I want to make with Delbanco's help (in the case of sports) is no less simple and no less telling: that the two groups of critics in question here have generally gone too far in the debunking department, with the predictable result that much of their work evokes pessimism rather than hope for the future.[12] Although I would not go as far as Rorty does in his criticism of what he calls the cultural Left in America – that they "can ridicule anything but can hope for nothing"[13] – there is enough truth in what he says to give us pause. For when social criticism succumbs to the urge to ridicule, which is just another way of saying that when debunking becomes not just one part of its critical repertoire but the whole of it, its often trenchant criticisms get lost in a fog of resentment, one that in lashing out at all that is wrong with sports and the world chokes off any belief that our best days lie ahead of rather than behind us. Too often, then, after reading some of these Leftist critiques of larger America and of contemporary sports, one is left with the impression that there is nothing redeemable about either, that both are too far gone to do anything about, and that, therefore, we all would be better off without them.

Consider two recent books, one a novel written by Max Barry entitled *Jennifer Government*, the other a Tony Award-winning play penned by Richard Greenberg entitled *Take Me Out*.[14] The first features sports – more particularly, the sporting industry – as viewed through the eyes of one of its most visible and morally challenged corporations, Nike, to slay capitalist America, the second features (homophobic) sports to slay sadist America.

In *Jennifer Government*, a dystopian tale set in the not-too-distant future, America is depicted as essentially one large market. In this setting, corporations have become so powerful that Americans derive their surnames (not to mention their personal identities) from the companies for which they work (which explains why the main protagonists of the story have such names as Gregory and John Nike and Billy Bechtel) and rename their central social institutions after their corporate sponsors (which explains the frequent references to McDonald Schools and Pepsi Schools).[15] The main plot of the book centers on a daring advertising campaign hatched by John Nike, a marketing vice-president of Nike, to promote the company's new line of shoes called "Mercurys." The gimmick he dreamed up to stir consumer interest in the new shoes, which will sell for the hefty price of $2,500 a pair and for which the labor costs are a paltry eighty-five cents, is to kill the first ten or so customers who turn up at Nike Town to purchase Mercurys on the morning of their public release and to make it appear that ghetto kids are the responsible party. In that way, the company gains, as one of the characters so indelicately puts it, "street cred coming out of our asses," which in turn helps it to convey the desired impression that people will stop at nothing to obtain a pair of Mercurys.[16]

Prominent American corporations that arrange contract killings to make a few bucks – actually a slew of bucks – is hardly an inspiring story of what we Americans have to look forward to. However, it is at least, in one important sense, a prescient story. For it picks up on our current suspicion that the government has already been bought off, that it takes its marching orders from the corporations that fill its members' campaign coffers with cash, and so, that what we should fear is not the old bugaboo against which such writers as Orwell so elegantly and passionately warned us – large, oppressive, tyrannical governments – but unfettered markets. In other words, what most threatens us today is capitalism itself: more precisely, capitalism run amok, in which everything is up for sale precisely because nothing is considered so sacrosanct that it cannot be subjected to the egoistic calculus of the business deal.

So, what *Jennifer Government* sketches is a picture of how America will appear after the private sector makes good on its goal to take over the public sector (i.e., after it has succeeded in shrinking the role of the government so that it is no longer able to interfere with its market decisions). And this is precisely the kind of no-frills government we get in the pages of *Jennifer Government*, one that no longer taxes people; no longer thinks it should be involved in any scheme, political or moral (or both), to redistribute wealth; and no longer wastes money in holding elections or passing legislation.[17] Rather, the only aims entrusted to government are stopping "people stealing or hurting each other" and outsourcing everything else to the private sector, including its police functions, "which everyone knows is more efficient."[18] The book pictures an America, therefore, that prides itself on letting "people do whatever they want" and that flaunts its infantile notion of freedom by invidiously wielding it against such European countries as France, where the government still taxes people and insists on regulating the private lives of its citizens.[19]

In keeping with the "America sucks" bent of *Jennifer Government*, the moral outlook of this imagined America is as off-putting as its version of market freedom and limited government. Of course, that is because its moral outlook is defined, like everything else in this depressing story, by its dominant market bearing. That means, strictly speaking, that there is no morality of which to speak here. Rather, what guides people's actions is nothing other than a crude cost–benefit analysis – one already familiar to us contemporary Americans – in which the unquestioned aim is to get what you want but to do so efficiently by weighing up the costs and benefits of each course of action, better transaction, acting when the benefits exceed the costs, and refraining from acting when they do not.

About this, *Jennifer Government* is unequivocal, as becomes clear when John Nike is asked by his corporate boss, Gregory Nike, whether it bothers him that he orchestrated the murder of 14 kids, the actual number killed when his plan was executed. His reply leaves nothing to the imagination: "It's my job to increase sales. Is it my fault that was the best way to do it? If the Government had the muscle to enforce the law, it wouldn't have made economic sense, but they don't, and it did. This is the world we live in. If you don't take advantage of the rules you're a sucker."[20] When confronted later in the book with the same question, John Nike's reply is even more chilling, because it comes uncomfortably close to the America in which we already live: "Lets not pretend these are the first people to die in the interests of commerce. Let's not pretend there's a company ... that hasn't put profit above human life at some point."[21]

Whereas *Jennifer Government* makes use of sports only incidentally in trying to skewer Americans' belief in America as a moral ideal (and some of the parallels between Nike's corporate moral and business dealings and those of contemporary sports are, though unremarked, striking, especially the notion that not taking advantage of the rules is something only suckers do and the practice of tagging social institutions with corporate names), *Take Me Out* tries to do the same using sports as its main vehicle. As noted, however, this time it is homophobic America that is savaged. This becomes crystal clear at the outset in the person of one Darren Leeming, the main character of the story and a very talented and very rich biracial baseball star who has, seemingly, the entire world at his command. Indeed, his present good fortune, as a talented, rich superstar, is matched only by his past good fortune, as a member of a fine middle-class family, which even this early in the story makes him something of an oddity: "a black man who had never obviously suffered."[22] However, as I said, this is mainly a tale about sexual identity, not race, as becomes clear when Darren, after a brief and perfunctory meeting with his teammates, publicly declares to a stunned world that he is a gay man.

His reasons for outing himself come across as capricious, certainly not born out of any moral impulse, say, to send a message to other kids who might be struggling with their sexual identities or to signal his solidarity with the gay community. Rather, it seems his personal "confession" was motivated primarily to draw attention to himself by provoking a reaction from the baseball community and America itself. And this it does in spades.

The first stirrings of homophobia come quickly and in a rather predictable and even humorous fashion. For Darren soon notices that his teammates are shying away from him in the locker-room, and that prompts him to ask one of his smarter and more reflective teammates, Kippy Sunderstorm, what is going on. Kippy opines that it is not so much that his teammates suspect Darren wants to have sex with them but that they might want to have sex with him, that deep down they, too, are gay men but, unlike Darren, are unable to face up to this evidently disturbing fact. However, Darren demurs and bases his demurral on his already apparent "narcissism:" "[E]verybody in the world is just a version of me … If I'm gonna have sex – and I am because I'm young and rich and famous and talented … I'd rather do it with a guy, but when all is said and done … I'd rather just play ball."[23]

This exchange is followed quickly by an encounter with one of his less intelligent teammates, Jason Chenier who, after regaling Darren with stories about the "Grecians" and the wonderful pyramids they built, complains that every time he's around Darren, he is "rackled with self-consciousness about my body." When Darren curtly replies, "Whyn't ya get dressed then?" Jason finds himself momentarily speechless.[24] However, he soon regains his composure and blurts out that there is one person who does not agree with his lifestyle, namely God, and then solemnly announces that he "can kill ya, man."[25] Things soon heat up, however, when Shane Mungitt, a poor white kid who has a wicked fastball and has just been called up from Double-A ball, tells a TV commentator, "Don't get me wrong. I don't mind the colored people – the gooks an' the spics an' the coons an' like that. But every night t'hafta take a shower with a faggot?"[26]

Even this crude display of homophobia, though humorless and hardly excusable, is at the very least forgivable. After all, what we have here is a poor, socially inept, white kid, a victim himself of the injuries of class, whose chief failing is not his undeniable prejudice but his lack of media savvy, his untutored sense of what can and cannot be said in the public realm. True to form, his crude prose ignites a firestorm both in the baseball community and the larger public, which allowed both to exercise their righteous indignation against the gauche and guileless Mungitt and conveniently ignore their own more-fine-grained but no less damaging racial and homosexual animus.

However, the more potent slings and arrows of humiliation loosed at Darren in *Take Me Out* come from more daunting and, therefore, more dangerous sources. They proceed in particular from Darren's best friend (at least before he chose to out himself), Davy Battle, no one's fool and a baseball superstar in his own right, and from Darren's manager, who also is no one's fool and worldly enough to know that in private he can say things – hurtful things – to Darren that he cannot say publicly. In the first instance, Davey Battle decides to confront Darren in his own locker-room, a breach of etiquette not even superstars are normally allowed, and assails Darren with the question, "What kind of sordidness is this you've got going on?" When Darren protests that "You told me to reveal my true nature. You said I could only do this through love," Davey angrily cuts him off and says, "That's before I knew you were a pervert." Davey continues his harangue by noting, "Oh, everybody knows Davey Battle's a religious man … nobody going around with Davey Battle's going to be whoring … was that the whole thing, Darren?"[27] With that, their longstanding friendship came to a screeching, humiliating end.

In many respects, Darren's confrontation with his manager over the impending return of Shane Mungitt to the team after his unfortunate remarks cuts even deeper. When Darren presses his manager that it is just not right to let this bigot back on the team, the manager at first reaches for the familiar bromide – "A lot of things aren't 'right'" – but he quickly makes things personal by pointedly saying to Darren, "Is it right … for somebody to land one of the fattest contracts in baseball history and *only then* reveal his interesting little personal quirk? Is *that* 'right'?"[28] Darren sloughs off the obvious insult and decides to change gears by, as he so bluntly puts it, speaking "as an African-American … not as a cocksucker" (i.e., by speaking out on behalf of all the black and Hispanic players on the team). To this, the manager replies that they are all fine with Mungitt's return. "They just want to play baseball. They just want to be part of this organization. They're willing to do what it takes, if it comes to that."[29]

What adds injury to insult in this second case is that it blots out the one seeming ray of hope Darren allows himself regarding his life as a baseball player, found in his already quoted response to Kippy's conjecture regarding the cause of the team's discord after the declaration of his sexual identity: "[W]hen all is said and done … [I and they would] rather just play ball."[30] What leavens this claim is its suggestion that despite the many differences that set him off from the rest of his teammates and the fans, there is at least one important thing that binds them all together: their shared love of the game. And more importantly, the evident binding force of this shared love transcends those potentially divisive differences without somehow either glossing over or impugning them.

No mean feat, to be sure. However, the manager's retort raises a less sanguine interpretation: that players are all too ready to sweep their differences under the rug rather than transcend them if the organization's financial success is at stake or – what comes to the same thing – if winning is at stake. This includes, evidently, the branding of players as coons, spics, and faggots. In other words, in the coordination of individual intentions, efforts, and actions to achieve a collective goal such as winning and the tangible rewards that follow in its train, cooperating with others is perfectly compatible with holding them in contempt. Unlike, then, Darren's seemingly uplifting claim that sports make it possible to achieve a kind of unity, a fusion of effort and purpose that encourages genuine fellow-feeling because it encourages a commitment and dedication to a mutually shared way of life, the manager's cynical reproof suggests that sports offer us at most a way to interact with others to get what we all individually want but cannot accomplish alone. This view does not encourage fellow-feeling, because it does not encourage anything more than that we do what is necessary, whatever it takes, to further our self-interests.

Worse, the manager's rendering of team (dis)unity and purpose suggests further that the Enlightenment project of self-enlargement was not just misguided but fundamentally flawed. That is because its claim – that self-enlargement is the key to enlightenment, that claiming a larger identity for oneself (as, say, a member of a baseball community or as an American) is a way to overcome a certain narrowness of purpose or concern – is a lie because it can be achieved only by denying one's local identity (i.e., by denying at bottom what one fundamentally is). In this view, true enlightenment can be had only by remaining true to oneself, where remaining true to oneself means clinging steadfastly to one's ethnicity, race, sexual identity, class standing, or some combination thereof. So understood, to attempt to submerge one's particular identity in the name of some larger identity or community is pure foolishness, because submerging one's individuality is tantamount to smiting it, to destroying one's core.

The resounding message that both books send, then, is that there is no pride, only shame, to be taken in calling oneself an American or in identifying one's self in terms of a cherished social practice, such as sports. And if that is the case, why trouble oneself with their attempted reform, why bother to lift a finger to try to make things better in or outside of sports? Better to embrace Heidegger's parting rebuke of the modern age, "That only a God can save us now,"[31] where the reference to God is not, of course, to be understood as an expression of faith that our salvation lies in attaching ourselves not just to something greater than ourselves but to something divinely greater, something nonhuman. Rather, it is a cry of exasperation born of our impotence, our lack of agency, to right the unforgiving times in which we live. This disbelief in our capacity to turn things around for the better is, I believe, the source of much of the resignation that permeates the American Left today and helps to explain its too-frequent resort to hand wringing rather than activism when confronted (almost on a daily basis) with solid evidence of the corruption of America and its sports.

Such, then, is the downside of counsels of despair in and outside of sports, of social criticism that leaves us without a proverbial leg on which to stand. None of this, again, is to deny that America and sports are in a socially and morally bad way these days or that critics are wrong to take them to task in this regard. Rather, it is only to say that what presently ails us is not anything that should paralyze us (i.e., lead us to wring our hands and retreat into a spectator state-of-mind and political stance).[32] Further, it is just another way of saying, of reinforcing, what I previously indicated were the difficulties that occasion social criticism of all stripes: that it is a little like walking a tight-rope, lean too much either to the criticism side or the hope side and all is lost.

Still, in one sense I have been guilty myself of leaning too much to the criticism side, at least in my treatment of Greenberg's *Take Me Out*. For though truly the main plot of his play actively discourages any belief in the moral healing powers of sports (or at least baseball), also true is that it does not leave us to wallow in our despair by claiming that sports are beyond repair. So, Greenberg does, in the end, give us something about which to be hopeful, even if he chooses a marginal and most unlikely source to be the bearer of these good tidings. The character in question is, of all people, Darren's business manager, Mason Marzac, a newcomer to the game and to the business of the game, but all the same a quick study and a resolute believer in the emancipatory elixir of baseball.

Mason's unabashed love affair with baseball can be traced to his conviction that "baseball is a perfect metaphor for hope in a democratic society," which he attributes to its rules of play and the equality of opportunity it makes possible. This is the kind of equality where "Everyone is given exactly the same chance. And the opportunity to exercise that chance at his own pace."[33] Sports further enliven our sense of hope, or so Mason proclaims, by providing a public forum in which we get to bear witness to and acknowledge the excellence of the play on the field and, in the process, get a chance to honor and respect one another.[34] It is this mutual honoring and respecting of one another, he opines, that draw us together into a tight-knit community, a community of likeminded lovers of the game who are ready at a moment's notice to "engage in learned debate" about last night's game.[35] This is a point not lost on Mason, given his heretofore perennial status as an outsider, someone who never before felt that he belonged anywhere, and a point made all the sharper by his disbelief in God. However, what is lost on Mason and those many like him is "Why?": why do we care as much as we apparently do about such seemingly trivial fare as sports? Mason spells out this shared perplexity well, and so I shall let him have the last word here: "I don't get it. I don't get any of it. I don't know why I feel exalted when we win. I don't know why I feel diminished when we lose. I don't know why I'm saying 'we.'"[36]

What is so striking about Mason's riff on baseball is how reminiscent it is of the previously discussed Progressive view of sport. Also, what is perhaps even more striking about it is how it taps the same egalitarian and communitarian impulses of sports that first attracted Progressives to them in their search to find something with which all Americans might identify and around which they might rally. That *something* might raise our moral consciousness so that, for instance, the plight of the least well-off among us might be seen as the common, moral concern of us all and not just a few do-gooders – whose pitifully small numbers causes the good that they seek to do to appear to the rest of us complacent folks as just so much moral brow beating. In other words, Mason's soliloquy on baseball starts us down the very same path that the Progressives tried to clear and explore as they entertained the admittedly grand idea that our caring for sports, which so many Americans seem to exhibit with great exuberance, might have some larger moral payoff.

So then, we have come full circle, back to the Progressive conception of sport with which we started this chapter. With that, we find ourselves face to face with the challenge that occupied many of the reformers of the Progressive movement and that I am presently arguing should occupy us now: what is the magic of the first-person plural "we" that is tossed around so freely and so confidently in our involvement in and discourse about sports, and what uplifting effect, if any, might it have on the moral soul of America itself? The answer to these questions, I am convinced – as many Progressive reformers of the past were – can go a long way toward telling us whether sports, despite their present morally squalid condition, might be a harbinger of morally good things to come.

In the chapters that follow, I will direct my critical attention to this "we" that seems so easily and naturally to fasten itself to our sporting endeavors as players and fans alike, and I shall inquire as to its moral fruitfulness. However, before I can address this matter headlong, I will first have to do some stage-setting. This will require, for reasons I will shortly explain, setting up an imaginary scenario that I call the *state of play*, to be followed by my own moral critique of contemporary sports and my critique of one dominant interpretation of that critique. With this accomplished, I will turn to the central issues at hand and assay the moral history of America, from the Progressive period to the present, and the moral history of American sports for the same period.

This will allow me in the concluding section of the book to make my case that the Progressive conception of sports captures about them important features that are still very much morally relevant to their contemporary conduct and to that of larger America as well. In this way, I hope to show that the moral criticism of sports is not for naught, because the forces of darkness are already on us. So, with apologies to F. Scott Fitzgerald and Karl Marx, I will argue that there are indeed "second acts in American lives" and that it is sports that not only prove as much but prove as well that second acts need not degenerate into farces.[37]

# 1  The state of play

## A genealogy

Genealogy is a way of trying to understand, explain, and evaluate a cultural practice by telling a story of how it came about or might have come about.[1] My use of this device in this chapter is to tell a story about the moral development of sport in contemporary America by resorting to an artifice that I call the "state of play." However, before I sketch out what I mean by the state of play, I first need to explain what sort of genealogical project I have in mind here.

### Historical and imaginary genealogies

Genealogy owes its critical progeny to Nietzsche, who used it to excavate the meaning of modern morality to his uncomprehending – because uncritical – nineteenth-century contemporaries. In particular, he was interested in investigating "under what conditions did man devise these value judgements good and evil? *and what value do they themselves possess?*"[2] What was at stake in such an inquiry, he opined, was nothing less than the value of morality itself or what he more colorfully called "the value of the 'unegoistic,'" which included such instincts as pity, self-abnegation, and self-sacrifice. For that, Nietzsche thought that an "actual history of morality itself" was required, a history of morality "that has actually existed, actually been lived."[3] What he claimed to have found is that our modern moral conceptions derive from hardly moral notions, such as resentment, malice, and hate, which were heaped by the weak on the strong to keep them in check, to stifle their vital, adventuresome impulses. In sum, he argued that a "symptom of regression" is inherent in our modern understanding of the good, in this effort by the weak to protect themselves against the strong by subjecting them to moral constraint.

In more recent times, Foucault has enlarged Nietzsche's genealogical project to show how we become subjects of knowledge, power, and morality. In this regard, he took over from Nietzsche the idea of lowly beginnings: that the genealogies of truth, power, and ethics uncover unlovely, even sinister motives that betray their supposed present nobility. He also clarified that this historical probing of origins is not to be understood as a search for essences, for the foundations of our most important conceptions and social practices. On the contrary, genealogy is intended to disturb "what was previously considered immobile," to fragment "what was thought unified," to exhibit "the heterogeneity of what was imagined consistent with itself."[4] Further, genealogy is not to be thought of along the lines of an unbroken story of the "evolution of a species" but rather as an attempt to effect discontinuity in the stories we tell about ourselves as agents of truth, power, and morality, to pick out the historical contingencies that shaped these practices and the ways in which we thought about them, and to do so by being "scrupulously attentive to [the] petty malice" of their every feature. In short, the point is to put history to use to destroy the "chimera" of the exalted origin, much as Nietzsche did when he tried to destroy the "feeling of man's sovereignty," of his much-claimed "divine birth," by showing how that claim cannot be upheld "since a monkey stands at the entrance."[5] In Foucault's hands, then, genealogy became a multipurpose tool by which to dememorialize rather than venerate the past, to forge a "disruptive countermemory" the critical promise of which lies in the challenge it poses to our stock conceptions and practices of truth telling, power mongering, and moralizing.[6]

However, genealogy has a long pedigree in moral and political philosophy as well. Here, its story line is more imaginary than historical, in which a narrative is contrived to explain how moral virtues might have arisen from natural ones or how the political might have arisen from the nonpolitical. Hume's derivation of the "artificial" virtue of justice is a case in point, because he sets this account up by narrating a story of people living in a state of "uncultivated nature" in which they govern themselves by natural, what he calls "partial affections." These partial affections strongly dispose people to favor their self-interests first, to consider less strongly the interests of their personal acquaintances, and to consider weakly – if at all – the interests of people outside their personal circle.[7] In such an uncultured setting, such virtues as justice have no purchase, because the "natural uncultivated ideas of morality" that guide them follow, rather than challenge, our partial appetites. The story concludes by showing that when people become educated and trained (in other words, civilized), come to see the "infinite advantages" that result from cooperating with others, and acquire "a new affection to company and conversation," they will come up with new moral reasons for action based on artificial virtues (social conventions), such as justice.[8]

Hume's idea that we can explain how modern conceptions of justice develop from imaginary genealogies, such as the state of nature, even if they did not actually develop in this way, is also the guiding idea behind the use of state-of-nature stories by political philosophers to explain how the modern state might have developed. Nozick's state-of-nature narrative is one such example: he tries to show how a political conception of the state could have arisen out of a prepolitical setting in which people are free to act and dispose of their property as they see fit without taking into account the interests and concerns of other people. The coda of Nozick's story puts forth and justifies a minimal conception of the state that accounts for our moral obligations to others without giving short shrift to liberty.[9]

Now, what Hume's and Nozick's genealogies share in common and distinguish them from Nietzsche's and Foucault's genealogies is, as noted, their fictional character. That is, Hume and Nozick tell stories of how modern moral and political conceptions and practices might have developed, mindful of the fact that they may not have actually developed in this way at all. More strongly, both thought that their respective state-of-nature sketches were not only false but, as Williams shrewdly observes, impossible – in other words, that they could not have been historically true because no societies that have ever existed were so morally and politically unsophisticated as these.[10] So, asking whether contemporary morality or the state could have come into existence in this way is for Hume and Nozick, and for those who follow in their path, a misguided question. That is because the explanatory role that such imaginative stories are supposed to play, as Nozick explains, falls into the category of what Hempel calls a "potential" explanation: "which intuitively … is what would be the correct explanation if everything mentioned were true and operated."[11] So understood, the "fact-defective" feature of these imaginary genealogies, the fact that they proceed from a "false antecedent condition," is not a strike against their theoretical or practical utility.

However, if their fact-defective character does not undercut their status as "potential" explanations, it does at least raise the question of what use "potential" explanations are in accounting for our moral and political ideas and practices. Williams, I think, gives the best answer to this question in claiming that fictional stories of this sort give us a functional understanding of morality and politics of which not everyone would expect to have a functional account and one that appeals to motivations that people have anyway. More importantly, Williams continues, the functional account that they offer is rational "in the sense that in the imagined circumstances people with the simpler motivations would welcome, and, if they could do so, aim for, a state of affairs in which the more complex reasons would operate."[12]

## The hybrid character of the state of play

The point of this survey of genealogy was to help to make clear the aim of my own genealogical project: to examine contemporary sports critically by use of what I am calling the state of play. Laying out the various senses in which my project resembles and differs from the foregoing genealogies, then, should clarify what I am up to here (in other words, why I have chosen first to tell a story that features certain moral and nonmoral qualities of sports before launching directly into a critique of their present low moral standing and a consideration of a possible remedy to revive them morally).

To begin with, in a number of important respects, my story coheres with the previous ones. Like all of them, its aim is decidedly moral, and it is pitched to a largely, though not completely, uncomprehending (because uncritical) contemporary public audience. Although history plays no direct role in my state-of-play narrative, it does not discount the importance of history, especially of historical accounts that follow Nietzsche's and Foucault's advice and take their point of departure from the actual moral lives of people in sports, though my narrative *does* defer this part of the analysis to another chapter. My story also does not seek, as Foucault counsels, to locate the essence or foundation of sport in play, to advance a play theory of sport of the kind, for instance, that Schmitz advances when he claims that "sport is primarily an extension of play, and … rests upon and derives its central values from play."[13]

I shall make no such claim, because I share no such aspiration to offer a theory of play, let alone of sport. In fact, the role that play performs in my sketch is purely a heuristic one, in which I stipulate that play is an intrinsically motivated way to engage in informal, unorganized, unstructured and, occasionally, elite forms of sport. However, my narrative does harbor, in the spirit of Nietzsche and Foucault, a subversive intent: it seeks to construct a counterstory and then deploy it against the dominant one in order to jar our present moral sensibilities regarding sports and, therefore, our stock moral conceptions of them as mainly instrumental pursuits chasing such external goods as money and fame.

Finally, the story I tell is, as already noted, partly fictional and, in the manner of Hume's and Nozick's state-of-nature stories, presupposes a simple, rudimentary conception of the social setting in which sports are played. It has an equally simple motivational set that guides its participants' actions – though, as I soon note, not the same simple social setting or motivational sets that Hume and Nozick incorporate into their stories.

In a number of respects, however, my genealogy of sports diverges from those previously canvassed. For starters, my narrative is more so a descriptive, quasi-phenomenological reckoning of our experience of sports in certain social settings and at certain stages of our lives rather than an historical reconstruction of a presocial and prepolitical state of play. However, to the extent that the social background of my narrative is a purposely scaled down and simplified one, it shares with Hume's and Nozick's accounts the feature of "fact defective[ness]." However, in this instance, the false antecedent on which the story depends does not consign it to the realm of the impossible. On the contrary, it sketches a state of affairs and an accompanying state of mind that, both from a phenomenological and a historical perspective, have been closely approximated and in some (admittedly rarer) cases actually achieved – even though seldom clearly articulated.

The previous point gives away a further distinguishing feature of my genealogy: that it seeks to reverse the order of regression that Nietzsche and Foucault sought to establish in their analyses by treating the moral regression evident in contemporary sports as a thoroughly modern development and one, therefore, that deviates rather than derives from the state of play. My genealogy also does not, in the manner in which Nozick tried to show how the political arises from the nonpolitical, aim to explain the development of sport from some nonsporting framework.[14] Rather, the state of play that I describe captures important features of contemporary sporting practices and of the kind of goods that they pursue as well as the motivations that certain of their participants have anyway. Finally, the rationality of the "potential" explanation of modern sport that I offer turns that of Hume's and Nozick's potential explanations on its head. This means not that the participants in the state of play would welcome the more complex reasons and goods that mostly inform the participants of contemporary sports but rather the other way around. In other words, the participants in present-day sports would welcome the motivations and goods depicted in the state of play and would strive to replicate those that they could. Obviously, the simplicity of that order could only be approximated – not replicated – by changing their present rational and moral outlook on sports.

## The state of play described

Any effort to patch together a hybrid narrative of this kind, trading as it does in both phenomenological description and fiction, is bound to be sketchy at certain points. And that is certainly true of my state-of-play story. Nonetheless, I shall try as best as I can to give a detailed description of this state. In so doing, I shall focus on and emphasize the important roles played by cooperation and trust in this account of sports and on the values that attend these qualities and together constitute a perfectionist way of life, one devoted to excellence. I first set out the social setting that I have in mind here, then the state of mind congenial to it, and finally the goods pursued in sports so conceived.

As for the social setting, I can do no better than Williams does when he describes a culture in which people "live under rules and values … [that] shape their behavior in some degree to social expectations, in ways that are not under surveillance and not directly controlled by threats and rewards."[15] It is not incidental to my account that Williams regards those who live in this society to be "living in an ethical system." For unlike Hume's and Nozick's state-of-nature stories in which people live in primitive (not ethical) economic societies that are long on self-interest and short on sympathy for others, Williams's society features one that is long on moral trust in others and short on insensate egoism. Just such a system characterizes the state of play I want to sketch, in which mutual regard for and trust in others typifies our general social engagements as well as our particular sportive ones. Further, precisely because such encounters are suffused with mutual regard for and trust in others, participants are disinclined to act unfairly, to try to gain an unfair advantage over others. Fairness is thus parasitic on solidarity in such a social system.

Now, it should not be conjectured that because my story is centered on such features as trust and cooperation, it is too far-fetched to have any explanatory or normative utility (in other words, that it is radically "fact defective"). For by featuring cooperation and trust so prominently, I could be accused of trying to eliminate competition from this picture of sports, of trying to pass off some fanciful version of sports absent their competitive element.[16] However, that would be a wrong conjecture for a rather simple reason: because competition itself in sports demands that we cooperate with others in accepting certain rules and conventions and – perhaps more importantly – in mutually agreeing, better mutually committing, to push each other to the limits of our capabilities, there is more than ample room for it in my narrative. What my genealogy clearly does rule out, however, is a certain kind of morally unsavory competition in which winning counts for everything and in which competitors are, therefore, reduced to mere obstacles to be overcome by hook or crook. For such competitive settings are seriously deficient in trust and cooperation and, therefore, are properly excluded from the story I tell.

Still, to the extent that most sports today are governed by such a Hobbesian war-of-all-against-all notion of competition, the state of play does come off, not surprisingly (and, of course, unapologetically) as fact defective. So, as a description of the social setting of contemporary sports, especially the elite, it obviously falls short. Nevertheless, it likely captures the spirit of most informal, unorganized youth sports, not to mention many recreationally oriented sports played with friends and strangers alike and what might be called "folk games." Those activities, though highly organized and institutionalized, are not commercialized and, therefore, do not offer their participants the promise of a professional career (e.g., such sports as men's and women's lacrosse and crew and – depending on your perspective – fortunately or unfortunately most women's college sports) and include, finally, a large number of master's sports played by adults intent on wringing whatever joy and meaning left them in their athletic lives.

That my genealogy is able to fit so many kinds and levels of sports into its story line is no mean feat, especially as it makes no pretense of its counter-factual, genealogical intentions. That it is able as well to accommodate certain elite sports, admittedly only when pursued under special conditions that go very much against the grain of the dominant ethos of these sports, is also notable. However, to see how these sports fit into the narrative necessitates shifting the focus from the social state of affairs that obtain in the state of play to the state of mind that their participants are expected to assume when they enter this realm.

What is perhaps most characteristic of this state of mind is its single-mindedness, its predominant focus on the excellence sought in sports and on the way of life required in order to attain it. It is this single-mindedness that marks the transition in a person's life when sport ceases to be simply one interest among other interests and becomes a passion. To play sports with passion, then, is to play them with a certain abandon in which the affairs of everyday life recede into the background, however fleetingly. It is this state of mind that allows players to telescope all their attention, effort, and concentration and to summon as much strength and energy as they can muster to meet the competitive challenges presented to them. And it is this state of mind that sustains players through the rigor and boredom that training for an athletic life requires and, more generally, the self-discipline and self-sacrifice that goes along with such a life.[17]

My description of this state of mind as single-minded is in one sense infelicitous insofar as it implies that I am talking about a single, individual mind. However, what I mean by *single-minded* has only to do with the highly focused perspective of the participants in sports and not with any claim that individual minds are the site in which such a focus is or should be located, expressed, and then coordinated with other individual minds. On the contrary, for descriptive and explanatory purpose, saying that the state of mind specific to the sports taken up in the state of play (whether individual, dual, or team sports) is a certain common- or like-mindedness would be more accurate. That is because when we attend to the challenges sports present to us and form certain intentions about how we might proceed on the basis of them and reason (both strategically and morally) about whether these are the appropriate intentions on which we should act, we do so mostly as a "we" rather than an "I." What is going on in each of these instances, then, is not simply the aggregation and coordination of separate attendings, intendings, reasonings, and actions that eventuate in a collective action but rather a mutual attending, intending, reasoning, and acting that eventuate in a common action. So, all these mental-conative operations are in some important sense intersubjective, operations that occupy a logical space between us and consequently matter not just to "me" or "you" but to "us."

The distinction that I am trying to draw here between collective action, the point and value of which are individual, and common action, the point and value of which are intersubjective, is very much like Baier's distinction between actions that are performed by more than one person but could just as easily be performed alone (though not, of course, as efficiently – her examples are painting a house or baking a cake) and actions that are performed by more than one person and could not have been performed otherwise (her examples again are performing a symphony or enacting a law).[18] What this distinction boils down to is that collective action, action carried out by more than one person, could be accomplished just as well, but just not as expediently, by one person, as the roles that each additional person plays in such activities are almost identical and thus call on the same kinds of competencies. This is why the sharing and mutual valuing of the task is for the most part incidental to its performance and to the character of that performance. By contrast, in common action, different roles are played by different persons and, therefore, call on different competencies. This is why the sharing and mutual valuing of this kind of activity is crucial to its performance and to the character of that performance.

What goes for symphonies here, I maintain, goes for sports as well. For sports are shared practices that are based on shared expectations and aims. Bill Bradley, former NBA basketball player, provides a nice illustration of this point. Bradley describes his state of mind in those moments when the play of the team came together, when, as he put it, "five guys moved as one." On those occasions, he goes on to say, "The only thing I had to do was allow the kid in me to feel the pure pleasure in just playing." And when he was able to do this, Bradley became so absorbed in the ebb and flow of the game and in the movements of his teammates that sometimes an entire quarter of play would go by before he even thought to glance at the scoreboard.[19]

Bradley's description nicely captures the common state of mind characteristic of sporting practices in the state of play. For what we see in action here is a group of people finely attuned to the thoughts and actions of one another, a group with a unity of purpose that defies any easy individuation: a meshing of wills and actions that makes it difficult to tell where one will and action end and the others begin. What we also see in action here is how that shared sense of purpose takes on a bodily form, how it is inscribed in the bodily comportment of the players.[20] So, this "commons of the mind" includes as well what might be called a *commons of the body*, which would account for the harmonious interactions that occur between players when they move and act as one.[21] Indeed, in such instances, it is as if they can feel in their bodies what their teammates are going to do next and can anticipate both where they will go before they get there and what they will likely do when they arrive. This is akin to being guided by what Hume referred to as "a kind of presentation: which tells us what will operate on others by what we feel immediately in ourselves."[22] Hence, in common athletic actions such as these, the feeling seems to be both immediate and felt by everybody concerned; how else to explain how five bodies are able to move in such seamless and complex ways as if they were one body?

As promised, in offering an account of the state of mind adequate to sports pursued in the state of play I have also managed to find room for elite sports within its boundaries: not just any elite sports, of course, but those pursued in the way in which highly attuned and sensitive athletes (e.g., Bill Bradley) and – come to think of it – highly infectious and joyous players (e.g., Magic Johnson) engage in them. That their numbers and the games on which they work their magic are small must be conceded at once, for nowadays they are clearly more the exception than the rule. Still, in my less cynical moments, I would like to think that there are a lot more Bill Bradleys and Magic Johnsons in the world of professional sports than most would suppose.

The more pressing question here, though, is what about these players and the games they are able to take over by the sheer integral force of their play warrants their inclusion in the state of play. Of course, I have already suggested that it has to do with the state of mind they bring to their games. However, what specifically is it about their state of mind that allows them to have such a transformative impact on the sports they play? Clearly, they are powerless to change the state of affairs that govern elite sports, and by this I mean principally the larger capitalist social system in which elite sports are presently forced to do their bidding. Just as clearly, the mores and values of this complex social system do not match up well at all with the mores and values I have cited as characteristic of the less sophisticated social system of the state of play. However, what such players as Bradley and Johnson are quite capable of accomplishing is bracketing and screening off this larger, intrusive social system, allowing both players and fans alike to forget the frequently off-putting business side of sports so that the perfectionist demands of sports themselves command our attention and scrutiny. That is, they are able to bring the game to life for us in ways that make it clear that sports are at their core more than an upscale market for the athletically gifted paid for by the economically privileged. (Of course, this is always at best a fragile achievement, as the imperatives of the market can undermine this delicate state of mind at a moment's notice.) Further, when such sports figures are able to pull this off – to put the dictates of the game first and those of its capitalization a distant second – I argue, the games that they play deserve some place in the state of play.

What, though, of the goods pursued in the state of play? Like their uncomplicated social setting, these goods are also uncomplicated in the sense that they take their primary marching orders from the goods internal, rather than external, to sports. That means that there are few goods in this social system, save in the special case of elite sports (about which I will talk shortly), that compete for the attention, not to mention the hearts and minds, of the players. Let me explain.

As in most other social systems, goods in the state of play come basically in two varieties: goods worthy of pursuit for the sake of something else and goods worthy of pursuit in themselves. The first kind of goods serve only temporarily as ends, because their chief value is as means that can be used to secure other goods. However, the second kind of goods serve primarily as ends, because their chief value is that they furnish ways of life, and corresponding aims and goals, that a sufficient number of people find compelling enough to pursue as ends in themselves – such that they are prepared to focus most of their attention on and sink most of their effort into trying to live up to the perfectionist life they require and to seek the sort of relatively autonomous goals they put into play. In the relatively simple social system of the state of play, participants would not be above treating sports as means to achieve other ends (say, participating in sports for their potential health benefits), but this instrumental interest in sports would be largely unobtrusive of the goods particular to sports themselves. At most, the modest social incentives operating in the state of play would impel participants to treat the goods of sports as mixed benefits (i.e., available for instrumental appropriation but certainly not consumed by such appropriation and available for instrumental use without crowding out or otherwise interfering with the pursuit of goods internal to sports). In short, these incentives would not pose a serious threat to sports as practices sufficiently compelling to elicit from participants an intrinsic interest in them.

Elite sports that fall under the state of play are something else again. For the larger social system in which these sports operate place an extraordinary set of demands on them, jeopardizing their standing as forms of life worthy of pursuit in themselves. Indeed, these complex and intrusive social demands introduce external goods (the chief one, of course, being money, especially large sums of it) into sports that not only open up sports for instrumental use but make it seem as if such instrumental use is the only one suited to them. That is why it takes a special athlete, one who understands and appreciates the fineries and nuances of sports, a similarly knowledgeable and appreciative audience, and strong institutional supports as well, to constrict the reach of such goods. Once again, Bradley's thoughtful analysis of his playing days strikes the right chord: "I felt about the court, the ball, the basket, the way people feel about friends, so playing for money seemed to me to be compromising enough. I never made any endorsements or commercials during my NBA career. To take money for hawking basketball shoes or shaving lotions would have demeaned my experience of the game, or so I felt."[23] However, the prospect of such athletes, audiences, and institutions lining up in the requisite way to exercise an appreciable deterrent effect on the influence of money in big-time sports, are growing dimmer every day ... and I consider this an optimistic estimate.

When all is said and done, then, elite sports can claim at best only a marginal and tenuous place in the state of play. Informal youth sports, recreational sports, and so-called folk games are on much stronger footing here. If pressed further, I would conjecture that informal youth sports are the most representative of the state of play. For sports at this level come closest to replicating the simple social system of the state of play described earlier, as the more complicated and competing larger social setting in which they occur are not yet a forceful reality – or at least not an intrusive one – for most of its participants.

What gives youth sports a leg up is that there is very little of the outside world that has to be bracketed here and, as a result, much more room for its participants to sample the intense pleasures that sports have to offer. For those of us who have come to sports relatively early in our lives, then (and we comprise a not-insignificant cross-section of the sporting public), the moral and nonmoral lessons we learned and the goods particular to sports that we managed to acquire, frequently played a formative role in constituting both our sense of self and our sense of community. That is because our initial foray into the world of sports, as more or less gangly, unsure adolescents, meant that we had at most a vague sense of who we were and perhaps an even vaguer sense of why we seemed so bent on gaining the recognition and approval of our peers. Sports thus became our crucible, a place to find out what we were made of and to gauge how well or ill others thought of us absent the paternalistic grip of the adult world. Typically, we competed hard and for hours on end, completely caught up in the game at hand. We learned to recognize when we had to tighten or let up on the rules in order to make the game more challenging, on the basis of our growing appreciation of the rewards of closely contested games. We also learned, often reluctantly, to trust one another to make the close calls that have to be made if the game is to progress smoothly. In the process, we crafted our argumentative skills so as to be able to press our claims as to the rightness of our calls as far as we could and at the same time our skills of compromise so as to cope with our more-than-occasional failures to sway others by the power of these claims. To be sure, there was plenty of griping and name calling in our games, and fistfights were not uncommon either. Yet, somehow through it all, these difficulties sorted themselves out, and we slowly but surely acquired a rudimentary moral sense of how to interact with one another, largely by gauging the reactions of our peers to the things that we did. We also bonded with one another, and more than a few of us formed deep friendships. Perhaps most of all, on the really good days – and we had more than our fair share of them – we experienced a joy and delight hard to put into words, emotions that more than compensated for all the time and effort we had packed into our athletic exploits and were unconnected to any thought of a possible instrumental payoff – primarily because there was little if any such payoff to speak of. Indeed, we commonly had a hard time recalling who had won the day before as we eagerly started yet another game, usually with a reworked or different cast of characters and as always in search of a good game.

This completes my rough sketch of the partly fictional (and partly not) state of play. It would be wise to reprise the two main reasons why I chose to begin my inquiry here. First, I wanted to set up the historical part of the genealogy of American sports to come; more particularly, to provide some critical perspective from which to examine the specific social and historical ways in which these sports actually developed. Second, I wanted to offer my own "potential" explanation of sports that turned on its head Nozick's deployment of this conceptual device with regard to the state of nature. The idea was that providing contemporary practitioners a view of sports in the state of play would lead them to see both those features of sports that have been either pushed to the background or simply sacrificed in the pursuit of the almighty dollar and why it would be rational and moral to try to redeem them, to find some vital role and place for them in the modern landscape of American sports.

I trust many will find these aims to be laudatory, but I also trust just as many will find them too high-minded (i.e., to be unreachable by today's social standards). What one can reasonably hope for in the way of significant social and moral reform in the case of sports (or for that matter, in any other valued human endeavor) is a vexing and mind-bending, if not mind-numbing, question, and one I specifically tackle in the last section of the book. For now, however, my tentative reply to this question comes in the form of a two-part conjecture. First, my hunch is that what it is about sports that attracts us so is bound up with just those qualities of sports that I have attributed here to our earliest experiences of them. The second, less happy, part of my conjecture is that it is these very qualities that drop out of the picture as one moves up the ladder of organized sports. However, what I am banking on in constructing the state of play and locating our first, inchoate dealings with sports firmly here, is precisely what Bradley banked on when his team played at its best: to bring out the child in all of us lovers of sports, to make more vivid our first, tentative step on the moral ladder of sports that propelled us on our winding athletic journeys. Aiming any lower than this, I conclude for now, shortchanges both the child within us and our adult capacity to reclaim that child for critical purposes.

# 2 The moral case against contemporary American sports

I begin this chapter with a sweeping but hardly controversial claim: American sports (i.e., actually existing American sports in most of their various forms) are in dire moral straits today. I shall have a lot to say later about what I mean by *moral* here (i.e., what makes a consideration, point of view, or judgment distinctively moral). For now, however, by moral consideration I mean one that gives pride of place to the good of others with whom we interact and the good of the projects we share and take up together. Morality, in other words, is importantly bound up with the first person plural *we* in a way that it is not with the first person singular *I*. This means, as Bernard Williams nicely puts it, that "simply to pursue what you want ... is not the stuff of morality; if [that] is your only motive ... then you are not within morality, and you do not have ... any ethical life."[1] So, to say that American sports are in sorry moral condition today is to say, among other things, that a thorough going narcissism permeates their ranks, a narcissism whose self-serving ways leave little, if any, room for consideration of the welfare of others in sports or for the larger good of these practices themselves.

Unfortunately, the moral status of present-day sports has sunk so low that merely documenting the extent of their corruption could easily fill an entire book or two or three. I shall, therefore, have to be more selective in making my case, as I want to say something as well about how the present corruption of sports might be undone. That explains why I devote most of my attention to professional and intercollegiate sports in this chapter, have much less to say about Olympic and high-school sports, and have next to nothing to say about adult master sports or youth sports. However, the reason why I chose not to limit my indictment of American sports to professional sports is because of the abysmally low moral expectations we have of them. This is because, as they continue reminding us, they are mainly businesses and, therefore, are usually content to let the market do their bidding for them unless they run up against something (say, trust-busting legislation) that threatens to compromise their market share; only then do they drag out their big guns and try to pass themselves off as respectable moral enterprises. Of course, their public relations approach to moral legitimacy only confirms my point here: professional sports are far too easy targets on which to pin a moral rap.[2]

However, even though any moral indictment of contemporary American sports must span more than the professional realm, starting with these sports still makes good sense. That is principally because they generally set the tone, morally and otherwise, for what goes on in sports at all other levels. As my opening remarks suggest, that tone is not a morally auspicious one.

## The brief against professional sports

Before I proceed, however, I should say that the unfettered role that market forces play in professional sports is not incidental to my moral critique of them here. For this is the main impetus, I argue, behind their excessive individualistic bent. The incursion of the market and the brand of instrumental reason in which it trades, therefore, go a long way toward explaining why in these sports winning trumps fair play; an assertive egoism triumphs over mutual moral respect; an anything-goes-as-long-as-I-don't-get caught attitude prevails over expressions of good will toward others; and a pervasive mistrust poisons most interactions and relations in sports, undercutting any sense of solidarity – of community – within them. To put it bluntly, this is not the kind of ambience that either inspires moral reflection or causes moral sentiments to well up within us. Also, I argue that it infects almost every feature of professional sports, from our interactions with others in sports to our regard for sports themselves. I should also say here that the discussion to follow includes the affects that the market has on both moral and nonmoral features of sports, with emphasis on those nonmoral features that are most complicit in the moral downfall of sports. Of course, this distinction between the moral and nonmoral is one that I will need to sharpen in due course.

The pernicious influence of money is no more apparent than in professional sports. For whatever market-averse motivational pull sports might have had on participants and spectators has been mostly laid low by the market. Basically, this means that in professional sports, just about everybody is (or is encouraged to be) on the take, whether it be to garner a larger contract or to land a lucrative endorsement deal or to secure whatever profitable end to which sports can be fitted. The result is that sports are treated more so as means than ends, as pursuits with a value to be instrumentally calculated in the same fashion as any other commodity: by the money they fetch. Indeed, the idea that professional sports could be ends in themselves comes off either as wishful thinking or as a willful distortion. This is why professional sports have become more and more like the rest of life rather than offering a welcome departure from it. For in both everyday life and sports these days, an instrumental regard for whatever people do is the rule rather than the exception, as is the concomitant rationalization of the unseemly dealings that are part and parcel of such a self-centered life. So, just as in sports, so too in everyday life: if one does not want to be taken advantage of, one would be well advised to look out for one's own good first and last. All this seems to go on without the slightest moral compunction in or outside sports.

One seldom-remarked result of the market's incursion into professional sports has been a decline in the quality of their play, in athletic excellence, and although excellence is, strictly speaking, a nonmoral quality of sports, it is, as we shall see, freighted with moral meaning. Understanding why this decline has gone largely unnoticed is difficult, as it follows as a matter of course that when winning becomes the primary or only thing because of the external goods it commands, the quality of play is usually the first thing to suffer. True, the fact that one can reap great rewards in select professional sports typically – but not always – does attract both the most talented and the most tenacious players to them. However, when that talent and determination are misdirected, as I am claiming they are in contemporary professional sports, the affect on the game is not the positive one most people suppose. Let me explain.

The decline in athletic excellence that I claim is a byproduct of the greater commercialization of professional sports is evident in the very conception of athletic excellence that informs these elite sports. As Dixon makes clear in his provocative and persuasive essay, "On Winning and Athletic Superiority," at least two rival conceptions of excellence exist in sports. The first holds that the most excellent players and teams are those that perform well under pressure over the entire course of a season. Assuming such excellence is adequately reflected in a team's won-lost record (which, of course, is generally – but not always – the case), this means that those teams with the best record should be regarded as the most excellent teams (i.e., as the champions of that particular sport for that particular season). A second conception of athletic excellence, however, holds that the best players and teams are those that play well when the stakes are the highest, which is in the postseason playoffs.[3] Of course, one cannot get into the playoffs unless one has played reasonably well over the entire season, but teams with less than stellar records are certainly eligible for postseason play and often (as a matter of contingent fact) do make the playoffs. In light of this second conception – but not the first – if they peak at the right time and defeat all comers in the playoffs, they are regarded as the best team, in spite of the fact that they may not (and often *do* not) have the best overall record.

Now, of course, all the most popular professional team sports in the United States – football, basketball, baseball, and hockey – operate under the second conception of athletic excellence, which is why they use a playoff system to determine the best teams. This is certainly an uncontroversial way to gauge athletic excellence, when the winner of the playoffs also happens to have the best won–loss record. And as Dixon duly notes, this is not an uncommon occurrence. Still, that does not change the fact that a playoff system is predicated on the idea that whoever is able, or fortunate enough, to save their best play for last – when everything is on the line – deserves to be called the best. So, we are left with the following question: which conception of athletic excellence deserves our support (i.e., which comes closer to capturing what true athletic excellence is all about)?

Dixon's answer, with which I fully concur, is that the first conception is clearly superior to the second: Assessing how well a player or team has played over the entire course of a season is a far better indicator of athletic excellence than largely limiting such assessment to a truncated playoff system. He offers two arguments to support his claim, both of which I find persuasive. The first is that by judging excellence over an entire season, one is able to give a far more comprehensive, balanced, and nuanced assessment of athletic performance, measuring not just those players and teams that perform well when the stakes are highest but those teams that are able to perform well under pressure day in and day out by wisely employing their athletic talents and strategic skills.[4] By contrast, the playoff system places far more weight on just one feature of excellent performance: those who perform best when put in do-or-die situations. While this is, no doubt, an important feature of athletic excellence, it is after all only one feature of what goes into an excellent performance in sports.

The second reason why Dixon thinks a comprehensive conception of athletic excellence is superior to a playoff system is that it is less vulnerable to elements that frequently affect the outcome of games but have nothing centrally to do with athletic excellence. Here, we enter more familiar moral territory, as what is at issue in this instance are such factors as refereeing errors, cheating, gamesmanship, and just plain bad luck. If they occur often enough and at propitious times, they can and frequently do play a role in determining who succeeds or fails in sports. Lessening the impact of these extra-athletic features over an entire season (in which they have a tendency to even out over time) is much easier than doing so in a short playoff system in which they may and often do prove decisive.[5]

Now, if Dixon is right about this (and I think he is), he raises the important question: why have all the major professional sports gone to a playoff format? What, precisely, does such a format have going for it that an entire season of excellent play does not? For the reasons just discussed, the answer clearly is not that such a system does a better job of assessing athletic excellence.[6] Nor can it be said that the playoff system is the only true and tested measure for assessing athletic excellence, because, as Dixon points out, professional soccer leagues in Europe and South America have for some time now recognized and awarded teams with the best record over the season as the most excellent teams.

However, a playoff system enjoys one distinct advantage, but it has nothing important to do with athletic excellence and everything to do with money. Playoffs generate more fan interest by giving even relatively poorly performing teams – who would otherwise have long since been eliminated by their season records – a chance to make the playoffs and by requiring superior performing teams (teams with the best overall records), who would otherwise have already been crowned champions, to prove their mettle all over again by submitting to postseason play.

So, there is a perfectly good reason for professional sports to resort to a playoff system, but the trouble is (to reiterate) that the reason is financial rather than athletic. For the allure of playoffs is that they attract large audiences and, in turn, large television revenues that would not be possible under the first, comprehensive conception of athletic success. And here is the rub. By opting for an inferior conception of and way to assess athletic excellence, professional sports are not just sending the depressing message that profits matter more than sporting excellence; after all, most of us knew this anyway. They are sending the far more worrisome message that at least when it comes to such things as athletic excellence, profits come at the expense of excellence, that the pursuit of the former cannot help but serve as an impediment to the latter, that profit and excellence are not only an unwholesome brew but a sulfurous and antiperfectionist one. And this proves my point: by putting dollars above excellence, professional sports have directly contributed to the decline in the quality of their play.

Further evidence of the decline of excellence in professional sports is apparent in the world of professional track and field. It is common knowledge in the track and field circuit, for instance, that world-class runners in hot pursuit of record-breaking performances more often than not stage such feats rather than compete for them. That is, they usually pick their fellow runners, better "rabbits," whose job is to set the pace necessary to run the sought after record time.[7] They then conveniently tuck behind the pace runners at each appointed stage of the race and dramatically break from the pack near the finish, setting up the spectacle of the solitary runner exerting herself or himself with every fiber of her or his being to breast the tape in record time. Now, of course, what we have here is not a footrace in any true sense of the term (i.e., a competition to determine the most excellent, in which the outcome is almost always up for grabs) but a carefully contrived time trial. To be sure, the result is often a superlative athletic performance, and in this sense at least we can say that a performance that has been achieved clearly has raised the level of past athletic accomplishment. However, the contrived, anticompetitive setting suggests at very least that we call into question its legitimacy. For it is also common knowledge that in such record-breaking quests, the very reason the appointed runners get to pick their "rabbits" is that their agents have cut a deal with the meet director to allow them to do so, to ensure that nobody gets into the race that their runners do not want into it – especially no one who might beat them. This is the Faustian bargain that any meet director of a major track and field event must make to guarantee the presence of star runners. Of course, the reason why meet directors are only too willing to make such odious deals is to bolster the marketability of these events.

Sometimes, however, the decline in quality of play is easier to see. Take NBA basketball as an example. It is hardly a secret that shooting percentages in the league are down, as are assists and other, general nuts-and-bolts basketball skills.[8] The same fate has befallen team play itself and the very idea of what it is. It is surely not what Bradley had in mind when he spoke of five guys playing as one but rather more like five individuals trying their utmost to separate themselves from the rest of the pack by their novel play or by some other eye-catching, marketable touch. In this setting, flair and panache count for a whole lot more than team choreography and feel. Cooperation is indulged only if it abets individual attention getting. Hence the preoccupation with feats of individual virtuosity, such as slam dunking and the decreased importance of team-oriented actions, such as assists and passing. Hence as well the attention lavished on individual stars and the relative obscurity meted out to solid, no-name teams.

In still other cases, the decline in quality of play seems more so a deliberate calculation. This, too, should come as no surprise because, as Sheed notes, market value is set by what draws crowds, and crowds are drawn to sport for reasons other than skillful play.[9] Television is one of the main culprits here, for in its quest to increase audience size for sports, it cannot but help to lower the level of understanding of fans. So, when such games as professional hockey are broadcast to regions of the country where the game has no firm tradition and where the fans lack even a rudimentary understanding of the game, it can hardly dramatize, let alone talk about, the fineries of the game. In order to promote such sports, the game is then reshaped to appeal to what such fans can appreciate. More than a few think this is one of the reasons why professional hockey does not do more to crack down on the violence of its games or on the goons who populate its ranks. In a word, violence sells.

Further, when professional sports expand into such areas to capitalize on television audiences, they dilute their talent pool and, therefore, the level of play. What is more, when television calls the shots, the times and seasons at which sports are played are affected as well: what makes for good television does not always make for good sports. Again, the emphasis is not on quality of play but on the size of the audience; if that means playing football games in cooler temperatures at night, or staging surfing events without regard for weather conditions, or playing World Series games in the cold weather in the fall, so be it.[10]

Finally, when corporations themselves get into the act and stage their own athletic events, quality of play hardly figures in the equation at all. Nike's "Hoop Heroes" basketball series, started in Japan in September of 1996, is a case in point. These games pitted Jordan, Barkley, and other Nike endorsers against 300-pound-plus Japanese sumo wrestlers.[11] The event proved wildly popular, but I think I am on firm ground in saying that its popularity had very little to do with even the basic skills of basketball, let alone its more fine-grained skills.

The emphasis on the star, the individual player, in most professional sports is also no accident but a consequence of the mania for cash and the marketing strategies hatched with that goal in mind that typify sports at this level. Of course, there is nothing worrisome or otherwise loathsome about individual expression itself, for one of the great achievements of modernity was the loosing of the bounds of the self from constraining cosmological schemes (e.g., the chain of being) that slotted individuals into certain realms, shaping and constraining their every move and opportunity. Likewise, the overturning of the reserve clause in professional baseball, which reserved a player's right to play for a specific team for his entire life, was a necessary and good thing. Free agency did not become a bad thing just because it also made many players wealthy beyond their dreams. Rather, it became a bad thing when it replaced the subjugation of the player to the team owner with the subjugation of the player to the dollar. As Susan Faldi notes, "money decoupled [players] from servitude, but also from the very idea of 'the team,' from any concept of loyalty to anything except perhaps their own agents, their own careers, their own images."[12]

The problem, then, is not individualism, which like most everything else is healthy when dispensed in the right dose; the problem is the kind of hyperindividualism to which markets give rise, wreaking havoc on sports because they turn them into crass exercises of self-promotion and self-assertion. This is why winning a championship in professional sports is nowadays viewed not as an occasion to build collectively on this achievement to attain yet another one but, as Sheed exclaims, as a "bargaining chip" that can be used by individual players "to raise their own price … cooperation is strictly ad hoc. No one wants to get bogged down in it."[13]

This further explains the misplaced allegiances of many professional athletes: why their loyalty is often reserved for the moneychangers of sports (owners, agents, corporations, tax accountants, public relations people, and the like) rather than for sports themselves or their teammates and opponents. Of this hardly distinguished group, professional agents are probably the most visible and perhaps the most transparent in their business dealings. Here, however, transparency is no virtue but simply a mark of the narrow world in which agents operate. For the agent's sole interest in the athletes they represent is, of course, financial, and this financial interest in lining their athletes pockets is predicated on lining their own pockets. This explains superagent David Falk's unabashed declaration to representatives of Reebok on behalf of his client basketball player Allen Iverson, that "Allen Iverson doesn't have to play great. He has to be a great personality on the court."[14] Perhaps I am crediting the forthrightness of such agents as Falk too much here, for when it comes to candor, it is hard to beat Robert Wright's observation, which nicely parses Falk's foregoing words: "Aside from athletic talent, nothing is more helpful in getting [an athlete] a big shoe contract than being an asshole."[15] That such market posturing only exacerbates the narcissistic tendencies of contemporary professional athletes goes without saying, but it is actually much worse than this. For the entire marketing ploy of professional sports agents is to gain for their athletes perks that single them out in no uncertain terms from the rest of the team. For instance, well known agent Scott Boros asked for the following in his negotiations with team ownership for star baseball player Alex Rodriquez: billboard space in the locale in which he plays, first-class airline tickets, offices for Rodriquez's marketing staff, and at spring training a tent in which to sell his memorabilia.[16]

It is little wonder, then, why Michael Jordan and Charles Barkley, both signed by Nike to promote their shoes, balked at wearing their Reebok festooned warm-up suits on the gold medal podium in 1992 and why Jordan was able to get out of this jam (cleverly, he thought; execrably, most everyone else thought) by draping the American flag over the Reebok emblem. Of course, we are not talking about small potatoes here, for when it comes to the financial clout of endorsement deals, the sky is apparently the limit. For instance, in the same Olympic year of 1992, Jordan earned roughly $25 million, of which only $3.8 million was his salary for playing basketball. By 1997, he earned as much as $100 million from endorsement deals spanning some 20 corporations. Though the sums of money cited here are staggering, the real worry is not just that for the right price athletes are willing to forsake their national and political identities – their standing as citizens – for flimsy corporate ones but that they are willing as well to forsake their very practical identities, those identities that underwrite what makes their lives in general (and their sporting lives in particular) meaningful, for a pot of money. This is, to put it mildly, scary stuff. For tethering one's identity to the vagaries of a fickle market is not only asking for trouble, for being sold out at a moment's notice when a better prospect comes along, but asking far too little of oneself (i.e., settling for a monetary calculation of the meaning of one's life). If this does not amount to moral suicide, I do not know what does.

I have already said enough to give the lie to Sheed's sunny consolation that "Fortunately for everyone, the best way … the player … can make some money … is to play the game as well as he can. And that is why the system seems to work despite itself."[17] Sheed is just plain wrong about this and not just from a narrow technical standpoint. For playing well means not just playing with technical precision or esthetic acclaim but with a moral sense of purpose as well. Of course, this feature of playing well is sorely lacking in modern professional sports and perhaps what is *most* lacking in them. That is why David Remnick was not exaggerating when he declared that in sports at this level, at least "goodness is a bonus, not a requirement." His immediate target was professional basketball player Latrell Spreewell, of coach-choking fame, whose suspect moral character was quickly forgotten when he helped his team, the Knicks, make a rare run at the NBA championship finals. Unfortunately, Remnick's point is easily generalizable to the whole of professional sports, as winning at this level seems to have the same morally anesthetizing effect no matter the sport, the team, or the locale. It is not that losers come in for closer moral scrutiny but only for more callow criticisms of ineffective or seemingly lethargic play. What passes for criticism in both instances, then, has scarcely anything to do with moral concerns.

This would explain the moral obtuseness of professional sports today; why, for example, such highly successful NBA coaches as Pat Riley can get away with fining his players for helping their opponents off the floor without so much as raising an eyebrow.[18] Print and media commentators of sports, who one might have plausibly supposed were supposed to keep tabs on such things, deserve criticism here as well, because they have long given up the mantle of moral criticism in favor of what can best be described as shrill carping: part of what some call the *outrage industry*.[19] Once such commentators found out that there was plenty of money to be made by delivering thoughtless, scandalous, off-the-cuff pronouncements about sports – pronouncements that (for those at least who worked in television) made up for their lack of critical force and then some by the high decibel level at which they were proffered – they gladly gave up the hard work of moral criticism.[20]

Of course, the commentators cannot, as already intimated, shoulder the entire blame, for when it comes to professional sports, it almost seems as if it is in bad taste to venture a moral view at all, to raise even the specter of moral wrongdoing. I am thinking, for instance, of why there appears to be no moral clamor for players to respect the close calls that referees have to make, rather than disputing them without a moment's reflection if such calls go against them or for respecting one's opponents rather than simply manipulating them, or for siding with the game when some policy or rule change is considered for the good of the game, though such might modestly dent the owners' considerable wealth or the players' substantial salaries.[21]

I fear that there is not much prospect of turning around this antipathy to everything moral in professional sports as long as playing well is crudely keyed to winning, which means, among other things, that playing the game well is not only compatible with cheating but obliges one to learn to cheat effectively – without getting caught. It scarcely needs saying that this sort of environment is not conducive to a moral life, to the cultivation of habits of moral reflection and the exercise of moral virtues.

Much of this moral malaise can be chalked up to the absence of a moral community in professional sports, to the mutual distrust of all parties concerned, which is the mark of a morally challenged community. And I do mean mutual distrust: one in which players can, without much effort, see through the aims of greedy owners; spectators and citizens can, again without reflective duress, see through the intentions of money-obsessed players; owners can readily detect players who are solely motivated by money; and – perhaps more important – unknowledgeable, entertainment-driven fans can go to games primarily looking for a good show (free beer, exploding scoreboards, side-shows and, of course, old-fashioned donnybrooks).

To begin at the top (or is it the bottom?) of this morally dysfunctional community: the owners' financial interests in the game color its every feature. It begins with the design of stadiums themselves and includes such breathtaking innovations as extraordinarily long dugouts (e.g., the dugouts in the Huston astrodome, measuring 120 feet in length, built not for the players' comfort but to ensure as many high-priced seats as possible behind each dugout) and luxurious sky boxes to entice business corporations to bring their most prized clients to sporting events without having to bother with the games themselves, because they are so far removed and insulated from the action. Once the stadium is built, there is the matter of naming rights, which so far has been able to attract a number of premium corporations who are only too willing to shell out whatever it takes to see their corporate name adorn an athletic stadium. The Chicago Bears, out of necessity, took this entrepreneurial step further. Barred by Mayor Daly from putting the name of their newly renovated stadium up for corporate bidding, the Bears (in what many in the business world considered a brilliant coup) instead put the name of their local community affiliation up for sale. Thus, radio and television advertising will from now on refer to the team as the "First Bank" Bears. The fact that all this private profiteering is mostly paid for by public money and that professional sport franchises are routinely afforded antitrust protections and other political privileges usually reserved for public utilities only makes things morally worse.

The erosion of a sense of moral community and the common good extends to the more particular sport community as well. I have already documented that professional athletes' primary concern appears to be furthering their own careers, even if it compromises the good of the sports from which they make their living.

That accounts for players' leaving teams and local communities at every chance they get simply to raise their salaries; professional sport franchises do the same, sometimes – despite the formidable logistical difficulties – with greater dispatch (think of the infamous overnight move of the Baltimore Colts to Indianapolis) if the decimal points on the check line up better somewhere else. Even those who stay put are not above blackmailing their current hosts to get a better financial package.

Where does this leave the fans? The short and simple answer is: in a lurch. The longer answer calls to mind Seinfeld's well-known joke that with players and franchises on the constant move, all that is left the spectators to cheer for is laundry.[22] However, even this joke falls flat because, as it turns out, clubs regularly change their team uniforms and logos to boost their merchandising profits. What this really means then is that fans are left out on the cold: the civic functions that sports spectatorship used to serve (mainly class and race mixing) it no longer serves, owing among other things to such crude, cash-raising schemes as professional seat licenses (in which people have to pay for the privilege to purchase tickets, a scheme that some have likened, appropriately, to renting menus in a restaurant) and escalating ticket prices.

Susan Fauldi observes a further fraying of the civic and moral fabric of fandom in her comparison of the fans of the old Cleveland Browns franchise to the fans of its new, present franchise.[23] Paul Brown, the founding coach of the old Browns, cut his teeth in the coaching field at Massillon High School, the football team of which gained national prominence under his tutelage. In the mid-1940s, he sought to forge a tighter relationship with the local community by turning fans into civic boosters. He did mean civic boosters, because the fans (given the times, of course, he was concerned only with the masculine gender) adopted players on the team and served as their surrogate fathers. This approach meant (among other things) spending time with them off the field, helping them if they got into trouble, making sure that they were in good scholastic standing, and occasionally even paying for food and clothing. As one might imagine, the bonding that developed between team and spectators by virtue of the latter's caretaking role was something to behold. What is more, given that America was just coming out from under a devastating depression, one would be hard pressed to overestimate the importance of this mutual bonding of team and community. As Fauldi writes, "For a man to have a hand in the making of a team's fortunes, at a time when the making of everything else was fast slipping out of his grasp, was the root of what it meant to be a 'fan'."[24] Brown was able to carry this paternalistic brand of spectatorship successfully for a time over to the professional Browns when he became their head coach – with the same strong communitarian results. However, in 1961, when Art Modell took over as owner of the Cleveland franchise, the NFL was in the full throes of transforming itself into a highly profitable business. Not long after that, most working-class fans of the earlier era found themselves priced out of the live spectator market, consigned either to watching the games at home alone or with friends or at their local sports bars. Needless to say, this did little to strengthen the bonds between the community and the team. Though those ties remain remarkably strong considering the shoddy treatment that these fans have received, they are less taut than they used to be, meaning that they still bind to a point but lack the moral cohesiveness they formerly had when they verged on the solidarity of friendship.

If one had to offer a *reductio ad absurdum* of the morally dispiriting effects of the wholesale marketing of professional sports, I suppose NASCAR auto racing would be a perfect candidate. The reason why is that the pandering of sports to money here is impossible to miss. To begin with the racing cars themselves, it is exceedingly difficult to find a space on them that is not taken up by some corporate name or logo; the same, by the way, goes for the racers' garb. The appeal to corporate sponsors is crystal clear: they get to display their brand name directly on the cars themselves so that they are constantly in the sight lines of the viewers for hours on end without having to lay out a significant chunk of change on an expensive commercial that runs at most for a few minutes. Of course, this is why different parts of the car fetch different prices. Not surprisingly, the most telegenic parts of the car command the highest prices (e.g., the hood and rear quarter panels of the car go for anywhere from $7 to $17 million). NASCAR drivers are also heavily recruited for television commercials, and they receive intensive media training sessions so that, when interviewed, they can effectively and seamlessly plug their sponsors' products. To make matters worse, corporate sponsors are also given considerable input on a racing team's choice of drivers to ensure that only the most media-friendly and savvy drivers represent that team.[25] This is, I think it is safe to say, professional sport in extremis, where the dominance of the market is so entrenched that one has to pinch oneself repeatedly to remind oneself that it is also a sport.

## The brief against intercollegiate sports

Unlike professional sports, college and university sports are freighted with both moral and educational meanings and values. This is why, to reiterate, I have singled them out, along with professional sports, for closer scrutiny. In my analysis, however, I target the moral rather than the educational dimension of intercollegiate sports, because that is my central focus and because the educational shortcomings of these sports have been well documented and widely discussed.[26]

The main difference between intercollegiate and professional sports is the very insistence by the former on this distinction itself, on not running together the aims of these supposed disparate athletic institutions. In fact, it says as much on the first page of the 1997–8 National Collegiate Athletic Association (NCAA) manual, which forthrightly declares that the purpose of sports at this level is "to maintain intercollegiate athletics as an integral part of the educational program and to the athlete as an integral part of the student body and, by doing so, retain a clear line of demarcation between intercollegiate athletics and professional sports."[27] The ethical part of this declaration is itself part of the demarcation effort in so far as it seeks to protect intercollegiate sports from commercial manipulation and exploitation by safeguarding their alleged amateur status, their supposed commitment to the love of athletic struggle rather than the love of money. What we have here then, at least doctrinally, is not only a decidedly ethical model of sports but one that presciently recognizes that one of the main moral evils befouling contemporary sports is their obsession with money. At very least, this should give aid and comfort to moral critics of sports, because they should have no reason to fear that in wielding their critical scalpels they will be regarded as interlopers. For the same reason, they should have no fear that in training their sights on the corrupting influence of money on sports and on subjecting their evidence of wrongdoing to the public, they have somehow deviated from their appointed role and committed some untoward act. After all, moral analysis and talk are built-in features of intercollegiate sports and one of the principal ways in which they represent themselves to the larger public so as not to be lumped together with professional sports.

Unfortunately, the reality of intercollegiate sports, as even the most casual observer of them will be quick to discern, is another matter entirely. For sports at this level are, in fact, almost indistinguishable from professional sports and certainly are driven by the same market imperatives. Indeed, intercollegiate sports is a multimillion dollar enterprise that is financed by large-dollar television contracts, licensing fees for athletic clothing, generous corporate sponsorships, and public financing in the form of bonds that are used, among other things, to build new athletic facilities. This would account for why most Division I athletic programs find it necessary to maintain their own extensive marketing divisions and why they pursue with gusto whatever capital ventures might be available to them: does the refrain *searching for new markets* sound familiar? The very same goes for the NCAA, which, despite its regulatory oversight role, is dependent for most of its funding on the financial success of big-time college football and especially basketball programs. Like professional sport franchises, it sold itself to the highest public bidder when it relocated its headquarters – the lucky (or unlucky) winner was Indianapolis, which offered the NCAA a whopping $50 million public subsidy.

That is not to say, however, that there is no important difference between college and professional sports. Indeed, there is an important difference between them, and it does have something to do with the professed moral aims of the former. However, in this instance the moral difference is of no moment because it merely serves as a cover for an economic difference. And a substantial economic difference at that, for by passing themselves off as amateur, nonprofit, ethically beholden organizations, college athletic departments are obliged neither to pay players for the financial bonanza they reap nor pay taxes on the lucrative television contracts, corporate sponsorships, and licensing deals they sign, which together number in the millions of dollars. What is more, they enable colleges and universities to install the same sort of cartel economic arrangements on which professional sport franchises pride themselves. What we have here, therefore, is moral tomfoolery of the worst sort, one in which greed is given greater scope in intercollegiate sports for ostensibly principled moral reasons.

If there is anything privileged about intercollegiate sports, then, it is their protected economic standing, not their moral standing. So, we have good reason to look with suspicion on their declarations of moral rectitude, as they merely confer legitimacy on all manner of moral mischief. This is, no doubt, why in his widely praised and read book, *Exploitation*, the moral philosopher Alan Wertheimer devoted an entire chapter to the moral chicanery of intercollegiate sports.[28] Further, this is, no doubt, why moral critics of college sports have to tread carefully within their precincts. For the empirical evidence is rather overwhelming that they are more likely to be regarded, on and off campus, as piranhas (under the circumstances, most would welcome the accusation of interloper as a blessing of sorts) and that their public declarations of athletic wrongdoing would be met, again on and off campus, with scorn and ad hominem attacks on their creditability, character, and (not least) mental stability. These are not only inauspicious settings for moral critics to do their work but – especially if the would-be critic is a faculty member – perhaps the most dangerous settings in which to do such work. I do not exclude here either financial or physical peril.

So, to pick up intercollegiate sports by the amateur handle is to pick them up by the wrong handle. It is no use, therefore, pretending that they swing free of the market, because it is principally there that they ply their trade and teach their lessons. As was the case with professional sports, the market is no less intrusive here, because it insinuates itself into every nook and cranny of intercollegiate sports.

This is no more true than in the practice of intercollegiate sports themselves. For the likelihood that sports will be treated as ends rather than as mere means is no greater here than it was in professional sports. So, once again, athletes are taught the not-so-subtle lesson that it is not only okay to be on the take but that it would be foolish (against their self-interests) not to be so, not to seize every available opportunity to parlay their athletic success into financial success and notoriety. In addition, why should we expect them to behave any differently when everyone else in college sports, from coaches to university presidents, is in it mostly for the money? As Sheed writes of the allure of money in college sports, "That's why the coach is doing it, with his [and her] contract on the side with the shoe company … And that's why the school is doing it, as it angles to get into the big-bucks tournaments and appear on TV."[29]

Speaking of coaches' shoe contracts (as I soon speak of televised sport tournaments), by the 1990s it was not uncommon for coaches to be paid in the $100,000 range to affix their signatures to such contracts, with successful coaches from high-profile athletic schools commanding four or five times that amount. Shoe companies also lavish college coaches with such perks as stock options and assists, financial and otherwise, and player recruitment.[30] Still other high-profile coaches have been offered executive positions with shoe companies (e.g., John Thompson, former basketball coach at Georgetown, appointed to the board of directors of Nike).[31] Because these lucrative deals are typically publicized by the local media, there is little chance that the players are oblivious to these cozy financial arrangements.

Of course, the NCAA forbids players from seeking their own endorsements, but this only makes matters morally worse because of the massive hypocrisy of such a restrictive policy. After all, if it is okay for coaches to make more than a little money on the side, why not the players? Hence, any invocation of the principle of amateurism in such instances is only likely, and rightly, to arouse moral derision, not moral compliance. For the message conveyed by these kinds of financial transactions, as already noted, is just too clear to be lost on players and, no doubt, instills in them the hardly moral incentive to cash in themselves even if it means breaking rules.

The long arms of the market are further corrosive of college sports because they raise the stakes of winning at the same time that they narrow our understanding and appreciation of the more complex notion of athletic success. It is just not good enough any more to play well – to play to the best of one's ability – if one loses. Despite all the flowery rhetoric to the contrary, players and coaches know that their jobs are on the line no matter how well they perform on or off the field if the board of trustees and college president look askance at their won-loss records. That is why such notions as tenure, so vital to academics who work on the political and moral edges of society, and loyalty, so vital to the maintenance of stable social relations, have no conceptual or practical traction in the sports world. And that is why, no doubt, to add fuel to the already white-hot competitive fire of college sports, the NCAA decided in 1973 to eliminate four-year scholarships in favor of one-year grants that are annually reviewed. In that way, athletes who are not up to the arduous task of playing top-level sports can be quickly dispatched and new, fresh, and more-promising talent can be brought in almost as quickly to right a listing ship. Why, indeed, should colleges and universities be expected to make four-year commitments to their student-athletes when winning rather than the fostering of athletic, moral, or educational excellence is their bottom-line goal?

In this kind of setting, it would take something akin to a miracle for players to come to think of sports as things worthy of pursuit in themselves. So, though amateurism may be the official ideology of college sports, it has next to nothing to do with the practice of these sports. On the contrary, the market reigns supreme here just as it does in professional sports; that is why athletes schooled in the ways of college sports learn pretty much the same lessons as professional athletes. Yet, there is an important difference here and that is that the opportunities afforded to college players are both more limited and more cruelly inflated than for their professional counterparts. Let me explain.

To be on the take at the college level means, above all else, grooming oneself for the professional ranks. The dream of turning professional and earning an extraordinary amount of money is powerful, especially for African-Americans who presently dominate, for example, collegiate football and basketball. However, for many of these athletes, the dream is just a pipedream and a savagely unkind one at that, for their chances of making it to the next level are miniscule. To be exact, as LaFeber notes, "the odds of a 20- to 29-year old African-American playing in the NBA was 135,800 to 1 (and for Hispanics, 33,300,000 to 1)."[32] Despite these formidable odds, few of these athletes are deterred from pursuing their dreams of turning professional and instead use their college careers to prepare themselves for making this transition. There would be something morally uplifting about their diligence, their resolve to chase their dreams no matter the cost, were it not for the fact that a disproportionate number of black college athletes (according to a 1990 survey, some 44 percent) as compared to white athletes (according to the same survey, 16 percent) cling to this dream.[33] There is clearly something quite radically amiss here and, to put it bluntly, it morally stinks. Somehow or other, and I clearly hold athletic officials and institutions at least partially to blame here (not to mention larger society), black athletes are being encouraged to view sports as their economic salvation, and this only compounds the moral offense of college sports players selling their soul to the highest bidder.

The very same can be said about the so-termed minor, or nonrevenue, college sports. For they, too, are a casualty of the market, as their numbers dwindle in order to stave off the financial drain they exact on the revenue-producing sports. As I mentioned in the introduction, it was a clever ploy on the part of athletic officials (mainly, male athletic directors) to finger women's college sports, and Title IX specifically, for their demise, but that dog won't hunt.[34] Rather, the main culprits are men's basketball and (especially) men's football programs, which are exceedingly expensive to maintain. Of course, they have been able to escape the wrath of nonrevenue sports advocates because of the large pots of money they supposedly contribute to the coffers of the athletic department. In other words, they are the ones – or so it is claimed – that make it possible even to field a program of college sports in the first place, an activity otherwise too costly to support.

However, one of the dirty, large secrets of intercollegiate sports is that most if not all athletic programs lose money. Part of the reason why it remains a secret is attributable to arcane accounting principles. According to Zimbalist, even in the case in which those principles are generally accepted (though they are not, except in one instance, in college sports), they can be used to turn a four-million-dollar profit into a two-million-dollar loss.[35] The other reason why it remains a secret, however, is because of the clever and altogether legal use of these cryptic accounting principles. This requires a little bit of explanation.

If we stand back for a moment, as Zimbalist does in his book, and survey the whole of college sports (in other words, not just Division I A,) we get a better picture of the economic plight of these sports. By Zimbalist's estimates (and this certainly is neither a secret nor a surprise), all the Divisions except I A failed to show a profit. To be more precise, of the 600 plus athletic programs in Divisions II and III, not a single one generated a profit; of the 200 or so Division I AA and AAA programs, again none showed a profit. By contrast, of the 100 or so Division I A programs, a hefty 43 percent reported a surplus.[36]

Now, if we cut the analysis off at this point, it would confirm the idea that close to one-half of the big-time programs are able to operate in the red, and it would also support the plausible inference from this that the reason they are able to turn a profit is because either (or both) their football and basketball teams are bringing in the necessary revenue to pay the bills for everyone else. However, as Zimbalist takes pains to show, any analysis of the economic impact of college sports worth the paper on which it is written must also consider the costs run up by money-making sports, such as football and basketball. Accounting for those costs, however, is easier said than done, owing once again to the clever but quite legal use of largely inscrutable accounting principles. However, it is also difficult to get a fix on their true costs because of a particular accounting technique that, though hardly inscrutable, is just the same very effective in disguising actual costs, something called "related party transactions." For example, athletic departments often charge their scholarship fees to the college's financial aid office, their substantial coaching salaries to the faculty pool, and their debt service on facility construction to the college's general facilities budget.[37] In addition, they frequently assign other big-ticket money items to off-budget accounts, such as the booster's club. However, once we take into account these related costs, as Zimbalist deftly shows, the profits reported by these Division I A athletic schools not only vanish but morph into an average loss of $823,000.[38]

Skeptics, of course, might retort that the reason why these schools run such deficits is that football and basketball profits can go only so far in supporting the increasing costs required to offer a full slate of men's nonrevenue and women's sports. The overall deficits, they might argue further, do not show that football and basketball are not doing their fair economic share, indeed more than their fair share but, on the contrary, that the rest of men's nonrevenue sports and women's sports are not doing their fair share, are not pulling their own economic weight. However, this claim is doubtful. The problem here is yet again – surprise, surprise – an accounting one. For when colleges report their expenses to the NCAA, as Zimbalist points out, they are not required to target those expenses to specific sports. So, for example, facilities maintenance expenses for football stadiums and basketball arenas are routinely charged to the entire program no matter that they are used exclusively by these teams. The same is true of the overhead expenses of the athletic departments, such as administrative salaries, travel, entertainment, advertising, utilities, and the like, which again are assigned to the entire program, even though the lion's share of those expenses is incurred by the football and basketball teams.[39]

When we factor in all the data, then, any notion that college sports operate only partially along market lines (e.g., share the wealth in a manner similar to nonprofits and dissimilar to markets) goes up in smoke. On the contrary, the only thing that distinguishes them from true markets is that they are legally allowed to run their affairs as cartels, which only worsens the moral predicament of college sports, not to mention the bleak economic outlook for African-American college athletes, men's nonrevenue sports, and women's sports. The problem is that there are not any other countervailing regulative forces in the vexed world of intercollegiate sports, on or off campus, to rein in these powerful market forces.[40]

The recent greater involvement of college presidents in athletic matters on their campuses is a case in point. When in 1996 the NCAA was persuaded (by the work of the Knight commission in the early 1990s) to give greater control to college presidents in running athletic programs, many thought this would go a long way toward eliminating abuses at this level. However, college presidents, already overextended and preoccupied with fundraising responsibilities for the general campus, were no match for the athletic juggernaut. In many cases, they proved to be allies, not critics, of the commercialization of college sports, evidently unable to resist the powers that be. As James Duderstadt, former president of the University of Michigan, plainly put it, "When push comes to shove and you put a lot of presidents around the table, they're going to go for the top dollar, whether it's TV negotiations or putting games on at 9 o'clock."[41] Perhaps their reticence to stem the influence of money in college sports is owed to their own complicity in the corporatization of the university itself or to their being star-struck fans themselves or to their toadying to the boards of trustees that they serve or to some combination of these factors. Whatever the reason, the commercialization of college sports grew worse under their watch, enough so to provoke yet another reconvening of the Knight commission in 2000, this time under the tutelage of Hodding Carter, to consider other possible reforms.[42]

It is equally clear that the conferences in which individual schools play and the commissioners who govern these conferences are neither equipped nor inclined to undertake significant reforms of college sports. Truth to tell, they are part of the problem, not the solution. The principal reason why is that conferences have become the main negotiating agents for the television broadcast rights of college games. It was not so very long ago that teams formed themselves into conferences based on athletic prowess and geographical proximity. Since the advent of televised sports, however, and the sculpting of sports into entertainment vehicles for students, alumni, and boosters, money and – as one athletic director crassly but honestly phrased it – "brand image" are the main concerns of conferences.[43] This is why colleges go to great lengths to align themselves with the richest and most powerful athletic conferences. This explains the recent spate of conference jumping by schools as well, in which Miami's and Virginia Tech's (the latter with the lobbying help of the governor) defections from the Big East to the Atlantic Coast Conference (ACC) are perhaps the most notable example. Their protestations to the contrary, cash is the main impelling force here.

The so-termed Big Six, which includes the ACC, the Big 12, the Southeastern Conference (SEC), the Pac-10, the Big 10, and the Big East, should be singled out here, as they attract most of the TV dollars and the teams with the best records from these conferences are guaranteed slots in the football Bowl Championship Series (BCS), thereby assuring them and the conferences they represent a large end-of-the-season pay off. Schools from other lesser conferences have an uphill battle to get into the lucrative football bowl series despite their records. For the BCS puts the accent less on maximizing the highest level of competition and more on advancing the economic fortunes of select schools, especially those with a large and profligate fan base. It is this built-in disparity that prompted Zimbalist's sardonic remark that "[t]he overall picture of bowl access in Division IA almost makes the income distribution in Haiti look equitable."[44]

So, not only are college sports market vehicles through and through but, especially in their conference getup, retrograde ones at that. Moneymaking and handling is their game, moral reform is not. Since conference commissioners answer to no one in the academic community and are evaluated almost entirely on the size of the television contracts they broker, there is little prospect that things will change for the better anytime soon. It should come as no surprise, then, that the largest moneymaker among the Big Six, the SEC (which took in $81.5 million in 2000), has the worst ethical record. As of 2002, six of the 12 member schools were either on probation or accused of unethical conduct, and since 1990, the SEC has been penalized nine times, far more than any other conference.[45] This is proof enough, I think, that money and college sports is an unseemly and unworkable moral mix.

Of course, I have only in passing mentioned the NCAA, whose main job it is to protect the moral and educational mission of college sports. I have, however, intimated that the NCAA is no moral savior of college sports. On yet closer inspection, however, it is evident that that claim is at best an understatement, as the NCAA is itself complicit in the morally benighted standing of these sports. The reason why is not difficult to discern because, as already mentioned, it depends for most of its revenue on the money generated from the television broadcast of its annual basketball tournament. In 1990, the NCAA signed a huge contract with CBS for $1 billion over seven years to carry the tournament, more than double the annual value of the previous contract, and in 1994 they renegotiated the contract with CBS for $1.75 billion again over seven years. Though that kind of money will not buy you moral integrity, it will buy you plenty of influence over the game. And the NCAA did not disappoint CBS when, in the first half of its 1997 men's final, it allowed an astonishing eight minutes of commercials to 20 minutes of playing time; not even the NBA tolerates commercial interruptions of this length.[46]

To say, then, that the NCAA is primarily a business association and that its main interest is less the moral integrity of the game than the financial returns it generates, is hardly an exaggeration. Of course, that it does not primarily serve the game or the athletes who play it was evident as early as 1953, when the NCAA coined the phrase *student-athlete* not to give voice to the academic commitments of college sports but to help their member schools to fend off legally the workmen's compensation insurance claims filed by injured football players.[47] Further, that the NCAA does not take its regulatory responsibilities for the ethical conduct of these sports seriously is also readily apparent by the resources it devotes to enforcement of its stated principles and rules. As Zimbalist forcefully writes, with around 1,000 schools to regulate, a rulebook that takes up three volumes and 1,268 pages of rules and regulations, and an annual budget in the neighborhood of $283 million, one would think that the NCAA would devote more than $1.5 million to enforcement, would hire more than 15 investigators to check on rule compliance, and would pay them well enough to ensure low turnover in their enforcement staff.[48] However, that paltry sum, woefully inadequate enforcement staff, and poor pay resulting in a large turnover of compliance officers is what the

NCAA actually commits to ensure that everything is up and up on the college sports scene.

To make matters worse, even with this pathetic attention to enforcement, the NCAA more often than not finds itself on the wrong side of the ethical divide when it comes to protecting college players from exploitation. For example, when some in congress became distressed with the scandalously low graduation rates of players in high-profile college football and basketball programs (which, as I noted before, is especially egregious given the insurmountable odds that most of these players face in trying to make it to the professional ranks), they introduced the Right to Know Act, which would simply require colleges and universities to publicize the graduation rates of their players. Leading the opposition against the passage of this act was the NCAA, who worked hard (fortunately unsuccessfully) to defeat it. All of this suggests that the NCAA is a regulatory body in name only and that its public moral posture is just a convenient ploy to divert attention from its ruthless economic agenda.

It is thus apparent that college sports are no more suited to a moral life than are professional sports. Indeed, how could they be, when everyone is too busy conjuring up ways to make money off sports or (what comes to the same thing) managing their own careers to give much thought or attention to the moral state of the games that they play or oversee. That is why cheating is as prevalent in college sports as it is in professional sports and why a technical regard has replaced a moral regard for such things as rule breaking and rule bending and the very notion of fair play itself. Those responsible would have us believe that it is aboveboard to break rules when it is to one's advantage and to refrain from doing so when it is not; this attitude reduces fairness to a not-so-fine-grained strategic sense that it is perfectly okay to take advantage of others as long as they are similarly disposed to take advantage of you. And that outlook, in turn, curiously means that what would otherwise be branded as unethical conduct if done in isolation is perfectly ethical if done in concert with others. It would also explain why the observance of even the most elementary moral norms in sports at this level, for example, the refusals of a player to take advantage of, say, an injured player or to accept a tainted victory are often touted or (as the case may be) hyped, as if they were supererogatory acts meriting the highest of moral praise, not to mention publicity. When it comes to the morality of college sports, therefore, the ordinary is made to appear quite extraordinary, and the extraordinary is made to appear as quite technically stupid. The exceptions are those sincere types looking for some moral consolation to justify their involvement in sports and for those less sincere public relations types groping for anything they can find to avert our eyes from the moral mess we call college sports. In other words, there is no reason to worry that fair play and sportsmanship will overtake cheating anytime soon.[49]

Unfortunately (but, of course, not surprisingly), the empirical evidence regarding the moral laxity of intercollegiate sports is rather overwhelming. As Louis Menand reports, college athletes are more likely than their nonathletic peers to regard being very well off financially as an essential or very important goal of life, which would further account for why male athletes at least frequently choose business-related fields for their majors.[50] Now, there is nothing wrong in wanting to make a lot of money – wouldn't we all in the right circumstances? However, there is something morally out of whack with rating this goal as an essential or even very important good, given the values of liberal arts institutions themselves, which place far more emphasis on the moral importance of a reflective life and on the value of public service.[51] It does suggest that there is something about the market trappings of these sports, as I have painstakingly tried to document, that prompts athletes not only to relegate too much importance to money making and not enough to the moral integrity of sports but too often to forsake the latter for the former.

When we couple this inflated importance of earning a lot of money with the further facts that athletes are also more likely than their peers to regard competition as an intrinsic good both on and off the playing field and less likely to assume responsibility for others, we have good cause to be alarmed.[52] Again, there is nothing wrong with competition per se, or at least a certain moral version of competition that is itself based on cooperation, on a consideration of the interests of others, but there is very definitely something morally worrisome about the kind of competition to which most of these athletes have been exposed, the type that places a premium on winning above all else. For when winning becomes this important, athletes and their "superiors" are more apt to cheat to get what they want and to disregard the harm that they do to others in the process, just as colleges are more apt, in Menand's words, "to put money into coaching and [athletic] facilities, and to trade academic promise for athletic talent in admissions."[53] Further, if this were not morally odious enough, a favorite ploy used by students to condone academic cheating – alas, presently on the upswing – is to point to the pervasive dishonesty of the campus athletic program, as if the moral failings of the latter somehow justify the moral failings of the former.[54] Though the students' moral reasoning leaves something to be desired in this instance, the conspicuous moral lapses of college athletic programs provide easy fodder for their sophistry.

The problem here is the same problem that beset professional sports, namely the absence of a moral community. However, unlike professional sports, there is not just a potential moral constituency for college sports but a fairly vocal one if only someone would pay it some mind. I am speaking here, among others, of faculty, alumni, and the general sporting public itself, all of whom are steadfast in their view that college sports are in moral trouble today and have encroached too far into the academic and moral mission of colleges and universities. For example, a 1989 Harris poll showed that 80 percent of Americans surveyed thought college sports have overstepped their proper bounds.[55] A more recent 2003 survey commissioned by the Chronicle of Higher Education reported a similar finding, with close to 70 percent of respondents registering their disapproval of the overemphasis placed on sports in colleges and universities.[56] This same poll showed that of 21 listed goals for higher education institutions, the goal of offering sports for the entertainment of the public ranked dead last by a wide margin. Alumni dissatisfaction with the attention that their colleges and universities shower on sports is also commonplace, no doubt accounting for why the old saw that "athletic success leads to greater alumni giving" does not accord with the evidence (despite unmistakable empirical evidence that enhancement of faculty and student quality does spur greater alumni giving).[57]

To reiterate, then: there is a moral constituency for college sports and one that has not been timorous in expressing its moral discontent with the status quo. What undercuts their moral clout, however, is the inner circle that pretty much rules the roost in college sports today, and the insularity of which largely renders them impervious to the wishes of the larger public. I am referring here to what are euphemistically called the "boosters" of college sports (many would reference them in far less flattering terms), made up of local wealthy businessmen whose ties to the university are typically not academic, meaning that they are for the most part *not* alumni but often find themselves, given their wealth and the influence that follows in its train, sitting on the boards of trustees of these same colleges. Make no mistake about it, however: sports are their bailiwick and what gives them cachet with the proconsuls of the university. In exchange for their generous financial contributions to the athletic department, they are treated as royalty and provided the best seats at athletic events, not to mention highly coveted parking places close to athletic facilities and select audiences with the head football or basketball coach, usually over lunch served in the athletic department. That these seats used to be occupied – before the untrammeled pursuit of cash became the mainstay of sports marketing – by loyal fans who had modest means and could be counted on to cheer for the home team come hell or high water no one seems to notice or care.

The problem is that these so-called boosters are by and large quite content with college sports just as they are and, as one might expect, with their privileged standing within these athletic hierarchies just as they are. Because it is this narrow (both in number and purview) constituency to which university presidents ultimately have to answer (not to mention on whom ultimately have to rely for their all-important fundraising projects), there is not much chance that the larger public's moral misgivings regarding college sports are likely to have any appreciable impact on the way they conduct their affairs. This goes to show that even when a moral community is on hand to register their moral disapproval with what is going on in sports (the same, by the way, goes for politics and practically everything else in contemporary society), markets are not in the least shy about ingratiating themselves with the powers that be to forestall such efforts.

## The brief against the rest of the sports world, or at least most of that world

I have already suggested that high-school sports and Olympic sports suffer from the same moral malaise as that of professional and college sports. The only thing preventing me from saying the same about youth sports and masters' sports for adult athletes is, no doubt, the market's thoroughgoing disinterest in their athletic exploits thus far and the lack of data on hand about these sports (itself revealing, as it seems to suggest that if the market chooses not to shine its light on one's athletic engagements, they must not be important enough to catalogue or document). In any event, I want only to sketch briefly for now the moral travails of high-school and Olympic sports.

As I have already intimated, the coupling of money and sports proves to be just as morally problematic at the high-school level as it has at the college and professional levels. The saga of basketball phenomenon LeBron James is a good illustration of this, as it shows that if your talent is large enough, the director of your high-school athletic program will not hesitate to capitalize on it by playing a national schedule at larger venues to accommodate greater numbers of fans and by signing a television contract to underwrite the costs and bring in a handsome profit to boot. When the money is this good, evidently any suggestion that high-school sports should comport themselves differently than the "big boys" because their aims are not the same is not likely to carry much weight. What is more, it is becoming more commonplace, particularly in such sports as basketball, for high-school seniors to jump directly to the professional leagues, a practice that transforms high-school sports into the same kind of feeder system as the college game, unfortunately with the same predictable and regrettable results.[58] This tapping of precocious high-school athletic talent has of late developed yet a new, more troubling, wrinkle, in the vernacular called "athletic leapfrogging." It involves players skipping their senior year either to play elite college football or professional baseball (for the boys) or professional soccer (for the girls).[59] The same sort of pump priming for athletic talent also goes on outside athletic departments in the schools themselves and in the formulation of educational policy. I have in mind here the increasing reliance on open enrollment policies in schools across the country. The main point of such policies is to make it easier for young gifted athletes to pick and choose the schools for which they want to play. If there is any doubt that the educational standing of these schools figures hardly at all in their decisions, we need only point to athletic powerhouses, such as Dominguez High School in southern California. For it is schools such as these to which talented athletes flock in order to jumpstart their athletic careers despite the fact that Dominguez's physical plant is dilapidated, its corridors racked by gang violence, and its basic resources so scant that students greatly outnumber available books.[60] Last, there are the off-season traveling teams and coaches sponsored by the Amateur Athletic Union (AAU), which compete with their school teams and coaches for their loyalty and commitment by, among other things, paying them under the table or by putting them in touch with professional agents.

Perhaps the worse moral offenders at this level, however, are the summer football camps run by prominent university football programs and the summer basketball camps sponsored (and run since the 1980s) by such shoe companies as Nike and Adidas. The purpose of the football camps is to bring in blue-chip prospects (in other words, whom the coaches are eyeing) where they are timed, filmed, and subjected to a battery of drills and tests to gauge their athletic mettle. In effect, these camps serve the same function as that of the combines for professional football teams: the careful evaluation of athletic talent so as to spend their scholarship money wisely. What is morally off-color about these arrangements is that they are used primarily as recruiting devices by major colleges in explicit violation of NCAA policy; worse, such arrangements sometimes operate as coercive devices in the case of athletes who are "on the bubble:" told in no uncertain terms they will not be offered a scholarship unless they go to camp. It should also be said that the other major purpose of these camps is to make money, and lots of it, for the coaching staff, as they attract a large number of lesser athletes as well, those willing to pay hundreds of dollars to hone their modest skills. It is no coincidence, therefore, that colleges stagger their camps to attract the largest pool of athletic prodigies possible, which also means that it is no coincidence that many of these athletes have little choice but to attend as many of these camps as they can afford (charged anywhere from $25 to $425) to showcase their skills. It is there that they learn to talk the talk and walk the walk, becoming street-smart self-promoters on the lookout for whatever favors, financial and otherwise, may come their way. A final moral worry about these summer arrangements is that the high-school coaches who are hired to help to run them are really being hired to bring their best prospects with them, not to mention being paid in large enough sums to cover the costs of bringing them (it is not against NCAA rules for high-school coaches to pay the camp fees of their own players).[61]

Basketball camps for high-school players sponsored by Nike and other athletic companies are even worse. The idea behind them is to gather the best high-school players from across the country under one roof to show their stuff, with most of the major college coaches in attendance watching their every move. However, the shoe companies relations with these players begins much earlier than this and is initiated and nurtured by street agents hired by these companies. Their main job is to scour playgrounds frequented by high-school kids, where they look for talented prospects. In addition to evaluating talent, they also play the role of soothsayer, trying to convince such kids that basketball is their future and that they would be well advised to attend schools that endorse the company's athletic products to ensure that future. This would explain why there is a strong correlation between the sneakers that these kids wear and the institutions of higher education for which they end up playing. If such talent scouts happen as well to come across players who possess extraordinary talent, their other, no-less-important job is to establish a relation with these budding stars with the idea of signing them later to a contract endorsing their products. For now, however, those talented kids have to be content with smaller perks, such as free shoes (which are also dispensed to the high-school teams for which they play) and to be emboldened by the promise of greater things to come.[62]

What Nike and others shoe companies get in return for their investment is not insubstantial and includes prominent advertisements for their shoes and athletic apparel, possible future superstar endorsements, and (not least) close relationships with college coaches who have the wherewithal to make those relations pay off in a big way. What the college coaches get in return is no less impressive: a central venue in which to scout the best players (which saves on travel and other expenses), lucrative shoe contracts, and company-based recruitment incentives for athletes to attend their schools. Finally, what the players get is less an honest evaluation of their basketball skills and fortunes than inside knowledge on how to game the system for their own benefit. Of course, no one who is a party to these transactions gets an education in the moral possibilities of sports or a greater appreciation of their internal goods, at least not in any direct or substantive sense. But then again, no one caught up in these affairs seems to have much interest in such moral lessons.

Finally, Olympic sports might be the biggest moral disappointment of all. For what is particularly galling about their mercenary conduct is that these sports were from the "get-go" supposed to be about ethics rather than pocketbooks, to be devoted to such lofty goals as the furtherance of international peace and tolerance than to enriching Olympic officials, sponsors, and participants. That is why the founder of the modern games, Coubertin, and his disciples never tired of promoting the games as a kind of secular religion, devoted in equal measure to athletic excellence and the triumph of a cosmopolitan state of mind, one respectful of different cultures and peoples.

The sad fact, however, is that the Olympics are no longer Olympian, at least from an ethical and political vantage point. For the only secular religion they seem inclined to support and propagate today (public relations campaigns to confuse us aside) is a suspect form of capitalism, which insists on treating and conducting the Games as if they were a string of fast-food restaurants. That explains why they get far more worked up about protecting their brand name and famous interlaced five-ring symbol (which, as Lipsyte ruefully observes, has become just "another sports logo, battling for the public's recognition with the Swoosh and the major league baseball batter's silhouette")[63] than by enacting true reform that would put an end once and for all to the graft and bribery of recent past Games.

If there is blame to be assessed here, it probably should be laid at the feet of past president of the International Olympic Committee (IOC) Juan Samaranch. For it was during his long tenure, beginning in 1980, that the Olympics went on a selling binge lending its name to any firm and product willing to shell out the requisite sum of cash. As a result, the IOC quickly transitioned from a cash strapped, aristocratic top-heavy organization to a cash-loaded, market manager-dominated one, presently presiding over an annual budget of $100 million plus.[64] It is no secret that very little of this money gets down to the grassroots level to develop exemplary sports programs or to disseminate the goals of world peace and respect. What little does trickle down allows the IOC to ponder its ethical dilemmas (mainly, performance-enhancing drugs because they most threaten its corporate image) at five-star hotels in such world-class cities as Paris. Who says doing ethics doesn't pay.

Of course, Olympic athletes are no paragons of virtue either. Most have professional agents at hand, not to mention a retinue of business types and accountants, to cash in immediately on their athletic triumphs. Endorsements, of course, are the major sought-after financial prizes in this regard, and winning a gold medal in the right event can bring in a number of these, not to mention a tidy sum of money. Money is not only a temporary distraction here; it upsets the entire Olympic apple cart, as the key to using sport as the medium to encourage respect for cultural differences is to have athletes bring their culture with them into the international athletic arena. The heavy symbolism of the athletes marching in unison together behind their flags and outfitted in a common national uniform in the opening ceremonies – and the no-less-heavy symbolism in which athletes drop their patriotic pose and in a cosmopolitan gesture mingle with members of all the other countries in the closing ceremony – crucially depend for their significance on the fact that these national and international identities and symbols really mean something to everyone concerned, especially to the participants. However, when athletes change countries to compete in the Olympics (as often as some change their clothes) and when their reason for doing so is based on financial calculations of success and the size of the markets of the countries they represent, these symbols become farcical. Of course, the same criticism holds for the countries that not only gladly accept these itinerant athletes but actively encourage them to jump ship and relax citizenship requirements to make the transition as seamless as possible.

The moral debaucheries of the IOC offering itself and its founding ideals up for sale and of Olympic athletes willingly forsaking their national identity for the right price are one thing (and as I have argued, a very bad thing), but the moral debauchery of the IOC welcoming into its ranks a well-known political thug is quite another thing – and, I want to argue (as if an argument is really needed in this case), a very, very bad thing. I am speaking here of the recent admittance into the IOC of a former Ugandan military commander who was Idi Amin's henchman during his infamous reign of terror. It is incredible, to say the least, that any organization – let alone one supposedly ethical, such as the IOC – could see fit to commit and then, most astonishingly, condone such a thing. But the IOC did indeed do such a thing and had the audacity to try to justify it. As one Olympic spokesman crudely put it, "Do you want to push for human rights around the world? That's Amnesty International. Or do you want African athletes at the Olympic Games?"[65] The appalling ignorance of this incautious declaration (for it is not only the job of the Olympics to promote human rights across the globe but one of its founding ideals to do just that) is matched only by its impudence. It tacitly proclaims that getting as many athletes from as many continents in the world to come to the Olympics (of course, of paramount importance to the furtherance of its financial ambitions) overrides its ethical commitment to do so in a way that promotes world peace rather than setting it back. It implies that there are not enough good and decent people from this part of the world to join the Olympic community without having to recruit and consort with hoodlums. To say this is a new ethical low for the Olympic movement almost sounds like a bad joke were it not for the moral *gravitas* of the situation.

## Where does this leave us?

My moral indictment of contemporary sports seems to have landed us in a most unsavory place. For there does not appear to be any form of sport today that has not been sullied in one way or another by the almighty dollar. This has the effect of making my sketch of the Arcadian-like moral ambience of the State of Play (offered in the first chapter) seem even more Arcadian and thus plainly unreachable by present standards (in other words, just another in a long line of useless utopian fantasies). My indictment also seems to suggest that what the market has emptied out of sports, precisely those moral qualities I claimed to discover in them in the State of Play, cannot be retrieved because they have been hopelessly compromised. All of which makes it difficult to resist Tannsjo's stunning claim that "if we are to grow as moral agents, we need to cultivate a distaste for our present interest in and admiration for sports."[66]

As one might suspect, however, I regard such misgivings and claims as (though understandable) plainly overstated, as too far removed from the facts to warrant our assent. For though the facts are not especially encouraging, neither are they so damning that we simply have to write off sports as a lost cause. My present assertions to the contrary, however, are just that: mere assertions. So, in the chapters that follow I will have to make my case, this time with arguments, that sports are not too far gone, that they can be morally rehabilitated by undoing their present marginalization.

I have no illusion, however, that making that case will be easy, will be anything other than a daunting and arduous task. However, as a first step in this direction, I need to provide some larger historical context for my moral critique of present-day sports. I must do so because all I have offered to this point is a synchronic glimpse of sports as they already exist, which – though it may give some tentative clues as to their future development – does not suggest how they have evolved to this point. For this, a diachronic perspective is required, one that situates my present morally disparaging story of contemporary sports into a larger, historically extended story. However, because this taking the longer measure of sports is so vital to making sense of their present moral standing, of how best to interpret that standing,[67] I want first to consider a well-known, if not hegemonic, diachronic historical narrative of sports: one that takes its point of departure from their complicity in the market but that I find unpersuasive and, therefore, reject.

# 3 Taking the longer moral measure of sports

In my closing remarks in Chapter 2, I noted that my critique of the morality of American contemporary sports needed further fleshing out: more specifically, needed to be incorporated into a longer historical narrative so as to understand better both how sports have arrived at their present lowly state and how to evaluate their prospects for the future. I also noted that the extended narrative into which I sought to place modern American sports ran against the grain of a dominant story commonly told about them and that I had first to dispatch with this latter story before I could tell my alternative tale. The aim of this chapter, then, is to accomplish this very thing: to take up this hegemonic story of American sports and to show why it fails to do justice to the moral history of sports that I want to tell.

## Contemporary sports: one story, two morals

The narrative of American sports that I am calling their *dominant story* actually comes in two different versions. However, as both versions share the same main plot line, I first direct my attention to it and only then attend to the different conclusions that each version draws from it.

What, then, is the common theme of this so-called dominant story? It is that the market forces and the monetary motives they unleash, which I have singled out as the source of the moral degradation of contemporary sports, have been an inextricable part of the American sport scene from day one. In a word, the claim is that there has never been a golden age of sports, one in which participants partook of them purely for the love of sport or in which spectators observed them simply out of a sheer love and passion for the game or in which owners or other athletic officials promoted and regulated them because of their dedication to the values of the game itself. Rather, they have always been bound up in one way or another with the pursuit of material gain. Any claim to the contrary, narrators of this story insist, is at best wishful thinking and at worst a willful distortion.

There is plenty of historical evidence that can be marshaled to support this version of events. For instance, at the professional level, they point out, owners as early as the 1880s were complaining about the high salaries commanded by players, and players of this era were similarly complaining that their fellow players were mainly in it for the money and not for the love of the game.[1] What is more, the practice of players selling their services to the highest bidders (not to mention gamblers trying to fix games) was well established even earlier, in the 1850s and 1860s, for example.[2] Fans of this period also considered winning to be extremely important, so much so that they not only urged the home team on to victory but took it on themselves to make sure that the home team prevailed by directly interfering with the action on the field. Surely one of the most astonishing examples of such fan meddling, to our modern sensibilities at any rate, was captured in the following account of a 1900 baseball game between the Chicago Cubs and Philadelphia Phillies: "Thousands of gunslinging Chicago Cubs fans turned a Fourth of July doubleheader into a shoot-out at the OK Corral, endangering the lives of players and fellow spectators. Bullets sang, darted, and whizzed over the players' heads as the rambunctious fans fired round after round whenever the Cubs scored against ... the ... Phillies."[3] Though contemporary fans of professional sports are not averse to making things more difficult for the visiting team by, among other things, trying to distract them when taking foul shots in basketball games or by screaming their lungs out and stomping their feet at football games to make it difficult for the players to hear the quarterback's signals, these measures clearly pale in comparison with those of their predecessors just described. So, though we have good cause to doubt the sanity and moral bearing of these earlier fans' actions, we have no cause at all to doubt that they took winning very seriously – indeed, just about as seriously as anyone could.

According to this same story line, college and other so-called amateur sports answer to the same capitalist gods. Indeed, as Zimbalist noted, commercial interests were evident in American collegiate sports from the very beginning. He is referring here to the first crew competition between Harvard and Yale in 1852, in which "lavish" prizes were furnished to the athletes by the organizer of the event, the superintendent of the Boston, Concord, and Montreal Railroad, who also plied spectators with "unlimited alcohol" to encourage their attendance. By the late 1880s, football games between Princeton and Yale were attracting upward of 40,000 spectators and generating revenues in the neighborhood of $25,000 ($420,000 in 1998 dollars). Around this same time, coaches' salaries began to eclipse those of the highest paid professors.[4] Cheating was no stranger to these times, either. Players were lured to play for particular colleges and universities by the promise of cash payments. These so-called tramp athletes moved back and forth from one team to another, sometimes in the same season, not just for money but for perks that almost approach those of modern-day professional athletes.[5] For example, Yale recruited tackle James Hogan "by offering him free meals and tuition, a suite in Vanderbilt Hall, a trip to Cuba, a monopoly on the sale of game cards, and a job as cigarette agent for the American Tobacco Company."[6] Even such much-revered coaches as Walter Camp and Amos Alonzo Stagg paid athletes out of secret slush funds of $100,000 or more to ensure that they attracted the most talented football players. No wonder that the 1929 Carnegie Commission's exhaustive study of college sports concluded that "the ethical bearing of intercollegiate football contests and their scholastic aspects are of secondary importance to the winning of victories and financial success."[7] And no wonder that as late as the 1930s, such films as the Marx Brothers' "Horse Feathers" parodied the moral duplicity of college sports.[8]

As I said previously, this plot line holds for both versions of this story. Where they part, however (as I also pointed out), is the different morals they draw from it. In the first, more benign but still damaging version, the claim is simply that money has always been a fixture of sports and, therefore, that any effort to pass them off as things *sui generis*, as morally exemplary practices, is a nonstarter. It also means that if there is anything that morally ails sports today that did not ail them earlier, it has to be something other than money. This makes my moral complaint that contemporary sports have become too cozy with the market for their own good not just off the mark but, as some of the just mentioned historical evidence suggests, simply another iteration of the same old and tired complaint that has been leveled against sports from their very inception. What I have to offer here, then, as a moral critique of American sports is, apparently, not only lacking in critical force but in imagination as well.

In the second, yet more damaging version, the effort to conjure up some golden age of sports in which only the love of sports guided their practice proves not only to be historically unsound and morally ill-conceived but worse – downright duplicitous. For according to the coda of this story, such efforts to burnish sports' moral image are themselves immoral, because their real purpose is to cover over all the bad things that go on in their name and, therefore, further the moral damage they do. This claim requires some explanation.

The first thing that those who favor this version of the dominant story do is to put a name to this "pathological" longing for pure sport, for sport willed and carried out only for the love of its pursuit, and that name is *amateurism*. The second thing they do is to heap further damning historical evidence on the already impressive body of evidence that gives the lie to such a conception of sport: this time trying to show that the more particular belief in amateur sport has no more going for it than the belief in such ghost-like notions as the tooth fairy. Two points of their indictment of amateur sports stand out here. First, amateurism was merely an afterthought of professional sport (i.e., something that was cooked up late in the nineteenth century well after playing for money had become the norm and after America's national sport, baseball, had crossed over into the professional ranks).[9] Second, this belated invention of amateurism began to pick up steam as a regulative ideal in collegiate sports only after the institutional control of collegiate sports had been wrested from students and turned over to college presidents and alumni.[10] This suggests that the cry for amateur sport was anything but a grassroots effort but simply another in a long line of top-down initiatives.

To make matters worse, however, these critics of amateur sports not only claimed that they played second fiddle, historically speaking, to their monied counterparts but carried the further stigma of being instruments of class repression. The roots of their class bias can be traced to their origins in elite English sports, the upper class participants of which were fond of belittling their social inferiors by claiming that they possessed no conception of sport for its own sake.

Presumably, this came about because most of their waking hours were devoted to back-breaking labor, the only recompense of which (owing to its execrable character) was the meager wages they were paid to do it, leaving them so little leisure time and energy with which to pursue it that they could not be trusted to engage in it "thoughtfully" or "ethically." At any rate, this was the reason they gave for banishing manual workers from their cherished amateur sports.[11] The spread to America of this invidious class practice, though less saddled by the rigid class practices of the English, proved no less invidious. For here, too, sports served as markers of class, this time privileging the upper and upper-middle classes by cultivating a distinctively bourgeois taste for sports, in which love of the game was supposed to trump any instrumental benefits they might bring, in opposition to the professional sports favored by the working class.

What is most important because most distinctive about this further assault on "pure" sports in the name of amateurism, however, is the important question it sets up, one that in turn sets up the charge of ethical duplicity on which this interpretation of the story rests. That question is – in light of the massive evidence that conclusively shows that sports have never been things *sui generis* and have never managed to separate themselves from material interests and mercenary motives – why do so many of its devotees continue to cling to and be captivated by purified, romanticized notions of sport, such as amateur sport?[12] Why, in other words, are they unable to see sports for the multimillion dollar industries they really are? Why can they not disabuse themselves of such plainly phony, not to mention grandiloquent, conceptions of sports? Finally, and perhaps most important, why can they not come clean and accept sports for what they themselves have helped them to become by virtue of their continued support and patronage of them?

Now, it is important to see how far reaching these sorts of questions are in their indictment of those who stand accused not just of being unable to answer them but of failing to grasp even the contradiction that underlies them, rendering their raising imperative in the first place. One way to accomplish this is to notice that these questions have been asked before of human enterprises other than sports but only of those human activities that (like sports) have been crowned with a sacred aura by the common but, apparently, benighted folk. I am thinking here, in particular, of Nietzsche's sardonic questioning of his nineteenth-century contemporaries regarding the death of God, which he puts in the mouth of a madman speaking to a crowd.

> "Whither is God?" he cried. "I shall tell you. We have killed him – you and I. All of us are his murderers. But how have we done this? ... Who gave us the sponge to wipe away the entire horizon? What did we do when we unchained this earth from its sun? ... Has it not become colder: Is not night and more night coming all the while? Must not lanterns be lit in the morning?"[13]

The parallels between this second rendition of the dominant story of sports and Nietzsche's story of the demise of God are, I believe, striking and, therefore, warrant our brief attention. Perhaps the best place to begin the comparison is with the two venerated human activities featured in these stories – religion and sport – which arguably exerted a strong hold on the publics that worshipped them and which were each regarded by their respective publics not only as pristine undertakings but as vitally important moral ones as well. Next, we are presented with the climatic death of God and the analogous precipitous death of (amateur) sports: fictional deaths, of course, because neither one was more than a figment of the public's imagination but important deaths all the same. Further, we are told that both these two deaths were self-inflicted – in the first instance, by Nietzsche's peers who slew God with their new science and reason; in the second, by aficionados of sports who slew (amateur) sport with their naïve adoration of them (only inspiring their avarice-minded contemporaries to turn them into full-fledged leisure industries). The mortal wounds suffered by these "holiest" of activities, in turn, dealt a death blow to the moral lives of these two peoples. In Nietzsche's case, without divine guidance and supervision, humans would be free to do whatever they wanted to their fellow humans without having to worry about divine retribution. They did so with gusto, fulfilling the first but, we can only hope, not the second part of Nietzsche's prophecy that the death of God would give way to the most terrible of moral spectacles for the next two centuries.[14] In the latter case of sports, without the moral guidance offered by amateur sport, the money changers in the temple of sports would be similarly free to do to sports whatever they wanted without fear of moral condemnation, as nothing of moral consequence was said to be going on there. As our previous chapter makes clear, they did so with gusto as well.

However, the most striking similarity between the two narratives (which I trust will further tamp down criticisms that this comparison is too far-fetched to entertain) is the uncomprehending manner of their respective publics. In Nietzsche's tale, the murderers of God did not have the faintest idea that in disposing of God they had disposed as well of their moral order. Likewise, the equally unwitting assassins of amateur sport were also clueless that the sports that they idolized had also lost their moral center. Of course, that does not prevent the more reflectively self-aware members of each of these publics from deceiving themselves and their compatriots by trying to smuggle in by the back door, on the one hand, Christian morality and on the other, amateur sport, claiming incoherently that though these practices have been thoroughly discredited, each society needs to preserve them for their own good. However, these deceptions only give Nietzsche and the chroniclers of this second narrative of sports further reason to question why societies such as these, which even in their brief and partial self-conscious moments prefer lying to truth telling, deserve our support.

Finally, the efficacy of this comparison is apparent even on the point at which their stories diverge significantly. That point concerns what we are to do once we have freed ourselves from the crippling illusions and falsehoods detailed above. For Nietzsche, the answer is to reinvent ourselves, to fill our lives with new meanings and values that do not depend on the pitiable and stultifying comfort provided by religion. For the critics of amateur sport, contrarily, the message is the more sober one: to fit our expectations to the prevailing social mores (i.e., to recognize that we live in market societies and, with the collapse of state-based East European alternatives to these societies, are likely to continue doing so for the near future). In a very Orwellian sense, then, such critics counsel us to face up to the social conditions that history has bequeathed to us,[15] requiring that we steel ourselves against the temptation to inflate sports with meanings and values that they can no longer bear. However, they ask us to do this in a distinctly un-Orwellian way by adapting to the status quo rather than by trying to change it, by reconciling ourselves to the fact that sports are just like the rest of life and, therefore, just as susceptible to the beguiling charms of money. As I suggested above, even this difference betrays an important commonality, namely, that both Nietzsche and the antagonists of amateur sport insist that there is no use in trying to remedy what has happened in the past, either by heroic interventions meant to alter significantly (or actually reverse) the course of history (interventions that usually succeed only in making things much worse) or by challenging the dominant tropes used to interpret the past so that they come out looking less grim than they presently do.

No doubt, there are likely other significant parallels between these two stories that should be remarked on as well. Perhaps, however, the best way to shake them out so that we can get on with this second telling of the history of American sports is by returning to that story at the point at which we left off: the public's uncomprehending understanding of and response to the ills of modern-day sports. We get a good sense of the depth of that incomprehension from the following remarks by the *New York Times* journalist, David Grann, regarding the public's reaction to the impending baseball strike in 2002. As Grann writes,

> [A]s the latest strike loomed, it has become harder and harder to deny the true nature of baseball – that it is, at its core, a business like any other, filled with labor disputes, petty disagreement, greed and drugs. Still, rather than view the strike as the ordinary jostling of competing self-interests, it has been spoken of as a moral catastrophe and a violation of some sacred trust.[16]

The message here is precisely the one that we earlier said it was, that the public simply does not get it, mistaking as it does here a quite ordinary and quite predictable market move intended to strengthen labor's hand against the capitalist owners for a full-blown moral crisis that betrays the public's trust in the game. These same fans have no difficulty in recognizing the workings of the market in their own personal lives but, apparently, as soon as they get to the ballpark, they lose all sense of perspective.

What accounts for these fans' extraordinary lapse in judgment, their inability to grasp what is going on before their very eyes, which even if dimly understood would in an instant pierce their grossly inflated moral expectations of sports? Steve Pope, one of the more forceful adherents of this historical take on sports, argues (persuasively) that it has something to do with larger America itself.[17] He thinks that the myth of amateur sport is inextricably bound up with the myth of America, with its effort to portray itself as something other that a nation of loosely connected individuals seeking only to enrich themselves no matter who gets trampled and harmed in the process. More precisely yet, sport pursued for the love of the game conjures up a decidedly moral image of America, one that would have us and the rest of the world believe that we are a nation of strivers moved not so much by greed and crass self-interest as by a larger vision of excellence, obtained only by arduous effort, social cooperation, and (above all) an abiding sense of fair play. Our blindness when it comes to sports, then, is a self-induced ideological blindness, one that is especially resistant to the light of day because it takes its lead from a powerful and unmistakably ignoble (or so say the critics) brand of American exceptionalism.

What remains to be said of this second narration of the history of American sports is the moral duplicity in which its narrators are charged with trading. Here Pope and kindred critics are quite explicit that the powers that run sports exploited the notion of amateurism to advance their own unmistakable financial agendas. For it was clear to those who organized and governed sports, such critics insisted – even if it were not clear to their adoring public – that amateur sports were really no different, in practice at least, from professional sports. This explains Pope's approving quote of distinguished journalist's Leonard Koppett's twin accusations against amateur sport: first, that "A more pervasive institutionalization of hypocrisy is hard to imagine," and second, that it "guarantees daily indoctrination in false values."[18] This explains further what would otherwise be inexplicable: why Division I A collegiate football powers continue to align themselves with such ostensibly amateur organizations as the NCAA and why professional baseball and other professional sports organizations raise the specter of amateurism whenever their bottom line is threatened by political and other forces that insist they are businesses that should be treated and regulated like all other businesses. In a word, they need the moral cachet that amateurism provides them in order to justify the economic privileges that have been wrongly bestowed on them for most of their history. On this reading of the history of American sports, then, what morally defiles sport is nothing other than the ideal of amateurism itself, which Koppett makes abundantly clear in his parting and unsparing shot: "Almost all the harmful effects of the sports establishment can be traced to this misnamed 'ideal' [and] poison."[19]

## Where does the dominant story go awry?

This completes my exegesis of the dominant story of American sports. I now raise some reservations about certain central features of the moral picture of sports that it paints. I should say at the outset, however, that my misgivings are not so wide ranging nor do they run so deep that they require the dismissal of this story in its entirety. Indeed, there are many features of it that I find compelling; I would regard as foolhardy even an attempt to gainsay them. Nonetheless, I am convinced, as narrative theory itself reminds us, that a phenomenon as deeply embedded in our culture and as complex as sport cannot be adequately summed up in one telling. Further, I am persuaded that there is another, more powerful moral story to be told about American sports, which the present one badly botches; it gives us far more reason to hope for a better future both for sports and for larger America than the despair for both engendered by the dominant story.

However, first my misgivings about this dominant story of sports: I can confidently say that they are almost completely interpretive in character. That said, I do not intend to quibble with the historical facts of this story, save to point out the obvious (that it is extraordinarily difficult, if not impossible, to attach precise dates to various periodizations of the history of sport or of the history of anything else, for that matter). With that in mind, I only parrot Zang's point and in the process set up some more precise historical markers. Prior roughly to the 1880s, sport was not widely regarded as a special undertaking in either of the two senses of special in question here: on the one hand, as a social practice unlike any other that requires exercise of the moral virtues and, on the other, as expressive of the larger moral ethos of America itself. This accounts for, among other things, Zang claims, the cavalier attitude of ballplayers and other athletes of this era who "carried pitchers of beer onto the field ... and fans [who] routinely stood on outfield turf, interfered with play, and sometimes chased umpires while brandishing guns."[20] This all began to change, at first ever so gradually, near the turn of the twentieth century, when people (including public intellectuals of the time) started to take notice of sports and of their supposed special qualities and how those qualities reflected something unique about the American character itself. However, because this more careful specification of historical boundaries is for the most part coincident with those drawn by the narrators of the dominant story as well, I am thinking especially of Pope's insightful connection of the amateur movement to a growing American national consciousness – after all, prior to 1880, America was mostly made up of newly arrived immigrants who possessed (understandably) no strong sense of national identity, it hardly qualifies as even a historical quibble.

The real problems with the dominant story, then (to reiterate), are interpretive and concern two related points: (1) the role of money in sports and (2) the public's stubborn belief that sports are special undertakings, that there is substantially more to them than the pursuit of material gain.

As to the first point, what the dominant story of sports clearly gets right is that money was their constant companion from day one. There is, then, no getting around this fact nor should we try, as money is not an unadulterated evil but, in fact – when dispensed in the right way and under the right circumstances (the specifying of which circumstances, of course, being no easy task) – a bona fide good. However, where the dominant story clearly goes wrong is in its failure to notice how the role of money in sports has changed of late in ways that morally threaten the integrity of contemporary sports. In other words, although money has always been a factor in sports, it is not until relatively recently that it has become a truly pernicious factor, one no longer content simply to be an occasional, on-again-off-again complement to sports but its main driving force.[21]

Without giving away too much of the story that I tell later, my criticism here is that money has become a dominant force in contemporary sports in two significant senses, first by virtue of the massive scale of its investment in modern sports and second by virtue of its intrusion into the internal affairs of these sports. Perhaps the best way to get at these two points is to imagine, as Gorn and Goldstein do in their fine history of American sports, what a nineteenth-century fan of sports would be most struck by if suddenly thrust into the contemporary sporting scene. Their answer, which I think is right as far as it goes, is that such a fan would be most surprised by "the vast increase in the amounts of money" poured into the modern game. The question this answer raises, however, is how we should interpret this expression of surprise. One possible response is that as money has been a constant fixture in sports, what we have here is at most a fillip, a brief and mild upsurge of excited surprise, because this increase in the outlay of capital ranks only as a difference in degree rather than kind, as more of the same-old-same-old, just in much bigger doses. However, another response is that this expression of surprise cuts much more deeply, because the magnitude of the increase in money expended on sports reflects a genuine difference in kind (i.e., something new under the sun about the way in which capital figures in sports).

I think the historical evidence clearly points in the latter direction – in favor of the idea that there has been a fundamental shift in the way in which contemporary sports are financed and marketed. This is borne out by Adelman's argument that whereas earlier sports were supported by individual, irregular commercial sponsorship, their contemporary counterparts are supported by a fully institutionalized and highly organized market-based sponsorship.[22] It is further borne out at the collegiate level by Gorn and Goldstein's point that the early history of football is replete with cases of colleges pulling out of league play for a year or two, which would be unthinkable today not for moral reasons but solely for economic considerations, because the economic stakes have become so great that the loss of revenue incurred by such a move would jeopardize the entire program.[23] Finally, this quantitative–qualitative change in the marketing and financing of contemporary sports is borne out at the professional level by Baker's observation that, in the 1940s, we begin to see a shift in the ownership of teams – from what he aptly calls "elderly gentleman" types, who despite getting rich from sports were still fans of the game and took pleasure in their fineries – to more entrepreneurial types who "had no fear of turning sport into a business [because] they assumed it already was." Thus, they not only had no real appreciation for the game but assumed that fans didn't, either, which is why they thought that their job was primarily to entertain the fans and only secondarily (if at all) to put on a good game, to show them a good time by treating them, among other things, to fireworks extravaganzas, gate prizes, plush seats, and plenty of cheap beer.[24]

However, if we were to go back to our historically transported fan and reprise Gorn and Goldstein's question regarding what that fan finds most striking about the modern game, I believe we would get another, perhaps even more important, answer as well. This time, the response would be not just surprise but agitation and maybe even shock and repulsion, which should leave no doubt in our contemporary minds that to this fan's mind something quite fundamental and even dreadful has happened to sports. For I think our nineteenth-century fan would be taken aback by the extent to which money insinuates itself into every nook and cranny of sports. I am thinking here especially of such things as television time-outs that are beginning to rival actual game time; of the lure of endorsements in which prominent athletes not only hawk products in and out of season but see their commitment to their corporate sponsors as both rivaling those of their teams and in many cases surpassing them (owing in no small measure to the fact that many of them make far more money off their endorsements than off the sports they play); of the constant presence and growing influence of professional agents and public relations types who are beginning to dominate the sports page as well; of professional seat licenses; of scheduling games at times not conducive to the skills they feature but entirely conducive to attracting mass audiences – in short, of all the things discussed in Chapter 2.

All of this suggests, then, that although the dominant story got it right when it declared that money was always a part of sports, it got it wrong when it suggested that this is pretty much the end of the story, that there is nothing much more to tell other than the fact that money and sports have consorted with one another from the very beginning. I am on record, of course, as believing that this is no small oversight, no minor blip in the historical reckoning of sports. The full argument for this, however, must await a later chapter. The upshot of that argument should already be clear, namely, that what used to be a more or less minor nuisance in sports has become a major corrupting force in sports, one that perhaps poses the most serious moral challenge they have yet confronted.

This brings me to what I regard to be the second major shortcoming of the dominant story: its claim that the modern sporting public is bedeviled by a rococo amateur regard for sports, which makes it oblivious to the most basic realities of contemporary sports, especially to their almost-impossible-to-miss market trappings. Once again, the dominant story's attribution of a deep-seated false consciousness to the connoisseurs of amateur sports is not wholly without warrant. So, it must be conceded at once that amateur sports are an atavistic throwback to elitist English class notions of athletic activity, notions that, in their expression of blistering contempt for the lower classes, betray their morally odious character. It must further be conceded that many governing organizations of sports at the professional and college levels have cynically exploited the ideal of amateurism to both conceal and abet their economic aims. Finally, it must be granted that the very notion of amateurism itself suffers from a fatal conceptual and moral defect: its absurd insistence that only those who pursue sports with the purest of motives (i.e., without the slightest material interest in them) are true athletes. What makes this ideal absurd is not only its utter unattainability, presuming as it does that morally flawed humans are somehow capable of morally flawless behavior, but its very touting of such purity of heart as a moral ideal worth striving for in the first place. For the idea that only a certain purity of will – a certain single-mindedness to will one thing to the exclusion of all else – is what morality requires of us in or outside sports strikes me not just as a doomed effort to deny one's finitude (what Sartre would call the ill-fated effort to turn oneself into an in-itself that is also for-itself, in other words, God) but as morally perverse.[25] This seems more so a guide for the seriously disturbed or, if there is a difference, the fanatic than for the athlete who wants to do right by sports or the nonathlete who wants to do right by others.[26]

This part of the dominant story, then, seems unimpeachable. However, what seems to me to be highly impeachable (indeed, highly implausible) is the dominant story's contention that it is something like this amateur state of mind that afflicts the public for contemporary sports, that accounts for its supposed deluded view that sports are more than just economic activities. Such a claim not only turns modern-day followers of sports into cultural dopes but it does so twice over, as it holds that they are captives of not only an outmoded, incoherent picture of sports but one that disables their empirical ability to detect what is going on before their very eyes in sports today. This is, to court understatement, an extraordinary (not to mention brassy) attribution to make, let alone contemplate, but it is plainly false.

It is plainly false because it runs together the belief that sports are morally different from the rest of life and the belief in their absolute purity, in their amateur standing. The argument that holds this conflation together is wrongheaded. Let me explain.

Let's begin with the silly idea that those who claim sports are things *sui generis* do so because their empirical apparatus is so damaged that they are unable to see sports for the businesses they really are. The idea is that no one of sound mind (whose mental capacities are ideologically and otherwise unsullied) or of sound body (whose perceptual capacities are likewise unsullied) could possibly sustain belief in such an ideal given the market's wholesale co-optation of contemporary sports. However, a moment's reflection shows this claim to be not only silly but plainly mistaken.

Perhaps the best way to see this is to take a page out of Gorn and Goldstein's book and to ask a hypothetical question, this time of the previously cited 2002 baseball fans' response of moral outrage to the impending strike. The basis of that moral response, it will be recalled from our earlier discussion, was that the players and owners were guilty of violating a sacred trust with the fans, a trust based on the idea that sports cannot be treated as simple business dealings without violation of their basic character. Now, if we were to ask these fans why they cannot fathom that the players threat of a strike amounts to nothing more or less than a "jostling of competing self-interests" – of the players' desire to make more money and of the owner's desire to hold down costs – and that this is what baseball has come to in the present era, I suspect the question would strike them at first blush as not only odd but ill considered. That is because they would be among the first to say (and to make a point of saying) that their cherished pastimes were being treated as one would treat a labor dispute in, say, the factory down the street. They would then likely say that this is precisely the problem, that baseball is being treated as if it were not appreciably different from the things that go on in that factory or in any other factory or business establishment. Their claim that it is a mistake to infer from their present shabby treatment that such sports as baseball are at their core mere economic transactions is not an empirical mistake then, but rather a legitimate objection to an illegitimate inference, an objection that maintains that sports ought to mean and stand for something more even if they presently do not (e.g., such things as excellence and such virtues as courage), which markets are not especially adept at understanding or valuing.

What is more, I suspect that on further reflection, these same baseball fans would come to regard the question as insulting; it cheekily assumes that, at least when it comes to sports, they are unable to see and think about more than one thing at a time. For to adhere to the idea that sports are more than businesses is, for their critics, a strong sign that these fans are incapable of seeing or recognizing them other than in these suspect idealistic terms, which, of course, denies what they plainly are, simple economic enterprises. However, these same fans would likely, and rightly to my mind, point out that such a single-minded, idealistic approach to sport is fundamentally at odds with their actual critical outlook on sports. For only a view of sports that is able to see them presently for what they are and morally for what they could and ought to be and that is able, therefore, to play off the latter against the former could adequately capture what it is that the fans presently object to regarding the status quo. This latter moral claim is, therefore, to reiterate, not to be understood as an empirical assessment of what they presently are but a normative assessment of what they could and should be at their best. It is only by illicitly conflating these two claims (i.e., by confusing the fans' moral assessment of sports at their best with an empirical assessment of their present state) that the critics of these fans are able to transpose their quite reasonable complaint – that sports remain moral projects rather than actual moral realities – into the quite unreasonable and massively mistaken complaint that sports are already moral realities.[27]

However, the critics might respond that I have conveniently elided a central feature of the fans' moral case against sports (i.e., that the intuitions that underwrite their case appear to be exclusively of the antieconomic kind, ones that would have us believe that the coupling of money and sports is a corruptive one, period). Of course, this view that any mixing of money and sports is strictly *verboten* is one that I explicitly disavowed in my opening remarks to this chapter, a view, moreover, that most people disavow, owing to its radically uncompromising character. To make matters worse, this hard-line take on the relation between sports and money not only treats that relation as absolutely corrupting but as absolutely corrupting as far as the eye can see: the triumph of capitalism across the globe means that any attempt to keep money and sports completely separate will come off as not just amusingly anachronistic but as not-so-amusing Platonist browbeating. If so, the fans' moral complaint against the intrusion of money into the internal affairs of sports can be written off as so much utopian nonsense.

I believe that the charge is misdirected, because the moral objection to the commercialization of contemporary sports does not rest on some unyielding, not to mention hopeless, aversion to money as such. To be sure, there is an antieconomic strand that runs through it, but it is not the purist strand that we earlier identified and criticized under the name of amateurism but the more moderate one that insists that sports cannot be treated exclusively as businesses without losing some important sense of what they are about. It does not regard the money-sports coupling, therefore, as a corruptive full stop but as corruptive only when the economic norms and ideals of the market get in the way of the perfectionist norms (excellences and skills) and ideals of sports. How to tell when the market saturation of sports has this unsettling effect on them is no easy matter, except in such obvious cases as Nike's "hoop series" (which, it will be remembered, pitted NBA stars against sumo wrestlers). However, try we must, I think it is safe to say our fans would retort, if we are reasonably to expect that such practices as sports are going to flourish in these hypercapitalized times.

More important, however, it should be pointed out that the intuitions that underlie the belief in the distinctive standing of sports range much wider than the antieconomic. In fact, the notion that sports are unlike the rest of life links up with a wide array of intuitions, all of which speak in one way or another to the standards of excellence that mark off sports from other forms of physical endeavor. By gathering them together, we can be understood to be doing something that Wittgenstein called "assembling reminders," the purpose of which is to draw out and articulate our often inarticulate yet intimate understandings of sports in order to put paid to representations of them, such as the claim in dispute here (that they are no different from the rest of life), that distort what they are principally about.[28]

For some, such as sportswriter Jay Wiener, the intuition of sports that nurtures our faith in their special-ness stretches all the way back to our childhood (the time, he claims, in which our deepest bounds with sports are formed) and to the extraordinary displays of athleticism they made available to us and that captivated us so.[29] For others, such as previously mentioned historians Gorn and Goldstein, belief in the special-ness of sports has to do with "the sense of limitless possibility" they arouse in us, which provide us "glimpses of a better world and nourish our hopes for much that is noble in humankind."[30] For still others, such as noted sports scholar Allen Guttmann, what singles out sports from other practices is the intuition that grounds their ethos of fair play, which "requires that athletes do their best because that is the only way to ensure that everyone involved achieves excellence."[31] Finally, for the American public and its intellectual spokespersons during the Progressive period of American history, which will form the centerpiece of the alternative historical account of sports to come, it was this same ethos of fair play as well as sports' uncanny capacity to forge lasting communal ties that accounts for our collective belief in their distinctiveness.[32]

Whatever the source and character of these intuitions, then, assembling reminders of them helps to explain our collective and apparently unshakable belief in their uniqueness and our equally collective and strong belief that the market, if left unchecked, threatens that uniqueness, seen in those features of sports that set them apart from everything else. As I indicated earlier, the alternative story I intend to tell about sports will take its point of departure from these intuitions. However, before I can tell that story, I must first tell a larger story about the recent moral history of America. And before I do *that*, however, I had better first make clear what force the adjective *moral* carries in both these stories. Doing so requires that I make explicit what I mean by *morality* itself (i.e., what counts as a moral consideration and what does not count as such a consideration).

# 4  Moral inquiry in sport

## What counts as a moral consideration of sport?

I have been insinuating thus far that ethical considerations of sports (and everything else for that matter) give pride of place to the good, where the good in question focuses especially on our noninstrumental relations to and interactions with others and on the noninstrumental goods particular to the social practices in which we collectively engage. To recall Nietzsche's pithy characterization, morality has to do with the "unegoistic" as opposed to the egoistic. However, I want to spell out more carefully and in more detail just what I mean by an ethical consideration and how it figures prominently in my present analysis of sports.

With this in mind, I borrow Habermas's tripartite division of the pragmatic, ethical, and moral spheres of life for two basic reasons: (1) it helps to clarify with reasonable precision the boundary between moral and nonmoral considerations, and (2) it is able to do so, as many moral theories are not, without eliding the most important and fertile realm in which our moral interactions with others occur. However, I also stress that my account of these spheres departs significantly from Habermas's account of them, differing most sharply from his account in trying to undo the distinction between the ethical and the moral that is the centerpiece of his (and many other contemporary moral theorists') effort to cast moral inquiry as an exercise in universal reasoning about values. Hence, my use of Habermas here counts more as a critical appropriation than as a faithful exegesis of his views.

### The pragmatic sphere

The subjective standpoint reigns supreme in this sphere of life for the simple reason that within its boundaries (which I have been insinuating all along and argue further have been stretched so far that they now encompass most of what we Americans think and do today), the first-person singular I is considered to be the source of all value and goodness. For it is only through such subjective expressions as "I want" or "I desire" that value or goodness in this sphere has any purchase in the world at all. So, it is my desire for something that confers value and goodness on it, rather than the value or goodness of the thing that confers value on my desire. Indeed, in this realm, to speak of the goodness of things independently of the agents who desire them is unintelligible, as the very existence of values, to say nothing of the place that they might occupy in our lives, depends – and depends absolutely – on individual valuers.

It follows from this that my desires here double as both preferences and reasons. Hence, my desire to acquire some belief or thing or to carry out some action counts itself as a reason, and a perfectly good reason, to acquire or do it. This simply confirms what has already been implied: that in the pragmatic realm of life, the I is considered a "self-originating" source of both reason and value.

Another way to understand this subjectification of desire, reason, and value is to put it in the "internalist" terms that Bernard Williams justly made famous. According to Williams, a reason counts as a bona fide reason if, and only if, it can be read off one or more elements of what he calls a person's *subjective motivational set* (SMS). The elements of such a motivational set include, besides the commonplace desires and beliefs, "dispositions of evaluation, patterns of emotional reaction, personal loyalties, and various projects … embodying commitments of the agents."[1] So understood, a person can be said to lack a reason to accept a belief or a value or carry out an action if that belief, value, or action does not hook up in the relevant sense with any elements of her motivational set. That pretty much describes life lived at the pragmatic level, in which I have reason to believe or value something or to perform an action only if it flows from some element or combination of elements of my motivational set.

Where do others figure in this self-interested calculus? Pretty much as Habermas describes them, namely, as limiting-conditions that I must take into instrumental account if I am to get what I want.[2] Nagel calls this the "free-agent" variable, and it colors every feature of our pragmatic, strategic interactions with others.[3] The basic idea is that I have reason to act on some element or other of my motivational set in seeking my good, and you have reason to act on some element or other of *your* motivational set in seeking *your* good, but I have no reason to value or promote your good and you have no reason to value or promote my good. Nonetheless, even though I have no reason to promote your good nor you mine, I do have a reason, and a particularly compelling one, to take into account your reasons and actions, and you have an equally compelling reason to take into account mine, as they are likely to affect each of our private pursuits of the good. In all such cases, of course, whatever interactions or cooperative schemes emerge will be predicated on each of us "using" the other to get what we want. So, if the benefits of cooperation exceed the costs for all parties concerned, each of us has reason to cooperate with the other; if the reverse proves to be true for some or all of us, however, our reason to cooperate simply vanishes. Cooperation in this pragmatic sphere, therefore, is strictly ad hoc, instrumentally based, and entirely parasitic on one's private aspirations.

What is more, because it is exceedingly rare that in our interactions with one another all of our actions will turn out to be equally cost-effective, cooperation in most instances will have a forced, manipulative quality about it: forced because others, as we have seen, will have no reason to cooperate with us if they think it is not in their self-interest to do so and so will have to be talked and cajoled into cooperating if it is not clear how their interests are being served; manipulative because almost all such efforts to convince and cajole others to cooperate are motivated by the effort of each party to further their self-interest at the expense of others. Hence the importance of defining the larger social settings in which we interact with others in ways that privilege our interests and abilities and of passing off private concerns as common ones on which we all should act. Hence, too, the importance of ostensibly moral utterances and claims the sole purpose of which is to get recalcitrant others to do things for the greater good that, in fact, only serve my good.[4] (I say *ostensibly moral utterances* because there is nothing morally substantive about them, given their self-serving, manipulative character and given that anyone moved by them in this realm will be so, despite the moral pitch, for decidedly strategic reasons, even though those reasons will be mostly mistaken if the effort to con others succeeds.)

From what has been said so far, it should be clear that pragmatically motivated actions are not those of an unreflective wanton (i.e., those of someone who acts on every impulse or desire that crosses his or her mind)[5] but rather those of a practical reasoner of a certain sort. Reflection, then, plays an important and prominent role in our pragmatic dealings with others, and only those desires and beliefs sanctioned by it warrant our acting on them. Of course, the model of practical reason appropriate to our pragmatic lives is shaped directly by the egoistic character of those lives, the egoistic character of which, in turn, is shaped by the social settings in which they are embedded and the social interactions and relations that they elicit. What we have here, therefore, as Habermas aptly puts it, is reason "placed at the service of a merely subjective self-assertion,"[6] in which the point of that self-assertion, as we have seen, is the decidedly instrumental one to maximize the satisfaction of the elements of one's motivational set by ordering them in such a way as to achieve this result.

It follows from what has been said thus far that practical reason and deliberation, although indispensable features of our pragmatic dealings with others, do not cut very deep. They do not cut very deep because their job is not reflectively to modify the beliefs, desires, dispositions, and values that make up a person's motivational set but only to ensure their satisfaction. To be sure, in the process of deliberating about how most efficiently to get what one wants, one or more elements of someone's motivational set may be modified or subtracted or a new element added. However, all such changes, subtractions, and additions have to do with the desirability of the choices and options before one (i.e., with considerations of whether they satisfy someone's wants and not whether those wants themselves should be satisfied or should answer to some consideration other than naked self-interest). So, what is at stake for the pragmatic reasoner is not the qualitative worth of his or her preferences but the simple desirability of those preferences, which is why Charles Taylor calls such reasoners "simple weighers" rather than "strong evaluators."[7]

This means that the main task of reflection at this level is to get a better handle on the elements in one's motivational set so that one can choose the most efficient means to realize them. Mistakes in pragmatic reasoning thus follow along two lines: (1) mistakes about what one believes and desires, about the elements in one's motivational set, and (2) technical mistakes in the selection of the means chosen to satisfy (reflectively clarified) elements of one's motivational set. It is mistakes of the former sort that concerned Williams in his analysis of internalist accounts of practical reason, and I begin with them and the example he uses to illustrate them.

Williams cites the case of someone who is about to drink from a bottle something that he believes is gin but which in fact is gasoline.[8] The question Williams poses is: does the person have a reason to drink what is in the bottle? In one interpretation, the person clearly does, given the fact that he desires to drink what is in the bottle. What could be said in favor of this answer is that it would certainly explain his action if he went ahead and drank the substance in the bottle. However, the problem with this answer, opines Williams, is that it supposes that internal reasons cover only explanations of action and are agnostic on questions regarding the rationality or normativity of actions, when in fact they are intended to cover both. What we need to account for in the latter is the role that reflection plays in such instances (i.e., that an agent performed some action, A, after deliberating appropriately and learning all the relevant facts). So, when we add reflection to this scenario, we can explain both why the agent did not drink what was in the bottle and why it was rational and good for him not to do so. We can also explain why it would be wrong to suppose that his subjective motivational set itself is impervious to change, that it must remain a static one. For when we deliberate about how best to get what we want, we must also consider whether our beliefs about something are mistaken (e.g., owing to our ignorance about some relevant fact), in which case, as in the present example, I no longer have a reason to do what I thought I had good reason to do. Conversely, we may find in reflecting further on our existing beliefs and desires that we have reason to do something, to satisfy some element of our motivational set, that we did not previously believe we had reason to do (e.g., to take up piano lessons because we did not fully realize or give sufficient weight to our musical interests). Of course, as already stated, in none of these cases does deliberation lead me to put in question whether I should be basing my reasons for action exclusively on my self-interest.

Technical mistakes in pragmatic reasoning, by contrast, have essentially to do, as we have said, with the faulty selection of means to achieve our purposes. Of course, poor "means" selection can result from confusion over elements of one's motivational set (specifically, about their character, their relation to other elements of the set, and their relative weightings) but, in that case, our selection of means proves to be inefficacious mainly because the ends we have posited for ourselves are inefficacious (to be sure, one can inefficaciously choose means to satisfy inefficacious ends and so commit a double error, but for a pragmatic reasoner, this is of no special moment, because a compound error is no more self-defeating than a simple, single end- or means-based one). Hence, when we have an adequate reflective grasp of our preferences and values but still fail to get what we want, the locus of the error is a means-based one. So, learning to be a "good" (technical) pragmatic reasoner means learning how to choose the most effective means and order them in the most effective ways to maximize our personal satisfaction. This is a lesson not likely to be lost on pragmatic reasoners, as the mark of failure in such cases is as simple as it is unambiguous: to fail to get what one wants.[9] In this instance, just as in the former, the idea that there might be anything untoward about channeling all our rational efforts to ensure that we satisfy as many of our preferences as we can is foreign to pragmatic reasoners for the very basic reason that their identity is constituted by such preferences.

It should be clear from what has been said so far that our pragmatic dealings with others in social practices strips them of any moral regard for those others and their practices. That is because no matter how much collective effort or collaboration (or both) is called for in such dealings, their point is unmistakably individual. For each of us have our own private reasons for involving ourselves with others and for taking up larger projects, and it is these private reasons alone that prompt us to do so. So, whatever purchase reason has in our pragmatic lives is bounded by and confined to strategic calculations of self-interest. Now, there would be nothing especially worrisome about any of this pragmatic posturing if the kind of reason and value it countenances were properly constrained to goods and interactions amenable to its instrumental take on things (e.g., if it were restricted to the market or to appropriate private satisfactions). However, if my diagnosis of the ills of contemporary American society and sports is anywhere close to the mark, what is cause for concern is just how far and wide it presently casts its instrumental net, how much its favored cost-benefit calculus insinuates itself into everything else we Americans think and do. For the more it so insinuates itself, as we have seen, the less ethical considerations will have any place in our lives – a point made all the more worrisome by the fact that there is no reflective route leading from pragmatic calculations of self-interest to ethical considerations of what we morally owe to one another.

## The ethical sphere

Ethical life replaces the dominant and domineering *I* that holds sway, as we have seen, in the pragmatic sphere, with its first-person plural counterpart – better counterweight – *we*. The basic subject matter of ethics thus concerns our significant relations and interactions with others, where those others no longer figure in my dealings with them as "limiting" conditions that must be reckoned with only in so far as my good is at stake but as constitutive of my own identity that must be reckoned with if our mutual good is to be realized. Hence, in the ethical realm, the question "Who am I?" is inseparable from the question "Who are we?" and the question "Who are we?" is inseparable from the question "What should we do?" The reason why this second question ("Who are we?") looms so large is that it asks after what it is exactly that makes us a coherent community rather than a mere assemblage of random folks (i.e., a mere aggregation of separate individuals with nothing more in common than the fact of our assemblage or aggregation). For it is not until we have asked the question regarding just what it is that we hold in common and that binds us together that we can consider ourselves as having a practical identity in the first place and one, therefore, from which we can potentially draw ethical sustenance.

This idea that ethics is bound up with the first-person *we*, that "What we should do" depends on "Who we think we are," is the same point that Annette Baier tried to drive home when she quipped, "[T]he secular equivalent of faith in God, which we need in morality … is faith in the community and its evolving procedures;" that Richard Rorty tried to make when he suggested, "[W]e cease to think of morality as the voice of the divine part of ourselves and instead think of it as the voice of ourselves as members of a community;" and that Korsgaard intended when she exclaimed that "The subject matter of morality is … how we should relate to one another … [and] find … reasons [we] can share."[10] Of course, not just any *we* will do here, for not only must it be a coherent *we*, one that confers a stable, recognizable identity, it must be a salient *we* that confers a substantive, binding identity, rooted in (among other things) mutual trust (which rules out fraternities, sororities, social clubs, and the like). It is this latter feature especially that warrants calling a particular community an *ethical* community.[11] It does so because it is only in such relationships that our interactions with others take on an unmistakable ethical character: ethical in part because I find myself no longer standing over against others pursuing private goals, which remain private however many others might be involved in their pursuit, but in unison with them in pursuing collective goals, which remain collective through and through, however few others are actually involved in their pursuit. It is also ethical in equal part because others are "internalized" and "idealized" in such a way that they become sources of special reasons and valuings not found in the pragmatic sphere.

In at least two significant senses, our relations with others become sources of special, distinctively ethical reasons and valuings. The first sense is that instrumental calculations of self-interest, rooted in private estimates of the good, are sidelined in favor of noninstrumental considerations of others, which are rooted in public estimates of the good. So, when the gratification of my private desires is no longer in point, using others to get what I want is no longer in point. When using others is no longer in point, connecting up with them in ways that require us to recognize what might be termed their *ethical substance* becomes very much in point. This means not only that the good of others must be accounted for and appropriately valued but that the good of others must in some important sense be regarded as indistinguishable from my own good. For an important feature of the good so conceived is its irreducibly social character, the fact that it is not so much good-for-me or good-for-you but good-for-us. What is perhaps the signature feature of such shared goods is the value vested in the sharing of the good itself, which permeates all our ethical relationships, be they friendships, or lovers, or (less intimately) those with whom we share a form of life, if not an entire culture or nation. This explains why voluntarist objections to such communal goods (to the idea that to ascribe ethical value to such relationships without the *consent* of each and everyone of the individuals involved is morally objectionable because it cedes too much control of our lives to others) miss the point.[12] For it is precisely the mark of an ethical community that not only are the boundaries where my good ends and those of others begin blurred – and intentionally so – but cease to matter, because the good in question is, to reiterate, not mine or yours but ours.

The second basic sense in which my relations with others become a source of special, ethical reasons is that they entail special responsibilities. Perhaps the most important of these is the willingness to come to the assistance, in every meaningful sense of that term, of others.[13] That is why cooperation is not an ad hoc matter here as it was in the pragmatic sphere. For others and for the common goods from which our relationships with them take their marching orders require a special kind of social interchange, one in which cooperation is not just a constant feature of those relationships but constitutive of those relationships. Take away this cooperative feature of our ethical interactions with others, then, and our community will fracture along atomistic lines as will our shared pursuit of the good and the special responsibilities that follow in their wake.

Now, it is in our noninstrumental relations with others that we come to see and appreciate the force of ethical reasons and are sensitized to the claims they make on us. It is in this sense that Oakeshott's likening of ethics to a "vernacular language," the point of which is to learn "to speak the language intelligently," proves especially apt.[14] For the space of reasons and meanings of a language is inescapably an interstitial one, which minimally presupposes a two-place relation between a speaker and a listener, and an intersubjective one, which cannot exclude members of the relevant language game nor what they have to say to us. This is why the words spoken, the meanings expressed, and the values conveyed in a language game are normative for all, not just for some of its players. Hence, just as "it is nearly impossible to hear the words of a language you know as mere noise,"[15] so it is nearly impossible to hear the reasons that make up the ethical vocabulary that we all know and speak as merely the private rantings of certain members of our ethical community, rantings whose private character means, therefore, that the members of that community can let them fall on deaf ears with ethical impunity. This explains why in the ethical realm at least, as Korsgaard writes, "We do not seem to need a reason to take the reasons of others into account. We seem to need a reason not to."[16]

Because the ethical realm is, as we have seen, an irreducibly social one in which cooperation and social dependence on others is of capital importance, it should come as no surprise that the relevant model of practical reason here will look substantially different from its pragmatic variant. That is to say, in our ethical relations with others, the "I want" and "I desire" no longer qualify as reasons for action but as simple preferences whose rational and normative appropriateness must now be gauged by considerations of the common good. So, the double role they played in the pragmatic sphere, as both preferences and reasons, is sundered in the ethical sphere so that practical reason can serve as a handmaiden of the common good rather than of the self-assertion of particular individuals. Put otherwise, the good is no longer good because you or I desire it but lies the other way around: we desire it because it is good. As the good is normative of our desires in this case, our failure to desire it counts itself as an ethical offense.

The forms of life and social practices that define and shape the ethical communities to which we belong are, therefore, what confer goodness and value on the things and actions we undertake within them. These valued forms of life vary, of course, from society to society, as does the particular moral weight attributed to them, but they typically include political, economic, religious, and other select cultural practices of which, or so I want to argue, sports are an important example. If cultural anthropologist Eduardo Archetti is to be believed, it is soccer, polo, and tango that come closest to revealing the ethical sensibility of Argentininans;[17] no doubt soccer plays a similar ethical part in most countries of Europe, as does politics and (especially in southern Europe) religion, whereas in America, politics and the holy trinity of football, basketball, and baseball (and to a lesser extent, religion) seem to exert an important ethical formative influence. The manner in which members of these ethically freighted practices relate to and interact with one another in trying to further the goods particular to them tells us a lot, then, about the ethical complexion of these different communities.

However, whatever social practices or combination of practices that a community singles out in this regard to register and express its ethical identity, the important task of practical reason is to make sure that the motivational sets of individuals chime with these forms of life to ensure their flourishing rather than, as was the case in the pragmatic sphere, simply maximizing the elements already present in these motivational sets. MacIntyre describes well the transition that must be effected in this regard: "The passage from desiring x to be satisfied, just because it is my desire, to desiring x qua good and wanting my desire for x to be satisfied, just because … it is a desire for what it is good and best for me to desire."[18] So, the subjective motivational sets of individuals must be brought into accord with the shared goods of the characteristic forms of life and practices of the community, as it is the latter rather than the former that determines both whether we have a reason to believe or act on something and whether that belief or action is an ethically good one. Further, as the good of these forms of life and practices cannot be constructed out of the private goods of individual members prior to and independently of their membership in them,[19] one cannot take for granted that the actual motivational sets of these individuals will be conducive to the larger good of these forms of life. Indeed, given what I have so far claimed with respect to the socialization typical of such societies as our own, one would be well advised to presume just the opposite: that they must be reflectively altered in order to be so conducive.

Now, whether the motivational sets of individuals will have to be modified reflectively or, more radically, reflectively transformed, depends (as I have just said) on the sort of ethical socialization, or lack thereof, that individuals receive. In either case, however, what is clear (also as noted) is that the members of the forms of life and practices of the ethical community must make the good of these forms of life and practices their own good. This is best thought of not so much as subordinating one's good to the common good, of suppressing one's own desires, but rather as enlarging one's sense of the good so that it now encompasses the common good; such enlargement, of course, is what is required if one is to be an ethical agent at all. What we have here, then, is an intersubjective form of internalism, what might be termed practice-internalism, which departs from Williams's previously mentioned subjective internalist account insofar as what we have reason to believe, do, and value is no longer read from the actual motivational sets of particular individuals but rather read from the goods internal to the forms of life endorsed by the ethical communities of which we are members. It is this reflective modification or bypassing of our actual motivational sets, then, that rules out egoism and the structure of motivation characteristic of ethical communities. This latter requires some explanation.

In the pragmatic sphere, where my desires are constitutive of the good, the projects I take up are taken up because I think they are good for me, because they are good in a subjective sense. This explains both why I want to be the one who achieves the good in question and why I do not want anyone else to achieve it. So, for example, my desire to compose a musical piece that everyone will want to hear is good if – and only if – I am the one who composes it. This gives me every reason to ensure that no one else composes it. My desire here, then, is a purely subjective one and, of course, a baldly vain one. However, suppose I now want to compose a piece of music that everyone will want to hear because of its high quality. Now, the structure of my motivation is no longer egoistic, as what I desire in this instance is the good intersubjectively considered, which gives me a reason and a motive to compose it without at the same time giving me a reason or a motive to prevent anyone else from composing it. Korsgaard nicely captures the relevant contrast in the two cases: "[T]o have a … project or ambition [in this latter sense] is not to desire a special object which you think is good for you subjectively, but rather to want to stand in a special relationship to something you think is good objectively."[20] This, in fact, is the structure of motivation required in one's ethical relations with others; for here it is essential that what I desire is the good, specifically the common good of the ethical community, in which the intersubjective character of the good enjoins my cooperation and dependence on others rather than my manipulation of them.

It should be clear from what has been said to this point that ethical reasoning is not concerned with desirability considerations but with what Charles Taylor calls *qualitative distinctions* in ways of living: specifically, qualitative distinctions in the manner in which forms of life are engaged and treated.[21] As such, the task of ethical reasoning is not to decide which of our subjective desires should be acted on owing to their attractiveness and which jettisoned owing to their unattractiveness but which should be countenanced or suppressed on the basis of their contributions to the good. This requires, again in Taylor's argot, not the simple weighing of desires but the strong evaluation of desires so that only those that are conducive to the flourishing of the forms of life that constitute our ethical identity are reflectively endorsed. In this regard, it is the normative standards of these forms of life, which both specify the goods internal to them and appraise their relative worth, that are the targets of strong evaluation. For it is by meeting these standards that we denominate them as goods of a certain kind and so deserving of a certain ethical respect. It is not so much that strong evaluation vies with subjective desires in the effort to overcome whatever pull they might exert on us (so that goods of these kinds are valued in the appropriate ways) but that it sidelines and thereby silences them. That is to say, subjective desires that would otherwise provide us with a reason to engage in a form of life without regard for its good are not only screened off from consideration by strong evaluation but are nullified as reasons as well.[22] In fact, the point of strong evaluation is to ensure that they count for nothing at all in ethical deliberation.

As the aim of ethical reasoning qua strong evaluation is to ensure the flourishing of the forms of life that mold the ethical character of the communities with which we identify, it is clear that justification must play an important role in ethical inquiry, one conspicuously absent in our pragmatic dealings. For the aim of ethical justification is to sanction reasons for engaging in these forms of life that contribute to their flourishing, and it must do so whenever those forms of life are reflectively challenged. And reflectively challenged they most certainly will be, especially because these forms of life do so much of the heavy ethical lifting for the larger community. Such challenges can come at a moment's notice and from almost every quarter: for example, when we realize ourselves that we might be in error as a result of some unexpected incident, when new members of the community think we might be in error because we have been blinded by our past socialization, when we are reflectively provoked by new conceptions of these practices either from creative insiders who have a novel take on them or from outsiders whose very outsider-hood sometimes makes them privy to conceptions of these practices that beggar our imagination.

However, it might reasonably be asked, how and with reference to what are we supposed to justify our ethical judgments? To begin with the latter question first, the answer is from the normative resources that are embedded in the social background of understandings and traditions of the forms of life of one's ethical community. For it is this background and these traditions that inform and underwrite our prereflective ethical intuitions regarding these forms of life and that allow us to make our ethical way around them in the first place. Part of the ethical know-how that they impart can be attributed to the fact that they themselves are often the product of previous justificatory efforts that, having passed initial muster, subsequently became part of the ethical background of these practices. It is in this postreflective form, then, that they get passed on to new practitioners as part of their initiation and induction into these practices. More important from our standpoint, however, is that when our ethical judgments are challenged, it is these background beliefs, values, and intuitions, as I have remarked earlier, that supply us with the evaluative resources and tools that we need either to vindicate these judgments or, if they cannot withstand reflective scrutiny, to replace them with judgments that can.

Now, while our justificatory queries begin with these intuitions, they do not end with them (i.e., they do not leave them as they found them untouched by further reflection). For reflection does play an important correcting role in sorting out and testing our ethical intuitions in an analogous way in which empirical inquiry plays an important role in correcting our sensible perceptions of the world: the case of the proverbial crooked stick in the water comes immediately to mind. However, reflection carries out its justificatory task not by taking leave of these intuitions,but by articulating them, by making explicit what they implicitly tell us. As a consequence, some of these background understandings will be foregrounded so that they can be subject to reflective testing. I use the word *some* here deliberately and carefully, as the background would by definition cease to be a background if it were entirely foregrounded. More important, because in ethical life the only resources we have to work with are the ones that life provides us and because even when we reflect on our life, we still have to live it, it would be akin to normative suicide to put in question all of those resources at one and the same time. This is the point Habermas was driving at when he argued that "ethical questions are accessible to rational discussion only within the unproblematic horizon of a concrete ethical life" and when he added that "problematization [of this horizon] can never be so profound as to risk all assets of the existing ethical substance."[23] This is the point of Bernard Williams's holism with regard to ethical questions, which insists that we can question and justify some of our beliefs and intuitions only by holding constant most of our other beliefs and intuitions. This is why he invokes Neurath's famous image of repairing a ship at sea to illustrate his ethical holism.[24] The same then goes for our ethical judgments, for these too cannot be repaired by suspending all of them at once in the effort to rebuild them in their entirely, because that would scuttle, not facilitate, the repair job and deprive us of any ethical rudder by which to steer our reflective efforts.

Now that we know by reference to "what" our ethical justifications must be pitched – our stock beliefs and intuitions – we can attend to the first question we raised as to "how," exactly, reflection is to do its justificatory work. Rawls well-known notion of "reflective equilibrium" provides the answer to this question.[25] Rawls's idea is the rather simple one that we try to bring our ethical intuitions into accord with our reflective articulation of them and our reflective articulation of them into accord with our ethical intuitions. By meshing our ethical intuitions and reflections in this critical back-and-forth fashion, some of our intuitions will drop out, because they do not survive reflective scrutiny, just as some will be modified by virtue of this same scrutiny (either by being given more prominence or downplayed) and some of our reflective efforts at articulation will be abandoned because they take us too far afield of our intuitions, just as some will be modified to accommodate better our intuitions. As the only test of reflective adequacy available to us here (given that efforts to step outside of our ethical language games is a nonstarter) is coherence, it is by finding the right balance between our judgments and intuitions that reflection is able to justify our ethical conceptions. To paraphrase Rawls himself, what justifies an ethical judgment is not its being true to an order antecedent and given to us but its congruence with our deeper understanding of ourselves and of the signature social practices of our ethical community and our realization that, given our history and traditions, it is the most rational conception for us.[26]

Two final points on the matter of ethical justification. The first is a corollary of the previous point that our stock beliefs and intuitions are the necessary starting points of ethical inquiry because these are the only ethical resources at our disposal. This means that justification in ethics is always a circular affair. For in starting with these stock beliefs and intuitions rather than others, we give them a normative prominence in our justificatory efforts that it would be foolhardy to deny. This normative prominence is further compounded and complicated by the fact that the norms by which we appraise these beliefs and intuitions are themselves built up out of these same intuitions, which means that in the process of trying to reflectively vindicate our beliefs and intuitions, we have no other option but to appeal to them. Hence the circular character of ethical justification. It would, however, be a mistake to treat this circularity as either vicious or the unfortunately steep price that has to be paid when doing justificatory work in the ethical realm, given its dependence on historically contingent starting points rather than rationally divined ones that are neither contingent nor hemmed in by concrete forms of life. For because our forms of life make little if any ethical or practical sense when viewed from the outside, from starting points that however rational in an abstract sense are necessarily external to and so out of touch with our basic ethical intuitions, it would be better, I believe, to think of the circular character of ethical justification in a more positive light as that which makes ethical inquiry relevant to our lives in the first place.

The second point is that it is important to remember that the point of justification in ethics is not to track the truth of our judgments, whether they accurately represent our forms of life, but to gauge their normative fitness as guides by which to lead a good (i.e., flourishing) life. Thus, to say that our values and judgments in ethics are justified is not to assess their truth and falsity as adequate accounts of what goes on in social practices but to say something about their goodness in terms of their contribution to the (ethical) perfection of these practices. As Korsgaard nicely phrases it, "To say that these sentiments and dispositions are justified … [is to say] we are the better for having them, for they perfect … and so promote … our [ethical] flourishing."[27]

It should be apparent by now that ethical reflection, unlike pragmatic reflection, cuts very deep indeed, because, as Habermas notes, ethical questions are at bottom identity questions, where the identity in question, to reiterate, is not mine or yours but ours.[28] In asking us what we should do, these questions thus force us to consider anew just "who we are," "how we got to be who we are," and "who might we yet become?" These are not trifling questions, as in addressing themselves as they do to our core ethical identity, they focus reflection on just those features of ourselves from which our lives derive whatever ethical meaning they possess and according to which we are able to distinguish what is the good and noble thing to do from what is the bad and ignoble thing to do. That is why in most cases ethical reflection should not settle for anything less than a reflective modification or, as the case may warrant, a reflective transformation of our individual motivational sets. That is further why the gravitas of ethical violations can and should not ever be doubted. For such transgressions mean that we are no longer able to think of ourselves as the ethical beings that we thought we were and so, as deserving of the ethical recognition, praise, and respect from our peers such thoughts confirm.

This fall from grace in the eyes of our peers, such that we can no longer credibly regard ourselves as one of them, is compounded by the fact that not only are we all too aware of their disapproving judgments of us but that we must concur in those same judgments of ourselves as well; after all, that is what it means to have one's ethical identity determined by one's fellowship with significant others.[29] In some senses, as Korsgaard explains, this is a fate worse than death itself, for "the only thing that could be as bad or worse than death is something that for us amounts to death – not being ourselves anymore."[30] All of which reinforces the point that the shame induced by such ethical violations, in which those from whom ethical recognition has been withdrawn find it increasingly difficult to live with themselves anymore because their own ethical self-worth is directly derived from such recognition, is no laughing matter.

Mistakes in ethical reasoning, therefore, are especially grievous ones. For what is at issue here is not the simple pragmatic mistake of not getting what we want but the much more momentous ethical mistake of failing to realize our ethical potential or – what is the same thing – of failing to impress on members of our relevant ethical community that we deserve to be thought of and treated as one of them, as their ethical equal.

Ethical mistakes of this sort are not the technical, means-based ones that plague our pragmatic lives but substantive, ends-based ones that roil our ethical lives. Such mistakes have less to do with a misidentification of our ends than they do with our reflective failure to specify them adequately. Hence, we are not, as Wiggins avers, talking here about deliberative mistakes no practical or ethical right-minded reasoner could or would make (e.g., doctors do not deliberate about whether to heal the sick, orators about persuading others, athletes about pursuing physical excellence).[31] However, all these practitioners do and should deliberate about what these respective aims come to and what they demand of us as ethical beings, not to mention what reasoned ethical ideals appropriately infuse them. So, it is no idle matter for them to ask to what extent, if at all, mercenary motives should play a part in their deliberations, when they should no longer try to heal the sick but make their death as comfortable and dignified as possible; when persuasion should yield to compassionate nurturance; when the pursuit of athletic excellence should be constrained for some greater good. All of these judgments turn on ethical ideals about which there are many substantive issues that warrant careful deliberative consideration.

What counts, therefore, as an adequate specification of our ends and of the corresponding ideals that figure centrally in their specification is a weighty ethical matter, indeed. So weighty that our reflective failures in this sphere have repercussions that overshadow anything that we have considered to this point. To see why, however, we need, first, to be clear about the sort of failure about which we are talking here.

In most cases, failures in ethical reasoning and deliberation, at least in market societies such as our own, involve a failure to see where our good qua member of an ethical community lies. This takes the form (as I have been arguing all along and continue to argue in ensuing chapters) of the contravention of *we*-intentions by *I*-intentions and the corresponding contravention of the inescapably social character of ethical reasoning by instrumental reasoning. All of which means that the failure to see where our good lies translates into our inability to see the force of reasons that can be seen only in terms of our noninstrumental social relations with one another, precisely those relations that are characteristic of (because constitutive of) our pursuit of the common good.

Now, what is so formidable about such missteps in our ethical reasoning is that they wreak havoc on both our conception and practice of the various iterations of an ethical life available to us. Of course, our conception of ethical forms of life cannot be so neatly separated from our practice of them in this regard, because the fundamental incoherence that they introduce into our conception of such forms of life (which would have us believe that our ethical lives are really no different from our pragmatic ones because both bottom out in the effort to get more of what each of us wants) is what induces us to practice them in incoherent ways (which would have us believe that we can achieve common goods in the same instrumental manner in which we achieve pragmatic ones). The double error here is easy to spot: ethical lives do, in fact, differ from pragmatic ones precisely because the former rather than the latter take their point of departure from shared goods and the common good of ethical practices can be achieved only if they are not allowed to be made the object of an instrumentally driven rational calculus. What is perhaps just as easy to spot is that such incoherences presuppose a wholesale breakdown in our ethical forms of life, in the mutual trust and bond from which such social unions draw their lifeblood, and in the social dependence on and cooperation with others that are indispensable to their flourishing. All of which underscores, as if it needed any further underscoring, our previous point of just how grievous the ethical violations that stem from such failures in our ethical reasoning are, for they disrupt our relations and interactions with the very people who are supposed to matter the most to us in ways that can neither be discounted nor overlooked.

Finally, as was the case with regard to the transition from the pragmatic to the ethical sphere, there is no reflective route leading from ethical considerations of the common good to moral ones of our obligations to humanity at large. For reasons that I explore in the next section, however, the lack of such reflective access is not as worrying as it was in the previous transition, if only because our ethical dealings with one another can proceed quite nicely, even when universal ethical considerations are called for, without invoking abstract moral notions of our humanity or what Feuerbach and Marx after him aptly called our *species-being*.[32]

## The moral sphere

Moral life is distinguished mainly by its abstract, impersonal character, which requires a complete break with both our pragmatic and ethical lives. It requires such a break because it insists that considerations and treatments of moral value must hook up with our basic humanity, with those features that we share in common with all human agents, not just some subsection of them. For it is only from this impersonal vantage point that we can discover what our moral obligations are to the rest of the members of the human species and grasp their binding force. This is why moral reflection cannot abide first-person considerations of value, which in speaking to our egoistic desires and ethnocentric attachments prevent us from seeing the larger moral picture. All traces of the first-person must, therefore, be exorcised from our moral reflections if they are to put us in touch with our core humanity; indeed, from this detached standpoint, as Williams avers, the "we can represent a self-interest as much as an *I*."[33] This is one important reason, then, why moral reflection must be accounted as impersonal reflection, for on its portmanteau conception of value there is no middle-ground between subjective and objective value, as there is in the tripartite division of value to which I have so far been appealing, and only objective value is properly considered moral value. It is no mystery, then, why moral inquiry must do its reflective work outside of the social practices in which we live out our lives and in which our being-in-the-world is firmly rooted.

However, another equally important reason why moral reflection is to be regarded as a species of impersonal reflection is that in its consideration of our moral obligations to humanity, it must proceed impartially. This means that morality is possible only if we are able to forsake the tendency to accord greater value to ourselves and our intimates from our own perspective and instead accord equal value to every one of our human peers from a perspective that is, again, neither egoistic nor ethnocentric nor (what comes to the same thing) subjective. Impartiality so understood, therefore, is parasitic on impersonal rather than personal reflection. Indeed, Nagel goes so far as to claim that it is only by judging others in such an impartial-impersonal way that we have any reasonable hope of checking our egoistic impulses.[34]

Another no-less-distinguishing feature of the moral realm is the relatively narrow normative scope in which it operates. This also follows from the impersonal bent of moral inquiry and its championing of objective value over subjective value. For if morality properly understood must address itself to values that are inclusive of the entire human community, it can only concern itself with evaluative questions and issues that admit of such wide generality. In other words, only those evaluative considerations that are amenable to universal treatment, that are expansive of the entire human race, are fitting objects of moral analysis. This obviously rules out once again pragmatic calculations of self-interest as well as ethical considerations of the good. For these sorts of evaluative matters defy universal treatment and can only be distorted by efforts to render them in such terms. That explains why questions dealing with justice, with the right rather than the good, are featured prominently in moral inquiry. For questions of justice and basic fairness permeate all our interactions with human agents, whereas questions of the good touch centrally on those particular others with whom we share a form of life and community.

It is not for nothing, then, that Habermas characterizes moral inquiry as "relatively narrow ... and uncompromisingly abstract."[35] However, it is the insistence that the last word be given only to our impersonal judgments as opposed to our first-person ones that primarily separates off the moral sphere from all other evaluative ones. Hence, it would be wise to reprise the two main reasons why this is so: why moral inquiry must be considered a failure if its reflective efforts fall short of universal judgments.

The first reason why (earlier discussed ever so briefly) is that moral reflection is supposed to tap our core identity as human beings, those features that we uniquely share and constitute what might be, and often is, called our *basic human nature*. What was left unsaid in this regard is that such reflection is considered an indispensable feature of human freedom, of our very autonomy as human agents. This is a Kantian notion and derives from his claim that a free will must be completely self-determining if it is to be truly free. It follows in Kant's argument that if the will is completely self-determining, it must be capable of causally ordering our lives by deciding which, if any, of our immediate desires qualify, after due reflection, as legitimate reasons for action and warrant our carrying them out. Finally, if the will is a causal force in our lives, it must act, obviously enough, in a lawful manner (it is also, of course, an important part of Kant's argument that in keeping with the self-determining character of the will, law must be self-imposed rather than imposed from the outside), which is just another way of saying that it must act in a universal manner, because that is the way in which all laws, whatever their kind, do their regulative work.

It is the way in which such philosophers as Nagel reinterpret Kant's linkage of universal reflection and personal freedom and autonomy, however, that best accounts for morality as presently understood. In Nagel's updated case, it is not considerations of causality but of what he calls "the externality of the reflective view" itself that sets up the connection between universal reflection and autonomy. The idea here is one that we have already come across and concerns the fact that what is the morally right thing to do can be answered only if we consider the matter not from our perspective but from an impersonal one. This means that we must suspend our own point of view, the site in which our immediate desires make their appearance and presence known, and consider the matter from the outside, from what he famously calls the "view from nowhere," if our reflective efforts are to have a moral payoff. For it is only by doing so that we will be able not only to distinguish between appearance and reality, between what seems the right thing to do from our personal perspective and what is, in fact, the right thing to do from a universal perspective, but to safeguard our freedom by making sure that we are not controlled by our desires, passions, or urges.[36]

The second reason why moral reflection must take on a universal form (which we also discussed) is because of issues of basic fairness, which highlights the connection between impersonal judgments and impartial ones rather than free, autonomous ones. What was left unsaid in this regard are the circumstances in which impartial judgments derive their moral salience. Habermas's take on moral inquiry is especially relevant here, because he has famously argued that breakdowns in what he calls *communicative action*, social actions oriented to reaching understanding with others, are the motive force behind moral reflection. The reason why is that such communicative breakdowns stem from normative failures in our social interactions, in which the norms that have heretofore governed these social interactions smoothly and seamlessly no longer do so, because they have for some reason or other fallen into disfavor. When this happens, argues Habermas, a different and higher kind of moral discourse is called for to remedy the situation, to ensure that such breakdowns are dealt with fairly rather than coercively or deceptively. The job of moral analysis, then, is to subject such disputed norms to a hypothetical, reflective procedure of testing that is free from the imperatives of action itself. The test that such norms must pass if they are to be reflectively redeemed (rather than banished) is a universal test, one that asks whether the norm in question meets with the agreement "from the perspective of all possibly affected" by it.[37] The idea, then, is that in such moral discourse, each of us is required to take the perspective of everyone else, which enjoins that we reflectively distance ourselves from whatever particular ethical communities to which we belong so that we can then reflectively wed ourselves to an ideal communication community in which universal principles of moral judgment rather than particular ethical intuitions guide our moral deliberations.

From what has been said thus far, it is apparent that there are at least two reflective paths that lead to this impersonal, universal moral standpoint. The first Kantian-like way is an introspective one that burrows deep within each of us in search of a primordial self. There is nothing personal or social about this core self or anything empirical in character that can be said of it, as it is claimed to exist prior to and independent of any personal or social roles it might come to play in the world. Indeed, how and what others may think of us is of utterly no moral significance on this view, as such considerations betray a heteronomous perspective that does not jibe with the autonomous standing of this self-legislating transcendental self. The only way to get a hold of this pristine self, therefore, to get a fix on its whereabouts and its constitutive powers and functions, is by a special reflective effort that does not cease until it successfully peels away all the first-person layers that conceal it from us and from our everyday, stay-on-the-surface reflections that regulate our socially laden, empirical selves. For it is in this deep, hard-to-fathom impersonal and authoritative part of ourselves that the universal standards of appraisal crucial to moral inquiry are located. This explains Nagel's cryptic remark that "I find within myself the universal standards that enable me to get outside of myself," as well as his no-less-cryptic further claim that freedom demands that I direct my life "from a point of view outside oneself, that one can nevertheless reach from the inside."[38]

The second, Habermasian reflective path to an impersonal, universal standpoint, requires a dialogical rather than a monological approach, one that demands that we reach out to others rather than retreat within ourselves in our reflective attempts. This is in part because Habermas hews to a social rather than an individualist view of autonomy, one that does not equate freedom with self-given laws or with individual reflective efforts to control our desires by getting outside of ourselves but rather one that regards the actualization of the freedom of any one individual as inextricably bound up with the actualization of the freedom of all.[39] This is why, then, Habermas seeks a universal foothold for moral inquiry by "moralizing" everyday communicative action (i.e., by continuing it in a reflective mode) rather than by isolating the reflective subject, as Kant and Nagel do. As Habermas notes in this regard, "Rather than ascribing as valid to all others any maxim that I can will to be a universal law, I must submit my maxim to all others for purposes of discursively testing its claim to universality."[40] So, in Habermas's view, the route to securing the much-sought-after impersonal-impartial perspective goes through our reflectively modulated discourse with others rather than the solitary, inward-turned reflective efforts of the individual self. However, in order for these social processes of reaching understanding to do their impersonal, justificatory work, they must be reflectively dislodged from the ethical forms of life in which they do most of their bidding and be relocated in a thoroughly moralized, idealized, and purified discourse. For it is only when placed in such a higher-order discourse, argues Habermas, that we are able to discover the "moment[s] of unconditionality" that are "built into" these very social processes. Further, it is only when moral discourse has put us in touch with these "moments" that it can do what Habermas thinks it alone is capable of doing: ensuring that whatever norms pass its discursive test truly transcend space and time even though they can not but help be "raised *here and now*."[41]

The model of practical reason put in play in the moral sphere must accommodate itself as well to its impersonal, universal character. Doing so means abandoning an internalist account of rationality, in which reasons for belief, action, and value are read from either our personal desires or the goods internal to social practices that serve as the focal point of some ethical community, for an externalist account of rationality in which our reasons for belief, action, and value are entirely agent-neutral. So neither *I* nor *we* intentions play any role in moral reflection, as what counts as a good reason and a genuine value is not to be determined by us but rather by an ahistorical tribunal of reason. It is the rational structure of reason itself, therefore, whether of a Kantian monological or Habermasian dialogical variety, that alone decrees what we have reason to do and value. The aim of moral reflection is to lay bare this rational structure so that we can discover what it is that anyone, not just me or you or us, ought to do. Hence, whatever fails to pass muster from these Olympian heights is to be regarded as lacking in reason, as congeries of mere inclinations and brute urges.

In this abstract picture, then, reasons and the normative spell they cast exert their authority independently of whether they are reflectively endorsed by individuals, groups, communities, or cultures. That is to say, they enjoy an intrinsic normative standing, the authority of which is not dependent in the least on individual or collective valuers. Whatever normative force moral reasons and values possess, therefore, they possess by virtue of being self-contained sources of rationality and value. That is why it is up to us practical reasoners and valuers to take the appropriate reflective measures necessary to discover them and form moral judgments based on what they have to tell us. "Discovery" rather than "making" is the operative word here, as in moral discourse any talk of making or inventing reasons and values is wrongheaded on its face. On the contrary, as

Rorty and others are wont to say of morality so conceived, all the logical space needed for moral deliberation is already at hand and so, too, "all the important truths about right and wrong."[42] It simply falls to us mortal beings, then, to avail ourselves reflectively of the moral truth they contain and save our imaginations for another day and for endeavors more suited to their idiosyncratic workings.

The high standard of (moral) objectivity claimed by this externalist account of rationality is every bit as unshakable and robust as what Bernard Williams claims befits what he calls an "absolute" conception of the world. As Williams remarks of such a conception, "There is no suggestion that we should try to describe a world without ourselves using any concepts, or without using any concepts we, human beings, can understand. The suggestion is that there are possible descriptions of the world using *concepts which are not peculiarly ours* … [and which are not] independent … of thought in general, but all that is arbitrary and individual in thought."[43] It is this idea that there are "concepts which are not peculiarly ours" that captures the independent normative force that moral reasons are purported to exercise. To see this, all we need to do is transpose Williams's example of trying to bring our concepts into accord with "what there is" in order to represent the world accurately, to our moral case of trying to bring our conduct into accord with concepts "which are not peculiarly ours" in order to get hold of a normative guide by which to lead our lives in an authoritative manner. This is why our rational standards must be impersonal ones and why it is necessary to divine such standards that we purge from our reflections and thoughts any "arbitrary and individual" features – whether we do so in proper Nagelian fashion by reflectively stepping back from our subjective perspectives or in proper Habermasian fashion by "moralizing" communicative action. Those of us unable or disinclined to carry reflection to these dizzying heights are thus condemned to lead our lives in the darkness that enshrouds the subjective point of view, forced to make do with subjective simulacra (assertions, rhetorical flourishes, imperatives, conventions, and the like) of objective reasons and with the no-less-subjective appearances that blind us as to the way things really are.

Justificatory efforts to secure the supposed moral truths in which moral inquiry traffics assume an importance here that would be hard to overstate. In fact, such efforts have an all-or-nothing quality about them, as they claim to leave nothing to chance. For the aim of moral justification is the unambiguous and unapologetically ambitious one of certifying norms that have absolute validity, that apply without qualification and equivocation to each and every moral agent on the face of the earth.[44] To say, then, of some moral norm that it passes reflective muster is to say that it provides a knockdown reason for someone to act in the way it prescribes regardless of one's subjective preferences, ethical commitments, or cultural attachments. The failure to be moved by such reasons is usually a sign of reflective obduracy, of the resistance to acknowledge a truth that is staring you in the face but, in moral matters, it is always a sign of irrationality, of the refusal to see matters aright.

It is for this and other reasons that holism, the previously discussed idea that we can reflectively probe some of our guiding values only by holding most of our other beliefs and values constant simply does not cut it in moral inquiry. For the justification of moral truths is not for the reflective faint of heart. Indeed, no stone can be left unturned in such justificatory efforts, least of all our socialization as ethical agents. The problem with such socialization and with ethical life in general is that the norms that guide it cannot be so much justified as recognized and followed. At most, the social background of beliefs and values that constitute ethical life admit of piecemeal examination, and whatever currency they enjoy is merely social in character. However, when it comes to moral life, such half-hearted, half-baked, piecemeal justificatory attempts simply will not do. That is why the moral justification of our social practices and institutions must appeal to principles that are outside and independent of such practices. Indeed, the point of moral justification, as Habermas aptly puts it, is to shatter the stability of the social and ethical world, of the habituated character of its forms of life and the complacency it encourages regarding long-held traditional beliefs and values, by asking it to put in question all at once the "unquestioned pre-reflectively given background" that informs whatever thoughts or actions are entertained there.[45] Because this is a move that no ethical agents can or will take up of their own (internalist) accord, the paramount aim of moral justification is to force argumentatively the hand of such agents, to employ whatever abstract trick it has up its sleeve to cajole them to ratchet up and stretch out their reflective attempts so that the good of all finally comes into view and with it the moral considerations that flow from such a panoramic view of moral life.

The objection that some universal truth sanctioned by moral inquiry is not universal at all but a local "truth" is, therefore, no small matter to would-be moral theorists. At the same time, it is not an objection of which they should be wary or from which they should shy away. As Nagel instructs us, if some of the moral reasons for action justified by moral inquiry prove to be parochial ones, moral theorists need only add them to their stock of beliefs about themselves, step back, and ask, "What in light of all this, do I [or we] have reason to do?"[46] The key here is not to cut off prematurely our reflective inquiries, to sustain them long enough so that we can locate the fact of the matter that settles the matter once and for all. Not to persevere in this regard, not to keep pressing this "recurrent normative question," amounts to, as Nagel sees it, "sheer laziness." In *The View from Nowhere*, Nagel dubs this unwavering commitment to and pursuit of the truth the "ambition of transcendence," a phrase that expresses well the resolute and unreconstructed character of moral justification.[47]

The same unswerving response is owed to another objection commonly leveled at reflective efforts to get at the unvarnished truth of some moral issue. That objection is that in trying to get outside of ourselves to justify our moral beliefs and values, again either by Nagel's preferred reflectively stepping-back from our personal perspective or Habermas's preferred moralization of communicative action, we will discover not universal principles of moral appraisal as promised but something altogether different, quite unexpected, and certainly unwelcome: that there are "no values left of any kind," as things can be said to matter only from some point within the world.[48] The idea that drives this objection is easy enough to understand, because when we view ourselves from a point outside ourselves, all the things that touched us and meant something to us in the world lose whatever sense they made and meaning they gave. Hence, the effort to justify our social practices by seeking principles that are independent of them leads us astray rather than to the truth.

Nagel has two responses to this objection. First, it mistakenly assumes that moral judgments are issued from the detached standpoint alone. If that were so, Nagel concedes, a conception of our moral lives from nowhere would lead to "objective nihilism." However, it plainly is not so, he insists, as the data with which the objective view has to work includes "the appearance of value to individuals with particular perspectives."[49] His second response to the claim that values vanish when they are examined from an external point of view is that we can certainly come up with impersonal *descriptions* of the world from which we can consider ourselves impersonally. If that is so, the only question is whether our moral evaluations of our conduct can keep pace with such descriptions. If they can, "we will finally have to evaluate our conduct from a non-first-person standpoint." However, can they? Certainly some descriptions outrun some evaluations. However, Nagel thinks it is unlikely that such is the case with our moral evaluations. Although he concedes that no "decisive proof" can be offered to support his contention, he continues to suggest that some evaluative questions simply cannot be answered by saying "this is the kind of person I am."[50] All of which is another way of saying that if we are willing to see our reflective queries through to their appointed end (i.e., if we suspend our disbelief and let the "ambition of transcendence" have its way with us), our reflections will eventually prove themselves worthy of the intellectual faith placed in them by yielding the universal moral principles of conduct that we seek.

The same "ambition of transcendence," of course, is what drives us as moral beings to shake off all particular conceptions of ourselves in favor of a much more expansive identity that accords with our basic humanity. Whereas, then, pragmatic calculations of self-interest only scratch the surface of who we are and ethical considerations probe only slightly more deeply until they make contact with a "practical identity" that is at one with the ethical community with which we affiliate, moral reflection goes yet deeper and higher; the two go hand-in-hand here, of course, until they put us in touch with a core identity that we share with all other human beings, and perhaps some other sentient beings as well. To be a member of a moral community, then, is to be a member of the human race, which gets you, if you reflectively grasp and embrace all that entails, admission into Kant's "Kingdom of Ends" or Habermas's ideal communication community (or both). Entrance into either or both ensures that you and everyone else will be treated as moral "equals" and, in more Kantian terms, that you and everyone else will be regarded as ends in themselves rather than as mere means. In either case, an "act of selfless empathy" is required on your and everyone else's part, not only going considerably beyond what is expected of anyone in the pragmatic sphere but going significantly beyond what is required of anyone in the ethical sphere as well.[51] It goes without saying that such moral communities are ideal ones that greatly exceed the bounds of any actual community, as it does to say that that point does not in the least count against such highly idealized communities.

As we have seen, moral reasoning is a fairly complex matter made all the more complex by its attempt to secure a universal foundation for our moral judgments. However, when it comes to mistakes in moral reasoning, moral theorists of this universalist ilk have surprisingly little to say, and what they do say is no less surprisingly simple and straightforward. For mistakes in moral reasoning evidently all boil down to reflective failures to attain the coveted impersonal-impartial standpoint. That is to say, they have to do with passing off particulars as universals, which most often takes the form of hypostasizing social practices highly valued by those doing the moral theorizing, so that they come to be erroneously identified with the universal itself. So, what moral theorists must be constantly on guard against is not to shortchange their reflective efforts so that they come up short of their foundationalist aims, which, to reiterate, consists for Nagel in "climb[ing] outside our own minds,"[52] for Williams in divining "concepts that are not peculiarly our own,"[53] and for Habermas in scaling the concrete enclosures of our ethical life so that we can discourse about what morally concerns us all. To put the same point otherwise, we must constantly be vigilant that no first-person considerations of an egoistic or ethnocentric character bog down and compromise our pursuit of moral truth.

What accounts of moral errancy lack in complexity they more than make up for in intrigue. For reflective failures to achieve an impersonal perspective are apparently not mere cognitive errors. They also importantly involve, at least to Nagel's mind, a failure of nerve, one that is sufficiently widespread in the intellectual circles of contemporary culture to rank as a sign of its "spiritual degeneration."[54] So, this reticence to follow the natural course of moral reflection as it wends its way into the impersonal logical space of reasons is not just a simple cognitive failing but something far more worrying and sinister: what Nagel calls an infantile rebellion against the "ambition of transcendence itself," one that brings in its train "intellectual repression" and a fanciful effort to wish away the complexity of moral problems and the arduous reflective effort needed to solve them.[55] If Nagel is right about this, this dumbing down of moral inquiry can be defeated only if we gird both our conceptual and "spiritual" loins. Otherwise, the moral problems that we face, which seem to grow exponentially as the world is made smaller by intercontinental communication and media systems (to say nothing of air travel), will easily crush our puny deflationist rational accounts and eventually crush us as well.

## The subsystem of morality and its objective–subjective picture of moral life reconsidered

I have already tipped my hand that the conception of morality that dominates much of moral theory today and that constitutes the third prong of my adaptation of Habermas's tripartite scheme leaves much to be desired. In fact, I am convinced not only that we can make do ethically without its vaunted claim to secure for us a neutral, impersonal standpoint from which to promulgate our moral judgments but that it obscures the one sphere of life without which we decidedly cannot make do, ethically speaking. I am referring here obviously to the intersubjective part of our lives that is the focal point of the ethical sphere and in which such social practices as sports do the brunt of their ethical work. However, before I spell out my reasons for thinking that the ethical sphere is indispensable to our moral lives and the moral sphere is extraneous and ultimately damaging to those lives, I want to sketch briefly the picture of moral life into which the morality system locks us and to suggest why we would all be better off if we were free of this picture .

It will be remembered that the primary reason why I tried to spell out the different senses in which we might understand our moral life was to see whether we could adequately distinguish between nonmoral and moral considerations. For unless we were able to make some such distinction, my claim that sports are in a bad moral way these days and desperately need fixing up could easily be dismissed as a rhetorical flourish rather than a call to action – something akin to the sort of public venting that ideologues and political pundits seem unable to resist for no apparent reason other than to hear themselves speak, to puff up their own self-importance. So, the effort to mark off where our nonmoral lives end and our moral lives begin is no idle intellectual question but a vitally practical one on which pretty much everything hangs.

Now, one thing the conception of morality has going for it is that it draws this line between nonmoral and moral considerations boldly and sharply. For according to this conception, all nonmoral considerations are to be accorded as subjective ones, be they first-person singular (I) or plural (we) expressions of desire, and all moral considerations are to be accorded as objective, impersonal ones, the universal scope of which is not to be doubted (provided the conditions for their application are suitably taken into account). Simply put then, nonmoral actions are all reducible to subjective preferences and inclinations, which give free reign to whatever it is we want and desire, and moral actions are all reducible to selfless expressions of altruism, in which the interests of all concerned are paramount and, therefore, always carry the day. The point is that once we have ordained morality as the domain of pure altruism, in which only other-regarding reflections and actions are allowed to be in play, it follows that the domain of the nonmoral is consigned to subjective expressions, in which only self-regarding reflections and actions are allowed to be in play. This is the sense in which the conception of morality forces us into a rather simple dichotomy between moral objectivity and nonmoral subjectivity. However, for all its clarity, boldness, and simplicity, it is a flawed and problematic picture for at least two reasons. First, it excludes any middle-ground, intersubjective notion of ethical life, in which beliefs and values "can only be mine insofar as they are also others,"[56] and second, its austere and exacting conception of moral life and its free-wheeling, anything-goes depiction of nonmoral life makes living up to the demands of morality well-nigh impossible. This requires a bit of historical background.

One noteworthy consequence of the Enlightenment that ushered in the modern era was what Weber famously called the *disenchantment of the world*. An especially important part of this disenchantment was the freeing of people from restrictive, hierarchical, and teleological religious, metaphysical, social, and moral orders, such as the "great chain of Being." In many cases, these orders were considered cosmic ones that were reflected in the divisions of society itself, and people lived out their lives according to predetermined purposes depending on where they were slotted in these grand schemes.[57] Though these cosmic and social orders were restrictive, they also imparted social and moral meaning to people's lives. What we gained in the way of individual and moral freedom, then, we lost in the way of moral meaning, as the moral dimensions of our lives were extirpated from the social settings and traditions in which they used to reside. In a word, the world lost its moral moorings, and it was now up to individuals to chart the course of their own moral lives.

So, the legacy of the Enlightenment was a complicated and ultimately tangled web. On one hand, it freed us to make our own social and moral way by giving birth to a new conception of the self that separated it from its social roles and embeddedness in the world; on the other hand, it forced the self to make its way in a forbiddingly disenchanted world stripped of all its moral magic. The effects of this disenchantment of the world on the contemporary social scene are most evident in the inflation of the significance and place of the pragmatic sphere in our lives and in the upsurge of undiluted subjectivity that is its trademark feature. This would explain the dominance of the market and of its instrumental brand of reason in present society and of its intrusiveness in most everything that we contemporary beings do. For when our forms of life are fitted to the imperatives of capital in this way, the goods that are internal to them and from which they derive their lifeblood are shunted aside in favor of such external goods as money, and the formative social and ethical roles that they play in the larger community are marginalized by their privatization (i.e., by their transformation into instruments of self-interest). Hence, "where the notion of engagement in a practice was once socially central,"[58] it has been almost completely supplanted by the notion of private self-aggrandizement.

The moral of this story is not that when given its chance, this newly minted autonomous self carved out quite an impressive and cavernous pragmatic life for itself and quite an unimpressive and diminutive moral life (or at least not just that); the moral is the impossible position into which this upsurge of subjectivity put moral life and reflection. For in giving such a wide berth to egoism and such a narrow berth to morality, it put the two in understandable opposition to one another, in which the objective tendencies of the moral sphere were supposed to act as a needed check on the hypersubjective tendencies of the pragmatic sphere but in such a way that the moral side was fated to lose this battle – and to lose it badly. As MacIntyre astutely notes, "[I]t was in the same period that men came to be thought of as in some dangerous measure egoistic by nature … that altruism becomes at once socially necessary and yet apparently impossible and, if and when it occurs, inexplicable."[59] In this epochal struggle, then, to rein in these newly unleashed subjective yearnings by making them answer to morally grounded appeals to altruism, the latter proved to be woefully overmatched. It is no wonder that moral concerns receded in importance as an effective regulative force in our contemporary lives, nor is it a wonder why people presently have a difficult time in even conjuring up why they should be moral at all if, indeed, acting morally means acting completely contrary to one's self-interests.

Of course, Enlightenment thinkers were not oblivious to this potential moral calamity, which is why they set out to do something about it. The basic problem that they faced was that if moral beliefs and values no longer can be read off the social forms of life and traditions in which people live (which before the disenchantment of the world helped human agents to transition from their "untutored" status as agents with certain brute subjective desires to human agents as they "could-be-if-[they]-realized [their] telos)," morality had to be somehow constructed directly from the rational capacities and desires of individuals just as they are.[60] Kant and his epigones focused on the rational capacities of human agents and argued, as we have seen, that by probing deep enough within ourselves, we could tap categorical (unconditional) rational principles of moral conduct by which to guide our lives. Such Utilitarians as Bentham focused on the desires of human agents and argued that once we see that the basic motives for action are attraction to pleasure and aversion to pain, we will be able to formulate principles of a self-enlightened morality based on a newly configured telos in which human agents are to seek the maximum pleasure and minimum pain for the greatest number of people. So, such moral thinkers as Kant and Bentham thought that they could compensate for the loss of traditional moral horizons by putting morality on a new and surer categorical and teleological footing.

However, it is now widely believed that neither thinker nor their successors succeeded in their efforts, which accounts for the long and ever-growing line of Enlightenment detractors who write it off as an abysmal failure. For instance, it has been persuasively argued that Kant's attempt to assign a categorical standing to morality by appealing to principles that rational self-legislating agents impose on themselves is unworkable. It is unworkable because if autonomous agents make their own moral laws, it follows both that they *are* bound by such laws (after all, they made them and, therefore, they should abide by them) and that they are *not* bound by them (after all, they made them and that gives them authority over these laws rather than the other way around), so they may break them whenever they see fit to do so.[61] There is also not much to be said for utilitarians' efforts to spin out moral principles by fashioning them from human desires, specifically the apparently basic human desire to increase our pleasure and decrease our pain. That is because pleasures come in too many kinds for them to serve as a stable moral arbiter of our lives. The main problem here is the evidently unsolvable one of just which kind of desire is to be considered normative for this purpose. Further, there is no way to get from my desire to maximize my pleasure to an obligation to maximize the pleasure of all.[62]

The discrediting of these Kantian and utilitarian efforts to salvage morality leaves us with three alternatives, broadly speaking. The first is simply to resign ourselves to the evident omnipotence and ubiquity of the modern individual and try to find some way to make morality amenable to its subjective desires and preferences. The second is to revive efforts to find a universal footing for moral judgments, as Nagel and Habermas and others like them do. The third alternative is to make the intersubjective precincts of the ethical sphere our moral guide and the place at which we draw the line between nonmoral first-person-singular subjective considerations and moral first-person-plural intersubjective considerations.[63]

As one can no doubt gather from my inhospitable view of the subjective-objective distinction favored by proponents of the subsystem of morality, I do not think the first two alternatives listed here offer much promise. Probably the least promising option, however, is the effort to square morality with our actual subjective desires, with our subjective motivational sets just as they are. There is every reason to regard such an effort as a capitulation rather than as a solution to the ethical problems that we face today as a result of the invention of the modern self-centered and self-sufficient self. Williams, I think, spots the glaring problem with such efforts to subjectivize morality:

> In any ordinary understanding of *good*, [I would add especially any moral understanding of good] surely, an extra step is taken if you go from saying that you want something or have decided to pursue it to saying that it is good … The idea of something's being good imports an idea, however minimal or hazy, of a perspective in which it can be acknowledged by more than one agent as good.[64]

There is the further matter of the meaning of such moral expressions as "stealing is wrong;" they resist efforts to equate them with such subjective feelings as "I don't approve of stealing." For even if I approve of stealing, that does not make it right. The converse, of course, also holds, suggesting that moral pronouncements always *mean* something more than and different from whether I find them or do not find them to my liking. That, of course and unfortunately, does not mean that moral expressions are not *used* to register subjective feelings of approval and disapproval, which is why emotivism, the moral theory that moral expressions are reducible to subjective expressions of approval or disapproval, pretty much dominates the contemporary moral scene (a development that more than a few moral theorists chalk up to the failure of Enlightenment thinkers to provide an objective foundation for morality).[65] For all these reasons, then, I think Nagel is right in warning us that "the temptation to offer an egoistic answer to egoism has been a weakness of ethical theory since the dawn of the subject."[66]

If the attempt to anchor moral judgments in subjective desires gets us nowhere, perhaps Nagel's admonition to be tough-minded in our pursuit of an objective, universal foundation for ethics, notwithstanding the failures of our predecessors, is just what the doctor ordered. However, I think this too is bad advice. A full explanation of why I think that would take me too far afield. Nonetheless, there are at least three important reasons why we should regard this approach as a nonstarter.

The first reason is that his tough-minded insistence that we follow our reflections through to the bitter end, to the point at which they yield up moral concepts that are not peculiarly ours, is actually a wistful yearning for a moral certainty beyond the reflective pale and grasp of us mere mortals. In a word, the quest to achieve an absolute, unconditional foundation for moral judgments is impossible. It will be remembered in this regard that Nagel conceded that his effort to pull off this Herculean, quixotic feat could in no way be argumentatively backed up but rather required that we steel ourselves against the failure of nerve that often stops reflection in its tracks before it is able to generate universal moral concepts. Short of a reflective guarantee, however, he does think that there is at least one argumentative thing that we can do to embolden us forward in this reflective quest: to refute arguments that try to show that such reflective feats are impossible, which should give us, he thinks further, the needed confidence to sustain our philosophical faith in the "ambition of transcendence."[67]

However, I am not at all convinced that he can succeed even in this more limited venture to disarm impossibility arguments against absolute conceptions of morality. That is because I do not think that such foundationalist moral theorists as Nagel have an answer, let alone a good answer, to a standard impossibility argument against such conceptions. Simon Blackburn's following rendition of the argument is, I think, especially good (because pithy): "[T]here is no way in which any mind can step back from its own system of belief, survey without its benefit a reality the system aims to depict, and discover whether it is doing well or badly."[68] Though Blackburn's main aim here is to discredit descriptive attempts to represent the world accurately, which means his main target is absolute conceptions of the world of the sort that we have already come across in Williams, his argument also has obvious implications for absolute normative conceptions of morality. However, first his descriptive point: that point is the simple one that there is no way to test whether our descriptions of the world are more or less adequate to it (i.e., get the world right), because there is no way we can climb outside of our descriptive vocabularies to get to the other side, the world's side, to assess how they are faring. The normative point to be drawn from this claim comes to much the same thing: there is no way to test whether our normative vocabularies are on the mark, because there is no way we can climb out of those vocabularies to get to the other side, to the not-peculiarly-ours value side, to assess how they are faring. The long and short of it, then, is that it is futile to try to bring our conduct into accord with impersonal moral reasons and values, because there are no such reasons or values to be had and there are no such reasons and values to be had because there is no elevated stage that we can reflectively scale to divine them and then somehow apply them from on high to our particular lives.

Another way to say this is to put it exactly as Nagel does: when we reflectively approach our lives from a point nowhere within them, whatever moral and other significance and value they might have had simply vanishes. However, if we put the point that way, doesn't that open us to Nagel's previously mentioned objection that it falsely presumes such external, impersonal views of our lives have nothing else to go on but their maximally detached views of the world, when in fact they also have the appearance of belief and value from our personal standpoint to go on? Nagel has a point but not, I think, a very telling one. For though it is the case that objective views such as his have something rather than nothing to go on (meaning that they begin their moral inquiries with our first-person perspectives on our lives), it must not be forgotten that the entire point of trying to view our particular lives from the outside is to free ourselves reflectively from the grip of these first-person perspectives so that we can get past the appearances they throw up to us and that prevent us from seeing things as they really are. In other words, the point of reflection for such moral theorists as Nagel is not to redeem reflectively whatever evaluative insights the first-person perspective might contain but the very opposite: reflectively to disengage that perspective and all that it shows and tells us, precisely because what it shows and tells us is unreliable, not to be trusted. After all, if the point were to recover rather than displace the first-person, there would be no point in trying to get outside of it in the first place, in trying to put reflective distance between it and us.

Nagel might complain, however (again, a point discussed earlier), that the conclusion of our argument that moral reasoning must be personal because it cannot be impersonal ignores the fact that we turn out highly abstract, impersonal descriptions of our lives all the time. If so, we certainly must be capable of such impressive descriptive feats, and if we are, the only relevant question remaining is whether our normative efforts can keep up with our descriptive ones.

However, I think Nagel's objection misses the mark again and by a wide margin. First, it is true that it is not difficult in the least to generate highly abstract descriptions of our lives. However, for the very reason that Blackburn states, such descriptions, though abstract, are not impersonal in the relevant absolute sense required by Nagel and likeminded moral theorists. The closest we get to such maximally abstract descriptions, I suppose, is the paradigmatic example of the alien visitor from space, which Searle nicely put to use to illustrate how such a stranger to earth might try to make sense out of such a game as American football. According to Searle, the best our alien visitor can muster is such descriptions as "circular clustering" to describe the huddle, "linear clustering" to describe the offense taking their positions at the line of scrimmage, and "linear penetration," to describe the execution of a running play.[69] There is no need to overtax our imaginative capacities in this regard, however, as to the culturally uninitiated, the descriptions I provide of football following Searle's are no more intelligible than his, and perhaps even less so. Surely the point here is not, as Nagel is wont to put it, whether our normative judgments can hold their own with our abstract descriptions but rather that at a certain abstract level (one, by the way, that falls well short of the impersonal mark), neither our descriptions nor our normative judgments can make intelligible sense of what they are supposed to be about anymore. This is precisely what Feezell concludes in his Nagelian-friendly analysis of sport when he writes that when viewed from an objective, impersonal standpoint, sports, as well as the rest of our lives, come off looking like wholly absurd affairs.[70]

Of course, none of these rejoinders to Nagel's Kantian, subject-centered conception of practical and moral reasoning detracts from Habermas's communicative conception of the same. That is decidedly not the case, however, for Habermas's moralization of communicative action, the intended purpose of which – purifying communicative reason of all first-person elements – puts it in exactly the same abstract bind as Nagel's account. That bind is simply that what it gains in the level of abstraction it loses in terms of its relevance to moral practice itself. That is, reflection that ranges too far from our first-person perspective of our lives loses all touch with those lives, which makes it both an unlikely and an ineffectual moral guide. Williams drives this point home: "There can come a point at which it is quite unreasonable for a [human agent] to give up, in the name of the impartial good ordering of the world of moral agents, something which is a condition of his [or her] having interest in being around in the world at all."[71] That unreasonableness is only exacerbated by Habermas's unconditional and unapologetic requirement that we leave the concrete ethical world in its entirety behind whenever our communicative norms are no longer in working order, as if efforts to repair them from the inside are a priori doomed to failure, and instead make ourselves at home in an "ideal communication community." For there is no moral substance, guidance, or least of all home to be found in such wide-ranging, universally extended communities for the reason that Walzer adeptly spells out:

> Societies are necessarily particular because they have members and memories, members with memories not only of their own but also of their common life. Humanity, by contrast, has members but no memory, and so it has no history and no culture, no customary practices ... no shared understanding of social goods.[72]

The upshot, then, is that although Habermas's turn away from subject-centered to communicative rationality was a step in the right direction, his moralization of communicative reason and action leaves us, alas, as morally clueless and lost as Nagel's view from nowhere.

So we are left with the ethical sphere as the site in which our reflective attempts to bring some moral sense to bear in our lives may find some sustenance. However, this is not a conclusion to which we need come timidly with our tails tucked between our legs, for any suggestion that the ethical sphere is merely a default position, a last-ditch chance for us to keep alive our fading hopes for a moral life, would be as misleading as it is wrong. On the contrary, the ethical life that we share with others seems to offer us precisely what we have been so far seeking in vain: a standpoint that allows us to ply our moral scalpels in a critical way to dissect and assess our bedrock beliefs, values, and actions. Better, then, or so I have been arguing, to look for ideals and values that are part of a community's repertoire of practices than to look for ideals and values that are independent of, and so not a part of, those practices or anyone else's practices (whether it be Kant's Kingdom of Ends or Habermas's ideal communication community). Further, the shared standpoint that defines our ethical life, which within, of course, certain limits can be enlarged just as effectively as it can be contracted depending on the relevant circumstances, ranges just far enough outside our subjective selves and the subjective motivational sets that we drag along with us as we pursue our different pragmatic agendas to provide us some much-needed moral perspective on those lives, yet not too far from our actual lives that all that morally matters to us disappears in one fell swoop. That means that there is no need to shoot from the hip, from whatever subjective preferences we might have at any one time, to assess our lives morally, or to shoot in the dark, from some view from nowhere, in search of abstract moral rules of conduct to guide our lives. That also means that the only line we need to draw in order to mark off nonmoral from moral considerations is the line that separates *I* intentions from *we* intentions. It also means (as I have been doing for the last few pages or so) that the notions of the ethical and the moral can be used interchangeably for one another without any loss of meaning or risk of confusion.

One last and immensely important matter – at least for the main thesis of my book. Fastening on the ethical sphere as the standpoint from which to launch our reflective efforts not only puts the moral spotlight back on where it should have been all along – our community's social practices and traditions – but back on such social practices as sports as well. At very least, it helps to make my case that glossing over any actual or potential moral role that sports might play in our own American community would be a serious mistake. For not only do sports install (moral and nonmoral) values and excellences that otherwise would never have seen the light of day, but the special mix of values and ideals they showcase come closer than many of our other practices to capturing what is morally best and most noble about America. Or I should say that sports used to be capable of such exemplar moral feats, notwithstanding its present moral malaise, and might once again, as I hope to show in ensuing chapters. However, there is enough moral substance there to make sports an ideal candidate for what Rorty rightly thinks is the best strategy for achieving moral progress today, which he argues involves "playing one part of a community's practice off against other parts."[73] When we play off sports in this manner, I want to argue in what follows, they more than prove their moral mettle.

Before I take up that charge, however, I first need to take a moral look at larger American society itself: in particular, important developments in American society of the last century or so bearing moral watching and scrutiny, not least because of their relevance to the moral case I try to build for contemporary sports.

# 5   A short moral history of America

The slice of American history that I want to make the focal point of my moral examination is not a very large one, running as it does roughly from the decade or so preceding the twentieth century to the present. So, most of the action to be surveyed and scrutinized took place in the twentieth century, which, if Jonathan Glover is right, was morally the worst century in human history.[1] Fortunately, though not untouched by some of these moral calamities, the moral condition of America and most of its citizens was considerably better by comparison. Of course, that is (to say the least) faint praise. Nevertheless, it is at least worth noting, if for no other reason than that it reminds us of the harsh moral background against which America's distinctive moral character was forged.

Any periodization of history, even one as circumscribed as the present one, is fraught with difficulty. The reason why, of course, is that history and the human life for which it tries to account are messy affairs indeed. Still, it is a worthwhile endeavor because it helps to set the boundaries of what is to be investigated, and as long as one keeps in mind that the boundaries discussed are loose and porous, any misunderstandings to which it might give rise will be easier to see and correct.

With this in mind, I divide this roughly 100-year swath of American history into two periods.[2] The first stretches from the waning years of the nineteenth century to the mid-1960s or so, which I simply call the Progressive-Liberal Consensus. More specifically, it chronicles the Progressive movement and its liberal evolution into Roosevelt's New Deal initiatives and Johnson's Great Society programs of the 1960s. This period was a rather heady moral time for much of America, with the usual important exceptions (African-Americans, native Americans, and women) and moral waxing and waning,[3] in which a national sense of moral purpose gripped a large majority of its citizens and in which much moral progress was made, particularly in stopping the rich from ripping off the poor. Some smaller though noteworthy moral gains were made as well in stemming the humiliation of African-Americans and women, but these came near the end of this period and were thus hardly more than incipient moral projects. Nonetheless, Americans were, or so I will claim, well on their way morally, to recall James Baldwin's famous phrase,[4] to achieving their country.

This first period of relative moral progress, however, was followed by a second period of significant moral slackening that started to take hold in the late 1960s, and that has largely become a dominant force in American life as we know it today. Despite some concerted and reasonably successful, though still quite fragile, efforts to reverse the humiliation of African-Americans, women, and gays and lesbians, the moral visage of America virtually disappeared in this era. This is no doubt why Lasch dubbed this period *The Culture of Narcissism*, and MacIntyre referred to it as the time *After Virtue*.[5] However, I think the better way to describe these later years, to steal the title but not the main theme of Paul Krugman's recent book, is to call it the Great Unraveling. For this is precisely what happened as the Progressive-Liberal consensus that had morally sustained America for some six or seven decades simply fell apart. What led to its unraveling and what has taken its place is the market, which looms large over everything it is that Americans do these days. Indeed, I think it is safe to say that for most Americans, and for that matter most of the world, America and capitalism are considered one and the same. That is, America is viewed by just about everybody as little more than a giant market in which the main aim in life is to get as rich as fast as one can and be dammed with everything else. If America is a great country in this view, it is principally because it not only gives more people a chance to get rich but gives more people a chance to get filthy rich, to accumulate wealth beyond their wildest dreams. It is as if the other Progressive and liberal America, the America that strove mightily to form itself into a more egalitarian and just society and that would never have dreamed of letting the market determine its moral fate, let alone its social or political fate, either never existed or was so hopelessly naïve and wooly as not to be considered worthy of even casual mention, let alone emulation. No matter, the consequences, or so I will once again claim, have been morally disastrous and explain, among other things, why the economic disparity between the haves and the have-nots is approaching a level in our country today that we have not seen since the bad old days of the Gilded Age. In short, America is in dire danger of becoming a plutocracy rather than a democracy, which threatens to undo most of the moral good it has accomplished in the recent past.

One further preliminary point before I get to the story I want to tell. The moral perspective that informs my analysis to come, as I hope I have made clear in the preceding chapter, eschews the sort of moral universalism that is characteristic of the Enlightenment and still in favor in much of contemporary moral theory. As such, it takes the view that the more impersonal, abstract, and detached one's moral standpoint, the less relevant it is to our lives, and so the less useful it is. To the extent that most critical theory practiced these days is similarly ill disposed to this Enlightenment view of moral and social theory, my moral vantage point will, I trust, strike a resonant chord with them. However, to avoid any misimpression at the outset, I should say further that the brand of moral particularism to which I am partial holds that we should seek as wide a moral consensus as we can get in working out our moral judgments and in trying to justify them. That means that it is not adverse, as I duly noted in Chapter 4,[6] either to the moral universalism of the sort John Rawls pursued as he tried to stretch his decidedly homespun American conception of "justice as fairness" to other liberal and even illiberal political regimes throughout the world or to efforts to make our moral judgments speak to entire nations and cultures. More strongly, my moral take not only resists the now fashionable view among most critical, postmodern theorists that the narrower one's moral focus the better (e.g., the idea that moral talk about "identity" groups – groups marked by their gender, race, and social class – is somehow legitimate because it comes closer to capturing our "authentic" moral identities), whereas moral talk about entire nations and cultures is less legitimate or even illegitimate because it strays too far from these "authentic" moral identities, but argues against it. Indeed, as I hope my moral narrative of America will show, one of the things that has gone terribly wrong in the last three and a half decades or so is that we Americans have lost our moral identity as a people and that we are unsure whether and how we might get it back again. This fact alone, I will argue, makes it imperative that if we hope to get out of the moral jam in which we presently find ourselves, we will not only have to dispense with (as noted) the universalist pretensions of Enlightenment theory and politics but with the identitarian tendencies of critical, postmodern theory and politics as well.[7]

## The first part of the story – progressivism

Progressivism is a notoriously difficult notion around which to get one's arms.[8] This is in part owed to the number of different views and ideas professed by its adherents, not all of which, by the way, were fully compatible with one another. However, if there is one thing on which most Progressives were agreed, it was the key idea that there is such a thing as the common good and that it can be distinguished adequately from special interests and market calculations of self-interest. Moreover, there was virtual unanimity among their ranks that cultivating this common good, instilling in Americans a national sense of purpose dedicated to the realization of this public good, was crucial to the survival and flourishing of the nascent republic. There can be no serious doubt, then, concerning the central agenda of the Progressive movement, which was to fashion America into a genuine moral commonwealth, one in which the common good of all takes precedence over the special interests of a few.

It is almost as difficult to pin down the various individuals and groups that aligned themselves with the Progressive cause. That is because they comprised a large cross-section of Americans from almost all walks of life. This included the venerable WASP elite, whose dedication to the solidarity and well-being of the country was based in its allegiance to the chivalric code of "noblesse oblige," not to mention forward-thinking businessmen who sought to give greater voice to those who toiled on their behalf. A not insignificant number of church and religious leaders should be lumped in here as well, especially the Social Gospel movement led by liberal theologians intent on bringing such issues as urban poverty to the attention of their mostly middle-class members. Disaffected socialists were a further important constituency; they found themselves supporting Progressive initiatives because they wanted to do something about the maladroit distribution of wealth generated by unfettered markets but had no socialist tradition or creed into which they could tap to channel their agitation. Such public intellectuals as William James and John Dewey were also well represented in this group, as were political types from both the grassroots and national political party level. By far, however, the largest bloc of Progressives were drawn from a wide ranging coalition of middle-class reformers, who were recruited from clubs, trade unions, settlement houses, and the like.

All in all, this was a formidable alliance of people who were convinced that America's best days lay ahead rather than behind her and were prepared to do whatever it took to make the American dream available to as many of its citizens as possible. In many ways, however, this period of moral ferment and political reform was remarkable, especially because these were not the most propitious of times to set one's moral sights high or to undertake significant political reform. For starters, the nation was still suffering the reverberations of a devastating Civil War, the many ill and divisive effects of which can scarcely be exaggerated. Further, the industrial revolution had dramatically changed the face of America in rather short order from a rural, agrarian landscape to a highly urbanized one in which massive waves of people crammed into the already densely populated quarters of cities. This led to overcrowding, crime, and immiseration all around. To make matters worse, coming as the Progressive movement did on the heels of the Gilded Age, most of the country's wealth was concentrated in very few hands; for instance, in 1896 the top 1 percent of the richest Americans owned more than one-half of the nation's total wealth, while the bottom 40 percent owned barely 1.2 percent of the total wealth. This was, after all, the era of such robber barons as Rockefeller, Morgan, and Carnegie, who had amassed unimaginable wealth in the midst of great poverty. They were, not surprisingly, more than willing to trade on their economic good fortune to gain favor from politicians eager to please their every whim. So, political graft and corruption were rampant, as was political apathy, as less well-off voters increasingly saw little reason to bother to cast their votes so long as politicians took their marching orders from their wealthy benefactors. This was also the time when the nation was inundated by large waves of immigrants who came from Europe and completely overwhelmed whatever meager social services American had to offer its tired and poor; their numbers, alas, dwarfed those select few capable of fending for themselves.

It is no small miracle that in these trying times, Americans in large numbers did not wring their hands in despair and declare that all was lost, that this great and noble experiment in democracy was doomed to failure. It was no less a miracle that the more well-off middle and upper classes did not turn their backs on the poor and immerse themselves in the pleasures their wealth afforded them. As Putnam nicely put it, "Then, as now, the comfortable middle class was torn between the seductive attractions of escape and the deeper demands of redemptive social solidarity."[9] History shows that, torn or not, then as opposed to now, a large majority of their numbers forsook the world weariness and fashionable despair of their European counterparts and opted for democratic solidarity. Why they did so and why their contemporaries show no sign of wanting to follow in their footsteps comprise, of course, the moral conundrum I address in this chapter.

What is no mystery, however, is that the Progressive movement was a moral one through and through. That is to say, it was steeped in unmistakable moral ideals that guided its reform efforts. What these moral ideals provided was a counsel of moral perfection rather than a description of fact, a point that put them in good stead with Rorty's own counsel, that "you have to describe the country in terms of what you passionately hope it will become, as well as in terms of what you know it is to be now."[10] The Progressives proved themselves adept on this score by not blurring Rorty's point as many would-be reformers are wont to do, by recognizing that staking out boldly what one hopes one's country will become almost always counts as a moral indictment rather than affirmation of what it presently is and stands for.

There were at least four overlapping moral ideals that played a formative and pivotal role for Progressives. The first was bound up with their effort to come up with a new social and moral conception of freedom, one that distances itself from ownership of property or the accumulation of wealth. They also sought a conception of freedom that underscored their separation from the hereditary caste system of the feudal and aristocratic traditions of Europe. With this in mind, they eschewed negative conceptions of freedom, which stressed the freedom of individuals to further their aims without outside interference, in favor of a positive conception of freedom, which was a thoroughly social notion that stressed how individuals working cooperatively and, therefore, in concert with one another could achieve aims and determine their fates in ways that would be unattainable if they acted on their own. In a word, they stressed collective self-determination over unimpeded individual action. In doing so, they provided a much-needed moral counter to the sort of self-serving behavior encouraged by markets.

The second ideal that served as a moral cynosure for Progressives was a commitment to an egalitarian America, to a social order in which our interactions with and relationships to one another would be permeated by a basic sense of fairness. This call for fairness in our dealings with one another brings to mind the famous first sentence of Alexis de Tocqueville's 1839 classic, *Democracy in America*, in which he observed that "Amongst the novel objects that attracted my attention during my stay in the United States, nothing struck me more than the general equality of condition among the people."[11] Of course, the United States of 1839 was a far cry from the United States of the late nineteenth century, in which a general inequality of condition obtained just about everywhere within its borders. However, in arguing for an egalitarian overhauling of our society, Progressives could not justly be accused of backward thinking, of a nostalgic longing for the good old days. That is because their pleading (e.g., for a more equal distribution of wealth) was a perfectly reasonable inference from their yet more basic commitment to furthering the common good. In short, they were keenly aware, as Delbanco nicely puts it, that "one thing fatal to democracy is a class of people without hope."[12] The best way to ensure that we do not consign our fellow countrymen to a life without hope is to ensure a reasonably prosperous life for all, which meant that the market had to be bent to the imperatives of social justice, not, as was the case at this time and especially today, the other way around.

This takes us to the third moral ideal embraced by Progressives: the moral reining in of the market. Unfettered markets were thought to be morally unwholesome in this vein, not just because they lead, *per necessity*, to inegalitarian consequences but because they induce a more pervasive – to invoke William James's famous phrase – "moral flabbiness." They do such because, once again, they militate against the common good in a number of menacing ways. To begin with, and to follow up on James's more specific point, the "squalid cash interpretation" that markets insist on putting on "the bitch-Goddess SUCCESS"[13] installs the private accumulation of wealth and its consumption as the be-all and end-all of a (nonmoral) good society. Markets wreak further moral havoc because the common good cannot be served if the pursuit of material advantage they sanction runs roughshod over, for instance, the right of workers to organize or have a voice in what they produce. Markets do yet further moral damage in privatizing whatever they manage to get their hands on, which means public discourse about what is our common good – without which we would not have the faintest idea of what that good is and what it requires of us – takes a second seat to the satisfaction of private preferences. Though they were not prepared to go as far as their socialist cousins, whose calls for a "dictatorship of the proletariat" and "nationalization of the means of production" were repudiated by Progressives as "undemocratic" and "un-American"[14] (prescient rebukes as it turns out, given the catastrophic fate of twentieth-century state socialist regimes), they were also not prepared to let the law of supply and demand erode the bonds that hold us together. This is why they insisted on ethical measures to contain the corrosive effects of the market. In this regard, as Foner astutely points out, Progressives created their own moral vocabulary, stringing together such prosaic but nonetheless forceful words as "standard of living" and a "living wage" to disarm any effort to pass off market outcomes as ethical and just ones.[15] By inventing these moral terms, then, they wanted to give the last word to such notions as the common good and social justice rather than to such notions as market share and the proverbial bottom line (i.e., to lard and thereby leaven the jargon of the market with ethical concepts to disabuse market actors of the idea that such terms have no place or normative force in the world of business).

The fourth (and for my purposes last) moral ideal of Progressivism is in many ways the most important and certainly the most encompassing one: to construct a vibrant, robust democracy in which all Americans could find moral and political solace and pride. According to Progressives, such a democracy must contain two essential elements: first, passionate, united, involved, and knowledgeable citizens who form a genuine body politic; second, a transparent, generous, responsive, expert, and morally oriented government-state. Because for Progressives the state can truly be democratic only if it is informed and held in check by the public, which makes the former parasitic on the latter, it is perhaps best to begin with their ideas as to how to mobilize such a connected and active public.

Progressives thought rightly that only if citizens feel some real bond with one another, some sense that they hold something important in common with one another, will they be more apt both to care for and cooperate with each another. In a word, Progressives believed that bonding with others lessens the chance that they will seek their own private advantage at the expense of others and increases the chance they will act in concert with one another for the common good. There are, of course, numerous (and, no doubt, special) obstacles that must be hurdled in order to get an entire nation to think of themselves as a genuine national community, as a bona fide moral commonwealth, as opposed, say, to a particular professional group or local community. The effort by Progressives to convince Americans that they should one and all enlist in the cause to further social justice, that social justice is a goal worthy of their collective attention and national aspiration, is one way in which they tried to prod Americans to think about something larger, much larger, than their own self-interests. The other way in which they tried to forge such ties was to take, once again, a page out of Tocqueville's *Democracy in America*. In particular, to follow up on his observation that

> Americans of all ages, all stations in life, and all types of disposition constantly form associations. They have not only commercial and manufacturing companies in which all take part, but associations of a thousand other kinds – religious, moral, serious, futile, general or restricted, enormous or diminutive … Nothing, in my opinion, is more deserving of our attention than the intellectual and moral associations of America.[16]

To be sure, the strong associational life Tocqueville so ably chronicled in his travels throughout early nineteenth-century America had nearly disappeared by the time in which Progressives made their presence known around the turn of the century. Still, the idea that they took from Tocqueville – that any democracy worth its salt must have a vibrant civil society in which people create and take part in associations of every kind and in the process learn to interact with one another in a cooperative fashion – was no anachronism. On the contrary, it was a brilliant insight into how to rouse a somnolent public into action, how, in effect, to turn a sleeping giant into a formidable moral and political force with which to be reckoned.

One of the factors that especially stood out to Progressives regarding such associations is that in goading us to cooperate with one another, they also goaded us to talk to one another about matters of mutual concern, the mutuality of which required that we converse in certain ways. Of course, simply getting people to talk to one another is an important first step, certainly no small feat in a society as splintered as America was at that time. However, for Progressives, that was only a precursor to getting them to talk to one another in ways conducive to democratic living. That was easier said than done, as only conversations that conformed to certain discursive norms, as they and their epigones quickly discovered, had any chance of succeeding in this regard. To begin with, it meant that our conversations should be directed to what is good and right rather than what is easy and expedient. It signified further that private dealing, bargaining, and use of power and force take a second seat to moral and political suasion. It also required that we not only know what we are talking about (which suggests that whereas it is perfectly appropriate to call on experts to gather such knowledge, it is entirely inappropriate, especially in political discussions, to have them act as our surrogates),[17] but actually listen and carefully consider as well what others have to say to us. As Gadamer was fond of putting it, that meant that we at least entertain the possibility that what they say to us might actually be right.[18] Finally, it also entails that we be reasonable in presenting our views to others (i.e., that whatever we bring up in public discourse has a reasonable chance of being accepted by others).[19]

As noted, however, an informed and active citizenry is not enough, according to Progressives, to ensure a true moral democracy. For that we would also need a strong, but not overreaching, state, one whose munificence would inspire our cheerful allegiance, not our fearful obedience. Such a state would be scrupulously fair and impartial and as publicly transparent in its dealings as is possible. It also would be populated by technical experts and organized into bureaucracies in order to carry out effectively its oversight role in regulating the economy. For the corporations and market actors that are the state's main charge to keep in check have their own retinue of experts (accountants, lawyers, statisticians, etc.), and only government agencies similarly staffed would be in a position to ensure that they conduct themselves fairly.[20] Finally, it would be the central role of the state and its technical agents, or so Progressives argued, to carry out rather than determine the will of the people.

This highly idealistic and complicated bicameral effort to form a moral commonwealth, which on the one hand seeks to instill in Americans a sense of belonging that transcends their private aims and their parochial attachments and on the other to put in place a strong but munificent state, is a delicate balancing act to say the least. That is to say, it can fail in any number of ways. For instance, the attempt to persuade Americans that social justice is the overriding aim of their moral and political life is liable to fall on deaf ears, especially given the cornucopia of goods regularly offered up by the market. Similarly, the encouragement of associations of all sizes and persuasions is perhaps just as likely to instigate internecine, sectarian struggle among them rather than to lead to their integration into an overarching community. Even more worrisome, a strong state full of technocrats is prone either to overstep its regulative role, to set public policy rather than execute it, in which case it becomes a tyrannical and not a democratic force, or to become just another self-promoting, ineffective bureaucracy, in which case it impedes rather that abets the public will and makes itself an easy prey for monied interests of all kinds.

Progressives were certainly aware of these pitfalls even if they did not have any surefire way to forestall them. To be fair, no one of their reform-minded peers did either, nor, I think it is safe to say, do we present-day Americans. However, they did have a method of sorts of dealing with them. As McCormick writes,

Progressivism owed much of its success to a distinctive method of reform, variations of which were adopted by the leaders of nearly every cause. They typically began by organizing a voluntary association, investigating a problem, gathering relevant facts, and analyzing them according to the precepts of one of the newer social sciences. From such an analysis, a proposed solution would emerge, be popularized through campaigns of education and moral suasion, and – as often as not, if it seemed to work – be taken over by some level of government as a public function.[21]

To give just one such example, women's reading associations that began as simple gathering places for reading literature soon morphed into social service and advocacy groups and then into national women's organizations that campaigned for stricter housing codes, safe drinking water, and services for the poor, sick, disabled, and children.[22] Many of these causes were subsequently taken over by various government agencies. Although this way of doing things did not always make for a seamless transition from the voluntary to the compulsory and the local to the national, it was more successful than not in effecting significant social and moral change.

Indeed, if the proof is in the pudding, as the old saying goes, the Progressives' reform efforts must be adjudged a resounding success, especially when compared to those of other similar reform groups in American history. A simple listing of their many social innovations and political accomplishments should suffice to make the point. On the social invention front, they established all over the country community centers that sponsored political debates in which social class mixing (and to a much lesser extent gender and racial mixing) were encouraged.[23] They also created a number of fraternal, religious, labor, professional, and civic associations, such as the League of Women Voters, the National Civic League, the National Consumers League, and the American Civil Liberties Union. These associations were not only sources of social and civic solidarity but often provided material benefits to their members in the form of insurance and the like. Progressives devoted an especially large share of their creative energies in this regard to founding youth-oriented associations, such as the Boy and Girl Scouts, the Campfire Girls, the 4-H, Boys Clubs and Girls Clubs, Big Brothers and Sisters, and the American Playground Movement. The idea behind these youth associations was to offer such enjoyable activities as sports and camping that also could double as places for the practice and cultivation of moral virtues. Further, Progressives were major players in the kindergarten movement, which (before they had been taken over by the state) offered many innovative educational programs to the poor. One of the more novel of Progressive's reforms was the settlement houses that they built in major urban centers, perhaps the most famous of which was Jane Addams's Hull-House in Chicago. Middle-class men and women who sought to educate and morally uplift poor immigrants ran these houses. They also taught English, set up debates and lectures, offered vocational training, and ran day care centers for the children of working families. On the more ostensibly political front, Progressives successfully agitated for women's suffrage, laws against child labor, a minimum wage, limits on the working day, and a progressive income tax.[24]

All in all, this is by any reasonable standard an enviable record of social and political achievements. However, just as important is the legacy of morally inspired reform that they bequeathed to their liberal-minded compatriots who continued their efforts to make America a moral beacon both to its own citizens and to those across the world.

## The rest of the story – the liberal consensus

It is no exaggeration to say that the next wave of reformist fervor and accomplishment – the liberal consensus – though enormously important in forging America's moral course for the next 40 years or so, is but a footnote to the Progressive era. After all, it was the latter that laid the intellectual foundation and set the practical stage for the emergence of the liberal consensus and the steady moral and political progress that it was able to make. Still, it deserves some separate mention and treatment for furthering the moral agenda of Progressivism and helping America to stay on track in its aspiration to become a full-fledged moral commonwealth.

As before, this period of social and political uplift was fueled by an unmistakable moral conception of American exceptionalism. The reigning moral view was that we are all in this noble and highly risky democratic experiment together and that if one part of us falls short of realizing the American dream, we all fall short. This time around, however, the moral responsibility and burden of realizing this dream fell more squarely and heavily on the state, owing (no doubt) to the growing complexity and size of the country itself, though neither the commitment to associational life nor its perceived significance as a bulwark against tyranny were overlooked or given short shrift by liberal reformers.

As Reich astutely pointed out, three pillars underpinned this moral conception of America.[25] The first was that as companies fared better so, too, should their workers. That meant that as the economic fortunes of the company increased the wages and benefits of their workers, not to mention that the company's commitment to and investment in the larger community, should increase as well. The second plank of the moral compact was that companies should pay workers enough to support themselves and their families. The corollary of this was that if there were not enough jobs for all or if workers became sick or otherwise disabled so that they could not work anymore, the government should provide a safety net in the form of social insurance programs (e.g., unemployment benefits) to prevent them from sinking into poverty. The third, and last plank was that all Americans should be given equal opportunity to receive a free public education to better themselves.

It would be wrong to presume, however, that the moral compact that impelled the liberal avatars of Progressivism forward was purely a moral one. Of course, that cannot be said of any reform movement, nor should it be, as moral purity is not, like everything else that claims to be such (in our case, the already discussed notion of amateurism), an unalloyed good.[26] In this particular case, what I have been calling the *liberal consensus* was also partly an economic and political compromise. On the economic side, working-class folks ceded control over their labor and what they produced to employers in exchange for relatively high wages. On the political side, conservatives accepted a reasonably strong welfare state as a concession to the Great Depression, and liberals accepted a strong emphasis on national security and a strong military as a concession to the Cold War.[27]

However, it would be equally wrong to suppose, for essentially the same reason, that these economic and political considerations somehow undermined or diluted the moral core of this liberal consensus. On the contrary, that moral core was very much in evidence, or so I claim, in the communitarian-inspired efforts by liberal reformers to soften the hard edges of market-based egoism by playing up the importance of moral fellow-feeling in our lives. Delbanco interestingly linked up this notion to Pericles's pithy point that "the last pleasure, when one is worn out with age, is not … making money, but having the respect of one's fellow men."[28] That moral core was also manifestly in evidence in the upsurge in social trust among Americans during this period, both in one another and in the government,[29] and in the impressive solidarity displayed by both American Catholics and Jews in support of African-Americans' struggle for equality, a struggle that would soon occupy the attention of the entire nation.[30]

Wolfe captures well the moral tenor of this age when he opines that the generation that endured the Great Depression and the Second World War "put its faith not in a vision of individuals as free choosers of their own moral beliefs, but … in [a moral vision rooted in] social cooperation."[31] That moral vision translated politically into such social insurance programs as social security, such subsidy programs as the GI Bill and low interest rates for housing (which gave returning servicemen a better-than-even crack at a middle-class life), and government monitoring and regulating of the market to guard against crushing economic inequality. These measures were mostly successful, as the ranks of the middle-class swelled, and great disparities in wealth were significantly narrowed.[32]

The coda of this Progressive-based and -led story can be summarized in a phrase: more of the same. For that was in fact what Johnson's Great Society programs of the 1960s amounted to in their enlistment of the government and the country in a battle to ameliorate the ill effects of poverty and in his and the Congress's related effort to provide a constitutional backing for the civil rights movement. So, once again the government, with the strong backing of the people, came to the rescue of the commonwealth by keeping the market in check and by doing their level best to stem racism and sexism. What we have here, then, is a story of continuing moral progress in which unemployment remained low, growth high, and wages robust. After all, this was a time in which highly educated professionals (college professors, lawyers, middle-managers) made about the same as unionized blue-collar workers.[33] The welfare state was further strengthened as part of the war on poverty and, as just noted, constitutional rights were extended to heretofore excluded groups, as African-Americans and women made their presence and political clout increasingly known. In addition, the civil rights and women's movements that they spawned kept alive the egalitarian ideals of the country. Of course, things were hardly perfect. America was still far from being a "classless" society, poverty remained a problem, and the sadistic humiliation of select groups did not cease. However, the ranks of both the superrich and the abjectly poor had shrunk significantly and, perhaps most important, a strong civic spirit that permeated the country was ever vigilant in spotting these problems and was committed to solving them. Indeed, the fact that reformers refused to consider them intractable problems is a testament to their civic pluck. As Putnam observed, the prospects for a strong civic life in the 1960s in America never "looked brighter."[34] Unfortunately, those prospects proved to be short-lived, as the country was about to go through a debilitating transition in which, with apology to Karl Marx and Marshall Berman, "all that was solid melt[ed] into air."

## The great unraveling

Just when this Progressive and liberal consensus in America started to crack is hard to say. Interestingly enough, more than one commentator tied its breaking apart to momentous developments in the world of sport. For instance, novelist Don DeLillo claimed that the last time at which Americans really connected with one another was in the fall of 1951, when Bobby Thompson "tomahawked" an inside fastball into the left-field fence in the ninth inning to clinch the pennant for the New York Giants. This stirring athletic feat, DeLillo mused, made "people want to be in the streets, joined with others, telling others what has happened, those few who haven't heard – comparing facts and states of mind."[35] Cultural critic Andrew Delbanco dated the end of Progressive and communitarian-minded America somewhat later but still in sporting terms, linking it to the advent of specialization in baseball (the designated hitter rule, middle relievers and closers) and its further commercialization (e.g., TV timeouts to air commercials that disrupt the rhythm and tempo of baseball),[36] both of which, he surmised, lessened the public appeal of the game, thereby giving the forces of privatization an important pass. However, noted cultural commentators Todd Gitlin and Richard Rorty saw the matter differently, both targeting the Vietnam War and its chaotic aftermath as the crucial period in which national pride in America fizzled out and, with it, the desire to perfect it morally and politically.[37] Finally, English critic Godfrey Hodgson attributed America's downward spiral more particularly to certain ominous economic markers that began to pop up in the mid-1970s (stagflation, the business class's opposition to further taxation and unions), which undermined Americans faith in a mixed, state-regulated economy.[38]

So, it seems that somewhere in the period between the mid-1960s and mid-1970s (DeLillo's conjecture aside) and for a variety of related reasons, "Something snapped in … the 'bands' that once connected us to one another," and the reform impulse gave way to "solipsism … installing instant gratification as the hallmark of a good life, and … repudiating the interventionist state as a source of hope."[39] The resultant picture was and is not a pretty one, as Americans lost their moral bearings (and show little evidence of having regained them) and as the country went into an atomistic tailspin from which it has yet to recover. As we shall see, this time around, there was no socially committed or politically activist middle class nor any significant social class coalitions (whether of the top-down or bottom-up variety) to bail us out. However, I am already getting ahead of myself and need first to sketch out in greater detail the economic, social, political, and moral features of this new and badly fractured America with which most of us are only too familiar.

To begin with perhaps the darkest chapter of the story, the economy, what these last three or four decades reveal is a virtual surrender – to the brute forces of the market – of everything that we Americans love and do. That is, having successfully convinced a worn down and wary public that the state had badly mismanaged the economic affairs of the country, proponents of the market relentlessly pressed their case that it should be left to its own devices. They reasoned that when it is not encumbered by, well, anything noneconomic – be it a bureaucratic state or a body of citizens with a political agenda – it does its best work, which is to allocate resources more efficiently than any other tool known to us. These market aficionados were especially contemptuous of any effort to import moral notions and ideals into economic matters, arguing that mixing such economic principles as the law of supply and demand with such moral considerations as fairness is like mixing oil and water: they cannot be mixed because of their fundamental incompatibility, and any effort to do so will lead to disastrous consequences all around. That is why they wasted no time in banishing such morally freighted words as a "living wage" (as noted, a favorite of Progressives) from the lexicon of the market, replacing them with their own unmistakably amoral neologisms, such as downsizing, outsourcing, leveraged buyouts, hostile takeovers, and mergers. These hard-edged, no-nonsense concepts made it clear, if it were not already clear, that conducting business is the only sensible and appropriate function of the market.

What the upsurge of this new predatory phase of capitalism signifies, then, is a major shift in the corporate ethos of the business world in which the old moral compact that had held the country together for the better part of a half-century was unceremoniously put out to pasture. Hence, the idea that companies were morally beholden to their workers and to the larger communities in which they resided quickly fell out of favor as corporate heads set their sights instead exclusively on raising the short-term profits of their shareholders.[40] As a consequence, profitable companies no longer saw any point in offering their workers job security, because cutting labor costs was one especially quick and effective way to enrich shareholders. This explains the rash of pink slips in the private sector during this period and the steady replacement of older workers pulling higher wages for younger workers pulling lower wages (the latter thankful just to have a job) not to mention the replacement of full-time workers for independent contractors and part-time workers. This focusing of the corporate eye on the bottom line also explains in part the draconian cuts in health and pension benefits over the last 30 years and – increasingly

– the elimination of these benefits altogether. Though the outsourcing of jobs to cheaper labor markets in Asia that began in earnest in the 1980s was spurred on primarily by the globalization of the marketplace, any lingering suspicions regarding its moral legitimacy were dashed as well by this change in corporate outlook. The formation of "foreign policy committees" by business elites in the cities of America's heartlands around this same time was similarly propelled by this lifting of moral constraints on the market; how else to explain their indifference to the human rights records of the countries they courted and continue to court?[41] Nothing of moral substance is to be found, either, in the narrative-poor symbols that the corporate world churns out to burnish its new money-isn't-everything-it's-the-only-thing image, the most conspicuous of which are "the logos of corporate advertising – the golden arches and the Nike Swoosh." As Delbanco rightly points out, these "symbols will never deliver the indispensable feeling that the world does not end at the borders of the self," nor do they in the least pretend or try to.[42] They don't try to because those responsible for them seem to think that the borders of the self really are coextensive with those of the world, which is why they do not think there is anything indispensable about any feeling that conveys the contrary, which suggests that self-transcendence is the prerequisite of a good life.

Perhaps the most disturbing consequence of this corporate turning of the Progressive and liberal consensus on its head are the startling economic inequalities to which it has given rise. Hodgson's stunning declaration in this regard, that contemporary America "is the most unequal society in the developed world in terms of both income and wealth,"[43] is no cheap rhetorical shot but a sober reading of what the data themselves reveal. What those data show is the hard-to-miss (because huge) differential between the wages, income (earnings from dividends, interest, and capital gains), and wealth of those at the top of the economic ladder from those at the bottom. If we start with wealth, it turns out that from 1989 to 1999, to single out just one decade from this post-Progressive-Liberal period, the top 1 percent owned 47.2 percent of all financial assets, the top 10 percent owned 83 percent of all assets, while the middle fifth of Americans saw their assets actually drop from 4.8 to 4.4 percent. What is more, today one in five Americans have zero or negative wealth (which means that their debt exceeds their net worth).[44] Things do not look much better from an income perspective. If we look first at those who are actual stockholders, what we see is that the top 1 percent own about 50 percent of all stocks, whereas the bottom 80 percent own only 4 percent of all stocks. Further, close to 52 percent of Americans own no stock whatsoever (not even in pension plans or IRAs or 401(k)s). Of those Americans who do hold stocks, 36 percent have $5,000 or less invested in the market. (As Hodgson sardonically remarks, the price of what a well-worn and well-traveled used car might fetch.)[45] Given these large disparities in the ownership of stocks, it comes as no surprise that the huge gains in the value of stocks in the 1990s redounded disproportionately, to court understatement, to the already rich. As Reich points out, the top 10 percent racked up 80 percent, and the top 1 percent gathered 40 percent of those gains, whereas the bottom 80 percent realized only 4 percent of those gains.[46] Of course, more than one-half of Americans, as just noted, realized no gains at all, because they owned no stock to begin with.

Things look that much worse when we factor wages into the equation. As Krugman reports, the average compensation of the top 100 CEOs in the last 30 years (adjusted for inflation) went from $1.3 million (39 times the salary of the average worker) to $37.5 million (1,000 times the salary of the average worker).[47] In that same period, the average annual compensation of the American worker, again adjusted for inflation, fell about 10 percent from its 1973 level. Worse, the real value of the minimum wage today is about 20 percent lower than it was in the 1970s.[48] Further, attempts to disguise or otherwise mitigate the force of these disparities, which principally take the form either of basing economic calculations on larger units of the population or arguing that those on the bottom do not stay there very long (i.e., are only temporarily poor), fall flat on their face. It is true that if income disparities are reported out in larger units, either by dividing the country into five quintiles (20-percent blocks) or ten deciles (10-percent blocks), they look less daunting. So, to borrow Krugman's example, if it is pointed out that the greater income gains realized by the top 10 percent includes everyone with an income beyond $81,000, it appears as if a goodly portion of those gains went to middle-class folks and not simply to the rich. In fact, however, that would be wrong, as those middle-class earners represent just a small portion of earners in this group and, of course, fall on the very bottom of its wage scale. When we take these points into consideration, what they show is that by far the largest share of those gains went instead to those on the very top of the heap, which means went to those at the top 1 percent, who make $230,000 or more, and went to those at the highest 0.01 percent level, whose income was $3.6 million or more and whose average income was $17 million.[49] Hence, it is clearly very wealthy, rather than middle class, Americans who are receiving the lion's share of these income gains. As for claims that things at the bottom look bad only in the short rather than the long run, once again the evidence suggests just the opposite. Consider, for example, the fact that 70 percent of Americans today remain in the same socioeconomic class in which they were born and that only 2 percent of the professional and managerial class comes from the children of poorly educated parents.[50] Hence, there is nothing transitional at all about the incomes of those at the bottom, which ominously suggests that social mobility in America, one of the main pillars of the American dream, may well be a thing of the past.

This is, to say the least, not a pretty picture, and it has only been made worse by recent government tax and economic policies that have abandoned any moral commitment to the redistribution of wealth in the name of equality and civic solidarity in favor of an economic commitment to fill the coffers of the wealthy investor class (hardly any of whose capital, by the way, ever "trickles down to the "little guy" and not just because a small but increasing portion of it goes overseas in hot pursuit of cheap labor).[51] Perhaps the most egregious example of such morally retrograde government policies was Bush's 2001 tax cuts, which gave the top 1 percent a not insignificant 6.3 percent cut (amounting to roughly a $45,000 bonus), and a 2.8 percent cut for everybody else (everybody, that is, save the poor, who pay little or no income tax but pay plenty in payroll taxes for which, alas, no tax relief was provided). However, the economic policies of Republican-controlled administrations from 1980 to 1992 were no less morally egregious, since they led to a drop of 5 percent in the median American worker's income, a rise of 30 percent in the income of the top 5 percent, and an eye-popping 78 percent rise in the income of the top 1 percent.[52]

What this means for the average working couple and family, where *average* means both husband and wife working full-time for production (nonsupervisory) wages of somewhere between $7.50 to $8.00 an hour to support two kids, is what Rorty grimly describes as a "humiliating, hand-to-mouth existence." For such a family would pull in a paltry $30,000 a year, which puts home ownership out of their reach and gives them barely enough money to rent a one-bedroom apartment (in fact, they would have to spend more on shelter than the 30 percent of income considered affordable for this purpose) and certainly not enough money to pay for decent child care or health care. So, a family with this level of income "will be constantly tormented by fears of wage rollbacks and downsizing, and the disastrous consequences of even a brief illness."[53] What we have here, then, is a new category of the poor, what Reich calls the "working poor," who have full-time jobs but do not earn enough to lift themselves out of poverty.[54] Their better-off but shrinking middle-class counterparts, many of whom find themselves in this more fortunate category (which among other things accounts for their flight to the more affluent, safe, and comfortable suburbs) in part because of the help their parents received during the depression from Progressive reformers and legislators, worry hardly at all about whether their government is morally committed enough but worry plenty about whether it will raise their taxes. Worried enough, in fact, that they can almost always be counted on to resist mightily, and usually successfully, whatever tax increases politicians propose, no matter how noble the proposals (for schools or the poor) and how well thought-out (cost-effective) they may be.[55]

Kruger was neither kidding nor exaggerating, therefore, when he wrote that "The America of [starkly presented in the 'greed is good' theme of the movie] 'Wall Street' and [Tom Wolfe's scary novel of the very affluent lives lived by rich Americans and the poverty stricken and very violent lives lived by poor Americans] 'The Bonfire of the Vanities' was positively egalitarian compared with the country we live in today."[56] This would explain why America, adjudged the richest country in the world at least by one crude measure (whose crudeness has to do with the fact that it does not explain that America's standing as the richest country on the planet is owed solely to one factor: our rich are considerably wealthier than the rich of other countries), has the highest poverty rate of 16 developed countries and the second lowest rate of escape from poverty.[57] It also explains why life in contemporary America falls short on other social, political, and moral measures as well.

The coming apart of the Progressive-liberal agenda not only wreaked havoc on the economy (installing, as it did, the market as its unrivaled arbiter) but on social life as well. For it severely depleted the social capital (roughly, the trust that we place in one another and from which we draw in our cooperative interactions with one another) that is vital to the flourishing of any society. Just as the market forced us to fend for ourselves, then – rewarding the relatively small number of winners with a life of material wealth beyond their wildest dreams and tormenting the much larger group of losers with a life of unremitting economic insecurity and incessant worry – so too did the larger social order shaped by these market forces further insulate and isolate us from one another. Indeed, the rate and extent of our disengagement from the public sphere and the various forms of associational life bound up with it has been so precipitous and pervasive that it is a wonder that we have any common life left to share at all with one another in this country. It is not for nothing, then, that Walzer characterizes present-day America as "perhaps the most individualist society in human history."[58]

This is perhaps nowhere as evident as in the major demographic shift that occurred in the last half of the twentieth century in America, in which literally millions of people left rural areas, and predominantly well-off white people abandoned inner cities to live in the suburbs. Though the population in the major center cities in America held steady, that of those living in the suburbs doubled in size during this period. As the primary form of segregation in the country today is by income, it is no surprise that almost 75 percent of welfare recipients live in the center cities and that most affluent whites live in the suburbs. This is the central reason why many social commentators equate the suburbanization of American life with its wholesale privatization.[59] For what happens when people flock to suburbs or alternatively are left stranded in central cities is that they end up spending almost their entire lives with people just like themselves, with people of their own "kind." The trade-off is significant, as the social class mixing that was often a feature of small-town life in America is now hardly to be found anywhere, in our cities or our suburbs. As noted, however, it is the clustering of people into single-class "isolated suburban pods" that is the main causal force behind this social schism and the main worry here.[60] For these suburban pods are nothing if not models of exclusivity, barring or discouraging, as the case may be, less affluent and less politically conservative folks and people of color (to be more precise, African-Americans, especially lower-class African-Americans). What is so worrying about this trend, of course, is the mutual incomprehension and social disintegration it spawns. For a nation that carves its people up into such homogeneous enclaves cannot expect anything other than social anomie (i.e., massive distrust, suspicion, intolerance, and virulent sadism all around). To be sure, it hardly needs saying that those at the bottom once again can expect to bear the brunt of these hurtful and destructive social forces.

The role that religion plays in contemporary life has undergone a similar metamorphosis that robs it of much of its bonding capacity as well. It will be remembered that liberal theologians in the Progressive period did much to sow the seeds of social integration and moral uplift in America. Today, that reservoir of social capital has practically dried up. The reason why is that religion, especially its emergent and thriving evangelical, born-again variety, has become as atomized as everything else. So, religion too has become mainly a private affair in which it is essentially left up to individuals to decide for themselves what counts as a religious form of life.[61] Just, then, as economic actors put a premium on individual freedom, so too do their religious counterparts, in their effort to personalize their relationship to God and thereby bypass the social institutions and traditions of the church and its appointed clergy as mediating agencies. Their objection to these institutions and traditions is precisely that they get in the way of religious self-exploration, that their institutional imperatives cramp the freedom of their members to forge their own religious paths. In a stunning reversal of the traditional notion of religious freedom, therefore, which was dedicated to assuring everyone the freedom to practice different religions, these new, contemporary evangelicals demanded and demand the freedom to determine for themselves what sort of religious expressions best suit their idiosyncratic desires and needs.[62] In their insistence that nothing come between them and their highly personal relationships to God, service to others got lost in the shuffle (i.e., was stripped of the considerable religious significance it used to enjoy).

Unfortunately, these desocializing tendencies were, as duly noted, not confined to life in the suburbs or religious practice. Rather, they ran and run through all the social networks that are integral to our present associational life. This would account for the marked atrophy of our most important informal and formal social and civic organizations, not to mention the steep decline in philanthropic giving and volunteerism. This weakening of associational life, however, has nothing to do with the actual number of these organizations, as formal organizations such as, for example, the Parent Teachers Association (PTA) or the American Association of Retired People (AARP) have actually increased over the last three decades or so; in fact, they have tripled in number. Rather, what is most noteworthy and worrying about these organizations is that membership in them has nose-dived. Indeed, they presently attract roughly one-tenth of the members they used to attract, which is why Putnam regards the escalating increase of these organizations but plummeting decrease in their members as indicative of a "proliferation of letterheads, not a boom of grassroots participation."[63] Moreover, there has been a steady decline as well in leadership roles played by members of these organizations. This is owed to a pattern of geographical and professional centralization, in which the conduct of the daily affairs of these organizations is delegated to professional staffs usually headquartered in Washington DC so that they can effectively lobby the government on their behalf. This reduces most participation in such groups to little more than writing checks to their national organizations.[64] What is true of formal organizations is no less true of informal ones, the number of whose members has also precipitously declined as well and whose leadership positions are shared among fewer and fewer people. The decline of giving and volunteerism can be similarly explained, as such activities correlate poorly, if at all, with economic capital and correlate highly with social capital. It is no mystery, then, why social trust in American life is in such short supply today.[65]

Of course, no society can survive without some associational life to keep it together, without a thriving civil society to support its political life and social infrastructure. That would also have to be at least minimally true of American society today despite its present highly riven state, for if there were truly nothing left that binds us together, we would simply implode. However, the fact that we have not as yet self-destructed is hardly consolation, especially as we seem to be moving ever closer and closer to our day of reckoning, and it is, more important, beside the point. For in many respects, how we think of ourselves now, following up on Durkheim's point that society can for the most part be summed up by the idea it has of itself, is even more important than what is likely to be our saturnine future fate if for no other reason than that it plays an obvious causal role in shaping that fate. That means that though there is still evidently some thread that holds us together, even if nothing more substantial than a gossamer thread, the real danger, as Walzer warns us, is that we may come to think of ourselves as even more fractured and disconnected than we actually are, so that we "deny the existence and legitimacy of these ties."[66] Once that happens, America might just as well write its obituary and be done with it.

Tocqueville presciently forewarned us, as he pondered the sort of despotism to which our unique social arrangements might give rise, that this sulfurous brew of real and imagined disconnectedness would be our ultimate undoing. As he sought, in his own words, "to trace the novel features under which despotism may appear" in our newly minted republic, he sketched the following troubling picture:

> an innumerable multitude of men … incessantly endeavoring to procure the petty and paltry pleasures with which they glut their lives. Each of them, living apart, is as a stranger to the fate of all the rest, his children and his private friends constitute to him the whole of mankind. As for the rest of his fellow citizens, he is close to them, but does not see them. … he exists only in himself and for himself alone; and if his kindred still remain to him, he may be said at any rate *to have lost his country*.[67]

That Tocqueville's remarks proved so prophetic is evident for one by the fact that they could easily pass, save the nineteenth-century prose, for Ehrenrich's contemporary eye-witness account of America's atomistic predicament. In it, she describes a country the rich citizens of which are so blithely unaware of its poor ones that they scarcely know they exist and attributes the reason why to the fact that the poor, though close by, are nowhere to be seen in the world of the affluent, who send their kids to private schools, spend their leisure time in private clubs as opposed to public parks, do not need or use public transportation, and live, as we have seen, in income-segregated suburbs.[68] If there is a special reason to worry about this kind of almost total separation of the classes, it lies in the fact that in erecting these kinds of feudalistic walls between the haves and the have-nots, we may well be setting the stage, however unwittingly, for a fascist-laced backlash in our country. For the rootless and despairing individuals, the predictable product of such class divisions, are easy prey for charismatic demagogues eager to fill their heads with all sorts of vitriol-laced nonsense to incite them to say and do horrid things that they otherwise wouldn't dream of saying or doing.[69]

Of course, the virtual collapse of civil society does not bode well for America's political soul, either. For without a fully informed, united, and engaged citizenry, as Progressive reformers never tired of reminding us, we cannot expect the public to perform its vital job of guarding against an overreaching and unresponsive state. Worse than that, however, without a common center that we can call our own and from which we can draw inspiration, it becomes highly presumptuous even to speak of a democratic public here or, for that matter, any kind of public. For the political reality in America today is that there does not appear to be a center anymore, and by that I do not mean a centrist politics that tries to balance strategically the concerns of the Right and Left but rather as a shared sense of tradition and common destiny that transcends party affiliations and narrow sectarian interests. To be blunt, we have indeed, as Tocqueville tellingly predicted, lost our country, our sense of being Americans first and foremost, and instead we cling to whatever special interest groups promise to make our particular lives better. I do mean *cling*, because most of us are free-riders content to sit back and allow those precious and harder-to-find few who are willing to take up the hard work necessary to advance our interests to do their thing.

So, the first causality of social anomie is patriotism itself. That is to say, love of country and the dedication and sacrifice to the greater good for which it calls, not to mention the ideals that it puts in place and demands us to reach and attain. Patriotism is the first thing to go when there is no longer anything that we as a people share in common, with which we can identify and around which we can rally. The sense, then, that imperialism is unworthy of America's democratic commitments or that no American should have to live in the way our present least well-off citizens do rings hollow when our own self-interest is all we really care about. This is just as true today for the Right, who confuse military jingoism for patriotism, as it is for the Left, who are convinced that the government acts at the behest mainly of large corporations rather than of the common folk and find it exceedingly difficult to summon any pride in their country. Certainly, the newest version of patriotism trotted out by the Bush administration during the initial phase of the war in Iraq, what has been contemptuously called "market" patriotism, which basically urged Americans to shop until they drop, is perhaps its most repellant one. It is little wonder, therefore, that Americans for the most part no longer trust their government or one another or that the poor and disenfranchised are the least trusting of all.

The sense, then, that we are all in this together, that our individual fates as citizens are ineradicably bound up with our larger and shared fate as a people (which Riech rightly claimed was the very core of the moral compact that prompted Progressive reformers to make America a better country for all its people and not just for a privileged subsection of them)[70] no longer rings true politically in our present circumstance. So, one important reason why those at the top end of the wage, income, and wealth scale steadfastly resist any tax proposal to redistribute wealth in a more equitable way is that they no longer see as one of them those poorer Americans that such proposals are meant to help out, as worthy of the political, moral, and economic capital that it would take to improve their lot in life. What goes for taxes here goes for everything else that is the proper province of political deliberation and negotiation: to include the funding of education, social insurance programs, welfare, public health, and retirement. Although, as Taylor astutely notes, such political fragmentation is compatible with a democracy dedicated to the defense of individual rights and the rule of law, it is fundamentally incompatible with a democracy based on common projects, a strong public and civic sense of purpose, and a flourishing political discourse. So, when it comes to the rallying and formation of "democratic majorities around meaningful programs that can then be carried to completion," for which some of our most pressing and urgent political problems (such as the ones just mentioned) cry out, we Americans have to settle for interest-based, advocacy politics that not only makes those problems increasingly intractable but further fragments and divides us.[71]

What we saw with the decline in our social organizations, then, we see once again with the decline in our political ones: a pattern of professionalization that encourages spectatorship and discourages participation in the body politic. This would explain, among other things, why it is estimated that somewhere around 14,000 lobbyists presently ply their trade in the nation's capital and why the number of people who vote in presidential elections has been declining steadily for the last four decades. This has been especially true of blue-collar workers, whose voting numbers have dropped one-third from 1960 to 1988.[72]

Finally, one important consequence of this splintering and professionalization of the political sphere was the eclipse of liberal by conservative politics that began in the 1970s.[73] The previously discussed suburbanization of America played a key role here not just by exacerbating an already badly divided body politic but further by giving aspiring political types and entrenched lobbyists a clear, identifiable, homogeneous, and (most important) politically ripe target to which to pitch their right-of-center appeals. This is perhaps most apparent in the House of Representatives, easily the most conservative branch of government, which not so very long ago (25 years, at time of writing) was evenly split in numbers among urban, rural, and suburban districts. Today, by contrast, suburban districts outnumber urban ones two to one and rural ones three to one.[74] That suburban advantage, of course, directly redounds to the advantage of conservatives and gives them the constituency that they so vitally need not just to gain access to political power but to wield it with authority. It goes without saying, of course, that this suburbanization of politics, just like the political fragmentation it encourages and from which it feeds, militates strongly against any politics oriented to the common good.

## The moral fallout of the "great unraveling"

What this economic, social, and political atomization of America betokens, then, is a colossal moral breakdown, a failure to realize the Progressive dream, which as we have seen was once the quintessential American dream: to fashion the country into a bona fide moral commonwealth. In short, we have indeed, just as Toqueville mused we might, lost our country and with it the moral compass we need to guide and track our moral commitments to our compatriots, to ensure that their lot in life never strays too far from our collective moral conscience. This loss of faith in America as a moral ideal is no small matter, then, but rather a loss the consequences of which prove ominous in a number of important respects.

Perhaps the most important and worrisome of these respects is the loss of any ethical sense of community in America itself (i.e., of a sense of community that asks us to identify with something larger and grander than our own particular, parochial interests). Instead, we have done just the opposite: either we pretend that what is good for a precious few of us must be good for all of us or we pretend that no one else but the particular groups with which we identify matters; thus, we can confidently and safely eschew any onerous consideration of the common good. The first way is the conservative way, favored by those who think that whatever serves the interest of our most prosperous citizens cannot help but be good for the entire lot of us. The second way is the one favored by many Leftist identitarian types, the way favored by those suspicious of any talk of the common good, because what is common among us always boils down in one way or another (or so they argue) to what the dominant group says is the common good. In other words, any talk of the common good is a sham, a ploy by which the strong exploit the weak. There is, of course, more than a grain of truth in their moral cynicism. However, by conceding rather than contesting the center and, therefore, who gets to define what the common good is to the Right and by insisting that progressive forces can be so only if they do not occupy the center but steadfastly maintain and proclaim their marginality as if it were some sort of badge of honor, the Left is making not only a grievous moral mistake but an equally grievous political one.[75] I have more to say about this Leftist version of the loss of country later, but for now I focus on the conservative one, because it is in fact the dominant view and especially morally disingenuous and dangerous, I might add.

What is so morally discomfiting about this conservative take is not just that it is self-deluded in trying to pass off market outcomes rigged in its favor as altogether just ones (representing as it does a half-hearted attempt by the haves to ease what little moral conscience they evidently have left) but is something far more troubling. The more troubling feature is that in peddling its claim that markets alone, rather than in concert with a socially connected civil society and a socially committed state, should be entrusted to allocate and distribute most if not all of our important resources, it effectively turns the ideal of a moral commonwealth on its head by cramming the larger good of the entire community into the much smaller and narrower good of a privileged subsection of that community. That such cramming manifestly ill suits the larger community goes without saying. What must not be left unsaid, however, is that this flattening and narrowing of the greater moral community carries with it ominous moral consequences. For the net effect of pushing the political community and the state out of the moral business of redistribution is to say to those who are not presently the main beneficiaries of the market (which as noted includes a sizable number of Americans) that we have nothing left to offer you, no other solutions that can ease or change your predicament for the better. This is nothing if not the language of moral abdication. For when we say such things as that, which today we say more baldly than we ever have before, we are in no uncertain terms writing off a large segment of our compatriots. As Rorty astutely reminds us in this regard, beliefs are habits of action, and when no actions follow from those beliefs, they turn out to be nothing more than empty platitudes.[76] So, the frequently heard market cry that the disadvantaged should pull themselves up by their own bootstraps, that government assistance of any kind, especially measures that require taxing some for the benefit of others, should not and will not be forthcoming, is a classic example of an empty moral platitude, a belief that demands no moral action, because it promises none but only more of the same. Indeed, its unmistakable message is that no help is on the way, because the only sensible and right thing to do is stay the course, further the status quo, continue doing what we have been doing.

It is for this reason that we, like Rorty, should not only be wary of any invocation of a *we* that offers no promissory note of help or action, whether it be to subsidize the poor members of that *we* or to combat the sadistic humiliation of its underrepresented members, but steadfastly should refuse to deploy the adjective *moral* to describe such a community. That is because the mark of a genuine moral community is that whatever happens to one of us happens to all of us – more particularly, that when something bad happens to one of us, the rest of us feel some commitment and willingness to do something to rectify it. The implication is clear: if America were a truly moral commonwealth, the market would be the last thing we would let do our moral bidding for us; moral talk would be plentiful and well regarded; and market talk would be sparse and, if not well regarded, at least viewed with appropriate suspicion when it intrudes, as is its main tendency, in noneconomic matters.

As I have been arguing for some time now, however, America is anything but a moral commonwealth today, which explains why it is that moral discourse rather than market discourse is sparse today and constantly suspect in our daily interactions. This is especially evident in the new generation of the amoral elite in our country, who attend the same prestigious private schools as their parents did, most notably such institutions of higher learning as Harvard and Princeton, but who unlike their parents regard the notion of noblesse oblige, at least those few who have ever heard of it, with detached bemusement if not studied indifference. From their perspective, they see no good reason why they should not cash in on rather than sublimate their good fortune to get ahead. Worse, it is not just the ideal of noblesse oblige that confounds them but anything that smacks of the moral at all. That is because they are not trying, as Brooks aptly puts it, to "buck the system" but to game it. In a word, they are full-time careerists hell bent on getting ahead rather than making the world a better place to live. It is not surprising, therefore, why they get tongue-tied whenever the conversation takes a moral turn (which, of course, does not happen very often) and why they have no faith in moral discourse or argument to speak of.[77]

The second casualty of the upending of the ideal of an American moral commonwealth concerns the severance of the all-important link between reward and effort (i.e., between work put in and wages received). It is difficult to overstate the moral significance of this link, as for many Americans it served as the cornerstone of their belief in the fundamental goodness of America: more specifically, its commitment to such high-minded principles as desert and distributive justice. As already noted, however, despite the fact that workers today are working longer hours than they ever have before, often hold down more than one job, frequently come from families in which both parents work, and are highly productive, they bring in less money and enjoy fewer retirement and health benefits than their predecessors did. It is, of course, no mystery why this has happened; after all, this is to be expected once the market is allowed to run roughshod over our productive lives. Nevertheless, it is more than a little shocking that this important staple of American-style distributive justice no longer seems to have any moral traction with its citizenry.

The last casualty of this loss of faith in America's basic moral goodness is less surprising but no less morally dispiriting. I am talking here about the bad behavior of the poor themselves and the moral resentment that lies behind it. The moral resentment is certainly understandable; after all, it's no picnic always being on the short end of the stick, especially when no one else seems to care, let alone notice. However, the deeds that spew from this resentment are hardly justifiable. So, when Putnam and others report that the have-nots that are crowded into our inner cities (for most the only place they can afford to live) are three times more likely to cheat on their taxes, insurance claims, and bank loan applications,[78] are more likely to engage in overt, often virulent, forms of racism, sexism, and gay-bashing, and tend to be even more conservative than their bosses on such cultural issues as abortion, affirmative action, and gun ownership, I trust few people are caught off guard by these revelations, and are even willing, with some justification, to forgive at least their dishonesty as a survival strategy. However, I also trust that few people are just willing to look the other way entirely. That is because the lack of virtue and the sadistic proclivities of America's poor do not speak well of them, and we should not shy away from saying so even if at least part of the blame for their moral failings can be attributed to the toxic moral environment in which they are forced to live their lives.

However you look at it then, contemporary America is sadly lacking in moral stature. If anything, we have regressed morally in the last 40 years or so, as evidenced by our creation of a society and polity that more so resembles the infamous state of nature, in which, as duly noted in Chapter 1, our natural appetites (those "partial affections" that prompt us to give our self-interests top billing) dominate, than it does an advanced liberal democratic society in which the virtues not only should hold firm sway over our natural appetites but have long since consigned their nettlesome partial affections to the dustbin of history. In short, by giving a long leash to our self-regarding interests and a short one to our other-regarding ones, we have wittingly installed a Hobbesian war of all against all, in which, especially for the losers, life is short, brutish, and nasty. When we add to this the utter arrogance of the winners (whose winning has often much more to do with their "connections" than their actual achievements),[79] which Delbanco nicely captures in his lament that "one of the startling features of the [recent] history of [American] happiness is the brazenness with which people in power have assured themselves of the happiness of the powerless," we can better appreciate just how close we have turned the fictional "state of nature" into an actual reality.[80] To say that we as a country have morally sunk just about as low as a developed liberal democratic nation can is, alas, more true than it is false.

Of course, it is not as if morality has vanished in America today; rather it has, like everything else, gone the way of privatization. That is, when such conservative moralists as William Bennett bemoan the "lack of moral outrage" in modern-day America, they are not referring to its citizens' turning their back on their poor compatriots but to their failure to get worked up over the private indiscretions of their prominent citizens, especially the sexual antics of such conservative political nemeses as former president Clinton. Make no mistake about it, however, it is not just the powerful and famous that are the targets of conservatives' moral ire, which explains their railing against such things as divorce and abortion, but as well the alleged slovenly work habits and sexual mores of the lower classes, which explains their unsparing attack on the welfare state and sexual education programs not based on abstinence. We should throw in here as well the alternative lifestyles of the counterculture and the gay and lesbian community, of which conservatives seem especially contemptuous.[81]

You might think that a moral system such as this one that banishes public (shared) conceptions of the good from its normative arsenal so that it can concentrate all its firepower on private indiscretions might sooner rather than later get around to condemning greed, which, after all, is as self-aggrandizing as, say, marital infidelity. However, you would be wrong on at least two counts, because this conservative brand of private morality first, subscribes to a highly selective conception of moral freedom that, as noted earlier, goes by the name of negative freedom, which stresses again what we as individuals can accomplish when we are not hindered by external forms of interference, and, second, evidently limits the legitimate exercise of that freedom only to certain, shall we say, privileged social settings: principally, of course, the market and the political sphere. So, the reason why selfishness gets a free pass on this account and sodomy does not is simply a matter of what we might call *moral geography*, of where it is and where it is not deigned appropriate for individuals to act on rather than constrain their private aims and concerns.[82] The more important matter of why the public good is not even a faint blip on conservatives' moral radar screen is because it is informed by a much different, positive conception of freedom, which, again as noted earlier, stresses self-determination and, therefore, what we can accomplish only by working cooperatively together.

This banishing of the common good from conservative moral reckoning is the more important matter because it explains why the government and its attempt to constrain or reorder our preferences for the greater good, not to mention the whole of civil society and the associations that operate within its precincts that one and all take their marching orders from distinctively collective aims and aspirations, are the principal targets of conservatives' moral wrath. For according to the conservative adherents of the morality of freedom, of course, all such efforts to reorder and or sublimate our subjective desires come across as mere moralizing, as nothing more than brow beating parading as moral uplift in which individuals are counseled to turn a deaf ear to their own innermost inclinations and desires and act contrary to their self-interests. It is not that what they say here is wholly without moral credence, for one of the morally undesirable side effects of the welfare state is that it did breed in some cases an unhealthy dependence of people on the government, and their wariness of government overreach, of concentrating too much political power in the state, is not something to be casually dismissed. Rather, it is the core moral idea that conservatives endorse: that freedom should always swing free of such notions as equality and fraternity, which distorts their moral outlook, and important, of course, our larger American moral outlook insofar as conservative moralists speak for the rest of us on these matters, in at least three important ways.[83]

It skews our collective moral outlook first by skewing our moral judgment, by falsely seducing us to believe that the triumph of the market and the negative freedom it encourages in our contemporary lives rank as moral achievements rather than the moral calamity that they really are. With nothing to go on but such a scaled-down, atomistically tailored conception of freedom, it is easy to see why we often run together an increase in selfishness with moral progress, fail to see that when the satisfaction of the private desires of individuals takes precedence over their collective good, morality can no longer be claimed to play much of a role in the life of such a society. For it is precisely when such things as a sense of community and reciprocal trust go, things that induce us to take others into account and accord them moral respect, that morality itself goes.[84] So, our often-fierce opposition to the welfare state and affirmative action are not so much owed to their imperfections, to the fact that they are sometimes poorly designed and not well thought out, but to the very idea of collective agency itself and the public good in which it trades. In other words, what sticks in our craw apparently are not principally the defects of such practices, which in most cases can, after all, be fixed with reasonable care and due diligence, but the notion that they keep alive: that there is something more to the idea of collective agency and the public good than the aggregation of individual actions or the summing of individual goods.

The second sense in which our conception of the morality of (negative) freedom skews our moral outlook makes us easy pickings for assertions of power and influence that do not take an explicit political form. When freedom is equated simply with the absence of constraint, the exercise of that freedom in various social settings turns out to have precious little to do with those social settings themselves and everything to do with what individuals do within them. To take just one example, academic freedom so considered has essentially to do with whether individuals are allowed to teach, study, and research what they want in the educational institutions where they are housed without outside interference from the state or religious authorities. To be sure, this is a cherished freedom and not one that any academic would or should take lightly. However, notice that academic freedom understood in this singularly individualistic way says almost nothing about the larger social contexts in which such freedom is exercised, about whether the academic practices that are, after all, the life-blood of universities are themselves in good working order. More precisely, it passes over in silence whether the integrity of those practices is threatened by forces that though not perhaps coercive of what individuals can do within them are subversive of their social purposes and so of the larger institutional aims of the university itself. This is especially the case when it comes to such things as money that, unlike political interference, corrupts not so much by limiting what individuals choose to do in such social settings as universities but by circumventing the collective character and point of those settings. As Walzer astutely argues, "What [political] power takes by force, money merely purchases, and the purchase has the appearance of a voluntary agreement between individuals."[85] So, the problem with negative freedom is not just that it misses these sorts of morally subversive influences on social practices themselves but that it makes them almost invisible by focusing our main attention on the coercive pressures exerted on their individual participants.

The third and, for my purposes, last sense in which this morality of (negative) freedom skews our moral outlook is that it leads to what might be called a *fetishization* of subjective preference and choice. That is, it would have us believe that moral judgments are reducible to subjective preferences, that when we commend to someone that they should do such and such, what we are really saying is that doing such and such meets with our subjective approval in the same sense in which we urge someone to try the chocolate ice cream because we like (approve of) its taste. The idea here is that the moral meaning and significance of what we do rest on nothing more substantive than our choice to do it, that choice itself confers moral worth. That is why on this conception of the morality of freedom everything hangs on our being able to make those choices unimpeded by outside influences (i.e., by influences that emanate outside our own subjective motivational sets).

However, this view of moral life is self-defeating in at least two important senses. First, it misconstrues the meaning of moral utterances. For when I commend to others that it would be (morally) good if they perform some action X, what I mean is not, as I tried to show in the previous chapter, that I subjectively approve of X but that I think they have good reason to do X, to carry it out in a certain way that is appropriate to it. In other words, what I commend to others with regard to X is not my personal stamp of approval but my considered evaluative judgment that they have good cause to do X and to do it in a particular way that it warrants. It thus follows that if my interlocutor challenges my moral appraisal, it is incumbent on me to make explicit why it would be wrong for someone to act in a contrary way, to make clear what my arguments are regarding such and why others should pay them some mind. So, the moral meaning of what we say to one another is a dialogical matter through and through (i.e., a matter of argument and persuasion) and not at all like my subjective concurrence that chocolate is a delicious flavor of ice cream – which would, of course, be absurd on its face to try to justify to others.

This fetishization of choice is further self-defeating in that it trivializes the moral significance of normative judgments. For the significance of our moral utterances is not, and can never be, a matter of simple choice. I can no sooner claim, to use an example from Taylor, that what makes me a significant human being is that I am the only person in the world with precisely 3,372 hairs on my head, than I can claim that what makes my moral utterances significant is the mere fact that I have chosen to utter them.[86] In either case, what confers significance or the lack thereof on my utterances, beliefs, and actions is not anything I feel or choose, not anything subjective, but rather their connection to what Taylor calls *pre-existing social horizons of significance*, to intersubjective social conditions of meaning. It is against the background of these latter horizons, therefore, that I and the other members who share those horizons with me can gauge the moral significance of what we say and do. To reiterate then, what proponents of the morality of freedom risk by reducing moral significance to choice is nothing less than the wholesale trivialization of moral life itself, the claim that we can make discriminating moral judgments about how to lead our lives in the same manner in which we choose the kind of wine to serve with our meal.

We Americans thus find ourselves at an unsavory moral place. For if we hope to become a true moral community again, we will have to reinvent ourselves morally, to trade in our moral self-image as a nation of individual choosers and purveyors of the good in exchange for some larger moral conception and vision of ourselves. Of course, moral projects of self-refashioning and self-redefinition on this scale are, to say the least, daunting tasks. However, the unenviable moral situation in which we presently find ourselves, I believe, requires nothing less. As I hope to show in the chapters to come, such social practices as sport have played an important role in such wholesale moral refashioning of our national identity in the past and, if properly understood and treated, are still capable of doing so in the future. Before I consider where sports fit into this moral picture, however, there remains some unfinished business with respect to my present moral history of America.

## Critical postscript

That unfinished business is essentially of a critical character. For a critic might reasonably take exception to my moral reckoning of America on at least three grounds. First, such a critic might note that my sober moral assessment of America is not sober enough, because it unaccountably spares Progressives of the same moral scrutiny extended to others in this period. That is to say, I might justly be charged of ignoring the racist and sexist tendencies of Progressives themselves and what many regard as their mainly middle-class representatives' efforts to control socially the "uncouth" ways of the largely immigrant working-class that they claimed to serve. Second, such a critic might take me to task for ignoring the

Left's own fairly recent and not altogether unsuccessful effort to undo the very sexism, racism, and homophobia that Progressives blithely overlooked. And last, such a critic might further object that at least in one important sense, my sober moral assessment of America is too sober, because it closes off any reasonable moral hope that we might be able to clamber out of the moral hole we have dug for ourselves. These are all forceful objections that deserve careful consideration, but I do not find any of them persuasive, for reasons I shortly adduce.

Let us begin at the beginning with the alleged free pass I give Progressives regarding their own moral shortcomings. The first part of that charge – that I conveniently gloss over their sexism and racism – is simply mistaken. For I have referenced these very moral debilities more than once in my otherwise highly positive account of the Progressives' reform efforts. The reason why is because there is no denying that the main beneficiaries of those efforts were mostly white males. As Rorty reminds us, however, their failings in this regard were not entirely owed to their own moral blind spots but as well to a basic theoretical miscalculation on their part. For they were convinced that if they could do something to lessen the economic inequality in the country, they could, as it were, kill two birds with one stone by eliminating the primary reason for sadism as well: economic insecurity.[87] Unfortunately, they turned out to be wrong about this – dead wrong – which is one of the reasons why Freud's writings started to show up on the reading lists of many folks on the Left.

That leaves the social-control charge, which is actually two charges, as it implicates the Progressives' reliance both on technical, government experts to help to solve social problems and on their recourse to middle-class social do-gooders to fix the working class's evident faulty beliefs, values, and actions.

With regard to the first of these charges – the Progressives' supposed technological elitism – what bothered many on the Left, especially such "radical" historians as Christopher Lasch, about their reliance on technical experts and government agencies (what Lasch liked to call contemptuously the "helping professions") was the bureaucratic paternalism that they preached and practiced.[88] Indeed, the idea that the government and its retinue of experts know better than the people they are trying to help what is best for them was repugnant to such Leftists as Lasch not only because it reeked of patrician contempt and arrogance but more important because it discounted the agency of those very people, treating them more or less as know-nothings and low-lifes constitutionally incapable either of understanding what was happening to them or of doing anything constructive about it. If this complaint sounds familiar today, it is because its attack on the government's supposed congenital inefficiency and its haughty high-mindedness has become a staple of neoconservative critiques of big government.

This criticism misses the mark for two reasons. First, as already noted, Progressives were only too aware of the paternalistic dangers of government overreach even if they occasionally succumbed to its bewitching charms. Dewey was certainly not alone among Progressive thinkers in this regard when he warned that, "Many a man, feeling himself justified by the social character of his ultimate aim … is genuinely … exasperated by the increasing antagonism and resentment which he invokes, because he has not enlisted in his pursuit of the 'common' end the freely cooperative activities of others. This cooperation must be the root principle of the morals of democracy."[89] What is more, Progressives were not only alert to the dangers of government-sponsored paternalism but, again as already noted, took active steps to rein it in by insisting that the government cannot act efficiently or morally unless it is held in check by civil society, by the strong associational life that one can only find in a well-ordered civil society. The second reason why this critique of technological elitism misses the mark is that it does not take into account how the government is supposed to carry out its charge of regulating the market, especially the large multinationals with their armies of accountants, lawyers, and the like, unless it, too, has at its ready an army of experts who can exercise oversight over its corporate foes. So, getting rid of government bureaucracies, as the critics are wont to do, rather than making sure that they do their important jobs well, as Progressives tried to do, is not a recipe for rescuing democracy but for jeopardizing it.

The second charge – that Progressive middle-class folks were more interested in socially controlling the working class than in helping them – is empirically weak and ideologically suspect. It is empirically weak because although the record shows that some Progressive initiatives were indeed motivated by class animus, a great many were not. That is to say, although there is something to be said for the critics' accusation that the Progressives' finding fault with the "unruly" behavior of the working class and their efforts to correct it was tainted by class prejudice, there is something also to be said for the Progressives genuine altruistic efforts to improve the working class lot in life. For instance, in the settlement houses run by such Progressives as Jane Addams, it is clear that great efforts were made to treat poor people with moral dignity, (i.e., to refrain from casting them as morally depraved people in need of the kind of moral uplift that could be provided only by their "betters") and to improve their unenviable living circumstances by taking their concerns and aspirations seriously.[90] So, though this charge is not without merit, a fair account of the historical record takes much of the sting out of it.

The ideological claim that lies behind this social-control charge, conversely, is wholly suspect. I am speaking here of the venerable Marxist saw that only bottom-up reforms authored and undertaken by the oppressed themselves are worthy of our support, because only they have the requisite epistemic, moral, and political insight needed to ensure their success. This belief in the innate good sense and goodness of the downtrodden by virtue of their social position as the downtrodden is, alas, nothing but Left-wing twaddle, as is its opposite New Left number, which would have us believe that the poor are predisposed to be dim-witted stooges rather than clear-eyed revolutionaries. The mistake that the Left makes here in both instances is to speak in the ex cathedra, ahistorical terms that they do; for the poor are not fated a priori to be either seers or dullards, because they are not fated to be anything nor, it should be said, is anybody else. The poor, however, are very much affected by the adverse contingent and historical circumstances in which they have to live, which does diminish greatly their ability to pull off their own liberation, to engineer and carry out unabetted their own reversal of their domination. That is to say, it is their immiseration that typically deprives them not only of the peace of mind, not to mention even the time to reflect, that they would need to hatch their revolutionary initiatives, but further of the resources (money, power, and security) that they would need just to get such initiatives off the ground, let alone to see them through successfully. Instead, they are often so resource-poor and so understandably racked by resentment and insecurity that they frequently act, goaded on and manipulated, of course, by conservative demagogues, in ways complicit with their own subordination.

The further and related misstep that the Left makes here in touting the privileged vantage point of the working class to carry out its own self-overcoming is an historical one. For the actual historical record of successful Progressive and liberal initiatives tells, as duly noted, a different story, one, as Rorty recounts, "of how top-down initiatives and bottom-up initiatives have interlocked." To be sure, as Rorty also recounts, most of the risks and heroic actions undertaken to see these reforms to their completion fell to those at the bottom. However, it is equally true that without the help of those at the top, without their financial and political clout and their efforts to publicize and articulate what those agitating for change were trying to do, there is little chance these ventures would have succeeded.[91] The message that transsocial class solidarity rather than heroic single-class revolutionary activity is the motor of progressive change is no small point then, as will become further evident when I turn to the next question of why the Left's admirable attempts to stanch sadism did not get bigger play in my own account.

I should say straightaway in this latter regard that the laudable efforts of the cultural Left, mainly those holed up in the Academy, to curb the sadistic exploitation of underrepresented social groups in our country was the one bright spot in the otherwise bleak period I have dubbed the "Great Unraveling." They recognized something that their Progressive predecessors did not regarding the humiliation of particular groups. Actually, I should use the plural *things* here, because what they recognized were three related things: first, that dissociated (because exploited) individuals could be rescued by hooking them up with social groups that have the capacity to compel their strong affiliation but only, second, if those groups speak in some direct and vital way to their exploitation and only, third, if the self-image of those groups can be successfully rehabilitated so that all traces of humiliation that they used to convey in the hands of their sadistic oppressors have been expunged. If we run these three things together, we can credit the academic Left with the following insight: that the atomizing effects of humiliation at being black or being gay can be reversed by cultivating pride in the very thing for which one is being exploited (one's blackness or gayness), provided the self-descriptions and self-conceptions that such identities convey are wiped clean of the hurtful stereotypes imposed on them from the outside. In sum, what these Leftists realized is that by focusing on those very differences and by, as it were, turning them on their head so that their normative valence changes from negative to positive, from something blameworthy to be sloughed off to something praiseworthy to be embraced, they could as well turn the tables on their oppressor's sadistic designs to stain them with their cruel stereotypes.[92]

Everything depends in this regard on enlisting groups that exhibit just the right blend of cohesiveness and exclusiveness. Put more strongly, such a remedy for sadism will work only if the binding force of these groups is parasitic on the differences that mark them off from other groups rather than the commonalities that connect them to other, larger groups.[93] Yet, it is this very insight that explains why neither they nor their largely successful remedy to stop sadism in its tracks does not get much play in my moral sketch of latter-day America. For the primary dissociative effects of this more recent phase of American history have primarily to do, as duly noted, with the growing proletarianization of its citizens rather than their sadistic isolation and humiliation. In other words, an increasing number of Americans find themselves cut off from others and thus forced to fend for themselves because of the selfishness of their more affluent citizens who no longer see any reason to come to their aid because they no longer feel any connection to them, at least not any important connection they are willing to acknowledge.[94] The politics of identity and its valorization of difference massively miss the mark here, therefore, precisely because in encouraging people to focus first and foremost on those features that separate them off from others, they only worsen the predicament of the immiserated masses by further splitting them off from one another, by prodding them to settle into their own isolated pods, what we might cheekily call *suburbanization in reverse*. This kind of disaggregation and monadic balkanization is obviously no match for the market-induced inegalitarianism that is rife in the land today, because it looks for solidarity in all the wrong places. To remedy this particular moral mess, a different sort of moral community needs to be summoned on our behalf, one that emboldens us to valorize what we share in common with one another (i.e., one that emboldens us to take pride in our being Americans rather than in some truncated, hyphenated surrogate).

This takes me to the third and last criticism that my moral accounting of America is too sober because it closes off any plausible hope that our best days lie ahead of us rather than behind us. I think this objection is wide of the mark, however, because it is mistaken about what I have tried to do in this chapter. For the point of my critical and historical excavation of the Progressive-liberal project was to show that the great importance it attached to our national identity – to the question of just what it means to be an American – and the egalitarian answer it gave to that question comprise precisely the question that contemporary America needs to ask itself and precisely the answer it needs to give if it hopes to right itself morally again, to recover from its recent and traumatic unraveling. Far from trying to twist Americans into a paralyzing moral knot, to drive them into moral despair and the inevitable hand wringing that follows in its train, I was trying to exhort them to embrace rather than reject the Progressive-liberal legacy, to see it not as an idle historical curiosity but a live option for the future. This is the main reason why I want to concede nothing to the Right as to how the composition of the moral center of America should look, to challenge rather than to accept complacently, as the cultural Left is wont to do as a gesture to the supposed moral superiority of resignation and marginality, what the Right tries to pass off as the placeholder for this center. Let me explain.

The Right's answer to the question of what the moral core of America is has always been some version, as previously discussed, of the negative freedom on display in the market. This is why the Right never seems to tire of extolling the virtues of the market, of its freeing us to follow our self-interests unimpeded by others, or of urging that the social practices that mean the most to us can endure and flourish only if molded in the image of the market. However, this claim that America is best understood and treated as the market writ large is absurd on its face. That is because the market acts, as we have seen, as a centrifugal rather than a centripetal force in our lives, something that forces us apart rather than together so that we can pursue our self-interests without having to worry morally about the interests or value judgments of others. In other words, the market is nothing if not an instrument of egoism, which means that the sort of freedom on which it prides itself could not be more unsuited to the moral role that the Right insists it must play in our lives. The idea, then, that it is the market and the kind of unbridled freedom it champions that best captures the moral soul of America, that provides the normative glue that holds us all together, is an easy mark for anyone interested enough to expose it for the ideological charade that it is. One would have thought those on the cultural Left would have considered this not just an appropriate target but a highly inviting one, as it would give them a rare opportunity to be a major player in the American political scene by challenging the Right directly over the presumptive moral center of America itself. However, and this is a crucial *but*, the Left can become a major player in this crucial struggle for the moral conscience of America, instead of a bit player in its cultural wars, only if it tosses aside its regrettable and stubborn conviction that at its core America is morally rotten.[95] If it were somehow able to overcome its bordering on a priori revulsion at anything that smacks of patriotism, of loyalty to an identity larger than one's ethnicity, race, and gender, however, there is every reason to believe that the Left could contend successfully with the Right as to who rightfully speaks for America's moral conscience.

Not that it will be easy task, though, for apologists on the Right are not unaware of the self-contradiction that shadows and threatens to lay waste to their notion of market patriotism. Indeed, how could they not, as despite the lip service they pay to freedom, their own privatized version of morality requires that certain individual preferences and impulses be curbed if they threaten the social fabric, which the Right narrowly conceives to consist principally of, among other things, two-parent heterosexual families, a chastened religiosity, and a willingness to bow when necessary to appropriate forms of authority. That is why they have not shied away from efforts at their own brand of social and moral engineering, of suffusing the market with their own "sociology of virtue,"[96] a sociology that they have variously associated with high-culture, a Victorian moral sensibility of shame, and most persistently and consistently a healthy respect for authoritative forms of religion. What the Right seems not to understand or appreciate fully, however, making the Left's task less daunting here, is that its advocacy of market patriotism is not only riddled with self-contradiction but is allergic to any sort of "sociology of virtue," no matter whether its pedigree is conservative or progressive.

This is perhaps easiest to see with regard to the Right's early and unmistakably Anglophile appeal to the binding qualities of high-culture, to Matthew Arnold's old and familiar bromide that culture is best understood as "the best which has been thought and said in the world."[97] However, the idea that it is, as Walzer sardonically remarks, "our shared commitment to Shakespeare, Dickens, or Joyce that has been holding us together all these years"[98] is thin gruel, indeed, as markets are not only categorically indifferent to qualitative judgments of worth no matter their object but downright hostile to them. It is, after all, the market that is largely responsible for what passes as mass culture today and that had more than a little to do with the waning of high culture in our country. The cultural Left deserves some credit here as well, as its adherents were never that enamored of high culture and so were eager to expose the numerous and various ways in which it divides us as a people along class lines rather than unifying us. Curiously enough, however, their uncritical and at times desperate habit of talking up the subversive qualities of the mass culture scene, its supposed, and often hard-to-see, except to the trained eye of the critical theorist, resistance to the status quo, actually played directly into the hands of conservative types, because it blithely ignored corporate America's uncanny ability to turn yesterday's cultural rebels and icons into today's cultural celebrities (those who, as Daniel Boorstein famously put it, are well-known for their well-known-ness) and hot commodities.

The Right's more basic and enduring appeal to authoritarian moral and religious codes fared, and continues to fare, no better, as its effort to yoke them to the market predictably led to their annexation by the market. That is because the freedom by which the market abides cannot abide, again, any "sociology of virtue" to include those of morality or religion. It is little wonder, then, as already remarked, why the resurgence of religion in our increasingly commercialized society today took the evangelical form that it did, in which so called born-again Christians claimed the right to decide for and by themselves what constitutes a genuine religious life and in which both they and their less religious and even nonreligious compatriots beg off any sort of moral criticism and judgment of one another and find especially abhorrent the kind of shaming tactics employed by Victorian practitioners of the moral art.[99]

To reiterate: what is inevitable about all this is that the market cannot avoid leaching the social and moral capital out of whatever social practices the Right affixes to it by virtue of what it is and how it conducts itself: which is to grant all agents who operate within its ever-expanding borders the freedom to ignore the normative judgments and claims of everyone else so that they can go about pursuing their self-interests unobstructed by those judgments and claims.[100] In other words, market patriotism is constitutionally averse to and corrosive of any "sociology of virtue" that tries to restrain or otherwise neutralize its self-seeking ways. This is why giving pride of place to the market, as the Right insists on doing despite its mostly ad hoc efforts to cordon off that place to accommodate its own narrow moral agenda, can do little to prevent market patriotism from turning into market fundamentalism.

This is true not just in theory but in political practice. For the odd political constituency that the Right has managed to cobble together is as unstable as the notion of market patriotism itself. A big reason why is that two of its largest constituents – the mostly male rich and the "anxious" middle class – have nothing in common with one another outside of, as Gitlin acerbically puts it, "the[ir] collective satisfaction of not being black or poor."[101] However, this is only the half of it, as the other important camp in this conservative coalition is poor whites. This would explain why, for instance, in such places as McPherson County in Nebraska, one of the poorest regions in all of America, Bush managed in 2000 to garner 80 percent of the vote.[102] Of course, an important part of the reason why poor whites overwhelmingly sided with the Right in this and previous elections is owed to their twin resentment at the recent gains made by people of color and women in the last couple of decades and the Left's failure, as they saw and continue to see it, even to factor their dismal life prospects into their oppression quotient let alone take up their cause; further, because Leftist intellectuals played such a pivotal role in the civil rights and women's movement, the poor also greatly resented and resent having their morals force fed to them by these academic, bookish types, whom the Right likes to call derisively *America's cultural elite*.[103] That said, there is no denying that the no-holds-barred conception of freedom favored by the Right does seem to resonate in one way or another with all these disparate folks.

Still, the fragility of this coalition is not to be doubted. For starters, the rich are so thoroughly enmeshed in the global market, whether it be in the management of their stock portfolios or in moving their businesses off shore (or both), that such writers as Alan Wolfe wonder out loud whether they even think of themselves as Americans at all,[104] not to mention the fact they are chary of the religious fundamentalism of their fellow conservative poor whites. The middle class is the anxious part of this coalition precisely because the freedom that the market bestows on the rich to exploit them to promote the short-term financial interests of their stockholders threatens to squeeze them out of the middle class and thus consign them, as we have seen, to a substantially lower standard of living. Finally, it is only a matter of time before the poor also realize that the "freedom [they enjoy] to defend [their] homes with assault rifles" is the very same freedom that the rich use to rip off both them and, as just observed, the middle class,[105] and the very same freedom that the middle class themselves invoke to justify their refusal to pay taxes in order to subsidize the welfare of the poor.

All this merely confirms my claim that it would not take much to overturn the Right's effort to install market patriotism as the presumptive moral center of America or to break up the strange factions that make up their present political constituency. However, nothing of this sort is likely to happen any time soon unless the Left resolves to take it on itself to vie for the hearts and minds of Americans and unless it has some morally persuasive and compelling alternative to offer the American people. This is where, to return to my main response to the criticism that my critique of America's recent past went too far because it left us without any reasonable hope, the Progressive vision of America as a moral commonwealth comes squarely back into the picture. For it is precisely this Progressive ideal, moral identity, and political program that I am urging the Left make its own and wield as a cudgel in its struggle against the Right to reclaim the moral soul of America.

A final doubt needs to be allayed. It is one thing to say that the Right's rendering of America is an ideological sham and one built on sand no less, and quite another to say that if we only look to our Progressive past, we can rediscover our real, as in genuine, moral identity and proceed to undo the damage that we Americans have inflicted on ourselves in the last 30 years or so. That is, what reason do I have to suppose that in suggesting such I am not falling prey to mere nostalgia or, perhaps what is worse, to wishful thinking of the sort we find in utopian writings that offer us only so much feel-good, pie-in-the-sky nonsense? After all, if the market has caused as much moral havoc as I have insinuated it has regarding all those things that we Americans hold near and dear, where do I get off thinking we can, as it were, turn back the clock and begin anew, without so much as taking a breath, precisely where the Progressives and their liberal epigones left off?

My answer is that the empirical news suggests that we can do just that. For among all the bad news that I have been ladling out in this chapter in rather heaping measures, there is some substantially good news to report regarding contemporary Americans' moral beliefs and values. In fact, recent surveys of those moral attitudes suggest the following: close to 80 percent of Americans think that our social and moral bonds are weaker today than they were in the past and believe we should, as a result, put more emphasis on the larger community even if it imposes more burdens on individuals;[106] 94 percent of us believe that if people work full-time, they should earn enough to live a decent life; 80 percent of Americans are in favor of raising the minimum wage;[107] rich and poor alike in large numbers believe that the gap between the income of the most well-off and the least well-off should be only a tiny fraction of what it is now; a great majority of Americans favor a society that is much more egalitarian than our present society;[108] 95 percent of Americans believe that corporations have responsibilities to workers and communities beyond simply turning a profit;[109] and finally, almost 80 percent of us do not equate success with the money we earn or possess.[110] The upshot of all of this survey data suggests at least three things: first, that most Americans are far more progressive and far less conservative socially and morally speaking than anyone might at first blush reasonably expect; second, that a great many of us are all too aware of our moral shortcomings, of how far we have strayed from our egalitarian roots, and seem determined to do something about it; and third, that the Progressive dream of America as a moral commonwealth has proved surprisingly resilient even in these highly jaded times.

This is more than enough evidence, I believe, to shake off any objection that now is not a propitious time to press the Progressive case, that trying to press that case as hard as we can on turf the Right has grown accustomed to calling its own, in part because of the Left's own moral lapses, should not be dismissed as mere nostalgic longing or fanciful utopian star-gazing. On the contrary, all the elements necessary to make such a push worth our while seem to be in place, awaiting only a more powerful articulation to make their presence more forcibly and coherently felt. So, another way, perhaps the best way, to describe what I hoped to accomplish by raising the specter of Progressivism in this context is to think of it in terms of what Charles Taylor calls a critical work of "retrieval," the purpose of which is to make "the force of an ideal [in this case, of course, the ideal of America as a moral commonwealth] that people are already living by more palpable, and more vivid for them; and by making it more vivid, empowering them to live up to it in a fuller and more integral fashion."[111]

Of course, it still remains to be seen what, if anything, this critical retrieval of the Progressive moral ideal of America as a cooperative commonwealth has to do with its major sports. However, before I can answer that important question, I first need to set the stage by sketching out a brief moral history of American sports.

# 6 A short moral history of American sports

I want to canvass the same period of American history as in the previous chapter, roughly from the last decade of the nineteenth century to the present, but this time with sports as my focal point. Of course, much of the latter part of this story has already been chronicled, not to mention criticized, in Chapter 2, where I detailed what I took to be the main moral failings of contemporary sports. So, the Progressive conception of sport and its liberal offshoot occupy most of my attention here,[1] and what I have to say about the unraveling of that conception of sport in the contemporary, market-driven era is confined mostly to an analysis of the major causal forces behind it.

## The evolution of sport as a "respectable" social practice

If, as is often said, the past is prologue, the past of the American sports scene gave not even the slightest hint of the heady role it was to play later in Progressive politics and morality. Indeed, at the turn of the nineteenth-century Americans attributed little significance to their sporting pastimes. That dismissive attitude dogged sports for most of that century, which surely has something to do with the fact that the sports of this period were mostly "tawdry, eccentric" displays that teemed with violence.[2] As Dizikes observed of nineteenth-century American horse racing, one of the dominant sports of the time, "It was rough and disordered because American culture itself was in many ways rough and disordered." Horse racing was rough and disordered in a quite literal sense: Cheating by all parties (owners, jockeys, trainers) was rampant, disciplinary action was rare and ineffective, spectators were unruly and regularly tried to interfere with the outcome, and the general public was indifferent to all the shenanigans that went on at the racetrack, because they considered it to be a private rather than a public matter and because they regarded the gamesmanship for which such hi-jinks called as the secret behind America's ingenuity and pluck.[3]

Nevertheless, this discouraging but altogether accurate estimate of the base moral standing of American sports was to change dramatically sometime around the late nineteenth century, in which "sports went from being a very bad thing to being a very good thing."[4] The reasons for this newfound respectability accorded sports by the American public can be traced to several social and historical developments.

The first of these developments was the growing national consciousness of the country itself, the budding sense that its citizens belonged to a bona fide national community. This was no small triumph, as in the nineteenth century, America was more of a work in progress, to use Benedict Anderson's famous phrase, an "imagined community" (in this case almost a wholly imagined community), than an actual historical and political accomplishment. Geography and population figures are telling in this instance, as at the beginning of that century, America was made up of a scant six million people and 16 states, and although it had grown considerably by midcentury, claiming 23 million inhabitants and 31 states, the course of nationhood still had a long way to go. Of course, the outbreak of the Civil War in 1861 was a cataclysmic event that tore the country literally in half, the divisive effects of which would take most of the remaining century for Americans to recover. That recovery was made all the more difficult by the massive waves of new immigrants that the country absorbed in the latter half of the nineteenth-century. The confluence of these factors, it is no exaggeration to say, threatened to end the American experiment before it had hardly gotten off the ground. It thus became increasing clear to Americans that they needed to find something that they shared in common and around which to rally, something that gave substance to their calling themselves Americans. Because they could not claim a native tongue or *Volk* for this purpose, latching on to the only genuine American native tongue and *Volk* (the Indians) was, of course, out of the question, they turned to such cultural practices as sports on which to pin their dawning and aspiring national hopes. Of course, only those sports whose American pedigree was considered beyond reproach could play this role, which in the case of baseball especially (and in football less so) meant cooking the historical books. In the case of basketball, however, no such historical revisionism was necessary, as this was the real thing, a genuinely homespun sport. In any event, all three of these sports attained national status in rather short order: to be more specific, somewhere between the closing years of the nineteenth century and the opening decade or so of the twentieth century. The fact that this was around the time in which Americans began to take their national identity seriously was no coincidence.

The resurrection of the ancient Olympic Games in 1896 also thrust sports into the national limelight. As it was necessary to compete in these modern games as a representative of some recognized country (of course, city-states had long since disappeared from the scene) and as spectators of them also quite naturally adopted a nationalistic frame of reference in viewing them, they raised questions about what role sports played in forming our national consciousness and about what national purposes they serve. That is precisely what they did for American participants and spectators of Olympic sports, who used these occasions to engage in national soul searching or national self-congratulations depending, of course, on how they fared in the competitions themselves. Of course, the national print media provided a further outlet for Americans to discourse about both their Olympic experiences and those of their supposed indigenous national sports, which, not surprisingly, contributed mightily to the growing prominence of sports in America.

The growing secularization of American society, hastened by new scientific achievements, also was a major force behind the precipitous rise in the respectability of sports. This was so in a number of instances. Perhaps most important, it helped to unseat religion from its place of dominance in the new republic, thereby freeing up other social practices, such as sports, to take over some of its key disciplinary and community-building functions. Secularization further helped to pave the way for American sports by ridding the body (and those practices, such as sports, that featured it) from the religious stigma foisted on them as "source[s] of sin and sign[s] of divine disfavor."[5] However, this scientifically backed legitimation of the body was important not only to the growing fortunes of sport but to those of science. That is because one important effect of the application of science to the productive forces of the country was a most unhappy and unwelcome one: the mechanization of labor that leached out of it the very uplifting qualities (skill, hard work, individual initiative) that had given it its social and moral cachet in the older and now quickly disappearing agrarian economy. The potentially devastating inference – that science was a source not of hope and liberation but of alienation and degradation – was avoided, because such practices as sports could, and were, plausibly cast as an unalienated alternative to this industrialized stultification of labor, as a way to further the development of our physical capacities and powers and the values associated with them without having to renounce or forsake the obvious gains that science provided. So, by coming, as it were, to the rescue of science, both sports and science gained significant stature in the heartland by resuscitating the idea of progress itself, the notion that America was on the right course even if not an entirely smooth one.

However, whatever confidence science gave to Americans that they were indeed making headway, it quickly chastened by reminding them that such progress could not be taken for granted, that it was by no means a sure thing, a point that once again, less obviously this time, redounded to the favor of sports. Here, Darwin's notion of the fragility of nature loomed large because of its obvious implications for the fragility of American society, to say nothing of human civilization itself. For if, like nature, progress in society could neither be guaranteed nor its extinction ruled out, the fate of such countries as America rested entirely on the shoulders of their members, on the thoughtfulness or thoughtlessness of their plans and actions. That is, the idea that some natural teleological scheme or invisible hand could be counted on to bail them out from any missteps that they might take no longer inspired their confidence. This scientifically fed anxiety regarding the fate of America and of its major social practices and institutions, coupled with the anomie that usually accompanies any major historical and social change of the sort that was occurring in the country at the turn of the twentieth century, thus touched off heated discussions among its members regarding strategies that might be pursued to ensure the survival and continued flourishing of the republic. That sports figured prominently in these discussions and in the strategies that came out of them is, therefore, additional proof of their newfound respectability.[6]

Finally, the growing influence of pragmatism in early America, which itself was a byproduct of its growing secular and scientific bent, especially its insistence on the inseparability of thought and action, on the meaninglessness of theory if it has no implications for or actual affect on practice, also served to catapult sports into the national spotlight and thereby helped to solidify their good name in the public eye.[7]

As we have seen, then, many social and historical forces in the late nineteenth and early twentieth century conspired to make sports an important cultural force in America. They did not disappoint in this regard, at least with respect to their rather remarkable capacity to capture the hearts and minds of most Americans of this era. For both intellectuals and the common folk alike became caught up in the world of sports and turned them into public forums for discussing and debating, among other things, what it meant to be an American and the standards and values for which the country should stand up. Of course, such topics were the favorite material of highbrow intellectuals and filled the various books, journals, and op-ed pieces that they authored. However, though Progressive intellectuals prided themselves on asking and articulating powerful answers to these kinds of questions, they could not be sure that any of their compatriots read or paid them any mind. What they could be sure of, however, is that their fellow citizens read the sports pages and read them voraciously if not carefully; indeed, newspaper coverage of sports alone exceeded that devoted to almost all other cultural fare.[8] So, while Americans were increasingly becoming, to borrow Max Weber's phrase, "religiously unmusical"[9] and never were especially intellectually inclined, they were decidedly not tone-deaf or oblivious to the charms of sports. Their athletic "musicality" goes a long way toward accounting for why sports became the lingua franca of the country itself, one of the primary sites in which discourse about who we are and how we should comport and conduct ourselves could be profitably, enthusiastically, and most important, democratically explored.

Sports, then, were not just an important part of American folklore and popular culture, not merely private pastimes that somehow managed to transform themselves into highly organized and highly visible public practices in a relatively short period but arresting interpretive vehicles of which Americans enthusiastically availed themselves to ponder the various issues and questions that confronted them as a nation. It is by serving as a sounding board for these kinds of questions that, as Mrozek avers, "a new interpretation of [sports'] utility to society" emerged,[10] one that became an important staple of Progressive reform efforts (to which I now turn).

## The progressive conception of sport

As before, it would be wise first to identify who exactly these sporting Progressives were before unpacking their conception of sports. Of course, most of these athletically steeped Progressives were the very same reformers we came across in Chapter 5, which included, to reprise that list, the well-to-do WASP elite, forward-thinking businessmen, liberal theologians, disaffected socialists, public intellectuals, and a large contingent of middle-class reformers. To this eclectic list, we can add what Dyreson aptly called the *new experts* in physical culture (physical educationists, coaches, trainers, nutritionists), collegiate and professional athletic administrators and players, members of elite sporting clubs, sporting entrepreneurs, sporting goods manufacturers, public health advocates, and last but certainly not least, sports journalists and editors.[11] What held this wide-ranging coalition of Progressive reformers together was their twin beliefs: the ideal of America as a true moral commonwealth and sports as a vehicle by which to make this ideal an actual reality.

Of course, the emergence of sports as respectable social practices in the late nineteenth century was what caught the attention of these Progressive types and what prompted their new interpretation of the social meaning and utility of sports: the idea that they could attract and mobilize a large cross-section of the country in ways that could be tapped to solve America's central social, political, and moral problems.[12] It is little wonder, therefore, why Progressives heavily recruited and enlisted sports in their efforts to reverse the worrisome antidemocratic tendencies that were loosed on the country and threatened to steer it in a most unwelcome, and for many of these reformers, unAmerican direction.

It would do well then to rehearse ever so briefly the main social, political, and moral problems targeted by Progressives as threats to the country and the main causal forces behind them, to understand better why they thought sports might well play an important role in their resolution.

The secularization America was undergoing at the close of the nineteenth century, as just noted, gave a large shove to human agency (i.e., to the idea that Americans need to take matters into their own hands if America was to make its mark on the world rather than to leave its fate in the providential hands of some divine agency). The problem, then, was not a lack of human agency but the narrow, instrumental form it took under the auspices of the capitalist market. That is, the agency that stepped into the breach created by secularization was inordinately devoted, or so Progressives tirelessly argued, to the unbridled pursuit of wealth. That pursuit elevated work to the top of the heap of important social practices at the same time as it deformed it by turning it into a mere means to accumulate capital, which led to its mechanization and inevitable alienation: in the sense that it became increasingly harder for people to identify with it, owing to its now largely lifeless, repetitive, and monotonous character. Progressives thus viewed the furious onslaught of capitalism in America as contributing to the growing irrationality of society itself, in which work was stripped of its uplifting qualities and tailored to wants rather than needs, which meant for those at the low end of the wage scale that their basic needs often went unmet in the effort to sate the wants of those at the top end of the scale, and in which sports and other leisure activities were similarly stripped of their ennobling features and instead reduced to providing amusement for the disaffected and the well-off. As Progressives saw it then, one of the principal dangers of an unfettered market is that it drains the "magic" out of all the social practices with which it comes into contact and installs in its place a "pleasure economy" that has no apparent purpose other than ensuring the self-gratification of those who can afford to traffic in its wares.

However, for Progressives there was another related and no-less-baleful threat posed to the country by the market and the "pleasure economy" that feeds it: that its hard-edged atomistic bent makes the effort to build a genuine sense of community throughout the land, to inculcate a sense of belonging that binds its citizens and their respective fates to one another, a daunting one to say the least. What is especially worrisome about this market-driven anticommunitarian impulse is that it works at cross-purposes to the egalitarian ideals of the country, to the idea that America stands or falls on how well the least well-off among its citizens fare economically, socially, politically, and morally. It should come as no surprise, then, to learn that Progressives were tormented by the idea that the freedom to do as one pleases without regard for others that the market encourages is fundamentally at odds with their hallowed conception of America as a republic (i.e., a country that prides itself foremost on the attention that it gives to the common good and on the importance it assigns to public deliberation in ensuring that the concerns of all citizens are given their fair and appropriate due).

So, whether it be the derationalization and alienation of social practices or the havoc it wreaks on our communitarian sensibilities, the problems that the market throws up to such self-proclaimed and heralded democracies as America, at least as Progressives of the time saw it, can ultimately be reduced to basic problems of human relationships, of how we interact and get on with one another.[13] The solution to those problems, again from a Progressive point of view, urgently required a new ethic, one that offers the promise of turning foot-loose individuals hell bent on pursuing their narcissistic agendas into fellow, fully committed members of a bona fide community.

However, Progressives were under no illusion that ridding America of its mostly market-induced bad habits would be an easy task. However, they were also not intimidated by the formidable obstacles that stood in their way, as they realized that the very same secular forces that had given birth to the market and given it such a wide berth to do its nasty work also generated points of resistance that could be counted on, if adequately protected and nurtured, not just to keep the market in check but to undo the damage it had already done.

The public enthusiasm for sports was a case in point. For their precipitous rise to respectability was also impelled by some of the same secular sources responsible for the domination of the market. In some respects, of course, they proceeded apace, as the holy trinity of American sports – football, basketball, and baseball – were able to achieve national prominence early in the twentieth century in part because of the professionalization they underwent during this time. However, in other important respects, the public thirst for sports answered to an entirely different set of needs and aspirations, ones that, as Progressives were quick to notice, spoke to a far less individualistic and a far more egalitarian America.

Perhaps this was most evident in the search for meaning, for a special national purpose that might serve as a call to action for Americans to change their distressingly undemocratic ways, touched off by the secularization of American society. One consequence of this secularization, as duly noted, was that religion predictably became less of a central force in most Americans' lives. This left a void in their lives that could not be filled by just any practice. For instance, work at this time was in no shape to take on such a role because of the alienation it had suffered at the hands of the market (i.e., because the market had made it exceedingly difficult for Americans to identify with their work). Sports, on the other hand, were not just able to fill this void but in many respects had been groomed to do so, as evidenced by their newly achieved respectability. For it was precisely because sports at this time had become fully respectable enterprises, practices that Americans could readily and completely identify with, that they were able to fill the deficit of meaning that resulted from the weakening of Americans' religious impulses. Because it was able to fill this deficit, it was also able to discharge other functions previously reserved for such practices as religion. Of pivotal importance in this respect was the disciplining force that sports were said to exact on individuals, on the "willfulness" that was blamed for their excessive self-seeking.[14] By requiring that individuals subordinate their own good to the greater good of the team, Progressives argued that sports were uniquely positioned to serve the public interest, to put a stop to the fulsome self-seeking ways of Americans. Further, they argued that sports' self-chastening effects, if appropriately articulated and championed, could serve as a much needed wake up call to Americans that they have a higher calling than ministering to the pleasures of their citizens (at least those with the cash to indulge them), than installing the world's largest and most formidable pleasure economy. Rather, Progressives insisted that America's true calling was to show the rest of the world what a country devoted to the common good of all – and so to democracy in its fullest and highest sense – could accomplish if it put its collective mind to it.[15]

Of course, the Progressive faith in sports' capacity to arouse Americans out of their slumber and to rally them around more-noble ideals was not a blind faith. Progressive types were well aware that sports were also damaged goods, that they, too, were exposed to the intrusive and alienating arms of the market, especially in being pressed into service as forms of mass amusement. However, their faith in the social, political, and moral rehabilitative powers of sports, in their capacity to right a country significantly off course, was attributable to features of them that they believed were unique to their practice, that distinguished sports from the other forms of life in which Americans engaged. That is why Progressives insisted that "[s]port was not a mirror of society" but rather, as Mrozek neatly put it, "a new pattern in the social fabric,"[16] (i.e., a social practice with distinctive properties, the very distinctiveness of which suggested an alternative way for Americans to make sense of themselves and their experiences, to tell stories about themselves that did not pivot around the pursuit of the almighty dollar).

What, then, were these distinctive features of sports that supposedly marked them off from the rest of life, that enabled them to introduce a new wrinkle into our social and moral relationships with one another, and in so doing helped to inoculate them against some of the ill effects of market egoism and freedom? Perhaps the best place to begin such an account is with what Progressives thought was the special rational character of sports: a rationality the main promise of which, according to these same Progressives, was its anti-instrumental pull, its threat to upend the monopoly that the market's brand of instrumental rationality enjoyed over the country's most important social and political practices. Williams James's claim is telling here: "The aim of a football-team is not merely to get the ball to a certain goal (if that were so, they would simply get up on some dark night and place it there), but to get there by a fixed machinery of conditions – the game's rules and opposing players."[17] By the "fixed machinery of conditions," James meant the rules and normative standards that govern what happens on the playing field and how it happens. Two features of these rules and normative standards deserve special mention here because they are the key, as I see it, to why Progressives believed that sports were both significantly different from the rest of life and, by virtue of that difference, could serve as a corrective to the irrationality spread by the market.

The first feature is the evident transparency of these rules and norms, which, or so Progressives claimed, was unmatched in the rest of life, where the welter of activities and their confusing and often conflicting norms make it difficult to know just what and how things should be done. Dyreson's astute comment on James's characterization of the "fixed machinery of conditions" of sports picks up on this very point, in which he observes that sports construct "prescriptive truths, what one ought and ought not to do … [that are] supposed to be readily apparent and rigidly followed."[18] Contemporary social critic Christopher Lasch also featured the clarity and lucidity of the normative structures of sports to account for their continued esthetic and moral appeal in the modern era, which he used as a cudgel to pummel such high-brow fare as the arts (dance, music, painting) in which the "constant experimentation" that goes on there created so much confusion about standards that the only surviving measure of excellence that they could countenance was the novelty and shock value of artworks, hardly standards, he continued, that further our commitment to or aspiration for genuine excellence.[19]

It is the second feature of these conditions (in the "fixed machinery of conditions"), however, that explains the importance of their transparent normative structures for reform-minded Progressives. That feature has to do with James's previously mentioned point about why the aim of football cannot be intelligibly achieved by getting the ball to the goal in the dead of night when the opposition, quite understandably, is nowhere to be found. That is to say, it is useful but proscribed to cross the goal line in football without opposition, because that would make the aim of football, not to mention any other sport, patently absurd.

It would make it absurd because, if that were all there was to football or again to any other sport endeavor, no one would find football in particular or sport in general worth the while. In a word, the game would cease to be a challenging one, a practice in which the generation of excellence is the entire point of the actions taken there. So, the only way in which sports can lay claim to being the forms of perfectionist life that they are (i.e., forms of life devoted to excellence and the skills and virtues such excellence put in play) is, in Suit's updated vocabulary,[20] if they rule out the most efficient means available to achieve the goals that they seek in favor of less efficient means. That means that sports must contrive the very forms of excellence for which they are noted and the forms of life that underpin them, and in order to accomplish this, they must be governed by a (technically) queer set of rules that Suits calls "constitutive" rules, aptly named, because these are the very rules that make sporting forms of life possible by (as already noted) proscribing certain useful ways to achieve their goals.[21] This is the point that Collier, one of the important Progressive writers on sport in the waning years of the nineteenth century, was driving at when he said of the sport of shooting that it "is shooting at a mark because there are no enemies to shoot at … now that the real necessity is gone."[22] In other words, unlike the practical difficulties that daily life throws up to us as we make our way in the world, sports create their own necessity and thereby a whole new way of life in which it is considered perfectly rational to pursue goals using means the disutility of which is their cardinal feature; their instrumental ineffectiveness is, therefore, no accident.

Now, what is of social, political, and moral interest about the inverted rationality of sports, about forms of life that measured by everyday rational standards come off as practically maddening, if not wholly irrational, and what caught the fancy of reform-minded Progressives, is how the kind of practical reason that sports put in play, which is unique to them alone, can act as a self-correcting guide both to the alienation of larger American life and to their own alienation.

We have already seen in this regard how the market makes our work servile by forcing it to serve exclusively as an instrument of capital accumulation in which wants rather than needs dictate its every feature and how it makes our sports servile by forcing them to satisfy the craven impulses for amusement and diversion that are a socially necessary offshoot of market societies. However, as work is itself a quintessential instrumental enterprise (i.e., not only one in which ends are separate from the means used to satisfy them but one in which the main point is to divine the most efficient means for the realization of those independent ends), its alienation is not synonymous with its being forced to play the role of a means rather than an end, with its mere instrumentalization. That is, its employment as a means in the capitalist scheme of things is the role that it would play in any economic scheme, even an authentically Marxist one. Nor is labor's being cast to play this instrumental role solely to accumulate capital the factor responsible for its market-induced irrationality; indeed, given the recent collapse of alternative state forms of socialism, it is eminently plausible to suppose that markets are a more rational way in which to meet the needs of the masses, even if their doing so is always a byproduct of their first and foremost commitment to satisfy the profit motive, because they outperform any alternative economic system so far invented when it comes to generating wealth. Rather, the irrationality that the market foists on work lies elsewhere, namely, with the convoluted and skewed way in which it rewards work and distributes the wealth it creates.

By contrast, sport in all its various forms, as just noted, is a quintessential anti-instrumental enterprise (i.e., not only one in which ends are inseparable from the means available to achieve them but one in which the crucial concern is to rule out "ultimate" means that make the attainment of its end less challenging, and so too easy to count as a perfectionist practice). That means that when markets press sports into instrumental service, as they inevitably do, to sate false cravings for amusement, cravings that if our work were meaningful and satisfying would, or so it is claimed, have no hold on us to speak of, that instrumentalization is synonymous with their alienation, with the breakdown and derangement of their internal logic of action. Comparatively speaking (compared to such other instrumental enterprises as work) then, sports wear – and cannot help but wear – their alienation on their sleeve. When one couples this fact about their logical character of action with the already addressed transparency of sports' central rules and norms, one can see why Progressives singled out sports for their reformist efforts. For the alienating and irrational effects of the market on such noninstrumental social practices as sports are easier to see and to get others to see than when they occur in such instrumental activities as work (which, because this point is to be taken in a strictly comparative sense, is not the same as saying that uncovering the market abasement of sports does not require the acute exercise of our critical faculties), not to mention the entire round of our other everyday activities that are created out of the same instrumental mold as work. Moreover, when one considers yet further that it is sports' very noninstrumental way of going at things, at its goals, that account for much of their attraction to the wider American populace (after all, it is their peculiar logic that accounts for the distinctive brand of excellence that they showcase), it becomes even clearer why Progressives were decidedly upbeat about the reformist potential of sports. That is because it means that sports are not only rich veins for social critics to mine but rich veins about which people care enough to notice what such critics might turn up.

The same goes, as previously noted, for the alienation of sports themselves. Here again, their noninstrumental way of going at things makes it relatively easy to see why when they are forced to do too much of the bidding of the market, things go downhill very, very fast. For when the economic stakes of sports overshadow their commitment to excellence, a condition all too familiar to Progressives even at the turn of the twentieth century, the pursuit of victory takes a decided turn that must be accounted as irrational (by game standards), as it forces apart the ends sought in sports from the rule-governed means that are themselves an integral part of those ends. In other words, when money speaks louder than excellence, a not-so-subtle shift occurs in our conception and regard for sports that, by wreaking havoc on the "machinery of conditions" to which they owe their distinctive rational character, sets them on a technical course for which they could not be more unsuited. This is just another way of saying what has already been said: that the instrumentalization of sports is synonymous with their alienation. For when the complex (because compound) ends of sports are reduced to simple, discrete ones, which is what follows when those ends are stripped of any and all specifications as to how they are to be attained, sports become essentially instruments for attaining certain states of affairs (e.g., crossing the goal line in football or the finish line in a footrace) as efficiently as possible. So, getting the ball across the goal line in football now can accommodate without theoretical or practical contradiction not just such things as rushing or passing but holding as well, and crossing the finish line in a foot race can likewise accommodate, again without conceptual or practical duress, not just outpacing but tripping one's opponents. Of course, the point here is that there is, in the case of sports but not in the case of such full-blown instrumental activities as work, hell to pay for swapping the standard compound ends of sports for simple, pared-down ones or, what comes to the same thing, for swapping the standard technically unfelicitous means deployed in sports for technically felicitous ones. That hell to pay is that incorporating these scaled-down ends and hyped-up means as part of the legitimate repertoire of skills, moves, tactics, and ends of sports makes a mockery of them, of their basic point and purpose. Here again, then, the key to resuscitating the rationality of sports is to stave off their instrumentalization, to make the pursuit of victory congruent with the distinctive ways in which they require their participants go at things rather that the dominant, technical way in which the market requires us to go at things.

The importance of sports for Progressives, therefore, is that they contained the key both to their own and society's social, political, and moral redemption. This is why Progressives, despite their partiality for sports, were never reluctant to criticize their shortcomings so that their ennobling qualities might stand out in even sharper relief. Also, that is why these same social reformers did not hesitate to hold up this critically vetted model of unalienated sports, of sports at their best, as a mirror to the larger country so that it might be able to see itself at its unalienated best as well.[23] Naturally enough, it was the latter task that took up most of their theoretical attention and practical efforts as they searched for yet other ideas and ideals that might be extracted from sports and enlisted to steer the country away from the dangerous path down which it was going.

However, all the Progressive efforts to remake America in the image of sports more or less took their point of departure from highlighting their distinctive noninstrumental rational and normative structures enunciated earlier so that they could be cast as an alternative to business as usual. In one sense, Progressives meant this quite literally, arguing in the spirit of America's foremost poet, Walt Whitman,[24] that despite their professionalization, such sports as baseball offered an important if ephemeral respite from monetary pursuit. In this, as in so many of their reform initiatives, Progressives were on point not just conceptually but socially as well.[25] For the idea that baseball and its ilk provided a healthy alternative to the market chimed with American public sentiment of the time. Indeed, as Brown points out, the theme that baseball provides a much-needed relief from money-grubbing business was a constant refrain of youth sports literature in the late nineteenth century, as evidenced, for instance, in the Frank Merriwell series and in Gilbert Patten's baseball novels.[26] By the turn of the century, these idealized stories about baseball became so popular that they outshone and outsold the Horatio Alger rags-to-riches stories that, of course, sketched the other side of the American saga, the side that Progressives were anxious to downplay by weaving it into a more comprehensive and coherent narrative about America.

The notion that sports were an alternative not just to work but to most of what passes for the status quo was taken up also by William James in his important and widely read essay, "The Moral Equivalent of War."[27] As his title announces, this time sports were seen as a moral alternative to war itself, to a military impulse capable of convulsing an entire people at a moment's notice and impelling them to do the most dreadful things. Progressives and such pragmatists as James were eager, naturally enough, to tamp down this incendiary impulse, but doing so, he and others argued, required that we account for the important social role and function that it fulfilled in American lives. That is, it requires us to take seriously what the apologists of war said about it, which came down chiefly to two things: first, that in rousing us to action, more specifically to strenuous action suffused with daring and, apologies to Kierkegaard, fear and trembling, martial activity saves us from a dull, insipid existence, what James aptly calls a life of "flat degeneration," and second, in rousing us to action in defense of our compatriots, war rescues us from a narcissistic preoccupation with self, with a life absent any sense of sympathy or any trace of fellow-feeling for others. Utopian peace advocates, who blithely dismiss the concerns that lie behind this apologist defense of war, who causally swat away its central point that "So far, war has been the only force that can discipline a whole community," should, James insisted, be taken to task. For though such "peaceniks" were right to shun war, they were woefully wrong, he argued, to think that we need no protection against our "weaker and more cowardly sel[ves]," that we can make do without some "moral equivalent to war."[28]

This is where sports come squarely into the picture, at least for James and his Progressive contemporaries. For sports at their best also incite people to action, to tempt the fates of excellence, to attempt grand feats. In short, sports are competitive affairs that entice – if not seduce – people to test their athletic mettle under difficult conditions, to see what they are capable of when pressed to the limits by others. In this sense, sports confirm James's claim that "Patriotic pride and ambition in their military form are … only specifications of a more general competitive passion. They are its first form, but that is no reason for supposing them to be its last form."[29] What we observe on our playing fields, therefore, is the same sort of heroic action and derring-do that we see in martial conflict but (and this is absolutely key to James) without the horrific consequences of military action.

However, sports not only stoke our competitive fires but inflame our civic tempers. That is, they save us from myopic self seeking by showing us the great things that we can achieve when we work together, when we collectively strive to realize a shared goal and aim.[30] Sports are able to do this because they have built into them an important and indispensable cooperative element, one premised on a mutual agreement to abide by rules that hamstring technically efficient ways of attaining their aims and on a mutually understood commitment by competitors to provide one another a good competition, a good test of one another's athletic prowess. This agreement, in effect, to forsake the instrumental calculations that facilitate most of what we do in everyday life just so that the competition can occur and to show up ready to give our opponents our best in order to prod them to do their best, does not, as Rawls notes in a slightly different context, presuppose "a deliberate performative act in the sense of a promise, or contract, and the like."[31] In other words, it is less a formal social contract than an implicitly understood condition of what it means to share a form of life with others, to aspire to a true community of people united by a common concern for, in this case, athletic excellence. It is because sports gesture toward just such a true sense of community, one with a commitment to reciprocity well beyond what any contractual arrangement might call for, that James and other Progressives thought sports could sublimate our willful insistence to put ourselves first in all things, that they might encourage us to seek "a higher social plane," one nurtured in "cooperation," and in "self-forgetfulness … [rather than] self-seeking."[32]

Sports were considered by Progressives to be an alternative to the market in the further sense that the lessons in civic virtue supposedly imbibed by their participants might rub off on the great throngs of their spectators and produce similar communitarian results. That is, just as the market is normatively ordered in ways that turn its actors into rational egoists and in so doing encourages them to view larger society in the same egoistic terms, so sports are normatively ordered in ways that turn their actors into communitarians and in so doing encourage those who watch them to see themselves and society in the same communitarian terms. It was such arguments as this that launched the Progressive claim that sports were a remedy for the social cleavages wrought by the market.

Of course, any claim that sports transcend social cleavages, that they build bridges between Americans and run across ethnic, social class, religious, and cultural lines is in part belied by the facts. As we shall shortly see, the racial and especially gender divides in sports were no less wide and in some cases even wider than those found in the rest of society at the dawn of the twentieth century and well beyond it. Still, there is no denying that sports of that time did create a strong bond among an astonishingly wide number and range of Americans. Even when the claims for their great inclusiveness were uttered by such sporting enthusiasts as Albert Spalding, a corporate magnate whose pronouncements on such matters are hardly trustworthy, who unabashedly proclaimed in his 1911 book, *America's National Game*, "Base Ball is a democratic game," they should not be rejected out of hand for precisely the reason just stated: baseball, and team sports like it, did indeed command the attention and loyalty of a wide swath of Americans. These claims on behalf of sports' ability to meld Americans together also should not be offhandedly dismissed, because the sentiment behind Spalding's utterance, notwithstanding his dubious credentials, was a genuinely democratic one, one that ran counter to, as Mrozek avers, "the political sympathies and social instincts of the rich."[33] That is because during this period, the rich fled in droves from sports played and admired by "ordinary" Americans, and sought out sports that only they could afford and, therefore, regard as fitting of their lofty economic standing in the social hierarchy. Their contempt for their "inferiors" was prominently on display, therefore, in the utter contempt they showed for the favorite sports of the common folk.

So, even if such proponents of sports as Spalding can rightly be charged for being disingenuous in extolling their civic value, such claims themselves, when considered apart from the suspect intentions of their authors, cannot be so reproached. Indeed, as Dyreson notes further in this regard, when the editors of the popular journal *Current Literature* urged their readers to avert their eyes from the presidential race between William Taft, Theodore Roosevelt, and Woodrow Wilson and instead train them on the 1912 Stockholm Olympic Games, where American Olympians were expected to reap more than their fair share of Gold Medals, they were not preaching political apathy. Rather, they were preaching the vices of partisan politics, which divides up the homeland into querulous and parlous factions, and the healing virtues of Olympic sports, which in melding them back again gives Americans some sense that they are compatriots after all, and so, perhaps, that they need not keep carping at one another or at least remind themselves that when they do they share an important larger identity in common they can invoke to temper their disagreements. When Progressives entertained communitarian aspirations of this grand sort and pinned them on the back of sports they did not have "kumbaya"-like notions of community in mind. For the sense of belonging inspired by sports runs very deep, indeed. Just how deep and strong are the attachments they form is captured well by Gorn and Goldstein when they observe how such in sports as baseball, "The identification of a 'home team' moves the private conception of home, as in the Victorian family circle, for example, into the public realm." The significance of this enlarged, public conception of home, they write further, is that it provided a "bridge by which Americans connected their family lives to the larger social world," such that by setting up a "relationship to a home team ... millions of uprooted Americans" were able to connect "to a sentimental language and cluster of values ... for which they hungered." So, the kind of allegiance that fans express for their "home" teams – who can forget the cries of "Red Sox Nation" following Boston's improbable winning of the 2004 World Series, especially in light of their remarkable comeback against their main rival the Yankees – and the sort of allegiance expressed by Americans and other countries, as noted earlier, in the Olympic Games when the "home" team is the nation itself, is powerful stuff indeed.[34]

Progressives considered sports ideal moral vehicles in the yet further sense that they not only excite our competitive and civic passions but promulgate a conception of fair play that the rest of society would do well to emulate. In many respects, it is this lashing of the perfectionist fortunes of sports to those of fair play that is for Progressives one of the most important moral features of sports. For without this emphasis on fair play, the competitive struggle on display in sports would differ hardly at all from the brute and hardly moral struggle for existence that Social Darwinists would have us believe tinctures all human striving. That the competitive strife of sports is morally leavened by considerations of fairness, therefore, is what gave William James and other Progressives hope that the cultivation of sports and other kindred practices might inspire in its citizens' pride in America's moral rather than its military might.[35] This hope was premised on two further factors: first, that America's national identity is not etched in stone, that whatever its past and present failings, its future is not irrevocably stained by them; and second, that individual character is not set in stone either, that character does not come already formed but is shaped by the actions we take, the corollary of which is that the more morally upstanding those actions, the more morally upstanding the character that results.[36]

However, what sort of fair play did Progressives believe that sports teach that might rub off on their fellow Americans and get them to honor their professed commitment to social justice? Two things can be said in response. First, sports' commitment to fair play can be understood as a commitment to equality of opportunity itself, to a common, garden-variety justice that mandates that everyone in the competition be given an equal chance to achieve athletic excellence. This is why in sports, it is crucial that everyone start from the proverbial same starting line, so that no one enjoys a leg up on the competition. At the very least, this entails an impartial observance and application of the rules to ensure that similar cases are treated similarly. It entails further that no arbitrary distinctions be drawn between and among competitors, where the term *arbitrary* refers to distinctions that have nothing integrally to do with the perfectionist point of athletic contests. So, to allow ethnic or social class distinctions to determine who can compete and how rules are to be interpreted in sports is a basic breach of fair play, a paradigmatic case of unfair treatment, one at which participants and observers alike have every right to take moral umbrage. It is no accident, therefore, that sports' commitment to open, fair competition became a favorite trope of Progressives anxious to draw invidious contrasts between America and its European counterparts (i.e., between America as a "city on the hill," where everybody gets a fair shake as evidenced by its favorite sporting pastimes and the rest of Europe, where class privilege rules as evidenced by its favorite sporting pastimes).[37] Of course, Progressives were never so brazen or loose-lipped as to suggest that fair play never gets short shrift in America and in her sports. Who would believe such an absurd claim anyway? Rather, they more soberly maintained that when it does get short shrift, fair play morally matters in a way in which it never could in a still aristocratic Europe riven by class distinctions that blind it to the cruelties of social injustice.[38]

The second thing that should be said about fair play in sport is that while it enjoins equality of conditions, it does not enjoin equality of results. Nor could it, as the entire point of making sure that no one enjoys an unfair advantage over anyone else, that everyone has an equal opportunity to succeed, is to expose the relevant inequalities in talent and strategy that sports are designed to bring out. As Hibbard pithily put it, "The chances must be equal, and then and only then, all may be done for victory."[39] That equal treatment does not mean identical treatment, therefore, follows from the perfectionist imperatives of sports themselves, which require that excellence be recognized, awarded, and so accorded a higher significance, and that deficiencies in excellence receive less plaudits, less reward, and so less significance. So, rewarding athletes for their perfectionist triumphs is no sin against equality as long as the conditions governing those triumphs, the procedures that gave rise to them, are themselves fair and equal ones.

This second feature of fair play introduces a somewhat new wrinkle into the conception of justice that is served up by sports and encourages a yet more egalitarian reading of it. The nuance in question is nicely rendered by Progressive athletic enthusiast Francis Tabor in his 1899 essay on the social and moral effects of what he called "true sport:" "The strong must help the weak; and the weak must be aroused, that they not be a drag upon the strong."[40] In one sense, of course, the upshot of Tabor's claim is no different from the upshot of the claim just made: equal treatment does not enjoin identical treatment. For the point of ensuring that no one is disadvantaged in the pursuit of athletic excellence, especially the more vulnerable weak, is to ensure a good competition, one in which competition is keen, excellence rife, and everyone is accorded her or his just dues. In another sense, however, Tabor's claim that fair play demands as well that the weak not act as a drag on the strong sheds, as intimated, new light on this notion, suggesting, as it does, that in sporting circles it is not enough that the weak be spared the indignities they face in everyday life, where they are forced to compete for their survival against rivals who enjoy any number of advantages over them, but that they be raised up, as it were, to a level where they can function as a worthy opponent: precisely the kind of opponent that can bring out the best in others. In short, athletic excellence depends for its generation on worthy competitors, on rivals who are capable of eliciting from one another the highest excellence that they can muster. That means that the strong should not only be restrained from disadvantaging opponents more vulnerable than they by requiring them to start at the same line as everybody else but that they be deterred as well from exploiting the athletically irrelevant misfortunes that befall their opponents in actual competition. What Tabor has in mind here is what fellow Progressive Collier has in mind when he counsels against seeking victory by default where the default in question can be easily corrected so that the pursuit of excellence can proceed apace. So if, for example, one's opponent is temporarily felled by muscle cramps that a suitable time delay can resolve (a real-life example of which I discuss in the Preface), one should not hesitate in the least to take corrective action so that the competition can be restored and the outcome duly contested rather than simply conceded. Exploiting weaknesses of this "unathletic" sort, unathletic because they have nothing important to do, or so it is claimed, with athletic competition, is manifestly unfair according to this Progressive reading, not to mention manifestly beside the point, as availing oneself of such measures proves nothing save, perhaps, one's lust for victory no matter how undeserved or impoverished. Understandably so, as it reveals a remarkable insensitivity to the purpose of sports themselves, to the perfectionist aim that endows them with whatever intelligibility they enjoy, and to the moral predilections that inform and shape that perfectionist aim.

Finally, fairness so understood further mandates that worthy competitors deserve our moral respect, win or lose. To put it more bluntly: winners should never lord their success over their competitors, as doing so shows a basic lack of moral appreciation for their competitors, without whom their athletic success, of course, would not have been possible, to say nothing of a lack of moral appreciation for the game itself, of a contest fairly and valiantly waged.[41] The will to win, therefore, amounts to little, esthetically and morally speaking, if such a will is not informed by a fair regard for one's opponents, by a will to win that does not transgress the rules or the boundaries established by moral respect for one's opponents.

The political implications of this Progressive conception of "true," fair sport are not hard to divine. Two such implications stand out in particular. The political significance of both is revealed by Sheed's trenchant observation that the regard for fair play and contempt for cheating inspired by sports were crucial to a nation that at the turn of the twentieth century was "on the verge of great transactions" and one that was "in the midst of a population explosion that might have reduced it to Third World." In such an unstable and highly charged atmosphere, argued Sheed, America "needed a citizenry it could trust," and sports, he surmised further, were precisely the tool needed to garner such trust or, to put it in a more contemporary idiom, to secure the social capital needed to make democracy work in America.[42]

The first politically pregnant feature of the kind of fair play wielded in sports implicates once again what James called the "fixed machinery of conditions" that govern their conduct. Of course, these are the rules that set out the aims of sporting practice and prescribe certain ways in which they are to be pursued. What sports reliance on such a "fixed machinery of conditions" suggests in the way of social justice is a kind of constitutionalism in which the rule of law is made the ultimate arbiter of fairness and in which strict adherence to that law is considered morally obligatory. The significance of entrusting fair decision making to such a corpus of law is that it prevents individuals and groups from taking matters into their own hands, from turning the law inside out so that it ends up promoting the interests of the privileged few over those of the not-so-privileged many. What is at stake here, then, is the very notion of fairness itself, because, like most other things, it is always prey to the sectarian interests of particular individuals and groups. What Progressives saw in sports was an instructive constitutional remedy, one mindful, as Dyreson astutely notes, of Madison's worry, which he articulated in "Federalist Number 10:" that unless individuals are bound by some such set of constitutional constraints, their considered judgments about what is fair or not will turn out to be not so considered, to be skewed by their understandable but unjustified desire to maximize their own self-interests at the expense of those of others.[43] Because, on this view, individuals cannot be deterred from acting on their egoistic preferences and groups cannot be deterred from acting as factions, the most for which we can hope in the way of justice is to regulate fairly their dealings with one another. Since the "fixed machinery of conditions" to which sports are wedded teach nothing if not "deference to constitutional authority,"[44] Progressives were eager to talk up and promote sports as popular models of how our political lives should look and how our main political practices and institutions should be rationally ordered – if, that is, fair political outcomes are how we want others to think of us when they do think of us.[45]

The second political value that can be read off the kind of fair play cultivated in sports harkens back to their previously discussed community-friendly character, to the cooperative thread that runs through them and that instills in their participants and onlookers a sense of belonging. Here the equality of conditions on which sports pride themselves and the social class mixing to which they give rise conjures up a less self-interested and factional notion of community, a true community in every sense of the term, as it is held together by a shared commitment to a highly valued form of life. Here, fairness comes off less as a constitutional remedy for the egoistic predilections of individuals and the factional ones of groups and more as a characteristic feature of communities whose commitment to the common good itself overrides such predilections, ensures they will not be given the final (let alone the first) say. On this view, the lessons in fair play learned in sports are politically valuable precisely because they encourage participants and spectators alike to see their own aims and ends as coincident with one another (because coincident with those of the game itself) of the perfectionist way of life particular to it. If, mused Progressives, political actors could learn from their widespread participation and great interest in sports to do the same, to see that their interests are bound up with rather than separate from those of their fellow countrymen and the government that represents them (in other words, that the government is never just "they" but always in some significant sense, if in good order, "we"), Americans could begin to live up to their democratic view of themselves. Only a staunchly Anglophile American, such as the following late nineteenth-century observer, whose words betray an unmistakable allegiance to the old aristocratic ways and prejudices, could fail to grasp this politically important dimension of sport that Progressives were not just quick to grasp but quick to capitalize on:

> Why there should be such constant strife to bring together in sport the two divergent elements of society that never by any chance meet elsewhere on even terms is quite incomprehensible, and it is altogether the sole cause of our athletic woe ... The laboring class are all right in their way; let them go their way in peace, and have their athletics in whatsoever manner best suits their inclinations. ... Let us have our own sport among the more refined elements, and allow no discordant spirits to enter it.[46]

Contrary to such Anglophiles then, whose elitist pretensions blind them even to the fact that social class mixing comes rather naturally to sporting enthusiasts, so much so that trying to put an end to such commingling almost always required resort to coercive measures of one sort or another, the insistence that fair play be extended to all in sports is quite comprehensible, as their Progressive opponents of the time could have well explained to them if they bothered to ask. This feature of fair play suggested to Progressives yet another way in which to quell Madison's worry about individuals letting their self-interested agendas get in the way of justice, one that unlike the previous insistence on rigid compliance to objective rules, which rather uncritically assumes that nothing can be done about our individualist and factional tendencies because they are constitutive of who we are, sought instead to tutor them in the cooperative ways of such social practices as sports that play to their communitarian sensibilities. Of course, if sports do play to such sensibilities as they seem to, the good news is that our egoistic and factional tendencies are decidedly not constitutive of who we are, and the even better news is that it is not asking too much of us to refrain from looking for loopholes and otherwise exploiting whatever rules have been devised to get us to act more fairly out of respect for the solidarity of the community to which we belong.

It was not lost on Progressives, however, that the constitutionalism and solidarity particular to sports were mutually inclusive rather than mutually exclusive of one another. That is, Progressives realized that any "fixed machinery of conditions," sportive or political, could do its legislative work if and only if the people that they were intended to govern had good moral reason to abide by them. Otherwise, compliance with these objective rules would either have to be forced by draconian measures, by penalties whose costs were so prohibitive that no one would dare run afoul of them, or would become something of a parody of itself by being made part of a self-interested rational calculus that insists that rules be followed only if they could not be successfully violated (which is code for *if they could not be broken without detection*). The problem with going the draconian-penalty way is that it conjures up a totalitarian rather than a democratic society, and the problem with going the self-interested rule-bending and rule-breaking way is that it conjures up the unfettered market society that Progressives were trying their level best to neutralize morally. On the other side of the coin, Progressives also realized that some enforcement mechanisms were needed to keep the peace, to prevent self-regarding free-riders from taking advantage of the other-regarding intentions and actions of their fellow citizens. This is why their deliberate and careful pairing of constitutionalism with belonging made not only good practical sense – the same practical sense noted in Chapter 5, in which Progressives first peddled their reforms through voluntary associations and then,[47] once they began to take hold in the people themselves, endeavored to make them the law of the land – but good moral sense. For it showed just how prescient Progressives were in anticipating Rawls's important argument that the principles of fair play or justice, at least those with democratic pretensions, must be capable of mutual acknowledgment and consent by all concerned, because only if such balanced reciprocity obtains "can there be true community between persons in their common practices."[48]

A final point before we move on to consider rivals to the Progressive conception of "true" sport: because most of these sporting Progressives, as we have seen, were either one and the same Progressive reformers discussed in Chapter 5 or mostly came from their same social ranks, it is not surprising that they shared the same moral blind spots. I am speaking primarily of their undeniable racist and sexist prejudices, their entrenched belief that people of color and women were at best second-class citizens both in and outside sports (a point of view that in the next chapter I argue is fundamentally at odds with the moral ideals they exalt and claim to find in sports).

On the racial front, Native-, Asian-, and African-Americans were not only marginalized in Progressive accounts of sports but largely excluded from them. That is because the moral, social, and political lessons allegedly learned in sports, it was claimed, were peculiarly suited to white males, which, therefore, made them peculiarly unsuited to their black or non-European counterparts (not to mention, of course, women). Further, pseudoscientific racist theories of black athletic superiority, which invariably tied their athletic prowess to their primitive backwardness, circulated freely during this period and were frequently picked up and regurgitated by sportswriters as unassailable facts. Hence, efforts to keep out people of color from such traditional pastimes as baseball were the rule rather than the exception. Those precious few who did manage to break through the racial barriers (e.g., the legendary Jim Thorpe) were typically greeted by racial epithets shouted at them by spectators indignant that racial "inferiors" were defiling their favored sports. Efforts by Progressives to suppress indigenous American and immigrant sports were no less common at this time and were part (but only, I hasten to add, part) of the same strategy to keep sports pure for white males.[49]

The fate of women in this Progressive scheme of things athletic was only marginally better, although markedly more complex because of its morally schizophrenic character. On the one hand, as Mrozek advised, if one compared the plight of women in the Progressive period to their former selves rather than to that of men in the same period, it could be plausibly claimed that women had made tangible moral and political progress.[50] One reason why was that some Progressives at least thought sports for women were a good thing, something from which they could substantially benefit, though mainly as participants rather than spectators. So, such prominent women Progressive advocates as Charlotte Perkins Gilman openly agitated for women's involvement in sports, arguing that it contributed, among other things, to feminine autonomy.[51] Women were further encouraged by Progressives to take up sports for their health and fitness benefits and because they helped to promote a conception of women as more physically active and vigorous, which could help to defeat the female stereotype of the "swooning damsel."[52] On the other hand, certain Progressives sought to use sports either to control women rather than liberate them or to exclude them from sports altogether. On the control side, sports were thought to contribute to the reinforcement of Victorian gender roles, to reinforce the quaint image of women as "creatures of the kitchen and fireside."[53] In this same vein, sports were pushed for women on the grounds that they would make them more compatible companions for men, tame their excess sexual desires, and turn them into better physical bearers of children.[54] Moreover, under the influence of bizarre, pseudoscientific theories of the time, which traced the source of many mental illnesses suffered by women to their sexual organs, certain Progressives advocated for women such sports as cycling as a way to ward off their predisposition to hysteria and insanity.[55]

As noted, however, Progressives just as often tried to bar women from sports. For instance, Collier furiously argued that women be kept out of sports so as not to jeopardize sports' distinctly masculine features, specifically their encouragement of rigorous and risky physical activity. This was no intellectual quibble, at least as far as Collier and many of his peers were concerned, because if America was going to stem the "softening" and "feminization" it was undergoing as a result of the Industrial Revolution, which had made most forms of hearty physical activity and daring practically obsolete, they argued that Americans would be well advised to avail themselves of masculine-friendly sports.[56] Such intellectuals as Veblen echoed Collier's concerns, arguing similarly that Americans needed to recapture their physical ferocity and cunning if they hoped to maintain their vaunted position in the world.[57] Hence, many Progressives convinced themselves that in order for Americans to pull themselves out of this dangerous downward spiral, this descent into pusillanimity, their favorite sports had to be scrubbed clean of the anticompetitive tendencies and sentimentalities of the weaker sex.

In this effort, they were joined by women physical educators of the era. Of course, the reason why these women physical educators rallied behind the effort to remove women from the dominant male sports scene was not ostensibly a chauvinist one, although it did, unfortunately and unwittingly further the cause of such chauvinist concerns. Their main interest was rather to shield women from the corrosive hypercompetitive, win-at-all-costs ethos that ruled most male sports. Since many of them were convinced that such sports were beyond redemption, they thought that segregating sports along sexual lines was the way to go. As I said, however, there would be something to say for this wariness regarding male sports, something of genuine critical import, were it not steeped in a no-less-damaging stereotype of women: the notion of "feminine moderation." This is the crippling idea that anything that women do full-bore (i.e., with arduous effort and great passion) is somehow destructive of their femininity, threatening to turn them into female eunuchs. Something very much like this prejudice dogged prominent women athletes of this time, such as the great Babe Didrikson, whose prodigious athletic skills and accomplishments were cruelly belittled by such sportswriters as Paul Gallico, who castigated them as a form of "compensation" for the fact that "she would not or could not compete with women at their own best game – man snatching."[58] Of course, these women leaders in physical education would have never put it this way and would not have stood for such demeaning accounts of women athletes. Still, their own skittishness regarding women's full-throttle pursuit of athletic excellence left such athletes as Didrikson virtually defenseless against such base attacks. That is because their embrace of female moderation indiscriminately inculpates not only morally dubious efforts to do whatever it takes to win but any otherwise morally exemplary commitment by women to excel in sports, to do something supremely well within their hallowed precincts. A more effective deterrent to women's self-overcoming in or outside of sports beggars the imagination. Not surprisingly, then, however well intentioned women physical educators might have been in promulgating this stereotype, the net effect of their efforts was to shut women out of most sports in the American public arena, not to mention the Olympic Games, until 1920 or so.[59]

The moral schizophrenia at work here is easy enough to spot. For the passion on display in male sports that these Progressive women physical educators tried their mightiest to curb by setting up separate sports for women was the very feature of sports that other Progressives isolated and extolled as the key factor behind American exceptionalism.[60] The moral inversion at work in this effort to exclude the second gender from the world of sports is also plain to see, especially when men further tried to justify such segregation by proclaiming that sports belong to the private, intimate sphere rather than to the public one. The purpose behind this privatization of public sport was the plainly transparent, even if topsy-turvy, one of providing men an escape from fuller social contact and relationships with the opposite gender.[61] That way, suitably transfixed by sports, men could, as Sheed indelicately puts it, "sleepwalk [their] way through … a marriage that could possibly use some attention."[62] It hardly needs saying that this very same privatization tactic also allowed men "to escape fuller familial relationships."[63]

## Rival conceptions of sports

The Progressive conception of sport was, to be sure, not the only game in town, or the dominant one. There were, however, a relatively small number of suitors vying for that honor, though each had formidable credentials that they brought to the table. In some cases, they acted both wittingly and unwittingly in cahoots with one another, which led, as we shall soon see, to some troubling developments both in and outside the world of sports. For my purposes here, four such rival conceptions of sports merit discussion.

The first conception of sport that I discuss in this regard, which was highly contemptuous of Progressive efforts to link sports to public virtue, came from the ranks of the so-called new experts of physical culture and largely centered on intercollegiate sports. As noted before, this group included male and female physical educators and overwhelmingly male coaches and trainers. However, it is the coaches and trainers who should be singled out here, as they were able to overcome the objections of male physical educators regarding the individual and social costs of pursuing winning too zealously, and because, as previously discussed, women physical educators essentially abdicated this turf to them by choosing to form their own, separate sports. These coaches and trainers, of course, like their other physical culture counterparts, did see themselves as experts of a sort and claimed that their supervision and training of athletes led to better performances.[64] However, their self-professed expertise was focused exclusively on turning out winning teams, which is how they justified the relatively high salaries that they were beginning to command. So, they did not trouble themselves regarding the larger social significance of sports but instead concentrated exclusively on producing teams that could be counted on to win year after year. In this quest, they proved to be unabashed amoralists, asserting without a hint of self-doubt that "athletic achievement depended less on the character of the man than on the managerial science of the new experts who regulated his life."[65]

The second notion of sport was peculiar to the ultrarich who had their own reasons for rejecting Progressives' efforts to view sports as sources of public virtue. On the contrary, their interest in sports was exclusively a private one: to partake of sports in which only people of their substantial material means could afford to engage and only in a manner that, once again, befit their lofty economic and social status. For these affluent folks, then, sports were nothing if not a conspicuous way to flaunt their considerable wealth, to lord it over others by choosing such sports as yachting, which no commoners could possibly take up owing to their great expense. When the expense of the sport alone was not sufficient to exclude their social "inferiors," the rich retreated to such private spaces as country clubs (the membership fees of which again put them beyond the reach of ordinary citizens) to pursue such sports as golf and tennis. When they could not find a way to restrict a sport to people of their refined ilk (e.g., baseball), they quickly absented themselves. As they saw it, therefore, sports were purely private entertainments best pursued and consumed for the pleasure and self-gratification they bring. They were also of one mind as well that their sports should be genteel in every respect and conducted strictly along amateur lines. However, there was no contradiction in their insistence that sports be pleasurable and genteel, as conducting oneself according to the strict dictates of amateurism enhanced the pleasure that they received from playing their idle pastimes. That is both because pay for play was considered socially uncouth and, therefore, most unbecoming of a social class whose wealth, as they never tired of pointing out, had nothing to do with the sweat of their brow and because, to their way of thinking, sports should also be done without any trace of laborious effort lest someone accuse them of – horror of horrors – turning their idle leisure amusements into work. There was never any question, then, of letting one's competitive ardor get the better of one in these sports, as the priority of social etiquette in all matters athletic was something every member of this privileged class had drilled into their heads from the first moment they decided to take up sports. So, while excessive competition was shunned, excessive frivolity was not. Indeed, it could not be, because in their view of the world, it made perfectly good sense to deploy the adjective *excessive* against the noun in the case of competition but not in the case of frivolity. That is because frivolity was the only way in which they knew how to make sense of their opulent lives, which means that it would have scarcely occurred to those traveling in this elite social circle that there was any reason to constrain their frivolity.[66]

The third conception of sport was, contrary to the second, strictly working-class in character and disposition. Pleasure had a privileged place here, too, but of a decidedly *lumpen* and masculine variety. That is to say, these folks openly spurned the Progressive idea that sports were a place in which one could learn to be a morally upstanding citizen and the well-to-do's penchant for genteel sports and instead went in for violent sports – the more violent the better. More specifically, they preferred such sports as boxing and blood sports, sports with a violent temperament that served to reinforce their hypermasculinity. They preferred to pursue and watch these sports in settings in which they were not likely to run into people who might spoil their good time by probing whether they should take pleasure in the misfortune of others or in the brutalization of animals, in such places as saloons, dance halls, and mining camps.[67]

Last, but certainly not least, was the notion of sports favored by the entrepreneurial class, by capitalists anxious to cash in on Americans' great love affair with sports. Here, the predominantly private predilections of those who were smitten with one or the other of the three previous conceptions of sports made them easy pickings for the private profit motives of these eager to please sporting entrepreneurs. This is why many Progressives considered commercial sports their most formidable and worrisome adversary and why they aimed most of their critical sallies in their direction.[68] We can count here such business savvy types as Richard Kyle Fox, who made a slew of money promoting working-class sporting amusements in his *National Police Gazette* by featuring such fare as "blood sports, tantalizing sexual pleasures, and illicit activities."[69] Of course, true to their well-honed market ways, sporting capitalists were not averse to exploiting the middle or upper classes either. This is why it did not take them long to get their own professional sport franchises up and running and why they did not have to be coaxed to help to finance and promote collegiate sports, not to mention the idle amusements of the rich. Of course, they were happy as well to sell to these various sporting enthusiasts all the athletic accoutrements after which they pined and made a tidy profit doing so. Commercial sports, we might say, then, and to reiterate our foregoing point, sealed the deal so far as the future direction sports were to take by providing the perfect private foil by which to co-opt and capitalize on the private aspirations that drove the other three conceptions of sports.

## The rest of the story: progressive and liberal sporting sentiments and their gradual demise

There is not much to tell regarding the rest of this post-Progressive saga, the period roughly between the 1920s and 1960s, save to mention the enduring but increasingly assailed conviction that sports still have something of moral import to teach the country. For the privatization and commodification of sports discussed earlier proceeded apace for these next four decades. The 1919 Black Sox scandal certainly did not get things off on the right foot, shaking to the core as it did the public's confidence in the country's premier national pastime, baseball. As Gorn and Goldstein point out, in the post-1920s, "big-time sports became a whirl of personality and promotion, cash and corruption."[70] This amoral trend persisted unabated through the Second World War era and picked up steam following it, as the pursuit of victory was ratcheted up yet another notch. The 1951 point-shaving scandals in college basketball demonstrated all too clearly just how high the stakes for winning had become. Despite all the bad news, however, Americans managed to retain their faith in the moral promise of sports, and many hoped against hope that the tide might yet turn in their favor and that America might once again find its moral bearings through the sheer moral example of her favorite sports.

That hope was nourished by the fact that throughout this period, Americans' fondness for their own sports, in particular the big three of football, basketball, and baseball, did not waiver. As Zang remarks more generally, up to and through the early 1960s, "Americans continued to reserve their greatest interest for activities they regarded as peculiarly theirs."[71] However, the decline in the moral salience of sports had reached the point at which it could not be hidden or ignored anymore, try as some mightily did. Simply put, the allure of money and the almost unimaginable sumptuous returns that the television broadcasts of sports made possible finally began to take its moral toll on them. Gorn and Goldstein were not exaggerating in the least, therefore, when they said of the contemporary sporting scene, "Nothing in the socialization and training of first-rate athletes, nothing in the culture of athletic boosterism, encourages honor over victory or rule-following over rule-bending."[72] Predictably, sports became more and more disconnected from the larger community, and the economic and social gulf between players and fans grew ever greater, so much so that the class mixing and sense of belonging that sports used to encourage were no longer possible because the wall that Progressives and other likeminded reformers tried to insert between sport and the market to resist its incessant and insidious advances came tumbling down once the full force of the profit motive asserted itself. Indeed, by the 1960s, things had deteriorated to the point that when the Vietnam War burst on the front pages of America's newspapers and on television screens, all hell broke lose, and nothing, not even American's moral confidence in their cherished sports, survived unscathed. As a result, the strong attachment that most Americans felt for their own pastimes began to slacken, as sports came under a heavy barrage of criticism previously reserved for what were considered to be less sacrosanct spheres of life: politics and the like. In fact, many Americans across the heartland openly questioned whether sports could withstand such a reflective onslaught, only adding to the growing suspicion that the country's best days might well have already passed them by. This would explain why social hope seems to be in such short supply these days.

## The postmortem: why did Americans' faith in the moral promise of sports nearly collapse around the 1960s or so?

I now dissect what I believe are the main causes behind the moral derangement of contemporary sports. Doing so will not only set the stage for my final assessment of the moral credentials of the Progressive conception of sports vis a vis the other main contending conceptions of sport in the ensuing chapter but help to fix more precisely the period in which America's moral faith in sports went into a steep decline, a decline from which it has yet to recover completely.

As I have previously remarked, trying to pin down the time in which a major social transformation occurred is a tricky matter, indeed. However, that should not stop us from at least trying to lay down some historical markers in this respect, as I did in the previous chapter and as I intend to do in this one as well. It will thus be remembered, I trust, that in that previous chapter, two of the authors discussed linked the unraveling of the Progressive-liberal era to certain momentous events in the world of sport. For the first, Don DeLillo, it was Bobby Thompson's 1951 winning home run that clinched the World Series for the New York Giants and convulsed, for the last time as he saw it, the entire country; for the second, Andrew Delbanco, it was the era in which specialization and commercialization overtook such sports as baseball and turned them into different games that lessened their national appeal, a development that he chose to leave temporally unspecified but which (it is generally agreed) ran its course from the 1970s or so on. However, I sided in that chapter with Gitlin's and Rorty's dating of the demise of the Progressive legacy, neither of which authors made any effort to hook up that demise with events in sports but both of whom conjectured, correctly to my mind, that the end of this period coincided with the onslaught of the Vietnam War. Further confirmation of Gitlin's and Rorty's periodization does, as it turns out, dovetail nicely with developments in sports, something that both authors would have, no doubt, readily discovered if they were interested enough to look. For there is good evidence to suggest that it was during the height of the Vietnam War that confidence in the moral powers of sports reached its nadir. As Lipsyte avers, for most of the twentieth century "The values of sport – honoring boundaries, playing by the rules, working together for a common goal, submitting to authority – were the same values that shaped the American character." However, he continues, "Somewhere around ... the middle of the Vietnam War," those values and the hopes to which they gave rise came crashing down.[73] Zang concurs, arguing that "nearly a century of consensus [in which] a widespread and unshakable conviction in sports' ability to build character" prevailed, was shattered in the Vietnam period. Zang goes on to claim, again correctly as I see it, that this period and its profound effects on the American *Weltanschauung* were not confined to the 1960s but extended into the mid-1970s.[74] So, the crucial period in which Americans' public faith in the morally redemptive powers of sports reached a precarious all-time low was somewhere between 1960 and the mid-1970s.

The more important question, of course, is why, and here there are at least three main reasons. The first and most important, not least because it is implicated in the other two reasons, was the increasing and unceasing commercialization of sports, about which I have had a lot to say in the previous chapters. It was during this 1960s period that money began to figure in just about everything that happened in sports, a change in *degree*, as sports were commercialized from the get-go, but one so massive in scale and so far reaching in its effects that it qualified, as I argued in Chapter 2, as a bona fide change in *kind*. That is not to suggest that the market proceeded merrily along its way gradually choking the air out of sports until it suffocated them in this sixth, decisive decade of the twentieth century but rather that it had its way with sports in fits and starts in which its influence mostly waxed but occasionally waned. It got a big boost, to reiterate, in the 1920s, in which sports, thanks to wealthy investors, went on a spending spree and such celebrities as Babe Ruth became household names, and again in the 1950s, in which television and mass advertising poured unheard of amounts of cash into their already ample coffers.

This commercialization of sports was also helped along by two unlikely sources. The first, early in the twentieth century, concerned the sporting habits of the rich, and the second was the sporting sentiments of the counter-culture that emerged in the 1960s and whose political passion was matched only by its passion for the pleasures of an unrestrained life. These are unlikely sources because, as discussed, the rich were nothing if not insular, dedicated foremost to making sure that whatever they did would not bring them into even remote contact with ordinary American citizens, and the counterculture were nothing if not rebellious and oppositional in every respect, or at least that is how they liked to portray themselves, especially when it came to the capitalistic practices of mainstream America. Despite their mutual disdain for mainstream America, however, both played a large role in shaping Americans' sporting habits. In the case of the rich, they successfully peddled the idea that wealth was its own reward, requiring, therefore, no justification, a quintessential feature of the market if ever there were one, and that sports served no moral interests but were just another form of consumption, just another way to pass the time by adding a little spice to the daily humdrum of life that not even the well-off could entirely escape. As Mrozek put it, the ultrarich put into circulation for all Americans to see and emulate "the prototype of the sportsman as an unrestricted consumer."[75] The counterculture, conversely, though they rejected the authoritarian and overt money-grubbing ways of traditional sports, especially the dominant team sports, were quite fond of such individual sports as jogging and more esoteric but such hardly less anarchic (because mostly ruleless) fare as earth ball. Their motivation again was as much political as pleasure seeking in character, as what "turned them off," to use 1960s argot, about traditional sports was precisely the subordination of the individual and the insistence on discipline that they required. However, this new focus on everything individual, as immortalized in the mantra of the time – "do your own thing" – and on the slackening of discipline to enhance the pleasure of the athletic experience was, despite its political antiauthoritarian overtones, music to the ears of ever-alert sporting entrepreneurs of the time. That is why it is not surprising, as Zang astutely observes, that in short order both sports and rock music became staples of the culture industry, which made more than a few corporate types obscenely rich. Hence, both the rich and the counterculture, each in its own inimitable way, hastened the commercialization of sports and molded sports into what they have become for a majority of Americans nowadays: a form of "passive consumption rooted in spectatorship and electronically simulated games."[76]

A second root cause of the decline of American's faith in the moral prowess of sports had to do with the managerial bent of the (already discussed) new experts of physical culture, principally the coaches. For it was their view that the technical expertise that they brought to sports, which, not coincidentally, was how, as also noted, they justified their high salaries, was the key to advancing athletic excellence. In the renewed attention and enthusiasm that they gave to winning, which they insisted was the only true measure of athletic excellence, technical expertise crowded out any moral concern for the welfare of sports. So, their taking over the reins of the sporting world, especially in the collegiate ranks, from male physical educators still receptive to the moral overtures of sports and keenly aware of the dangers of excessive devotion to winning (as already discussed, women physical educators were no less alert to the moral possibilities of sports and to the pitfalls of athletic success, but their desire to disassociate themselves entirely from anything having to do with male sports made them essentially nonplayers in this public fight for the moral soul of sports), contributed in a not insignificant way to the demoralization of sports. Today, the reign of these coaches and their growing retinue of technical experts, which now prominently features members from the emergent sport sciences – principally exercise physiologists, biomechanists, and sport psychologists[77] – has only tightened. As long as their preeminent position in the athletic food chain remains unchallenged, especially because they command the strong support of those who financially underwrite the large expenses they run up, the chance for any genuine moral reform in sports is exceedingly unlikely.

A third, and for my purposes final, important cause behind the waning moral influence of sports had to do with the gradual withdrawal of Progressive and liberal-minded public intellectuals' support of them, which was followed in the 1960s by the emergent student Left's abrupt break with anything having to do with sports. This third cause warrants more extended comment, because I have to this point barely touched on it.

To begin with the Progressive-liberal loss of faith in sports: the key event here was undoubtedly the outbreak of the First World War, which upended the 1916 Berlin Olympic Games and sowed the seeds of doubt in these intellectuals' minds about whether sports could, in fact, serve as a moral deterrent to war. Whatever moral and political curative powers they thought that sports possessed were dealt an early setback, therefore, by the seeming impotence of sports to mobilize Americans against martial conflict.[78] However, their disappointment might have been lessened somewhat had they been aware of and taken to heart some of the stories that came out of that awful war, which have only recently been documented in a serious way, regarding the pacific effects that one sport in particular, soccer, had on the British and German combatants. The most noteworthy of these stories had to do with the so-called Christmas truce of 1914, in which soldiers from both sides cleared away the carnage that lay between their two trenches (which they had fittingly dubbed "No Man's Land") and remarkably engaged each other in a soccer game played with a makeshift ball made out of a cap-comforter stuffed with straw. These games, which took place all along the front line and were initiated by the soldiers themselves in defiance of their superior officers and in which both sides played in front of peers lined up on each side of their respective trenches with armed rifles slung over their shoulders, must have seemed as surreal to them as it does to me now recounting them.

However, there is no doubting their profound effect on the soldiers themselves, which, as one of the combatants turned player related in a letter to loved ones at home, "Even as I write, I can scarcely credit what I have seen and done. It has indeed been a wonderful day," helped to drive home to all concerned the utter insanity of war.[79] Even when their commanding officers, once they learned of their unofficial truce, angrily ordered them to retreat to their respective redoubts and recommence firing, most of them aimed their rifles well above the heads of the troops on the other side to ensure that their bullets fell harmlessly to the ground. Of course, even if these and like stories had filtered their way back to Progressive reformers, the huge loss of life suffered in this war would not likely have stilled their lingering doubts regarding sports, especially their inability to avert the war in the first place, even though they provide wonderful confirmation of some of the morally uplifting features that they attributed to them.

This crisis of faith in sports experienced by these first-generation Progressives intellectuals only deepened when their second-generation liberal counterparts came on the scene. They had to contend, of course, with a major war of their own, the Second World War; however, the course of events that led up to America's involvement in that war were altogether different and considerably less damning of sports and cultural practices like them. Rather, the main culprit in this instance was the continuing and steady commercialization of sports, which had progressed to the point that once these liberal reformers came of age, they pretty much took it for granted that sports had been hopelessly compromised by the market and, therefore, wrote them off as just another example of the misguided, entertainment-driven activities that make up mass culture. This is why one prominent liberal could write so off-handedly "that literature and politics are the spheres to which contemporary intellectuals look when they worry about ends rather than means."[80] This predictable turn to more high-brow fare to rescue us from the hardly upstanding consumers most of us Americans had become, to activities that because of their supposed status as ends could not be easily manipulated to serve the whims of capitalism, followed, of course, from the view that sports and their ilk were firmly and irretrievably ensconced in the dead-end enterprises of the culture industry.

In the 1960s, this depreciating picture of sports painted by intellectual types took a radical turn that made sports, hard as it might at first blush seem, look that much worse. I am speaking here of the student radicals who were the product of the civil and political tumult of the 1960s and energized by their unwavering conviction, now widely shared by most Americans, that America's entry into the Vietnam War was an ill-conceived and manifestly unjust military intervention. The growing debilitating effects of capitalism and its erosion of our political sensibilities, of America's claim to be a democratic nation above all else, played a large role here as well, as did the financing by the captains of industry of this disastrous war. So, this emergent Left not only took aim at sports but at their Progressive and liberal reform-minded predecessors as well for being much too timid in their opposition to the antidemocratic forces that were spreading throughout the country at this time. Indeed, their take-no-prisoners style of social criticism, which attacked not just the abuses of sports but everything about them, and their insistence on revolution over gradualist reform, were symptomatic of what Bernard Yack unflatteringly called a "longing for total revolution."[81] This longing itself was a product both of the "radical interactionist" theory of society with which they came armed, which insisted that all the important practices of a society are interconnected with one another,[82] and the claim of corruption that they directed at the very heart of American society. This meant that if any part of American society was infected, the entirety of it was, as nothing that occupied an important space within its precincts, as sports clearly did, could claim any degree of autonomy from the rest of society. So, it was not only sports that were defenseless against the market forces arrayed against them but everything else, including the system itself. It is little wonder, therefore, why these campus radicals scolded their Leftist predecessors for trying to work within the system to eradicate the injustices they found there, as they believed that any such efforts were only bound to strengthen the very capitalist forces that they were trying to weaken by softening the conflicts that would otherwise have inevitably burst the entire system apart.[83]

That is not to say that these New Left adherents had no legitimate beef against American society or its contemporary sports; how could they or any other semiconscious observer not given that the sorry moral condition of both, or that most of their criticisms were not in point. On the contrary, their critique of the Vietnam War helped to hasten its end, for which we can all be thankful, because it saved America from itself, from its bad, militaristic, imperialistic side. Many of their criticisms of sports were trenchant ones that revealed for all to see the extent to which sports had been savaged by the market, not to mention by the still-dominant patriarchal tendencies at work in larger society. Hence, their taking modern sports to task for the cult of manliness that they encouraged, for the violence to which they too often catered, for the joy that they gladly sacrificed as the necessary price to be paid for pursuing victory at all costs, for the unquestioned allegiance to authority that they too quickly passed off as virtuous, and for the money for which they prostituted themselves,[84] all found their mark. More importantly, they had a lot to do with subsequent efforts to address and remedy the racism and sexism still raging within America's sports.

That said, the student Left's unsparing and ruthless criticism of sports contributed in its own way to the moral leveling of sports, to a deflationary account of them that gave further traction to the idea that any belief in their moral gravitas was at best wishful thinking, the stuff of utopian flights of fancy, and at worst a blatant lie, the stuff of ideologically laden stories intended to deceive us as to the unsavory position in which we presently find ourselves. That is why, or so I argue, their critical efforts in this regard proved to be stillborn and, alas, played right into the hands of their bourgeois detractors.

Let me try to be more precise here. Although there is no question that these Leftists were on solid ground in rejecting any quasimetaphysical claim that sports are not of this world, they were skating on very thin ice, indeed, when they went on to claim that there is nothing special about sports in any respect. That is to say, it is one thing to criticize sports for falling short of their moral promise, and an altogether different thing to claim that they never had any moral promise to begin with, or at least no more than other everyday activities, as according to these Leftists, sports were so similar to these activities as to be indistinguishable from them. So, though it is not only unobjectionable but good, sound social criticism to smoke out connections between significant events in the world at large and the sporting world, to point out, as these campus radicals astutely did, that some of our overzealous urging on the home team to victory can be chalked up to the growing realization that we were not only entangled in a dubious war but were also losing that war,[85] it is objectionable to suggest that the complicity of sports in that war was somehow inevitable, given its basic character and given the state of the social world at that time. Similarly, there is no question that this Left's criticism of the Right's use of sports to stifle legitimate critical interrogation both of sports and of the war effort itself was on target, but there is equally no question that its assertion that the brutality of sports was somehow intimately bound up with the brutality of the Vietnam War itself was not on target, in fact, was so wide of the mark as to invite its own refutation.[86] The first set of claims, as I intimated, is what good social criticism of sports, or of anything else for that matter, is all about, whereas the second is what bad social criticism all too often devolves into: ideological cant borne both of a refusal to appreciate the complexity of the social world in which we live and a stubborn belief that whatever captures the hearts and minds of the many cannot possibly have anything morally or politically going for it.

What accounts for the New Left's overreach here? Mainly, two things. The first was the understandable passion in which they prosecuted their attack on sports and America. After all, it was they and their peers whose lives were being sacrificed on the killing fields of Vietnam, not only without their consent but contrary to their ferocious opposition. By comparison, student activist exuberance for desecrating the American flag, which understandably agitated Second World War veterans, and their general delight in poking fun at all the sacred cows that their adult counterparts held dear, which made enemies, among others, of members of labor unions, most of whom never went to college and so greatly resented being singled out by middle- and upper-class long-haired youth, seemed tame stuff. Of course, one of those sacred cows was sport, which the students also seemed to relish debunking every chance they could. Now, in one obvious sense, their youthful taking to task of the older generation and their fondness for traditional American sports was indeed tame stuff, as it seldom led to carnage though it did occasionally lead to bloodletting and often hard feelings. However, in another moral and political sense, it was nothing short of disastrous, estranging this emergent New Left, as it did, from labor unions and other usually democratic-leaning groups that had for the better part of a half-century formed a formidable Leftist coalition that successfully opposed and held at bay conservative countermovements. Indeed, this unfortunate splintering of the Left is something from which it has yet to recover, and judging from the inroads that American conservatives were able to make in politics and just about everything else because of their fractured and significantly weakened state, there is good reason to regard this breakup and its aftermath with considerable alarm.

However, the second reason behind the New Left's overreach in the case of sports was a self-inflicted one that was prefigured by the theory of society that they, as already noted, clung to. This was the idea that society is all of a piece and, therefore, that neither sports nor anything else can enjoy immunity from what goes on around them. So, if capitalism is the monolithic force in American society that everyone nowadays thinks it is, cheerfully in the case of the Right and, of course, forlornly in the case of the Left, that means for this particular radical Left that anything that goes on there has to be regarded by sheer theoretical dent as wholly compromised by the market. It could not be otherwise, as in its view, all social practices, as we said, are radically bound up with one another, so that once such a potentially disruptive force as the market gets its foot, so to speak, in the door of a society like ours, there is nothing standing in its way to stop it from having its way with everything with which it comes into contact. This puts paid to any account of social construction that makes room for, rather than rejects out of hand, such notions as relative autonomy on the grounds that not all practices are alike because not all of them are put together in the same way using the same materials, which at least opens up the possibility that some of these practices may well be formed in ways that make them less vulnerable to market incursions. Something very much like this, of course, is what Progressives believed, which is why, as we have duly documented, many of them singled out sports for closer scrutiny. Such extended scrutiny convinced them that sports do indeed possess certain distinctive features, like their own scrupulous brand of fairness, that other cultural practices do not, which means it would be sheer folly not to enlist them in the effort to hem in the market to prevent it from wreaking further havoc. In other words, their view of the open-ended character of social construction gave them a reason to believe that they could make a bad situation better and the hope and resolve to try to do just that. However, if, like the student Left, any talk of relative autonomy or of alternative forms of social construction must be avoided like the plague because of an overriding commitment to such a social theory as radical interactionism, reflective scrutiny of such a social practice as sport can lead only to the opposite conclusion, to the denial that any practice is more distinctive than another and, therefore, that all are equally susceptible to market entreaties. When all is said and done, therefore, the New Left's theory acts more like a black hole than anything else, sucking all the light, as it does, and the optimism that comes with it, out of such reform-oriented projects as Progressivism.

The student Left's political passions and theoretical predilections, then, explain its dour outlook on the moral and political potential of sports, which contributed, as I have been arguing throughout, to a growing skepticism about that potential across the heartland. However, to make matters worse, what scant attention these campus activists did pay to possible replacements for our present roster of traditional team sports, scant because they were too preoccupied trying to take down these "old" sports to be bothered to puzzle out their rightful successors, played, as I earlier said, right into the hands of bourgeois apologists of sports. For when they did get around to talking about this important topic, they usually ended up lauding individual sports played in virtual solitude (i.e., without teammates, opponents, or coaches) and made a point of stressing that private pleasure is the most compelling motive for pursuing these sports.[87] If this picture of sports appears familiar, that is because it should, for though some of these sports, such as Frisbee, were relatively recent inventions (of course, many others they advocated, such as running, were not), the style of play and individual bent of these athletic enterprises were strongly reminiscent of the prevailing contemporary sports scene. That is to say, these supposed alternative sports betray the same atomistic outlook of their opposite bourgeois number, which means they are long in freedom, construed narrowly as the absence of external constraints, and noticeably short on everything else that might clip its wings, especially our social relationships with others that come off, on this solipsistic interpretation of sports, exclusively as dependence relationships that cannot help but crimp our desire to do whatever we please in sports. That rules out both in and outside sports any notion of rational authority or of positive discipline or of a shared conception of the good that has a higher claim on us than our own private conceptions of the good. The fact that the New Left is unapologetically opposed both in its conception of sports and of social life to those very things that require us to take a larger, less egocentric perspective on our own lives is proof enough that its radical agenda for sports and American society is in this crucial respect at least hardly radical, as it so closely resembles the top-heavy market society and sports that we presently have. This is just another way of saying that its alternative rendering of sports is not sufficiently different from the status quo to make a difference, either theoretically or practically speaking.

## A parting shot or two and a final nod to the resilience of Americans' moral hope in their sports

It hardly needs be asked what these various causal forces, all of which I have claimed came to a head in the 1960s and led to an unprecedented market saturation of sports, have wrought. I have, of course, touched on this question in much detail in Chapters 2 and 3. Those chapters did not leave much room for hope in sports and, of course, neither does our present discussion of the root causes of the precipitous fall of contemporary sports from moral grace. Perhaps Guterson put it best when he said that it was during this period that "the economics of sport began to proliferate with such Malthusian energy that the real players – networks, the shoe companies, the owners, the agents, the ad agencies – could no longer allow the game to be dictated by, well, the games themselves."[88] This ominously suggests that once the market had managed to insinuate itself into the interior workings of the games themselves, any moral faith in their progressive promise could no longer be credibly sustained, as there was nothing evidently left to them that had not already been profaned by this profit motive. And I do mean nothing.

So, I don't think it is an exaggeration in the least to say that most Progressives, even the more sober and realistic among them, would have turned over in their graves had they known what was in store for sports and America in the last four decades or so of the twentieth century and beyond. Indeed, the present regime of sports and Americans' attitudes toward them are about as far removed from the Progressive view of sports as one can get. By comparison, the Progressives' sunny, but to their minds fully justified (because reflectively secured), outlook on sports comes off as hopelessly romantic. Of course, it was not to be, as we have painstakingly detailed, upended as it was by the market, the new cult of athletic managerial experts, and the tell-it-like-it-is version of social criticism embraced by the New Left, which in condemning sports root and branch undercut not only the moral hope that Progressives placed in sports but the very different way in which they did their critical work, which was predicated on balancing hard-headed critique of sports and America "As They Actually Exist" with, as noted in Chapter 3, a normative assessment of what they could and should be at their best.

We are once again faced, therefore, with the daunting question: where does this leave us? Is it as hopeless as it all seems, and are sports and America too far gone, no matter the theory or form of social criticism to which we subscribe, even to try to revive them? These are the final decisive questions I take up in the concluding chapter. By way of a prelude, however, I echo Zang's prescient remark that though

> No one at the turn of the [twenty-first, unlike the turn of the twentieth] century is calling sports 'the glue holding the nation together'… we still seek parables and lessons that give our games a meaning that can't be explained by a vault full of money, multiple camera angles, or press conferences. The Vietnam era made the search harder.[89]

This is, as I see it, exactly right and should give us some solace that all is not lost as long as sports are capable, however ephemerally, of summoning in us the resolve needed to undertake meaningful reform. To sustain that hope, it is not necessary to drag out the old and thoroughly discredited homilies and mythologies regarding the phony purity of sports nor to invent new ones along this or other as yet undreamt themes but rather to latch on to and articulate more forcefully the Progressive conception of sport and America that these reformers have bequeathed to us. For it is my firm conviction, one I try to back up in the ensuing chapter, that this dual conception of sport and America is the last conceptual revolution we need to right what presently ails both[90] and that if we have the gumption and reflective acumen it requires to infuse it with new life, it just might help to launch the last political effort we need to make it a reality.

# 7 Progressive sport and progressive America

## A dialectical summing up

At the close of the previous chapter, I argued that Progressives provide sports with the last conceptual but not, alas, the last political revolution they need to play their part in giving credence to the idea that America is best thought of as a moral commonwealth. The reason why Progressives were not able to deliver the political goods as well is because, as I have been arguing, the political outlook of the country has shifted of late – decisively to the Right – for reasons that are difficult to divine.[1]

With this in mind, I set two aims for myself in this concluding chapter. First, I revisit the foregoing conceptual claim, in support of which I have offered nary a snippet of argument thus far, and flesh out in just what senses sports as conceived by Progressives captures not only their moral soul but that of America itself, or at least the America, rightly to my mind, championed by Progressives. In particular, I want to show that contrary to what those on the New Left claim, such a conception of sport can indeed survive reflective scrutiny and, therefore – contrary to what those on the Right claim – can be effectively deployed to tell a story about an America in which democracy is not just another name for the freedom to exploit others in the marketplace. This sets up the second aim I set for myself in this chapter: to address the country's previously mentioned shift to the right in matters political and athletic, its baffling rejection of its political and athletic progressive past. I wish I had some new, imaginative, and interesting things to say on this latter score. However, unfortunately, I do not. Yet, I remain convinced there is still something important to be said here, indeed, that the best antidote to this tilt to the political and athletic right is to expose its reflective weaknesses as an adequate conception both of sports and of America. In other words, it is this economic conception of sports and America rather than its Progressive rival that cannot withstand reflective scrutiny and, by driving this point home, I am persuaded that Americans can be disabused of the notion, for the most part uncontested today, that markets are the best way to run their sporting and political lives. Finally, as what needs changing here is Americans' social and moral outlook on themselves as reflected through the forms of life that they share, if we can make some headway in undermining this outlook we should be in a much better position to crank out a political solution to our present difficulties.

## Sports and the social imaginary

I begin by sketching out just what hurdles a conception of sports must clear if it is to do the kind of moral and political narrative work that Progressives think that it not only can do but is uniquely equipped to do. First, it must be able to furnish a persuasive account of sports themselves, of the special features that they possess and make them stand out from other forms of life that slip under the radar of our social consciousness, that do not excite our attention or captivate us in the way that certain sports, such as football, basketball, and baseball, manage on the home front and Olympic sports manage mostly on the international front. In other words, such a conception must explain why such sports resonate as they do with the larger American public, why it is these sorts of athletic enterprises that pull on Americans' hearts and beget their passionate attachment often to the point where nothing else seems to matter in their lives, at least not to the same feverish degree. At the same time, such a conception must explain how it is that in capturing the imagination of the public in the way in which these sports do, they are able at the same time to express something distinctive about our national character, about the qualities that make us stand out as a nation from other nations. Hence, an adequate account of sports so conceived faces a dual challenge, one that requires not just a philosophy of sports but, even more important, a political philosophy of sports.

What a conception of sports that aspires to the moral and political heights sought by Progressives must accomplish, therefore, is to explain how these sports become firmly lodged in what Taylor calls the "social imaginary" of a culture. By the social imaginary, Taylor means "the ways people imagine their social existence, how they fit together with others, how things go on between them and their fellows, the expectations that are normally met, and the deeper normative notions and images that underlie these expectations."² What the social imaginary is not, therefore, is a worked-out theoretical or intellectual account of our public understanding of ourselves, or at least not at first. Rather, it is the prereflective way in which we envisage ourselves and our interactions with one another; it is how we understand what it is that we do in public and how we should go on in this social space in a way that is intelligible to our compatriots and meets the normative expectations we set for one another without having to make any of this explicit among us. So, when everything is going smoothly in our ongoing forms of life and the relationships to which they give rise, the penumbra that this social imaginary casts need not and should not be reflectively engaged. For instance, when some action on my part clearly violates the normative expectations of some well-defined practice – say, insulting a new colleague at a faculty reception – my insistence that being rude to one's colleagues in such instances is not an obvious moral offense but something that after due deliberation might even warrant praise rather than reproof is not only likely to be regarded by my colleagues, especially the one wounded by my remarks, as disingenuous but as compounding the original moral offense committed. In short, insisting that explication precede rebuke in such clear-cut instances only adds injury to insult, only makes a bad situation worse. However, when genuine breakdowns occur, as they are inevitably bound to from time to time in this mostly inarticulate and unstructured social space of reasons and values, such that it is no longer clear how it is we are supposed to understand one another or how we ought to act towards one another, careful deliberation, and following it either repairs to or innovative changes in the social imaginary, is itself a normative expectation and a paramount one at that, which overrides practically everything else. It hardly needs to be said in this regard that such reflective recovery work cannot be executed by somehow stepping outside the social imaginary that frames our lives to survey the damage, for that is not an option for us finite, socially bound creatures, because we have to make our way in life normatively and otherwise in the grip of some social imaginary or other, nor are our reflective efforts able to grasp the social imaginary in its entirety, for then it would not be a social imaginary at all, something that in encompassing the whole of our lives gives it whatever sense it possesses, but a simulacrum.[3]

So, to say that a conception of sports of the scale on which Progressives insisted, rightly I believe, is required to account for both their relative autonomous standing with respect to other social practices and their capacity to spin a yarn about what it means to be an American in the best sense of that term, is to say that such a conception must account for how sports have been able to insinuate themselves in the social imaginary of America itself. That is to say, it must show that when Americans engage in sports and observe them, what they see, understand, and grasp in the way of the meanings that they evoke and the values that they generate could not "be in the minds of certain individuals only."[4] Rather, the meaning and value of such social practices as sports must be such that, as Descombes aptly writes, it "outruns each individual mind, in that individual participation in [such] a practice expresses not only the way in which a given person sees things ... but also the way in which society considers things ought to be done."[5] Sports could play such a role, therefore, only if the meanings and values that they convey incorporate common social understandings as to how things are and should be done in larger society and if those common understandings are vetted in a public setting where they can be appropriately acknowledged and affirmed (and, of course, at times occasionally, but only occasionally, if they are to claim their rightful place in this social space of reasons and norms, disconfirmed). In other words, sports can rightfully be considered an integral part of the social imaginary of America as Progressives claim if – and only if – they can be appropriately considered part of the "social repertory of actions" by which Americans express who they are and for what they stand, which would put them on a par with such other forms of life as marriage, funeral practices, elections, and the like.[6]

We can begin to appreciate, then, the complexity and wide scope of the Progressive thesis that sports are special undertakings and that by virtue of their "special-ness" are capable of pulling off what many, many activities are not (i.e., articulating in the form of narratives, ritual expressions, symbolic action and when these fail, spirited conversations that require argumentative give and take, what it means to be an American). A final point should be made, however, before I move on to spelling out what particular meanings and values are expressed by certain sports that speak to America's progressive legacy. That point is that not all practices that rightly belong to the social repertory of actions by which Americans telegraph to themselves and others who they are and what they stand for are equally expressive in this regard. In other words, some of these practices speak more passionately to, and are more revelatory of, the social imaginary of America than others. This point is also central to the Progressive argument that such sports as baseball deserve closer scrutiny and appreciation than they typically get, given the special narrative role that they play in laying out the political philosophy of the country.

The best way in which to make this point, I believe, is to compare sports to other estimable social practices such as law. Law is a good place to start such a discussion, as there is no doubting that legal practices belong to America's social repertory of actions, expressing as they do important American views about justice, such as that every person, guilty or innocent, deserves legal representation by competent lawyers. This places a heavy onus on lawyers, as they are obligated to defend clients even if they believe (or worse, somehow know) that they are guilty. Further, because their defense of defendants, guilty or not, requires that in the course of a trial they might well be called on to impeach witnesses who have damning testimony to give against their clients and because carrying out this task more often than not mandates that it be done in a vigorous, aggressive, not to mention sardonic manner that transgresses the boundaries of everyday civil discourse, even lawyers who represent innocent, highly sympathetic figures are likely to engender some public discontent. So, efforts to impugn the reputations of adversarial witnesses, to undermine their credibility, which efforts within certain hard-to-define limits are not only considered perfectly appropriate lawyerly conduct but professionally exemplary behavior – often come off to the general public as unsavory efforts to smear good people.

That Americans have a love-hate relationship with lawyers, of course, does not warrant the banishment of law from the social imaginary of America. Far from it; justice American style, though not always a pretty sight or matter, constitutes an important part of our American identity, of our claim that ours is a nation in which no one, not even the chief executive of the land, is considered above the law. Nonetheless, it does mean that the practice of law takes some getting used to, that it requires an adaptation of sorts on the part of most Americans so that certain unattractive features that seem intrinsic to it do not overshadow its larger social and political importance.[7] That is, Americans have to learn, as it were, to disregard certain things that go on in the courtroom as a matter of course, such as the just-mentioned defense of guilty defendants or the harsh questioning of witnesses (that lawyers who are especially good at getting off guilty defendants and smearing witnesses often become quite rich as a result only exacerbates the problem), in order to maintain a healthy public respect and confidence in the law and those who practice it. However, such special adaptations as this one, which require the public to become inured to what would otherwise be considered offensive behavior, are at best tenuous arrangements that have clear limits. And when those limits are breached (the infamous O. J. Simpson trial comes quickly to mind), it becomes practically impossible, psychologically and sociologically speaking, for ordinary citizens to continue to tolerate the disagreeable behavior that they frequently observe in courtrooms. In other words, at some hard-to-measure point, the esteem that lawyers typically enjoy is put under some strain, which is just another way of saying that the general public starts to see them as importantly different from the rest of us, as practitioners of a craft that turns them into the sort of people that make us uneasy to deal with them or be around them. To reiterate, this does not in itself invalidate or undo the special adaptation responsible for the law's still-impressive standing in society, but it does explain the present morally schizophrenic public view of lawyers who, on the one hand, continue to attract wide public acclaim, which is why so many of us evidently are tripping over one another trying to get into the most prestigious law schools, not least aspiring politicians (which, of course, is another can of worms) and yet who, on the other hand, find themselves the butt of seemingly endless jokes (surpassed only perhaps by the proverbial dumb blond jokes). It also explains, more important for my purposes, why it is that the expressive capacity of such practices as law to tell an uplifting story about America that might inspire it to reform itself, despite its continued good press, is not up to snuff in most people's eyes.

The case is different, or so I argue, with respect to sports, not in the sense that they require no special adaptation to be fully palatable to the general public, for most "American" sports demand some sort of adjustment in this regard. Further, some sports, particularly those such as boxing where violence is not an incidental matter and where, therefore, its place in a liberal democratic society that makes no bones about its opposition to gratuitous displays of violence immediately casts a negative pall over it, cannot get by without some significant adaptation on the part of the public.[8] The problem with boxing, of course, is that it involves not just the use of physical force but the deliberate intent to inflict physical harm on another, in which even the euphemisms employed to mask the violence – punches, knockdowns, and the like – are only able to do so in slightly muted tones. In the case of America's three quintessential sports (baseball, basketball, and football), however, only football, the dependence of which on physical aggression is undeniable, requires anything like the adaptation accounted boxing. Of course, it helps that any attribution of intentional use of physical force to harm others in football does not wash when critically probed. That is not to say that the other members of this athletic troika – basketball and baseball – do not require getting used to in other ways, given, for example, their history of sexism and racism (football, of course, is no exception here either), nor that these sports are beyond moral reproach in every other respect, which as I tried to show in Chapter 2 is manifestly not the case. However, it is to say at least two important things: first, that these sports enjoy the public's affection and trust to a degree that most other social practices can only envy but not come close to emulating, and second, that one of the reasons why this is so, why the public reputation of sports is better than that most other endeavors and probably better than it currently deserves, is that Americans are more apt and willing to separate out the good things from the bad things that occur in sports. That means that they are less likely to do what they typically do with respect to other spheres of life: to run together the former with the latter, to assume, as they do in the case of law and lawyers for example, that the bad things that happen in sport cannot be helped, because they are peculiar to its practice. How long the public's romance-like embrace of these sports, warts and all, will continue is anyone's guess. However, we can count on one thing, or so I have been claiming throughout: that we are most assuredly headed for a moral train wreck here, a point at which the market's saturation of sports will make it extremely difficult for anyone, let alone the general public, to believe that there is not a causal relationship between the bad things that happen in sports and how it is, owing to economic imperatives, that we must make our way within their no-longer-hallowed precincts.

## Sports and freedom-in-equality

I hope I have said enough so far to show that sports are an important part of America's social imaginary, of the way in which Americans think and imagine themselves, especially when that thinking and imagining figures importantly in their conception of themselves as free, democracy-loving people. However, establishing the place of sports in the cultural firmament of America is only a necessary first step in getting the Progressive account of sports off the ground. It is the next step that is the most crucial one, and that is to show that the Progressives' heady treatment of and healthy regard for sports as a moral anodyne for atomism, a persistent affliction, I have been arguing, of market societies that has once again reared its ugly head, can be rationally and normatively vindicated. In trying to press the case that it can indeed be so vindicated, I of necessity cover some of the same ground over which I have already gone in previous chapters. However, as my focus here is principally a justificatory one, to establish that the Progressive take on sports is as crucial now as it was before to the success of the Progressive effort to refashion America into a moral commonwealth, most of this rehashed material will be presented in a new light, and some of it will be original.

Any such account of sports must address sooner rather than later the notion of freedom, which is perhaps the single most important feature that marks us modern agents off from our premodern predecessors and which is absolutely central to the self-image of such liberal democracies as America. For if America is anything, it is a child of modernity, more precisely, a child of the Enlightenment, the main aim of which, it will be remembered, was to loosen human agents from hierarchical societies and from, in particular, the hierarchical schemes that such societies entertained in order to maintain dominion over people's lives. As heirs to this Enlightenment tradition, therefore, Americans and their modern counterparts were socialized to avert their eyes, initially at any rate, from the heavens when considering their lot in life and their particular life-plans, whether it be some authoritarian religion or some complicated cosmological scheme, such as the "great chain of being." Instead, they were directed to look to themselves, to decide for themselves what kind of life they want to live (including whether they want to live a religious life) and to build social and political institutions that accommodate those human yearnings and the freedom that gives rise to them. In a nutshell, the idea was "to create heaven on earth: a world without caste, class, or cruelty."[9]

This Enlightenment counsel that human agents should take matters into their own hands, should spurn the heavens above in favor of building a heaven on earth – one in which individuals make sacrifices for one another and for future generations so that they might all lead better, more decent lives – was, to say the least, taken to heart by the early founders of the American republic, especially the idea that a free society could not be free unless all its citizens were free, unless the social and political institutions that they erected were egalitarian ones that ensured everyone an opportunity to exercise that freedom. Fortunately for my purposes, this project to create a model society based on freedom and equality was not always tied up in the minds of these early Americans with another piece of advice that can also be traced back to the Enlightenment: the thoroughly rationalist claim that building a truly free society required a new philosophic world-view, one "which would replace God with Nature and Reason."[10] This intellectual battle between Enlightenment rationalists, who insist that democratic politics be grounded in universal principles of human conduct, and Enlightenment historicists (to include their postmodernist successors), who "hope to do to Nature, Reason and Truth what the eighteenth century did to God,"[11] is, of course, still being hotly waged today. As I said, however, that need not concern us at present, because though Jefferson and his ilk often liked to speak and write in such rationalist and universalist terms, they did not always feel obliged to do so.[12] This would explain why in his *A Summary View of the Rights of British Americans*, a precursor to his penning of the Declaration of Independence a couple of years later, Jefferson offered what Hitchens indelicately called a "tribal" defense of human rights, which consisted of a simple but completely persuasive two-step argument. The first step noted the ancient Saxon settlers voluntary relocation from the European continent to the island of England and then likened it to the American settlers' voluntary relocation from that island to a new continent; and the second step simply pointed out that no loss or infringement of liberties or rights to form "self-ruling and autonomous communities" could be divined or incurred from such voluntary relocations. So, in two deft moves, Jefferson was able to show, without waxing metaphysical in the least, that Americans enjoyed the same liberties and rights as English citizens did.[13]

That means that Jefferson and those like him made it possible for Americans to talk about freedom and to design social institutions that featured it without having to pay homage to Reason (as we have noted, modernity's substitute for God) in order to justify their doing so. That also made it possible to concentrate their moral and political attention on a simple social fact: that our freedom to live our lives as we see fit always gets exercised in some social practice or other. That means that what goes on in these social practices is essential to our agency, to our capacity to accomplish the aims that we set for ourselves within them. So, how these practices are put together and what institutional safeguards are in place that ensure that they are in good working order, are crucial to our effort to create a meaningful life for ourselves. Hence, we ignore these social practices only at our own peril, only at the expense of the very freedom that we claim as our birthright, and of the social and political institutions that we erect in its name and on which we stake our reputation as an authentic democratic republic.

Now, let us grant that all of our home-grown social practices and institutions either are or should be ones that further our thoroughly modern determination to live self-determined lives. That said, however, are there some of these practices and institutions that are better suited than others to realize such an autonomous life, that, in other words, take us farther down the path of freedom? This is an important question not only because in answering it we can get clearer about what, exactly, we are calling freedom here and about how we might best secure it, but because given the modern creatures we are, it is not only *verboten* to look to the heavens for an answer but *verboten* as well to look to a single, all-encompassing form of life for an answer. We cannot give ourselves such latitude in the latter case, because any liberal democratic society rightly so called is not likely to have such authoritative, all-encompassing forms of life around in the first place. In other words, it is no accident that such modern nations as America that take pride in the freedom that they provide their citizens to forge their own lives are almost always radically pluralistic societies, societies in which no social practice can claim a monopoly on the desires and aims of their citizens as, for example, religion did in premodern times.

Interestingly enough, however, this very point about the necessarily pluralistic character of liberal democracies provides the normative yardstick that we need to answer our foregoing question regarding whether some social practices are better equipped than others to deliver the kind of autonomous lives that we associate with such societies. For the reason why genuinely democratic societies are necessarily pluralistic is the same reason why some social practices register higher on the freedom scale than others: because they comport better with the model of agency that modern self-conscious autonomous individuals would recognize as valid for themselves. In other words, these practices come closer to the ideal of human agency that members of democratic societies would accept as authoritative for themselves, as they best capture their understanding of just what sort of free, autonomous agents they are. Another, perhaps better way to say this is that forms of life that reveal what William James called the *trace of the human serpent*, of self-conscious human agency, on both their ends and means afford individuals greater freedom, and so self-determination, than do forms of life in which that human trace is evident only in their means but not their ends.

This suggests that we can profitably arrange social practices (i.e., put them in some normatively compelling order) according to whether they fall under the realm of necessity, which is characterized by the fact that the ends pursued there are not the product of human willing so much as they are dictated by certain natural facts about human agents (principally that they are finite, mortal beings and as such must assume and maintain an instrumental relation to the world and other human agents in order to secure their own existence) or whether they fall under the realm of freedom, which is characterized by the fact that the ends pursued there are wholly the product of human willing, because these ends exist only because these practices do, only because they were created by human agents to express themselves in ways that would otherwise not be possible. This arrangement leads us back, admittedly after a long but not, I think, circuitous line of argument, to the Progressive conception of sports. For it is evident from the way in which Progressives pitched their account of sports that they firmly believed sports should be slotted into the realm of freedom and, therefore, that they have only an incidental connection to the sorts of things that we do to secure our existence as natural beings. Of course, it goes without saying that this normative placing of sports is one of the primary factors that recommends the Progressive account to us today and is, therefore, central to my effort to vindicate their use of sports as a narrative vehicle by which to remind Americans of the moral ideals that come with citizenship in a democratic social setting.

No less a figure than Hegel himself worked out an almost identical account of sports from his interpretation of the ancient Greek games, which at first, he noted, were strictly private affairs but soon turned into "an affair of the nation." Though I later argue that the Greek's conception of sport falls woefully short as an adequate account of sport when stacked up against the modern, Progressive conception, Hegel's rendering makes a decidedly modern point about the sort of freedom sport offers human agents, notwithstanding the ancient source of his reflections, that is, as I said, illustrative of the Progressive's conception of sport. As Hegel writes,

> If we look at the inner nature of these [Greek] sports, we observe first how sport itself is opposed to serious business, to dependence and need. This wrestling, running, contending was no serious affair; it *bespoke no obligation* of defense, no necessity of combat. Serious occupation is labor that has reference to some need. Man or nature must succumb; if the one is to live, the other must fall. In contrast with this kind of seriousness, sport presents the higher seriousness; for in it nature is wrought into spirit. In this exercise of physical powers, man shows his *freedom* [my emphasis], he shows that he has transformed his body into an organ of spirit.[14]

What is more, the distinction that Hegel draws here between such activities as work that are rooted in necessity and such activities as sport that are rooted in freedom, is remarkably similar to a distinction that Marx was to make not long after in *Das Kapital*. I air Marx's rendition of this distinction first before I comment on Hegel's, because it helps to clarify the thrust of Hegel's argument here and adds an important feature to it. Marx's gloss thus goes like this:

> The realm of freedom actually begins only where labour which is determined by necessity and mundane considerations ceases; thus in the very nature of things it lies beyond the sphere of actual material production … Freedom in this field [of necessity] can only consist in socialized man, the associated producers, rationally regulating their interchange with Nature, bringing it under their common control, instead of being ruled by it as by the blind forces

of Nature … But it nonetheless still remains a realm of necessity. Beyond it begins that development of human energy which is an end in itself, the true realm of freedom, which can blossom forth only with this realm of necessity as its basis. The shortening of the working day is its basic prerequisite.[15]

What do these two passages tell us then, when conjoined? The first and most obvious, if not most important, point is that unlike activities that are beholden to aims steeped in our need to produce and reproduce the material means of our existence, the aims that govern sports are beholden to nothing save the constraints that we build into these forms of life in order to give them some discernable shape and in order to make it possible for us to execute our agency within them. That suggests that because those aims and ends are part of the social space that we create for ourselves in these practices, they cannot help but enhance our freedom rather than impede it, as they are constituted through and through by our agency. That means further that because the constraints and imperatives that partly define that social space are as well things that we have put there rather than things that have been imposed on us, these constraints cannot be treated as if they are obstacles that stand in the way of our self-determination but only as contrivances that further, as they were expressly designed to do, our self-determination. So, literally everything about sports – the ends that they pursue, the excellences that they stand for, and rules that govern them – are human creations, are artifacts suffused from top to bottom with the stamp of human agency. It is no wonder, then, that Hegel portrayed sports as one of the preeminent places in which human agents get to showcase their freedom, where human willing and striving rather than something external to them, something overpoweringly nonhuman, such as Nature or Reason, are properly regarded as the animating force of these sports. It is no wonder further why Marx thought that "true … freedom … can blossom" only in such practices as sport that lie "beyond" the realm of necessity, practices that exist only because we have willed them into existence in order to activate certain human capacities and realize certain human aims that would not only otherwise be unavailable but unknowable to us. In this sense, the limits of our freedom, what we are capable of and what we are not, are coincident with the limits of the forms of life that we have created for ourselves. To sum up this first point, then, it is precisely because sport and their ilk are in this sense entirely optional affairs, endeavors that we can take or leave, attend to or not, pursue or ignore, without apparent consequence to our survival (but with, I argue shortly, great consequence to the quality of our lives) that they are entirely free, self-determining affairs and why they were singled out for this very reason by the likes of Hegel, and perhaps even more remarkably, given his great preoccupation with labor, by Marx and, of course, by American Progressive thinkers and reformers.

What Hegel's and Marx's distinction contributes further to the vindication of the Progressive take on sports is that it suggests the relation that ought to obtain between them and activities like work. In this regard, it is not so much that such things as work offer us no glimpse of freedom, that self-determination plays no role in the world of work, but that it offers us at best only a partial, incomplete liberation. That is because the ends that work serves are not artifacts but, as I have been arguing, natural facts, facts about human agency that are not of our own choosing or making and that, try as we might, we cannot make our own in the way in which we can make the ends of sports our own. Still, the means that we devise to realize those ends are of our own self-choosing and are, therefore, self-constituted.[16] So, when we reflect and decide on what means to employ to achieve our natural ends and when we do so in the rational manner that Marx suggests as associated producers, we win for ourselves not only a temporary reprieve, as it were, from nature – our survival – but the leisure to pursue forms of life in which freedom is not circumscribed by ends imposed on us.

This is the way in which things ought to go in a well-ordered democratic society in which free self-determination is the be-all and end-all of such a society. This is what Marx meant when he said that beyond the realm of necessity "begins that development of human energy which is an end in itself," which is, in other words, not geared to our self-preservation but our autonomous self-assertion. Something very much like this is what Hegel meant as well when he argued that "sport" in contrast to work "presents the higher seriousness" and when he went on to claim in a related vein that in sport "man shows his freedom" by showing "that he has transformed his body into an organ of spirit." Sport presents the "higher seriousness" to Hegel's way of thinking, and by implication to Marx's and Progressives' as well, because the seriousness of work is parasitic on that of such practices as sport. For there would be no point in working, in securing the conditions of our material sustenance, unless life were worth the candle in the first place, and it is precisely such things as sport that make life worth living, in part by making possible an unfettered form of self-determination that work and such instrumental activities as it cannot deliver on their own accord save by making themselves unnecessary, superfluous. In other words, the entire point of life is to get to the point at which we do not have to work anymore, so that we can exercise our freedom in contrived social settings in which the natural imperatives that life throws our way can be safely ignored because safely disposed of.

Now, it is when we come to this realization about our lives, about the way in which they should be normatively ordered so that we can live a truly fulfilled and good life, that what we set out to do in our work and everyday lives, that is, what we do intentionally in those lives, is suffused with a self-understanding that makes it apparent to us *why* we are doing what we are doing there: to work so that we can spend most of if not all our time occupied in one or another practice in the realm of freedom. Another way of saying this is that when we come to see both how to achieve an autonomous life and the point of doing so, we become self-conscious beings rather than merely conscious ones, or as Hegel would put it, we make the all important leap from consciousness to *Geist*, Spirit.[17] That is the point behind his claim that in sports we are able to transform our bodies into organs of Spirit, as by doing so we come to see the proper rational and normative relation between what we do in the realm of necessity and why and what we do in the realm of freedom and why. In coming to see this, we are able to see further how it is that our activities in the realm of necessity can go wrong (again, rationally and normatively speaking) by not living up to the instrumental standards that we build into these activities and thus hold over our heads when engaging in them and how things in the realm of freedom can go wrong by not living up to the decidedly noninstrumental standards that we build into these social practices and thus hold over our heads when engaging in them. This is no trivial point, nor a merely theoretical one, because what rides on our coming to understand why work cannot and should not be regarded and treated as an end-in-itself and why such forms of life as sports can (indeed, must) and should be so regarded and treated is the difference between a life riddled with contradiction and incoherence that undermine our self-determination and a life free of such contradiction and incoherence that underwrite our self-determination.

That is not the half of it, however. As this pivotal connection between sports and freedom, which I am touting here as one of the important points that the Progressive conception of sports has going for it over its rivals and is also the reason why, to reiterate, I am pushing their account of sports as our best hope for turning around the present morally disquieting state of the contemporary sports scene, implicates as well our relationship to others in sports. It cannot help but do so, because the very features of sports that are responsible for their inclusion in the vaunted realm of freedom are also responsible for the joint action that they set in motion and the special interactions with others that they elicit that strengthen the self-determination sports offer those who take them up.

To see what role these relationships with others play in bolstering the free self-determination that sports make available, we need to pick up our discussion of the distinctive social composition of sporting ends at precisely the point at which we left it: the fact that these ends are wholly human contrivances. It was this fact about sporting ends, we noted, that explained how these forms of life are able to advance us farther down the path of freedom than such activities as work are able to, given that the latter are tethered to ends that exist independently of them. Further, it was the contrived character of these sporting ends that also accounted for, as discussed in Chapter 6, their complexity, the fact that these ends are inclusive of the means permitted to achieve them and, therefore, inclusive of the rules that tell us which of these means are permissible and which not. As the complex makeup of these ends also pushes us in a noninstrumental direction, because they militate against, on pain of contradiction (both conceptual and practical), any effort to pry the goal of the game (winning) loose from the play that leads up to it so that the latter can serve as a means to the former, this fact about them also serves notice that they best fit in the realm of freedom rather than the realm of necessity. That is why trying to win a footrace by tripping one's opponent, to reprise the example I used in the previous chapter, although a perfectly intelligible not to mention morally unobjectionable thing to do (presuming it is ever appropriate to treat others exclusively in this way) from an instrumental standpoint, is a perfectly unintelligible not to mention morally debauched thing to do from a game standpoint.[18] Its incoherence in this instance is a matter of its goading one to pursue an end (winning) in a way (instrumental) that makes its attainment not just improbable but impossible. The nub of my argument so far is thus that the noninstrumental manner in which sports are put together, socially constructed, has everything to do with the greater freedom they afford those who take them up. What should now be obvious but which still needs some argumentative shoring up is that what goes for the distinctive social composition of the ends of sports and, so, their means and rules, goes as well for the human relationships that they engender, which, true to form, betray a similar noninstrumental construction.

This point regarding our interpersonal relationships in sports comes clean if we note yet a third important feature of sporting ends, a feature that kicks in only when the perfectionist character of these thoroughly contrived ends is acknowledged. For in their best perfectionist form, these sporting ends qualify as full-blown shared ends, a fact that further strengthens my earlier appropriation of Descombes's argument as to why such aims cannot exist just in the head of particular individuals, in what, as discussed in Chapter 4, Williams labeled our individual subjective motivational sets, but rather must permeate the "general mind" of the relevant sport practice community, what might be called their intersubjective motivational set, which in our case includes those untold numbers of Americans for whom certain sports are, for all intents and purposes, their national religion. We can see this most clearly in the case of team sports (a further nod to the Progressive account here) in which individuals map their individual life projects and aims onto the common projects and aims of sports themselves and, in doing so, take those collective aims as their own, something that they can do only, of course, because, once again, those aims are quite literally human artifacts. What we have here, then, is perhaps what can best be described as a process of self-enlargement by which an *I* becomes a *we*, the consequence of which is that it becomes next to impossible to tell where the agency of one individual leaves off and that of another begins. That is why it is an exercise in futility in such instances to try to draw a line between the agency of individual participants in a practice and the agency, the irreducibly social agency, that the practice itself exacts of its participants, because when individuals make the ends of sports their very own, the actions that they undertake in their name, in compliance with what they demand of us, are every bit their (individual) action as they are the collective action of the practice community. That is as it is and should be when the rightful author of a social action is a communal *we* rather than an isolated *I*. Of course, that does not mean that one cannot for analytical purposes differentiate between the relative performances of individual participants, but it does mean that one cannot plausibly assess the strength or quality of those performances or make any similar substantive judgment of the joint action that takes place there in this disjointed, atomistic manner.

What goes for qualitative judgments in sports goes in spades for the collective agency that they generate, because the actions and effects of each member of the practice community, as argued, cannot be sundered from the actions and effects of every other member of that community without distortion. So, we see once again a familiar pattern emerging here, in which the noninstrumental character of the ends of sports rubs off on every other feature of athletic agency and further on the kinds of human relationships they require and where this leads in each case to a further enhancement of our self-determination. For it would be just as much a deterrent to our freedom to pursue athletic excellence by treating sports as means rather than as ends in themselves, because that would connect them up to (natural) ends over which they have no say and, therefore, no control, as to pursue excellence by treating one's teammates and opponents in sports as means rather than ends in themselves, because that would fragment the common agency of the practice community and, as a result, diminish what they would otherwise be capable of achieving together. In both cases, then, the firm stricture against instrumentalism that sports enforces bolsters rather than weakens our freedom.

This explains why I cannot be said to be acting against myself, to be contravening my own freedom, when as a member of such a practice community I act in a certain way that it calls for, in a way that its rules, norms, and aims prescribe. For the unity of purpose that suffuses and guides my actions and those of every other member of that community ensures that we are not working at cross-purposes to one another, that we are indeed a genuine community bound tightly together by our common aspirations to achieve excellence. This is, after all, what the transformation from an *I* to a *we* (which we referenced earlier) comes to, as when we engage in sports and appropriate the forms of life that they make available to us, the actions that we undertake in their name can no longer be broken up and assigned to you or me but must be regarded as our action, as something that can only be appropriately assigned collectively to us. Something very much like this displacement of an atomistic *I* for a communitarian *we*, or as Hegel put it, an "'I' that is 'we' and 'we' that is 'I,'"[19] I think, is what Spinoza had in mind when he exclaimed, "None but those who are free are united by the closest bond of friendship," to which Baier fittingly and helpfully adds, that in such close bonds, there is an "awareness of increasing freedom, accompanied by the idea of another as the cause of that increase."[20]

It is no wonder, therefore, why the first-person plural *we* gets tossed around as frequently as it does in sports settings by both players and spectators alike, a point I have occasion to examine more closely later. However, I mention it here only to underscore how tight a weld it is that holds the respective members of sport practice communities together and how the tightness of that weld gives greater scope to our self-determination. For what goes on in sports, both the actions that take place there and the meanings they evoke and the values that they put into play, is not just a shared affair but, additionally, a very public one.[21] This is important because it not only shows that the actions, meanings, and values that sports excite are common, shared ones but that a mutual understanding and public acknowledgment of the shared character of these actions, meanings, and values is itself a crucial feature of any athletic *we*. This is obvious in the case of the players themselves, who by virtue of the way in which sports are structured, let their actions do most, if not all, of their talking for them (of course, many elite athletes talk a good game as well, but most of this talk is for private consumption and, if it is not backed up by athletic prowess on the field, is usually dismissed as idle chatter) and in which public recognition of what those actions convey is paramount. In other words, it is very much a part of the excellence generated in sports that it is generated for us, the sporting public, which means that an important part of the intentional apparatus of players is focused specifically on creating excellence for public recognition.[22] This is no less true of spectators, who sometimes let their emotions and passions do their talking for them but just as often vocalize these emotions and passions and, when necessary, which seems most of the time, are more than willing to argue with one another about the significance and value of what they have witnessed on the field. Here, too, the passions vented, the meanings vocalized and then debated, are meant for public consumption, are a matter for us, the sporting public, to take up mutually. Whether what gets said in such contexts is worth listening to is for my present purposes beside the point. Rather, what is of interest here is the extent to which both players and spectators alike are willing to go, and in the particular case of players structurally obliged to go, to circulate in public space for others to take notice of and respond to the passion and love for the game that they hold in common. This is yet another sense in which sports encourage interpersonal relationships that tilt toward friendship and, as just noted, even love, or at least friendship and love writ large, as what is crucial to all of these bonds is that some mutual acknowledgment of what ties them together is incorporated into, and thus constitutes an important part of, the bond itself. What is unique to sports, of course, and central to my championing of the Progressive view of sports here, is the scale of that acknowledgment, which must be, if I am right, a public matter and at opportune times a national matter.

As we have seen here and in the previous chapter, then, this talk of a *we* in sports is not mere rhetoric but the real thing. That is perhaps most obvious when we ask more specifically just what sort of interpersonal relationships sports enjoin? The answer is first and foremost that everyone cooperate in the mutual effort to realize the in-built perfectionist aims of sports, that everyone collude in what Rawls calls "the common desire … that there should be a good … game."[23] The cooperation called for here cuts across that which one would naturally expect from one's teammates and encompasses, per necessity, one's opponents as well, because without their mutual agreement to seek excellence, the game could not honor its perfectionist aims. Indeed, in the absence of such mutual concurrence, one would have less reason or incentive to appropriate the ends of sports, to make them one's own.

In order to avoid any possible misunderstanding on this point, however, it is important to be clear as to what is precisely the object of this requisite mutual concurrence. What that agreement is decidedly not reducible to is simply the common desire for the same thing or end, because, as Rawls adroitly writes, "Grant and Lee were one in their desire to hold Richmond but this desire did not establish community between them."[24] In other words, some social (shared) intentions, like Grant's and Lee's, are downright unsocial in their effect, as they drive a wedge between people and communities and impel them to act at cross-purposes to one another. In the case of sports, such intentions are, of course, what make most sports the competitive affairs they assuredly are, in which players act in opposition to one another, which means that one cooperates with one's teammates but frustrates, or tries to frustrate, one's opponents. That is why it is wrong to say that players cooperate in the sense intended here in their shared desire to achieve the specific state of affairs that define particular sports, what Suits calls the prelusory goal of games (prelusory because it includes only the exact specification of what these varying states of affairs consist of, for example, crossing the finish line first in a footrace) and wrong or at very least misleading to say they cooperate in their shared desire to win the game, what Suits calls the lusory goal of games (lusory because it includes a specification of the rules and so the permissible means that must be followed to win a game, for example, crossing the finish line first in a footrace by, among other things, running around the track rather than across it).[25] The reason why players cannot be said to collude with regard to these game goals is because the achievement of either one of them by a player or a team precludes their achievement by everyone else. In other words, whoever achieves the prelusory or the lusory goals (or both) of sports does so, strictly speaking, exclusively, which is just an elliptical way of saying sports are zero-sum games, that there can be, to be technically exact, only one winning player or team.

So, what players must cooperate about if the game is to be what Rawls calls a "good" one, is not, strictly speaking, the prelusory or lusory goals of games but the perfectionist aims that inform or should inform these goals. It is not enough, therefore, that competitors simply have a shared desire to achieve the prelusory goal of a game, because one can do so by cheating, and excellence in cheating is not the (perfectionist or, for that matter, lusory) aim of sports, and it is not enough that players simply have a shared desire to win a game, because sometimes winning and excellence are not synonymous (owing to sloppy play, or to mismatched opponents, or to ruthless play, etc.). Rather, the concurrence mandated here touches on something that runs much deeper, on a resolute commitment to nothing less than a shared way of life that defines itself by and prides itself on the excellence that it engenders.[26] It is this shared commitment to a perfectionist form of life and the cooperation it entails, therefore, to which all must mutually subscribe in sports if, that is, they are to fulfill their esthetic and moral potential.

To focus for the moment on the moral potential of sports, it should be said that this shared commitment to give one's competitors a good game is what softens the hard edges of the competitive striving that is no less a central element of sports, because sports are, after all, quintessential competitive endeavors. What should not be lost sight of here, however, is that the competitive fires that sports deliberately set and fan would quickly flame out were it not for the fact that they are parasitic on the kind of cooperation that follows from a mutual commitment to the perfectionist constraints that define an athletic life. That is to say, my effort to frustrate my opponent's actions takes place itself in a cooperative framework not only in which it is mutually understood that each of us will try to parry the other's every move but in which it is mutually understood further that this competitive posturing back and forth is the way in which things are supposed to and, therefore, should go in sports if the excellence attained on the playing field is to amount to anything worthy of public recognition. Hence, the competitive strivings that sports provoke are provoked in this larger cooperative context, and it is this context from which they derive their moral orientation.

The kind of cooperation that sports call for, however, should be distinguished from two other cooperative schemes with which it is commonly but wrongly confused. The first such scheme with which it should not be conflated is the sort of ad hoc cooperation that goes on, as discussed in Chapter 4, between freestanding individuals (i.e., individuals whose overriding aim is to satisfy their own private preferences). It is, of course, a commonplace in such instances that cooperation is often a necessary vice if I am going to get what I want, as my efforts to do just this often require the witting or unwitting compliance of others. This is why the relationships that are a product of such egoistic efforts are always of the instrumental kind, wherein we try to use one another to achieve our private ends and often have a manipulative cast, because the point of my interactions with others is to get them to act in ways that further my ends and so my best self-interests and not their ends and so their best self-interests, which is, of course, precisely the point of their egoistically driven interactions with me. There is precious little if anything mutual or shared in these sorts of quasicoercive cooperative arrangements, as their point, no matter how many people may get caught up in them, is always individual. I say *quasicoercive* here because, of course, if there were any way for me to get what I want without having to depend on others to do so, to get out from under the dependence that they foist on me, I would gladly and quickly break off all such interactions. That there is as well hardly anything that would remotely qualify as moral about these interactions is also evident, but what is, unfortunately, especially in these market-saturated times, less evident is that sports fare very poorly indeed when they have to do their bidding in terms of such stilted relationships.

The cooperative arrangements characteristic of sports should also not be run together with those associated with contractual relationships, a point we had occasion to mention ever so briefly in the previous chapter. For sports are not a species of social contracts for at least two important reasons. First, they are not, as already noted, the product of what Rawls calls "deliberative performative acts," the kind, for instance, of performative acts involved in promise making. Rather, the cooperation that sports call for issues directly from the perfectionist way of life that they embody and which we as members of the relevant practice community appropriate and thus internalize, make our own. So, they are not the product of some explicit compact that I am sworn to uphold in the presence of others but rather part of the (ethical) know-how that any member of the practice community is supposed and expected to pick up in order to navigate their way in sports. That is not to say that sports are constitutionally allergic to such quasicontractual promises (the Olympic Oath to which all Olympic athletes swear comes quickly to mind), only that they are practically and normatively unnecessary and where enacted are derivative of the collective commitment that sports ask of us.

This point becomes clearer when we consider the second way in which the cooperation elicited in sports differs from that elicited in contracts. Contracts bind us in formal and formulaic ways that demand strict reciprocity, such that if X does A, Y is obligated to do B. These obligations are typically spelled out for all concerned so that the expected obligation incurred from the performance of some action is not lost on anyone and so that reciprocity is repaid in a timely fashion. However, the cooperation peculiar to sports borders more so, once again, on friendship, wherein the bonds of reciprocity that tie us together are neither formal, formulaic, or impersonal, and where the reciprocity that obtains between friends and competitors alike is rooted in the confidence and trust that we have gained in one another by virtue of our special relationship rather than any contractually wrung obligation. Just, then, as friendships do not abide algorithm-like calibrations of the sort that we find in contracts, neither do sports. On the contrary, what draws and holds us together in friendships and sports is, in the first instance, the unique, inimitable qualities significant others present to us and in the second, the unique, inimitable qualities of the form of life that sports present to us. That is why it would not only be highly inappropriate but also highly insulting to insist too strenuously that I pay exactly half the tab for a lunch to which my friend has invited me and fully intended to pay for, or, short of that, to let it be known that the first chance I get I will take my friend out for a lunch of comparable monetary worth and pick up the tab in order to return the favor, to, as it were, balance the books of reciprocity. Similarly, it would be highly inappropriate and highly insulting for me to demand of my competitors before the competition an eye-for-an-eye strategy for getting on with one another, such that if I compliment or, as the case may be, slight my competitors they are obligated either to return the favor or the insult. Friends who consistently act in these over-the-top, rigidly reciprocal ways will soon have no friends left them to insult, and competitors who insist on behaving likewise will, depending on the circumstances, either soon find themselves without competitors too or engaged with competitors in which the relationships between them does not remotely resemble those akin to friendship. That is why friends, true friends, are loathe to treat each other this way and, therefore, predisposed to act in ways that affirm the personal bond that exists between them and why competitors, true competitors, are loathe to treat each other in this way either, and, therefore, predisposed to act in perfectionist ways that affirm the interpersonal bond that exists between them as well.

I think I am on solid ground, then, in claiming that the cooperative character of sports not only softens their agonistic tendencies but, more importantly, moralizes them. The noninstrumental bent of that cooperation suggests as much, because it is, as noted in Chapter 4, an important element of any moral relationship properly so called. Hence, it should now be clear why, in addition to what has been said thus far, yet another necessary condition that must be met if one is to attain excellence in sports is that it be achieved fairly. Fairness so understood means, of course, that everyone be treated equally in sports, that with respect to opportunity and conditions but not, as we have seen, results, everyone be afforded a fair chance to contribute to athletic excellence. Indeed, this is the only way to ensure that sports live up to their perfectionist aims, as equality denied in this regard is tantamount to excellence denied. This is why Taylor's expression "freedom-in-equality" is especially felicitous in the case of sports, because freedom in this realm cannot be secured unless everyone is treated equally, and as athletic excellence cannot be achieved unless that fairness is conducive to our self-determination. I would be remiss if I did not note further that it is because freedom, equality, and the excellences sought in sports all line up in just the right way here that not only is Taylor's at-first-blush curious coupling of freedom and equality given the credence it deserves but the Progressive's effort to find egalitarian confirmation for their forward-thinking moral and political views in sports given its just due as well. Fletcher's following apposite observation clinches, I believe, the Progressive case for sports on this very ground. For I think he is right to say that the heavy employment of "sporting metaphors" to carry out the daily transactions of life in such English-speaking countries as America discloses "a striking feature of English and American culture. We cannot think about human relationships without thinking about sports and the idiom of fair and foul play." William James could not have said it any better. The fact that this heavy linguistic reliance on fair play, which would not obtain unless it did substantively figure in our everyday lives in just the way in which Fletcher intimates, is not the case in "French, German, Russian, Italian, or any other major language or culture of the West," only makes the prescience of Progressive thought on this important matter all the more impressive.[27]

The upshot of my argument so far has been devoted almost entirely to showing how the all-important link between sports and self-determining freedom, which, of course, Progressives made the centerpiece of their account of sports, is owed principally to their noninstrumental social composition (i.e., to the wholly self-contrived character of their ends, means, and rules) and to the noninstrumental relationships with others that these self-made features of sports encourage. It is true that I have paid some mind to the instrumental things that go on within the noninstrumental, institutionalized shell of sports, as apparent, for example, in the competitive striving that defines most sports, which explains further the heavy reliance on technology and strategic thinking that goes on within their "sacred" precincts and which are all paradigmatic examples of instrumental reasoning not to mention the self-assertion of the *I* that resides in and partially animates the *we* that is the trademark of athletic agency. However, there is another sense of freedom important to sports about which we have not as yet talked and which bears witness further to the instrumental calculations and individual predilections at work there, all of which, of course, must do their bidding within the noninstrumental and communal space marked out by sports. The freedom that I have in mind here is an offshoot of the notion of equal opportunity, which we have already discussed at length and is most commonly referred to as "the career open to talents." The thoroughly modern idea that something such as sports could be plausibly regarded as an example, indeed a paradigmatic example, of a career open to talent adds something genuinely important to the sports and freedom connection that I have been touting for some pages now in an effort to showcase the normative potency of the Progressive conception of sports. As always, however, what it adds to this connection requires not a little explanation.

The idea of a career open to talents goes right to the heart of how we moderns and especially we members of liberal democracies think of ourselves as subjects, as the authors of our own lives. As John Stuart Mill famously put it, such modern agents as we require foremost the liberty "of framing the plan of our life to suit our own character" as long as no one else is harmed in the process.[28] So, the notion of a career suggests at once both the importance of having a plan for our life, which evidently ranks above a wholly random life, one predicated on chance, and the importance that that plan, and the life from which it takes its cues, be a self-chosen one, dictated by individuals in accordance with their desires, beliefs, and reasons, rather than, as was the case in premodern hierarchical societies, those of some external agency. Therefore, careers must necessarily be dissociated from any form of social hierarchy, which is one of the reasons why they are central to the way in which members of liberal democracies conceive of themselves. Of course, the point of separating careers from hierarchy is to make them open to talent, to a free competition in which everyone is given equal opportunity to obtain some office or reward and in which those offices and rewards are meted out based on merit rather than, say, nepotism. That is why the equality of opportunity by which such competitions must be governed is, as Walzer astutely writes, "also an equality of risk," as the linkage of rewards to talent expended eliminates any guarantee that one is going to obtain what one sets out to obtain.[29] Everything depends on the competition itself if, of course, things go as they are supposed to go.

The relevance to sports of a career open to talents is an easy enough one to fathom in our contemporary era, because that is the way in which not just athletes but, as we have seen, most of us think of our lives these days, and because sports are prime examples of what are known as *meritocracies* (i.e., places in which talent and its judicious cultivation and application are supposed to count for everything). I have not yet got around to thinking about sports in this sense, as I have already conceded, given my exclusive focus on sports as social practices. What now needs to be said, however, is that this latter conception of sports itself prefigures rather than rules out thinking of sports as hooked up in one way or another with the life plans that individuals bring with them into sports. This is again easy enough to see, because when individuals hitch their life plans to the contrived forms of life of sports and thereby make their agency indistinguishable from the agency that sports wring from us, not to mention their respective fates, what remains an important factor in this transition from an *I* to a *we* is, among other things, the place that sports occupy in the lives of these individuals. Of course, this all-important determination is not anything that can or should be sloughed off to a *we* but must recur, per necessity, to individuals. Here, then, is the *I* that Hegel insisted lurks within every *we* and whose deliberations about what sports mean are intimately bound up with the plans of life that individuals envisage for themselves and with the careers they fashion out of those plans. It would be not only sheer folly to discount this *I* and the sense of agency it brings to sports but a basic mistake the consequences of which range from the relatively benign to the truly grievous.

The first error incurred from slighting the importance of individual self-assertion in such collective projects as sports is that it entraps us in some bad arguments that put in question some of what I have said thus far about the ways in which sports aid and abet our freedom. I should make clear first, however, that none of these so-called bad arguments have anything to do with the lame idea of amateur sports, which blithely dismisses the very idea that sports could be careers because the purity of heart they allegedly enjoin would be profaned by such a conception. As I have already made abundantly clear, I regard this idea of the pure amateur as so much sanctimonious piffle and, therefore, as not worth even discussing. So, if the idea that sports can rightly be thought of as careers can be put to use to discredit further the cogency of the amateur conception of sports, to my mind that is all to the good. Nor is this mere wishful thinking on my part, for surely one of the things that the notion of an athletic career has going for it is precisely that it punctures any idea that sports are Pollyanna-like endeavors suitable only for the faint of heart. This is no small feat, as it frees us to take seriously the notion that sports can indeed be plausibly thought of as vocations, as the sort of things around which it makes sense to build a life and customize a life plan to match, rather than leisurely avocations, mere pastimes that must be jettisoned the moment the affairs of daily life break their spell and compel our attention.

Rather, the first error with which I am concerned here is one that puts in question the conceptual soundness of Hegel's and Marx's distinction between the realm of necessity and freedom, a distinction pivotal to my argument so far regarding the important link between sports and freedom. For when we factor into the athletic equation that sports are not just forms of life but vocations at which some very gifted individuals (elite athletes, after all, are genetic outliers) are not only able to make a living but a substantial one at that, then the matter of just where sports belong in this two-pronged scheme gets suddenly dicey. On the one hand, at least from the perspective of professional athletes, sports are their livelihood, which it would be not only wrongheaded for them to deny or discount unduly but foolhardy, because most everyone else involved in one way or another in staging these sports consider them a business and often a rather unpleasant and cut-throat one. Of course, athletic entrepreneurs would not likely furrow their brows if professional athletes were gullible enough to believe that what they do is not in any way economic activity nor, I suspect, would corporate titans of such retrograde companies as Wall-Mart object if their employees actually believed what they were told: that they were all happy members of the same corporate *family*, as that would make them ripe for the picking, for being exploited by these business-savvy types. On the other hand, even at the professional level, sports are to most players and spectators alike, save the most jaded among them, much more than a business; they are indeed a captivating, engrossing, and compelling way of life. If sports are indeed both practices and vocations, it seems that sports can be, and perhaps should be, slotted in both the realm of necessity and freedom.

However, if that is so, Hegel's and Marx's important distinction between them, and, alas, much of my argument to this point is reduced to rubbish, to linguistic gibberish.

So where, exactly, did the argument go awry? The answer requires that we take a second look at the distinction. It will be recalled that the main reason why Hegel and Marx consigned labor to the realm of necessity was that it answers to natural ends that, even when they are morphed into human wants, act as an external fetter on our agency, as something that directs and controls us rather than something we direct and control. At most, we do not so much act as react to what they throw up to us, as these ends are not and cannot be our ends, because the trace of the human serpent is nowhere to be found on them. Rather, they are irrevocably bound up with our biological inheritance as finite creatures whose very survival depends on our instrumental interchange with the world or, what is the same thing, our labor. Contrarily, as the ends of sports are our ends, the product of our human agency, they are directly subject to our will and control and, therefore, or so the argument goes, belong to the different realm of freedom. This, then, is the argument that both certifies that there is an important distinction to be drawn here and that (once it is drawn) provides one of the props that holds up my argument and, as I have been claiming, the Progressive argument that sport and freedom form an inseparable pair.

That said, however, it is not difficult to locate the shaky premise that causes all the trouble here. For what the argument does not take into account, as G. A. Cohen for one argues in taking Marx to task on this particular point,[30] is that just because an activity such as labor has to be done, presuming we are not independently wealthy or have a death wish, does not mean that one's primary motive for performing it is because it has to be done. To assume otherwise, as the argument seems to, is plainly false. For one may well undertake a particular line of work because one finds it intrinsically interesting and challenging, and the fact that one is able to make a living at it is an added and most welcome bonus, something we can indeed take to the bank. There is, of course, nothing contradictory in choosing a vocation that one enjoys and that provides enough money on which to live a reasonably prosperous life. If anything, doing something one would enjoy doing even if one did not get paid for doing it and getting someone to pay one for doing it seems the most rational strategy, in every sense of that term, to adopt for anyone who lives in a market society; indeed, it seems a surefire recipe for living a good life, not to mention a happy one. However, again, if all this is true, it does not seem to leave much hope for Hegel's distinction or for my championing of the Progressive case for the sports-freedom connection.

Or does it? In fact, I think the distinction can meet this objection without in any way denying that such things as sports can be both vocations and perfectionist forms of life. All we need to do is qualify the claim rather than to reject it. However, it is important first to remember that on both Hegel's and Marx's rendition of this distinction, labor and its ilk do not come off as unfree, alienated activities but as activities the composition of which, the way in which they are structured, puts a cap on just how self-determined agents can be under their sway. So, though it is not to be denied that labor is grounded in (natural) ends over which it has no say or control, it is also not to be denied that overcoming the obstacles that such ends put in our way is itself, as Marx says, "a liberating activity."³¹ The distinction does not, therefore, rest on a caricature of labor as bereft of any trace of freedom or even creativity but only as not as suited as such practices as sports are to extend our freedom to the same degree because of the (natural) ends with which they have to contend. This is the reason, and the only one, that is being appealed to in the distinction at issue, as to why sport belongs in the realm of freedom and labor does not.

Despite this clarification, however, the objection still stands that if sport can plausibly be construed as both a vocation and a social practice in the special sense intended here, the matter of where it should be placed is still up for grabs as well as, of course, the distinction itself.

There are at least four things that, I think, can be said in response to rescue both the distinction and the place of sports in the realm of freedom without denying the obvious: that it is also a vocation. The first thing should be said is that this criticism runs together two things that should be kept separate. What it conflates is careers, the plan of life that individuals forge that determine where certain things and such practices as sports fit into people's lives and what meanings and values they attach to them, and labor, the manifold ways in which people earn a living. This is a natural enough conflation to make in capitalist societies such as our own, wherein one's career is most often associated with one's line of work, with the things one gets paid for doing. However, it is a false conflation all the same, as the place and meaning of work in people's lives is no less shaped by one's life plan, one's career, than the place of sports, or politics, or friendships, or whatever. Rightly understood, then, careers are as Walzer says of them, a "set of our activities, extended over time, planned in advance, [and] aimed at a goal,"³² and the cardinal point not to be lost sight of here is that overarching goal may or may not have anything to do with the activities for which one receives monetary compensation. That careers are not reducible to monetary pursuits is, therefore, not in any way compromised by the contingent fact that in market societies people's careers are most often lumped with the exchange of money for services rendered for the simple reason that in such societies, most of their lives revolve around the things they get paid to do, which is, I think, one of the chief shortcomings of these societies. Hence, if sports are vocations (i.e., the sort of things around which individuals plot out the course of their lives and assign meanings and values to the various things they undertake) and if sports can figure centrally in people's lives in just this way without receiving monetary compensation for their involvement in them, Hegel's distinction is in no way jeopardized, nor, therefore, is my Progressive-inspired location of sports in the realm of freedom.

It will surely be objected, however, that in the case of professional sports, equating the idea of an athletic career with the performances that professional athletes are paid to produce is entirely in point and, at least in this sense, therefore, most definitely does wreak havoc on both Hegel's distinction and on my use of it to position sports in the ensemble of free endeavors.

However, I remain unconvinced of even this. The reason why, as Cohen raises in his criticism of Marx but rejects in short order,[33] is that there is indeed a fundamental incompatibility, as the objection holds, between the unadulterated instrumental activity that goes on in the market and the free and creative activity that goes on in sports and similar cultural fare. However, against that objection, this incompatibility does not work against the necessity-freedom distinction but rather against the idea that economic activity can be given a dominant role even in the life of professional athletes, not at least without undercutting the perfectionist demands that sports make on these and all other athletes. In other words, the premise of incompatibility on which the objection is based is on the mark, but the inference drawn from it without which the objection cannot go through is well off the mark. Let me explain.

The first thing to notice in this regard is, unsurprisingly, that the premise of incompatibility is common both to the objection and to the two-realms distinction. For Hegel's and Marx's account of this distinction presumes that the compatibility between economic activity and free, creative activity is at best slight, so that if it obtains at all, it would obtain only in a very few cases and even then would be highly unstable. Cohen's objection to this is that there is no way in which such compatibility can be judged a priori,[34] which suggests that the only way to test it is to do so on a case-by-case basis, a fact that would, evidently, defeat any attempt to generalize from such finely grained data. I think he is right about the a priori bit but overlooks the important point that we can assess this compatibility between instrumentally necessary activity and free, noninstrumental activity in large-scale sociological terms rather than discrete empirical terms, and doing so does allow us to generalize. That is, it does seem to be the case that the way in which labor is socialized in market societies turns it quite wittingly into a less-than-free or creative activity. I am talking about the widely noted de-skilling of labor that occurs matter-of-factly in capitalist economies and which invariably makes work for large scores of people more tedious, less craftsman-like and, last but certainly not least, as its recent globalization bears out, cheap – so cheap in fact that many people cannot get by, as discussed in Chapter Five, unless they take on a second job. By this not-insignificant sociological measure, then, the likely compatibility between economically valuable activity and free and creative activity does not look promising in the least. What goes for labor here, it seems reasonable to suppose, surely goes for athletic labor, which does not look like it would fare any better on this compatibility quotient given the deadening effects that greet the capitalization of most human endeavors. If I am right about the social conditions in which labor must suffer under the auspices of a capitalist economy, the necessity–freedom distinction seems not so vulnerable after all, nor does the placement of sports firmly in the realm of freedom.

However, it is likely to be objected further, are not professional sports the important exception here that prove rather than refute the compatibility rule: that objectively instrumental activity and free, creative activity complement rather than contradict one another. For the professionalization of sports has not led to a decline, precipitous or otherwise, in the extraordinarily high level of skill required to play them well, nor has it reduced the no-less-extraordinary price that elite athletes are still able to fetch on the open market these days, which, if anything, is trending ever higher as we speak. Indeed, as matters presently stand, professional sports sit at or very near the top of the heap of those handful or so of ways in which to make a living that have not seen their position in the labor aristocracy diminished. So, in this case at least, it seems far-fetched to suppose that athletic labor cannot be free, creative activity.

I have two responses to this, which constitute my second and third responses to the criticism that the necessity–freedom distinction and what follows from it does not ring true. The first of these is to emphasize the miniscule number of athletes about whom we are talking here, even at the professional level (i.e., athletes who are able even to eke out a living, let alone a substantial one, playing sports). Indeed, in a number of sports, rowing for instance, there is at present literally next to no market for them, which means that the chances of pursing a career in these sports in the economic sense meant here is practically nil.[35] To be sure, the American triumvirate of football, basketball, and baseball do offer accomplished athletes a lucrative standard of living but, again, this is true of only a minute percentage of such athletes. Part of the reason for this, of course, can be attributed to the vagaries of the market, which play to the advantage of certain sports such as football but to the disadvantage of such sports as rowing, and to the no-less-fortuitous workings of the genetic lottery, which churn out so few truly gifted athletic types. However, a substantial part of the reason why athletes have a hard time making a living off the sports they play is directly owed, once again, to the way in which they have been socially constructed. For instance, the peculiar logic that governs sports and the way in which they get patched together, in which such otherwise ridiculously easy-to-attain goals as putting a ball through a hoop are made exceedingly difficult to attain by arbitrarily adopting rules that prevent the most expeditious way to achieve them, does not especially fit them for the instrumental tasks that it is the main function of labor to carry out. Ironically enough, if sports are market-friendly, it is because they are different, because their noninstrumental complexion is what catches the eye of so many people and draws them to the playing fields of America and which the market, as in all things that promise a handsome financial return, is only too happy to exploit. That does not change the fact, though, that they are not made, as other forms of labor are, to be economically productive activity, which puts a strain on, or so I argue, their instrumental transformation into economic activity and partially accounts for why so very, very few athletes are able to earn a living from their athletic exploits.

The other thing I want to say in this respect clinches the case, I think, for why sports cannot completely accommodate themselves to the notion of an economically grounded career as opposed to a career in which economic calculations play at most a subsidiary role. This has to do with the fact that sports cannot be made to conform too much to market imperatives (how much is too much is, as conceded earlier in the book, difficult to pinpoint with any precision but is easy enough to spot once the disastrous consequences that follow in its wake are too noticeable not to alarm even the most casual observer), without undercutting the perfectionist form of life that they instantiate, without, that is, selling their soul. That is because work is beholden to a bottom line that it cannot ignore without ceasing to be the quintessential instrumental activity that it is. Abstractly speaking, that bottom line is that it satisfy the needs that gave rise to it in the first place and for which it was expressly designed; more concretely speaking, that bottom line in the present capitalist setting is that it satisfy the principal aim of its capitalist owners to realize a profit off the labor of their employees. Of course, that does not mean, to reiterate, that honoring this bottom line is the only motive that one may have in engaging in or hiring others to engage in labor, but it does mean that it is the one reason why all those so engaged must have if what they are doing is to count as labor. This is precisely the point of Marx's quip, "If the thing [labor produces] is useless, so is the labor contained in it; the labor does not count as labor, and therefore it creates no [economic] value."[36]

The problem, of course, is that sports are beholden to a bottom line as well that is not an economic one but a perfectionist one and one on which its very standing as a special form of life is predicated. This is a problem, because it puts in stark relief the incompatibility between sports' perfectionist ambitions and the economic ambitions they are sometimes made to serve, as sports cannot accomplish their perfectionist aims if those financial interests are given top billing. That is not because professional athletes are by virtue of their commitment to an athletic way of life constitutionally incapable of or prohibited from entertaining other motives for pursuing their athletic craft, for like workers, they may well engage in sports for a variety of reasons. However, the one reason that they must have for engaging in sports if what they are doing is to count as genuine athletic activity is to pursue the standards of excellence for which sports were expressly designed and to which they owe their peculiar, from an instrumental standpoint at any rate, social composition, which is to say their very existence as perfectionist forms of life. If economic motives get in the way of these perfectionist aims, if, in other words, profit becomes their bottom line, which seems, by the way, the unkind fate that awaits most everything that goes on in market societies, the sports in which they are nominally engaged no longer qualify as genuine sports, and they create none of the social, political, and moral value that Progressives and others have at one time or another attributed to them. This is exactly the reason why I took Sheed and other commentators like him to task in Chapter 2 for falsely claiming that "Fortunately for everyone, the best way … the player … can make money … is to play the game as well as he can. And that is why the system [of economically financed and contoured sports] seems to work despite itself."[37] Sheed is dead wrong about this for precisely the reason he cites later in his essay, apparently unaware of the contradiction: "[M]arket value is determined by what draws a crowd, and crowds are drawn by all sorts of things besides skill."[38] Most of the abuses of contemporary sports at all levels, as I have tried to document in Chapter 2, stem from this very point, which is what follows when the market insinuates itself, as it is wont to do, into the internal workings of sports, into the very heart of sports where it has no business (no pun intended) being. Unless, then, playing well is mistakenly confused with playing well in a technical, instrumental sense, in which bending and breaking rules is considered merely a strategic, cost-benefit decision rather than a moral one, in which winning is routinely separated from the play that leads up to it, in which if violence is what it takes to draw spectators to games they know little about, then rules are relaxed and, if necessary, even brazenly ignored, in which the moral hardening of athletes so that they become oblivious to the harm they inflict on others and find it difficult even to think in moral terms let alone act on them is encouraged rather than frowned upon – I could, of course, go on and on here, we have every reason to wall off sports so as to make them less vulnerable to this insidious profit motive. All of which means, of course, that we have good reason to suppose there is indeed a basic incompatibility between our work and the kind of free and creative activity that goes on in such social practices as sports and that if we pay this incompatibility no mind, we risk leaching out of sports and their kind the distinctive qualities that make them the special undertakings they are.

If the three arguments I have marshaled thus far find their mark, the sport-and-freedom connection that I believe is the hallmark of the Progressive account of sports, and so the source of its moral and political promise, looks to be, critically speaking, on solid footing. That means that we can take on board the sense of freedom introduced by the notion of a career, in which the *I* that lurks within the *we* of the athletic practice community makes its presence known through the plans that it draws up that tells us where, precisely, sports fit into that life, thereby further strengthening this all-important connection. In order to incorporate this individual strand of self-determination into sports, however, we had to reject the idea that it was an either-or matter, that sports are either social practices or they are vocations, for they are clearly both. We were able to accomplish this, of course, only by defusing a tension that remains when careers are too given over to economic concerns, insisting that athletic careers and the perfectionist forms of life that sports embody nicely complement one another when economic concerns are not permitted to play a dominant role in the formulation of people's life plans, to be sure a delicate balancing act in any capitalist society.

So far, then, so good. However, we are not entirely out of the woods yet, as there is one last matter that needs to be addressed if this sport-and-freedom argument is to avoid being impaled on one other tension that the idea of a career introduces. That tension has to do with the fact that a person's life plan can for purely personal reasons that do not necessarily have anything to do with matters economic make sports hostage to other ends (i.e., require them to serve second-fiddle as means to secure other ends). This is another way in which the fragile balance that keeps sports alive as viable forms of life, in which what is instrumental in them is, to parrot Suits, "inseparably combined with what is intrinsically valuable" about them, is upset by turning them into "an instrument for some further end."[39] In one sense, of course, this is a harmless enough matter, as in the course of anyone's life, a person may take up sports to enhance health, improve social life, to relax, you name it, and may well take up any number of other things for both related and different instrumental reasons. In such instances as these, a person's life plan is filled in by a number of what can best be described as hobbies, which would, of course, accurately describe their athletic ventures as well, none of which need be taken all that seriously and none of which touch on the grander social, moral, and political themes of concern here. Similarly, sports can be used as private vehicles in harmless ways, again to prepare one for a career in music, in which the self-determining effects of a life plan simply redound to the benefit of a social practice different from sports, and no one seems the worse off, including sports themselves. However, things do get a bit wooly when sports and other endeavors that properly belong in the realm of freedom are turned into instruments to replenish, for example, our appetite for such instrumental activities as work. For one, this is one of the classic ways in which capitalist economies exploit workers so as to extract every last ounce of labor out of them. For another, this inversion of the necessity–freedom scheme looks like a recipe for an irrational life, to say nothing of an unhappy one, as it claims that the point of a life devoted to work is to make it possible for us to work some more is a perfectly sensible way to think about and order one's life. However, it clearly is not, least of all from the standpoint of work, the overriding aim of which, it will be remembered, is to secure the conditions necessary for our survival so that we do not have to work anymore (i.e., so that we have the leisure to do those things we truly want to do rather than those things we have to do).

The problem with which I am concerned, however, arises when the subjective move that careers introduce, the self-assertion of the I to which they give credence, goes too far. This happens when the ideal of a self-chosen life, which as we earlier observed is what gives the notion of a career its particular force, illicitly, as Taylor felicitously puts it, "slides towards an affirmation of choice itself."[40] When this slide occurs, choice begins to figure in our lives in a way that makes little rational or normative sense, as it would have us believe that it is choice itself that confers worth and value on the projects that individuals plan for themselves as well as the social practices in which they engage. If this were true, sports and the entire ensemble of practices that comprise the realm of freedom would be subjectivized beyond recognition. That is to say, sports and their kindred practices would be transformed into wholly private affairs in which their participants would be free to do not only whatever they please *within* them but, what is worse, whatever they like *to* them. In effect, sports would become the playthings of fancy-free, footloose subjects intent only on following their preferences wherever they may lead them. It hardly needs saying that this untrammeled brand of freedom is not the sort that is central to the Progressive linkage of sport and freedom that I have been trying to explicate here and goes well beyond the individual freedom implicated in the idea of a career in which it still makes sense, as it does not in this privatized rendering of sports, to talk of an I doing its bidding within a *we*.

Part of what is problematic about this subjectivization of sports, this promotion of an unattached private I, is that it coincides with rather than militates against the privatization of sports associated with its present capitalization, against which I have been railing for some time now. The other part of what is problematic about this subjective turn is the seductive intellectual appeal that it has had on a surprising number of theorists of sports, who normally would look askance at any such privatization of sports but who, under the influence of especially Richard Rorty's writings and his account of what he calls the "strong poet," end up endorsing a subjective account of sports that is almost indistinguishable from its dominant commodified form. We get a good idea of the subjective bent of Rorty's "strong poet," of the Nietzsche-like effort at self-overcoming that is its trademark, when he tells us, using the poignant words of famous literary theorist and critic Allen Bloom, that the worst nightmare of the strong poet is "the horror of finding himself to be only a copy or a replica" rather than an original.[41] One can get a similarly good idea of the subjectivist flavor of Rorty's influence on sport philosophers by sampling some of the best of that work; I am referring here to Terry Roberts's provocative attempt to cast sports as fertile terrain for athletic strong poets to do their subjective thing. I begin with Roberts's approving quotation of Paul Weiss's curious, markedly anti-Progressive remark that "the athletic goal rarely allows a man to work toward the achievement of any one but himself, except incidentally as a means." If Weiss errs here, he does so in Roberts's eyes only for thinking that such other strong poets as the scientist and musician are not as self-centered as the athlete, for mistakenly believing that in both of these nonathletic pursuits "though never freed from a reference to the self, [the goal] is one in which their own completion is inseparable from the completion of others." Weiss's slight against these latter strong poets, his underestimation of their burning private desire to reinvent themselves, can easily be corrected to Roberts's distinctly Rortyan way of thinking by simply pointing out to Weiss that in sports as well as in music or science, or presumably, again, in the practices attached to the realm of freedom, "strong poetry is necessarily solipsistic because it can occur only when the individual triumphs over the self."[42] Here, then, is a heady, highbrow recipe for the transvaluation of sports as private enterprises that, though in one sense far removed from the economic machinations of the market is, nevertheless, in another sense quite congenial to their inveterate and evidently unbreakable habit of, no matter the circumstance, always giving top billing to private preferences.

It would be a mistake, therefore, to treat this inward turn apparent in and outside sports lightly, as a whimsical passing threat. However, it would be a worse mistake to swallow whole its mistaken view that the importance that a life be chosen means that it is choice itself that must be singled out as our rational and normative yardstick, as the standard by which meaning and value are conferred on what we do in and with our lives. For this is a self-defeating idea if ever there were one. The reason why is that self-fashioning is not and cannot be an entirely private exercise because it depends in part on our dialogical interactions with others and in part on the practical and normative landmarks furnished by social practices, which, in turn, form the backdrop against which our efforts to invent ourselves derive their meaning and significance. If it were just a private matter, it would be possible to define myself by claiming that what makes me unique, and so significantly different from others, is the fact that, to borrow an example from Taylor, I am "exactly the same height as some tree on the Siberian plain."[43] This is, of course, a nonsensical claim precisely because significance and meaning are not things that anybody can just choose to attach to their self-definitional efforts and expect anyone else to take them with a grain of salt. If, on the other hand, I define myself by my musical talent or my ability to hit a 90-mile-an-hour fastball, these self-definitions now do mean something, as they fall within what Taylor calls "the domain of recognizable self-definitions."[44] Like everything else, then, self-fashioning is something that can be accommodated only within some social framework or other and the we-intentions and meanings that they install. It is not the actual choices that go into self-fashioning, therefore, but the frameworks in which they get worked out that confer on them whatever rational and normative salience they possess.

What goes for self-fashioning here goes doubly so for such social practices as sports. For these, too, are not and cannot be mere private exercises and thus do not lend themselves exclusively to private self-definition because what meaning and significance they possess is as well an unmistakably social, intersubjective matter. I can no more claim that what makes me the distinctive person I am is that I am the same height as some tree on the Siberian plain than I can claim that what makes American football a distinctive game is that it satisfies some deep-seated sexual fancy that I have to dominate others. What makes this claim about football nonsensical is the same thing that made my foregoing effort to define myself by the height of some tree somewhere nonsensical; these are just not the sort of things that can be decided privately without taking into account the rational and normative landmarks that such social practices as football on the one hand and those bound up with our self-identity on the other (which, if my argument to this point goes through, would surely include sports for many, many people) lay down for us to help to make sense of who we are and what we are doing. Deprived of these landmarks, of the normative orientation that they furnish, I would not have the faintest idea "who I am" let alone how to make myself more self-determined, nor would I have any idea where I stand in such social practices as sports. So, this strategy of self-detachment, whether offered in the prosaic name of the market to grease the skids for entrepreneurs bent on squeezing every last dollar out of sports and their kind or in the more exotic name of Rorty's "strong poet" to pave the way for athletic and other similarly inclined entrepreneurs of the self bent on recreating themselves, is a fundamentally misguided one. That it is not a strategy for securing our liberty should be obvious by now, because as we have seen, it is in the social spaces that such forms of life as sports carve out that individuals' bids for freedom, their effort to effect their self-determination, is won or lost. That it is not a strategy around which we can plan a life and engage effectively in such social practices as sports but, in fact, a strategy for self-estrangement and for the alienation of everything that such an *I* touches (presuming it can touch anything without compromising its solipsistic effort to reinvent itself), should also be readily apparent at this stage of our argument, as an *I* that swings completely free of a *we* has no rational or normative rudder by which to steer its life in one direction as opposed to another and is left clueless as to how to navigate its way in any social practice on which it happens.

That said, the sense of individual freedom that the notion of a career brings to the table, if not shorn of a *we* that can appropriately shadow its every move, adds an important element to the Progressive freedom–sport tandem that I have been pushing here. This is true in one further, and for my purposes, final sense. For we need not only worry about an *I* that somehow manages to slip the grasp of any *we* but as well about a *we* that suffocates each and every *I* with which it comes into contact. This is a real worry for any polity, especially a democratic one, and should lead us, even in these extreme atomistic times, to appraise carefully any communitarian scheme that comes our way to ensure that it provides ample room for individuals to express themselves. The same caution, of course, should be extended to my own support of the Progressive heralding of sports' community-building prowess. Exercising caution in such instances, however, is easier said than done, because safeguarding the individual aspirations of members of such communities requires more than granting them simple egress from groups no longer to their liking, because no longer responsive to those aspirations. For there has to be some place for such individuals to go once they have exited practices in which they no longer feel affirmed, some place where they can consort with others either for purposes of solidarity or for purposes of figuring out who they are (or both). That is why when even one of our important social practices goes overboard in this communitarian direction, we should be careful that there is not something larger afoot that might similarly affect our other social practices; otherwise we may find ourselves without any place to go, shut out, as it were, from any place in which we might be able to find or create a niche for ourselves. Rousseau's famous notion of the "general will," inhospitable as it was to the claims of individuals, gave us a theoretical glimpse of how forbidding such a place could be. The Jacobins and their epigones, who were hell bent on turning Rousseau's "general will" into a political reality, only confirmed in starker, because now concrete, practical terms our worst suspicions of what Taylor aptly called the "terrible forms of homogenizing tyranny" characteristic of such regimes.[45]

The only effective remedy for such tyranny, therefore, is to ensure that the *I* in the *we* is not expunged or unduly rebuffed, that no community, large or small, is permitted simply to have its way with those who people it. If the notion of a career and the individual self-assertion from which it takes its marching orders is an important one, it is precisely here that its importance is manifest. No matter how large or small a part it may play, therefore, in our lives in general and in our sports in particular, we should not begrudge but rather celebrate the fact that it does indeed still play a part in them, because it still very much resonates in such self-proclaimed democracies as America. To the extent that it does, it bolsters the sort of free self-determination that such social practices as sports make possible, which in these depressingly and increasingly undemocratic times is no small achievement.

## Caring, seriousness, and sports

With this last bit of the Progressive sport–freedom connection secured, my effort to vindicate the Progressive conception of sport normatively has come full circle. If the long and at times complicated argument I have offered on its behalf is persuasive, it seems it has accomplished what it set out to do, namely, justify what to many at the time and, as I have insinuated throughout, perhaps even that many more today, must have seemed, and seems, a curious place to go looking for the democratic soul of America. After all, who would have thought that something as trivial as sports could play such a major role in reviving Americans faith in their democratic selves. That it once did just that, as spirited along by a social movement whose intellectual leaders were not afraid to sing the praises of sports, seems to be ancient history for many Americans today, which, considering that contemporary Americans are not especially fond of history, theirs or anyone else's, only seems to confirm how dim their moral and political hopes for the future really are. How to activate those democratic dreams once again through the prism of sports remains the great conundrum and, of course, the great political task, about which I will have something to say (but, I'm afraid, not nearly enough) in my closing remarks. For now, however, the claim alleging that sports are too trivial a fare on which to pin our moral or political hopes raises another obstacle that must be cleared if the Progressive argument is to go through.

As I said, that obstacle is precisely that sports themselves are not serious affairs, that the freedom that they win for us is too trivial an accomplishment to support the grand moral and political role that Progressives asked them to play in the past, which would offer one not implausible explanation why that effort ultimately failed and that I am once again, in their name, asking them to play in the future. The argument can be couched in many ways, but one especially formidable way in which it can be put, which is in fact how David Miller, in his important book *Principles of Social Justice*, and Simon Keller, in his incisive essay, "Patriotism as Bad Faith," frame it, goes as follows. Because sports are entirely optional affairs, a claim confirmed, or so Miller argues, by the fact that "participants are not required to engage in them, either by physical necessity or by a sense of moral obligation,"[46] it follows that the imputation of any moral or political qualities and such virtues as courage to them is simply wrongheaded. In short, as nothing is really at stake in sports, getting worked up by the qualities of action they excite is not called for, and getting so worked up about those qualities that one begins to throw around such high-minded adjectives as *moral* or *political* to characterize them is even more uncalled for, in fact, it would be laughable were it not for the fact that throwing around such words as these constitutes a grievous misuse of our moral and political vocabularies, vocabularies about which we can hardly afford to be cavalier if we expect to take ourselves seriously, let alone expect anyone else to take us seriously.

Keller adds to Miller's argument the important point that because being a supporter of a sports team such as "Geelong," a fictional name of a football club he coined for illustrative reasons, "does not influence any really important decisions of mine or result in any important change in my view of the world,"[47] my defense of Geelong, say, of the excellence of its players or the moral character of their conduct, is not what I ostensibly present it to be, a reasoned justification of their actions, but a biased, partisan interpretation of those actions that reflects, not incidentally, my attachment and loyalty to Geelong. As Keller smartly sums up his point, "the purported facts to which I appeal are not really what lead me to hold them. Really, I hold those opinions because I am a Geelong supporter. It would spoil the fun for me or anyone else to point this out, but we nevertheless know it to be the case."[48] Evidently, then, at least if Keller is right about this, sports are more like obituaries than they are moral justifications, as what is said in both of the former can be counted on, as it turns out quite explicitly for both those doing the telling and those for whom it is intended, as falling well short of the unvarnished truth. That it also falls well short of lying should not come as a surprise, as there is no need to lie, to deceive when writing an obituary or supporting a sports team, because truth telling is not what anyone in either instance is pretending to do, is not the aim of the writer or the supporter.[49] That is why when they, in effect, airbrush the truth to suit their purposes, they cannot justly be accused of moral wrongdoing, of breaching anyone's moral trust.

On the other hand, the exercise of courage in "saving [a] life or the defense of one's homeland" are serious matters, especially because these things are motivated both by a sense of "physical necessity" and of "moral obligation," which makes it not only appropriate but imperative to talk about them in moral and political terms. In fact, not to talk about them or consider them in such terms is not only a conceptual mistake but, no doubt, a moral offense to boot. Hence, as these are the genuine articles and not some simulacrum, features of some social practice contrived merely to display courage "for its own sake" as opposed to displaying it "in the service of a valued end," such as saving a life or defending one's country,[50] it is important both that what anyone has to say about these events be said at least in part using unmistakable moral language and that whatever is thus said be backed up by reasons, reasons that show that the actions that took place there were justifiable ones.

This argument that sports are trivial matters that should not be taken too seriously, that neither warrant using moral language to characterize them, except in negative terms where devotion to sports is claimed to interfere with the fulfillment of more pressing moral obligations, nor involve reason-giving of the sort that is required in moral and political circles, is no trivial objection. But I also don't think it is a forceful objection. That is because it relies on an account of seriousness that is itself suspect precisely because it does not take into account, but merely dismisses, the important sense in which sports or any other practice slotted in the realm of freedom qualify as serious endeavors, as endeavors in which both moral talk and reasoning are integral to their flourishing, and by extension integral to the flourishing of democratic societies like America. To build my case and help my criticism stick, I reprise Hegel's distinction between the realm of necessity and freedom, but this time I do so by asking what each side of this distinction tells us about what makes for a truly serious and meaningful life.

Asking the question in this way, of course, will yield two answers but, I contend, one of those answers gets, argumentatively speaking, the better of the other one.

The sense in which the instrumental activities that make up the realm of necessity are serious affairs can be read directly from, as previously noted, the ends that give rise to them and color their every feature. Those ends, of course, are the natural ones that characterize our fundamental dependence on the world in which we live and the others that co-inhabit that world with us and to which we must be responsive if we are to be in a position to produce and reproduce the material conditions of our existence. Hence, because those ends are not truly our own ends, aims that can be attributed to our own self-fashioning, they not only put a cap on our self-determination, as earlier argued, but require that their importance be gauged independently of and antecedently to our desiring and valuing them. In other words, instrumental activities are important and compel our attention and agency for strictly objective reasons (i.e., for reasons that do not stem from the fact that we human agents care about them). As Baier helpfully puts it, instrumental activities are "things which are important to us, because they *affect* our lives in ways we *find* important" [my emphasis],[51] rather than our *making* them important by intending, desiring, valuing, wanting, or producing them. So, such instrumental activities as work or social engineering or political diplomacy or war are serious matters, even at times deadly serious matters, because in one way or another, what they are intended to bring about is crucial to our very survival and because the conditions of our survival are not anything with which we human agents had anything directly to do, are not social preconditions but rather natural preconditions of human agency.

The fact that these instrumental ventures are objectively important to us does not mean, of course, that we can be indifferent to the demands that their (natural) ends make on us, not at least if we want to live, but only that we need not care about them and the ends they serve. Whereas, then, the claims that they make on us compel us to action, they do not compel us to desire or value or care for them but simply to take notice of them and respond accordingly. That, of course, does not prevent us from desiring or valuing these activities, so long at least as such desiring or valuing does not get in the way of the instrumental tasks with which they are charged. However, it does explain why when such an instrumental activity as labor is drained of any and all features that might touch off such desiring or valuing, by dint, say, of the social conditions under which it is required to meet the ends thrown up to it, nothing about its complexion has changed to suggest that it is no longer and should, therefore, be treated no longer as merely an instrumental enterprise. Further, that we need not care about labor and its kind to account for their importance or the seriousness they warrant is no knock against them but something that very much counts in their favor in these particular respects. For it is because they are necessary to our survival and at various times and points morally obligatory, for instance, to use Miller's example, when we are morally obliged to protect our country from external threats, that they are accorded the great seriousness they typically receive. That is, it is because the ends that they serve are indifferent as such to human desiring, willing, and valuing that we cannot be indifferent to their importance nor the seriousness that we are required to accord them.

When we view our life from the realm of necessity, therefore, what makes life serious is what is instrumental to our survival, is what is required of us in order to produce and reproduce the material conditions of our life. What things are and should rank as important from this same perspective are those things that are likewise bound up with our survival, that figure in central ways with securing the natural preconditions on which our brute existence depends. It is easy to see why, from this vantage point, sports must be regarded as Miller and Keller regard them, as trivial matters that should always take a second seat to the more important and serious instrumental concerns of life. It is also easy to see what it would take to turn sports into serious and important human enterprises in this view, which is as simple as turning them into our means of livelihood or, short of that, to make them instrumental to our survival by playing up their potential health benefits or the instrumental social skills they teach. What is clearly beyond the pale on this rendering of seriousness, however, is any idea that the perfectionist life that sports offer to us is in itself anything that warrants our serious attention or anything to which we should accord importance, not, at least, without turning the world on its head.

To turn to the opposite pole of human life, then, to the realm of freedom, the sense in which sports and their kind are to be considered as serious and regarded as important human undertakings can also be directly read from, as earlier discussed, their ends that color as well their every feature. The reading that we get here turns out to be much different from the previous one precisely because these ends are the product of our human agency, are indeed our ends, as they exist only because some not-insignificant subset of the human species bothered to create them in the first place. Hence, because these ends are wholly owed to our communal self-fashioning, they not only extend our free self-determination, as previously argued, but require that their importance and seriousness be gauged solely by our caring for them as we do. Here it is our caring for and valuing sports and their ilk, and not something independent of or antecedent to such caring and valuing, that confers their importance and the seriousness they are owed. Accordingly, those things that are important and serious to us in this sense are not so by virtue of the fact that "they *affect* our lives in ways we *find* important" but by virtue of the fact that our caring "*makes*" them so [my emphasis].[52] So, such noninstrumental practices as sports, art, music, and the like are serious matters in their own right and sense, seldom, if ever, deadly but more often than not all-absorbing, because of the care we extend to them, and because their status as ends in themselves is a social rather than a natural feature of human agency.

Whereas, then, we can be indifferent to the ends that instrumental activities serve in terms of how we engage them but not, of course, deaf or unresponsive to the demands they foist on us, we cannot be so indifferent to such forms of life as sports, because if we were, they would count for nothing with respect to both their importance and seriousness. Here, the fact that it is our caring for and valuing sports that is the source of their importance, rather than something independent of and antecedent to such caring, often does count as a knock against them, specifically, against their substantive heft and moral standing. This is in part because of the beguiling appeal that the first, objective account of importance and seriousness holds over us contemporary folks, beguiling because it is not an especially cogent account to begin with (more about this in a moment) and in part because of a misunderstanding of how the way that we care about such things as sports confers their significance. So, we need to say something more about what we mean by *caring* here and what, exactly, it has to do with the importance of such things as sports.

When we care about things, as Frankfurt tells us in his seminal essay, "The Importance of What We Care About,"[53] we become "invested" in them. To be invested in the things about which we care means that we identify strongly with them such that whatever befalls them, good or bad, befalls us. That is why when we care about such practices as sports, whatever happens to them makes such a difference in our own lives and cannot help but do so.

Further, caring about things should not be confused either with simply liking or wanting them or with deciding to like them.[54] For there are many things that we may like and desire but about which we do not especially care in the sense that we are significantly affected by their ups and downs. For example, I may like movies that involve political intrigue but not care a whit whether another one ever gets made, as there are many other things that I may watch or do that I find just as pleasurable. When I truly care about something, however, and appropriate its aims and goods as my own, its fate gets utterly entangled with my own, which makes it well-nigh impossible for me not to get caught up in the good and bad things that happen to it, because in a very real sense they are happening to me as well. What is more, as the things I care about guide my actions, they must have, as Frankfurt notes, "a degree of persistence about them."[55] That is why a person who cared about something for only an instant cannot be said really to care about it, as that would reduce caring to acting on impulse, to the sort of thing that a "wanton" does.[56] Finally, deciding to care about something should be distinguished from caring about it for the simple reason that the intention embedded in such decisions may not pan out, because what we decide to do we may not end up acting on – unfortunately or not, a rather common occurrence. For example, I may decide to become a vegetarian, but actually becoming one is another matter. For that to happen, I must fulfill the intention, and whether or not I am able to do so is not to be confused with my merely intending to. Interestingly enough, it is this feature about caring for something that speaks to our free self-determination, as it is my "will" that moves me to do something and that is directly implicated in that about which I care, which means that unlike my decisions, which "may pertain" to what I will, what I care about reveals "what [my] will truly *is*."[57]

Now, one of the knocks against the idea that some things are important only because we care about them – think, for instance, of your parents or children – is that it relies on a kind of subjectivism of which we had earlier found it necessary to disabuse ourselves. In the previous case, it will be remembered, it was the subjectivist idea that choice itself is what confers the significance of the way I define myself and the life plan that I construct for myself that had to be gotten rid of to explain properly the role that the *I* plays in any *we*. In the present context, the suspect premise turns out to be roughly the same one but now directed to the notions of importance and seriousness. This time around, it is packaged in an argument that claims that whenever we are confronted with, as we inevitably are, determining what things are important in our lives and should be taken seriously, the best answer we can give is the subjective one whatever we decide. To be sure, this answer is different from the previous one given by those who view such matters through the prism of practically and morally obligatory activities, but it is hardly a persuasive alternative to that objective answer, because it proves no more intelligible on issues of self-identity and life-plans than it does on assessments of importance. Let me explain.

What is so unsatisfactory about this subjective answer is that it would have us believe that when judging what things are important in our lives, practically anything goes. How could it be otherwise, because if importance were only a subjective notion, only a matter of determining whether something mattered personally to someone or other at some point or other in time, it would be an utterly trivial notion because an utterly relativistic one. In other words, what is missing in the answer is any evaluative dimension, any way to deal with the surely uncontroversial fact that people often care about things that they should not and, conversely, fail to care about things they should. Some people, for instance, take their careers too seriously, to the point that they end up neglecting their parental responsibilities, and some people do not take their careers seriously enough and waste a goodly portion of their lives as a consequence. The fact that they should not do these things, that their failures here are genuine moral failures, shows that importance and seriousness are normatively loaded notions, that they have an evaluative element built into them that cannot be ignored without misconstruing what they are fundamentally all about.

That this subjectivist rendering of importance does simply bypass this crucial evaluative feature of caring is, therefore, what proves to be its undoing. For without that feature, there is no way to generate a hypothetical of the form "if I care about this thing," then "this thing must be important." Of course, for my present purpose, this normative gap in the account of caring is a fatal defect, because my entire reason for casting about for a persuasive alternative account of importance and seriousness was to dispel what I claimed was the bad idea that sports themselves are trivial practices, that the free self-determination that we secure in their name is, therefore, an important accomplishment and nothing to be sneered at. However, if the only rival account of importance available is itself a trivial one, there is no way to make good on this claim.

Fortunately, for me at any rate, there is another nontrivial account of caring that it is not an objective or subjective account, but an intersubjective one. The best way to tease it out is to consider an example of subjective caring that Frankfurt uses in his essay for illustrative purposes and show how by making an intersubjective adjustment to it we can divine a notion of importance that can withstand reflective scrutiny.

Frankfurt's example concerns an obviously eccentric man whose main care, at least when he takes his daily morning walk, is not to step on any cracks in the sidewalk he traverses.[58] The point of this example, according to Frankfurt, is the simple one that because the man cares about avoiding the cracks in the sidewalk, it obviously matters to him. Indeed, the claim that it matters to this person is for Frankfurt conclusive evidence that merely caring about something makes it important at very least to that person. In one sense, this is as clearly unassailable as Frankfurt says it is, for there is no denying that it matters to the person in the example. However, a point that Frankfurt does not fully seem to appreciate himself and with which he chooses to deal in another way, is the point that we just made: that from the mere fact that the man cares about not stepping on the cracks in the sidewalk, we cannot infer that it truly is important to him or anyone else, as no validation of its importance has been made. That it subjectively matters to him is one thing, a subjective issue about which there can be no dispute, which is just how things go when we are dealing with subjective states of mind, such as someone's pain; that it is important to him is another thing, an evaluative issue about which there can be and should be questions, which is also just how things go when what is in question is not anything that can be subjectively adjudicated, such as the meaning of words that cannot have purely private meanings and still qualify as bits of language.

This raises an obvious question: where do we look to find the evaluative dimension that is evidently missing here? The answer is to recall a yet earlier discussion that we had about self-identity, specifically Taylor's example of the individual who claims that the fact that he is the same height as some tree in the Siberian plain shows he is a significant individual. The mistake that this misguided soul commits is the same subjective mistake that Frankfurt's eccentric walker commits. For the idea that avoiding stepping on cracks in a sidewalk is an important thing to do and the idea that defining myself by the height of a tree comprise a significant self-definition are both utter nonsense, because they both falsely presume that the importance of "who I am" or "what I do" is something we can decide for ourselves as individuals qua individuals. As this mistake can be rectified in just the way in which Taylor recommended on that earlier occasion, the missing evaluative element for which we are looking can be found by taking his advice and dragging into the picture the background of things that matter, the intersubjective dimension of what relevant others think about the way in which we define ourselves and ascribe importance to the actions that we undertake. As Taylor so succinctly puts it, "to bracket out history, nature, society, the demands of solidarity, everything but what I find in myself, would be to eliminate all candidates for what matters."[59]

What communal caring on the scale of a culture or society (or both) has going for it that individual caring does not, therefore, is that it comes already packaged with a set of evaluative standards that include, among other things, the settled judgments of the culture that are themselves the product of the conversational give and take and argumentative back and forth of its members. It is by virtue of the evaluative standards embedded in these cultural traditions that when appropriately invoked, they are able to validate and thus confer the importance or lack thereof of our actions by whether they measure up to those standards or fail to. Hence, although what individuals care about can err, as we have seen, in the particular estimations of importance that they generate, the same cannot be said of entire cultures, at least not of those that are genuine communities of inquiry. To be sure, cultures and societies can err in mistaking what their true normative standards are or in trying, as often happens, to slough off their normative standards as universal ones, so that what is important to them becomes all of a sudden and by an abstract sleight of hand important to any rational agent rightly so called. However, absent these and kindred errors of interpretation and hubris, what entire cultures and societies cannot get wrong, because they are the standard bearers themselves, is what counts as important or unimportant for the people who live in them.[60] That is why we can say with some confidence with respect to the settled traditions of our own culture that Frankfurt's sidewalk-cracks-averse-walker and Taylor's tree-based-self-definer are deluded because they both mistakenly think that because they care about these (strange) things, they must be important to them and to everyone else, when they are most assuredly not.[61] Hence, although the importance of something is independent of the particular intentions, desires, motives, and cares that are stuffed into our subjective motivational sets, it is not independent of that about which *we* as members of particular communities care.

We should now be in a better position to see how such practically and morally optional forms of life as sports qualify, nonetheless, as important features of our lives that warrant our serious regard, a serious regard that not only differs from the seriousness rightly accorded practically and morally obligatory activities but one that is able to account for their seriousness in a way in which they are not able to account for the seriousness of sports. What we need to show here is how such activities as sports that are optional in the sense that we need not ever engage them are nonoptional in another important and morally compelling sense. This will require showing how they, as it were, shed their pure optionality as things that we can take or leave and become practices that many of us come to think of as indispensable to leading a good, meaningful, and, therefore, full life.

It might help to begin with a nonsporting example. Neither I nor anyone else is practically required nor morally obligated to become, say, a sculptor. However, once I become a sculptor, it is no longer, practically or morally speaking, an incidental matter, for me or the artistic community, that I aspire to the highest standards of excellence so far achieved and morally acquit myself well in doing so. For these have now become expectations, full-blooded normative ones, to which the art community quite rightly holds me and to which I hold myself. Hence, what was once merely one option among many others of how I might choose to lead my life has become the way whereby I and relevant others assess what meaning and substance my life actually has or might potentially have. That is to say, in some sense being an artist has become a weighty matter indeed, one central to my own identity and to how others size me up and one central to my sense of self-importance, which is, as we have seen, inextricably connected to how others view the importance of what I do. In this way then, being an artist becomes a necessary feature of the way in which I express myself and how others respond to my artistic expression of myself. It goes without saying, of course, that this necessity has little if anything in common with the practical or moral necessity that might lead me to enlist in the armed services to protect my country in a time of war.

Now, something very much like this transition is what takes place when we care in the requisite manner about sports. For sports are also not practically or morally necessary endeavors in any straightforwardly instrumental sense. Once we engage them, because we care about the forms of life they make possible, they cease being merely one option among others of how I might live my life and become central to how I live my life, define myself, and assess the importance of what I do. What is going on in such transitions and shifts of meaning is, as Raz writes, something very much akin to this: "Once a value comes into being, it bears on everything."[62] Simply put, that means that when we invent such practices as sports, we bring the values peculiar to them into being, and those values then contend with the other values circulating in a given culture. We play these various values off against one another and some of them, for reasons just as inexplicable as everything that came before it, start to catch on with the larger community. Before long, they assume a hallowed place in that culture and, therefore, come to be revered by a large cross section of its members. When we get to this point, those sporting values take on a social, political, and moral valence that they previously did not enjoy commensurate to their newfound importance.

Raz even suggests that such transitions can be broken down further into three stages.[63] The first is that we begin to think about and regard sports in accord with their purported special value. The second step is that the values that sports introduce begin to command the respect of the members of the relevant culture, as values that should not be violated and, perhaps, even promoted. The third step is that in which members of the culture are moved to engage, again in an appropriate manner, the values that sports make available to them, which is the most important stage, because the only way to realize the values of sports or any other such practice is to engage them. Once these three stages are successfully traversed, such practices as sports attain a moral and political importance in the culture in which they are practiced, that it singles them out for distinctive treatment and regard, which is what Progressives detected and to which they were responding at the time when they focused the spotlight on sports for these very reasons and on which I, following their lead, am trying to argue we Americans should now, especially now, be focusing our attention for precisely the same reasons. It is, then, much in the manner that Raz outlines here that we can explain how sports in and outside America have achieved a moral prominence that rises to the level of something that approaches a moral obligation. In one sense, this is a misleading way to put it, because it puts too much stock in the importance of moral obligation, as if it is the be-all and end-all of matters moral, which it plainly is not.[64] For is quite enough for my purpose that sports be considered a key moral player in prodding Americans to think of themselves as members of a moral commonwealth, which means that, although no one is morally obligated to engage sports (though they are morally obligated to respect the values for which they stand),[65] for the simple reason that no one can engage all things of value because of the standard variance of subjective interests and the pluralistic character of a society such as ours, enough Americans must find them sufficiently morally engaging to rank them as important human undertakings.

The upshot of my argument, therefore, is that sports have been wrongly accused of being trivial activities because the wrong standard of seriousness has been habitually applied to them. Measured by the same instrumental standards by which we assign the seriousness of such practically necessary activities as work and such morally obligatory ones as saving someone's life, it is understandable why sports rate hardly a second look. For their social constitution, the way they are put together, does not suit them in the least for such straightforwardly instrumental purposes save, as already noted, in incidental ways that casually bracket their main importance (e.g., using sports to promote physical fitness) or in not-so-incidental ways that compromise their importance (e.g., the wholesale commodification of sports). However, the peculiar character of their social constitution suits them just fine, uniquely in fact, for the politically and morally important role that Progressives and I think they can play in our lives. That is because their made-up social standing, the fact that their ends are artifacts that I can readily appropriate and not just call my own but actually make my own, allows them to insinuate themselves in what Korsgaard aptly calls *our practical identity*, which she just as aptly defines as "a description under which you find your life to be worth living and your actions to be worth undertaking."[66] For when we truly care about sports, we internalize the perfectionist features of their way of life and the moral qualities they demand of us and, by virtue of internalizing them, make them an important part of who we are, of the very features and qualities by which we define ourselves and gauge the meaning, importance, and seriousness of our actions. This is what explains the importance of sports and why they captivate so many of us and why, when we yield ourselves up to them and are, as it were, overcome by them, we do not feel in the slightest constrained by their strange rules or alienated or disenchanted by their perfectionist demands.

It also explains why, when we appropriate the ends and values of sports and make them our own, there is nothing that strikes us as either optional or arbitrary regarding our involvement in sport no matter as a player or a spectator. This change in perspective is, as we noted earlier, a byproduct of our engagement with sports. However, how deep this change in perspective goes and what a radical shift it represents can be appreciated fully only if its affect on our practical identity is noted. For when we take on board the perfectionist imperatives of sports and the moral qualities that they require and, as it were, write them into our own description of what constitutes a life worth living, sports exert an influence on our lives that rivals that of Frankfurt's intriguing notion of "volitional necessity," a notion that he thinks underpins Luther's famous declaration: "Here I stand, I can do no other."[67] The incapacity of which Luther speaks here, as Frankfurt tells it, is not that exhibited by, for example, the addict who is unable to resist the urge to use drugs because he is too weak to counter them. On the contrary, Luther suffers not from any weakness of the will, for it is because his will is strong, ready to crush any contrary impulse that might cross his mind, that he is able to proffer the bald declaration that he did. Rather, the necessity that prompts him to say that he can do no other than take the stand he has taken is not of the instrumental sort that one might expect to hear from someone carrying out the daily tasks that need attending to in ordinary life but rather a necessity that one would expect to hear from a man such as Luther who, at a pivotal point in his life, realizes "that every apparent alternative" to what he must now do is "unthinkable" because it would betray who he is and all for which he stands.[68] Much the same can be said, I think, of the engaged athlete or the engaged musician or the engaged writer, who can do no other than what he or she is doing when engaged in sports or music or writing, because the alternatives, although perhaps not "unthinkable," are nonetheless deeply unsatisfying. That is because for them, as for Luther, who they are and the magic elixir that gives their life meaning, importance, and substance (i.e., makes their life worth living) are intimately bound up with what they do and accomplish on the playing field, in the concert hall, and at their desk.

Perhaps this explains why, on the participant side of the ledger, athletes, musicians, and writers who are no longer able for whatever reasons to perform at the exquisite levels of which they once were capable are often given to view their imminent departure from these practices more so as a kind of death than as mere retirement. It would not be wise, I think, to belittle them for thinking so, to ask them to be prudent rather than self-despairing, not at least until they have had sufficient time to grieve. For once one has to forsake through no initiative or fault of one's own what has been, so to speak, etched into one's soul, to give up what it is that gave one a sense of worth and importance, what one experiences is, as Korsgaard reminds us, "something that … amounts to death" because it means "not being ourselves any more."[69] Perhaps this explains as well from the spectator side of the ledger why the attachment and loyalty of fans to their sports teams can be justifiably likened, as Dixon neatly shows using Nozick as his guide, to people's love for their romantic partners. For the trajectory of most healthy romantic relationships begins with an initial appreciation of their partners' good qualities and then grows and deepens into an appreciation of their "unique instantiation of those qualities … their special identity." Similarly, the trajectory of most healthy relationships of fans to teams begins with an initial appreciation of the good qualities of the teams for which they root, which, of course, involve a mix of such qualities as excellence and fair play and then grows and deepens into an appreciation of their "non-duplicable" instantiation of those qualities, their special identity. This is why true fans, like true lovers, do not "trade up" to a different team or partner who scores higher than their current team or lover on some relevant evaluative scale but remain steadfast in their loyalty to their team and their love for their partner. For a "willingness to trade up" as soon as our team falters or one or more of our lover's attractive qualities wane is a sure sign that our attachment to our team or our love for our lover is not genuine.[70]

Last, the "volitional necessity" that powers the claim that "I can do no other" further explains, contra Kellor, why players and spectators alike go out of their way to argue and debate endlessly the significance of what happened at last night's game and to justify their views to one another for the same reason, as Scanlon tells us, that motivates people to justify their moral actions to their peers: "We have a basic desire to be able to justify our actions to others on grounds that they could not reasonably reject."[71] In other words, the motivation and effort to justify ourselves to others comes naturally to individuals who view themselves as members of a community bound by a shared love for something that touches them all deeply. Indeed, not to defend one's views to such peers is tantamount to denying one's membership in the group. We should not be surprised, then, to hear noted American literary critic Gerald Graff recount how he had to defend himself against criticism from his boyhood friends when he shifted his allegiance from the Chicago Cubs to the Chicago White Sox: "Challenged to defend myself daily during the summer of '51, I struggled for persuasive reasons in defense of my new faith." Nor should we be surprised that this very same Gerald Graff, now all grown up, not only remains fond of arguing about sports but attributes his present professional interest in critical analysis to his long-term critical interest in sports. As he writes, "It was through debates over sports … that I learned to form arguments and analyses that I would later produce as a professional academic … It was through reading and arguing about sports that I learned what it felt like to propose a generalization, restate and respond to a counterargument and the other complex operations that constitute what we call 'intellectualizing.'"[72] Is this not why so many of us adults still follow our childhood habit of turning to the sports page first where we invariably find discussions and arguments, to be sure of varying quality and thoughtfulness, regarding such issues as race, gender, and drugs and which the first chance we get are only too willing and eager to try out on our friends and colleagues to see whether they have any critical traction?

So, it seems that sports can be, very often are, and rightfully deserve to be treated as serious affairs, indeed, very serious affairs, after all. Of course, that is not to say that things cannot go awry in this regard, that they cannot go terribly, terribly wrong, in which our justifiably serious interest in sports shades into something unjustifiably sinister, indeed, into dangerous obsessions that crowd out legitimate moral obligations and claims that emanate from what I have been calling the *realm of necessity*.[73] Still, most things that touch human agents as deeply as sports do are no more or less susceptible to such worrying distortion. In any event, my intent here was only to show that sports are capable of and should be treated as seriously as the other practices that make up the realm of freedom. So, I concede the criticism that our serious fixation on sports might become a problem itself if it is taken to extremes. Still, if there is a problem with sports today, that problem is not that they are taken too seriously but not taken seriously enough, by which I mean they have too often and for too long now been wrongly cast as instrumental affairs and evaluated as such. Though they can sometimes hold their own when subject to such misguided estimates of their importance and value (e.g., it has been lost on practically no one that sports are now an economic force to be reckoned with in big business circles today), what such comparisons gloss over is practically everything about sports that account for their distinctive and special character. That is why I claimed earlier that the kind of seriousness owed to sports and their kind is not only different from the seriousness of everyday life but serves as its ultimate justification, because the only justification of the former social practices is, to quote Suits, "that they justify everything else."[74] In other words, the seriousness of such instrumental pursuits as work, political diplomacy, and social engineering is owed to the role that they play in securing our survival, but whatever seriousness or importance that can be imputed to our survival depends in the final analysis on whether life is worth living. If my account is on the mark, it is forms of life such as sports to which more Americans than we might at first like to admit turn for an affirmative answer. However, if my account is on the mark, there is no reason to bemoan Americans' enthusiasm for sports, especially at their best, as such enthusiasm is not only fully justified but is a possible harbinger of good things to come.

## Concluding remarks

With this last objection out of the way, my effort to vindicate rationally and normatively the Progressive conception of sports is now complete. If my extended line of argument here has, in fact, disarmed the relevant objections to it, I will have succeeded in showing that the Progressive account of sport is, conceptually speaking, truly without peer. For there is no apparent rival conception of sports with which I am familiar, at least one that can similarly pass critical muster and that, on the one hand, offers as cogent an account of the distinctive features of sports and that, on the other hand, is able to show with the same critical acumen how those very features of sports go a long way toward explaining why America is best thought of as a moral commonwealth. A cursory review of some of the main alternatives to the Progressive's account should suffice to make the point.

The much-heralded and bandied-about alternative of amateur sports is still frequently brought up even in present discussions of the fate of contemporary sports. As I have been arguing throughout, however, it is pretty much a nonstarter. The obvious reason why is that the purity of heart that amateur sports extol is linked to a political philosophy that is much closer to an antediluvian aristocratic conception of society than a contemporary democratic one. Hence, the contempt that the enthusiasts of amateur sport willfully direct at working-class folks (e.g., that they are incapable of conducting themselves in accordance with principles of fair play, that they have no clue as to what sport for sport's sake means),[75] is an indelible feature of their genteel take on the world, and, therefore, nothing that they can correct, let alone realize that they need to correct, given their anti-modernist outlook. Moreover, their suspicion of emotional commitment and devotion to a single way of life and to extending oneself physically and spiritually in any pursuit (with the possible exception of conspicuous consumption, which they never tired of trying to outdo their peers at), let alone a lowly one such as sports,[76] rules out by conceptual fiat rather than argument the notion that sports might be serious affairs (callings or vocations) that figure prominently in what makes for a good life.

Efforts to import religious ideals into sports prove similarly problematic. Of course, the ancient Greeks' anthropomorphic conception of religion, which led them to worship the divine in man, was not only conducive to such competitive activities as sports but essentially gave competitors a free pass to do what they must to win. Moreover, in Athens at least, a quasidemocratic form of government reigned for a time. Of course, the distance that separates us moderns from these ancients is too great in every respect to attempt anything more than a partial and heavily sanitized emulation of some of their practices. However, even the latter must be ruled on at least in the case of sports, because the main distributive principle of justice by which the ancient Greeks abided, that the race should go "not to the swiftest but to the divinely favored,"[77] is antithetical to the principle of justice that governs modern sports. Even less of a positive nature can be said regarding the compatibility of Christian conceptions of justice, which one finds, for instance, in chivalry, to the notion of fair play in which modern sports trade. For as the New Testament parable of the laborers in the vineyard teaches, no legitimate claim of unfair treatment can be charged when those hired last and worked the least are paid the same as those who were hired first and worked the most.[78] That is because the sense of fairness appealed to in this story is not anything that we moderns would recognize, let alone endorse, for the reason offered to explain why no one can legitimately claim to have been cheated here is the seemingly arbitrary one that everybody agreed to be paid the sum that they received for their labor. By modern terms, this looks a lot more like exploitation than it does fairness. Things only get worse when this notion of fairness is applied to sports, as it implies that, in competitive sports at least, the last shall be first and the first last.[79]

That the New Left conception of sports is merely, as we have seen, a curious amalgam of quasiamateur sports and private versions of more traditional individual sports, most of which have long since faded from the scene, suffices to rule it out, I believe, from further consideration. Finally, that the professional conception of sports has nothing to recommend it to us either needs no further demonstration, because that has been the central argument of the entire book.

It seems, therefore, that we have nowhere to turn except to the Progressives for a notion of sport adequate to the moral and political goals for which, I believe, America stands or, at very least, America is supposed and ought to stand. In saying that, however, I do not want to suggest that the conceptual superiority of Progressive sports in this regard suggests in any way that they are beyond critical reproach. Far from it, because, as I pointed out in the previous chapter, they were beset by their own problems of class (more so the middle class in this instance) and were further tainted by racism and sexism. The difference, however, is that the way in which Progressives conceived of sports and the moral ideals they divined within them gave these reformers all the critical ammunition that they needed to reform themselves from within. That in many cases they failed to do so is not an indictment of their ideals but only of their own argumentative resolve and imaginative powers. For the best criticism as to why, for example, sports should be free of racial and sexual bias can be derived directly from such Progressive ideals as fair play. The same cannot be said for the other accounts of sports that we have canvassed, the failings of which can be traced directly to their founding ideals, which is why their failures are appropriately treated as internal, self-inflicted ones. So, when I say that Progressives have provided the last conceptual, but not political, revolution that sports need, what I mean by that is precisely what Taylor meant by what he calls "supersession" arguments: that there is a rational path from A to B but not from B to A.[80] Let A stand here for rivals to the Progressive conception of sports and B for the Progressive conception of sport, and what we have here is a supersession argument that claims as follows: the transition from A (amateur sports, chivalric sports, professional sports) to B (Progressive sports) is an irreversible rational advance in the sense that the latter better explicates than any of the former the social, moral, and political aims of sports, just as the same transition viewed from the larger perspective of the societies that hatched these conceptions of sports from A (premodern, nondemocratic societies) to B (modern, democratic ones) marks an irreversible rational advance in the sense that the latter better explicates than the former how societies should be morally and politically ordered. Arranged chronologically, of course, the rational advance of which I speak here is not a pristine linear one and almost never is when moral ideals take on messy historical forms, because, as we have seen, the transition from Progressive sports to private, professional ones is, if my account is not wide of the mark, an indisputably regressive one. That is precisely the political predicament in which we presently find ourselves.

Whereas, then, the Progressives' take on sports and larger America seems to have the most going for it in terms of the conceptual resources and moral and political ideals that it has at its disposal to correct whatever missteps it might take, the present political plight of sports and America is another matter entirely and a far less sanguine one. This is a predicament precisely because there is no good reason, in the best sense of that term, why we should not proceed with the Progressive agenda for cleaning up the moral and political ills that plague sports and larger society today, but there are plenty of political obstacles that stand in our path to dissuade even the fiercest proponents of change from prosecuting such an agenda.

What to do politically speaking, therefore, is the ominous question that we must ask ourselves here, a question that defies any easy answer. For though the conceptual transition, as we said, that needs to be made here is all too clear, as is the moral and political necessity of making it, the way to bring it about socially, to make it a political reality, is anything but. There is, nonetheless, a perfectly good, even if not spine-tingling, answer to this political question about which we should not be shy in throwing out for consideration and adopting wholesale. For it cuts to the very heart of social criticism itself, to the much ballyhooed but little understood intersection between theory and practice, and provides, I think, the only reasonable hope that practitioners of this highly fragile and fallible craft can and should allow themselves. What it lacks in predictive power, simply because critical efforts to effect real political change require social assists that seem to come out of nowhere, that are owed to contingent historical events that no one can adequately foresee and, therefore, get a handle on, it more than makes up for in the historical successes that it has, despite the formidable odds, racked up.

What I am talking about here is the important role that argument plays in changing people's social outlook, in getting them not just to see the error in their ways but to correct those errors where it most counts, in the so-called real world in which we live, work, and play. Taylor provides a nice illustration of this deceptively simple point.[81] It surely is astonishing, as Taylor writes, that the extension of political franchise to women in this country took as long as it did considering that in the nineteenth century a large majority of both genders agreed on the moral desirability and political necessity of gender equality.[82] Before gender equality was a social reality, or at least a well-entrenched political position, arguments against it were not, as Taylor notes, "decisively refutable," though arguments for gender equality were able to weaken somewhat the conviction of many of these deniers of women's equality. Still, so long as these barriers excluding women in political circles were in place, the idea that women were inferior to men seemed at least halfway plausible. After those barriers were removed, however, this idea of women's inferiority and the arguments offered in its defense seemed just "weird," not to mention "bizarre." In other words, once the argument for gender equality picked up social steam, once the favorable social conditions it in part helped to create gained momentum, there was just no going back, assuming, of course, that we can hold the Taliban and their kind at bay. Once we reach this point, as Taylor nicely puts it, the argument against gender inequality "is not just de facto irreversible ... the rational argument is unwinnable by any partisans of reversal."[83]

The moral of this story is precisely what we said it was: social criticism and arguments are an important way to agitate for and effect genuine, long-lasting progressive change. The bewitching factor will continue to be what social assists such criticism might be able to generate and marshal on its behalf, given the historically contingent factors that also play an important role in changing people's social outlook. Everyone, and I do mean everyone, was caught completely unaware by the sudden favorable mix of social conditions that led up to the incredible historical events of 1989 and 1991, which completely changed the face of Eastern Europe and led to the collapse of the Soviet Union. Why the familiar arguments against such totalitarian political regimes as these that had been percolating for some time suddenly took hold is anyone's guess. However, the important point here is that what happened in 1989 and 1991 is very much relevant to the situation that we are presently facing, both with regard to the antidemocratic winds swirling around America today and sports' place and role in this whole sordid mess. This is, as I said, no reason to despair but, contrarily, a good and powerful reason to stay the course, to remain on the offensive in prosecuting our case that sports contoured along the lines sketched by Progressives are the better way to go here. What social efficacy this case and the arguments that power it might have in charting a new democratic course for America in these trying times no one, least of all me, can say for sure. However, if, to reiterate, the past is prologue, we have every reason to press on, to hold to the fire the feet of the desecrators of all that is good in sports and in this grand democratic experiment that goes by the name of America. To be sure, this is a slim hope, but it is, I think, hope enough.

# Notes

## Introduction

1  I should say at the outset that I am sensitive to some on the Left who object to using America to refer exclusively to the United States of America, as I do here and throughout the book. Their criticism – that America is an idea that transcends the United States of America – is well founded, but it is complicated by the fact that Mexico and El Salvador are both formally referred to as "Los Estados Unidos de Mexico" and "Los Unidos de El Salvador." So, there are complications no matter the locution employed, and as America is the more grammatically felicitous, I have favored its usage here. I owe this point to Christopher Hitchen's fine book, *Why Orwell Matters*. New York: Basic Books, 2002, p. 103.
2  Richard Rorty. *Achieving our Country*. Boston, MA: Harvard University Press, 1997, p. 14.
3  For the features that distinguish an identity group from, e.g., an interest group whose members can move fairly easily out of such groups, see Joseph Raz and Avishai Margalit, "National Self-Determination." *Journal of Philosophy* 87 (September, 1990), pp. 439–61.
4  Rorty, *Achieving our Country*, pp. 80–1.
5  However, I will not be talking about sadism in this book for at least two reasons. First, for much the same reason that I confine my attention here to American sports, because I am more familiar with them, I will confine my attention primarily to the money issue, because I am not as familiar with the sadism literature nor can I claim any expertise in the critical theories and tools such critics bring to bear on their work. Second, for reasons that I raise in the ensuing chapters, I believe economic issues are presently the greater threat to our country and our major sports.
6  Andrew Zimbalist. *Unpaid Professionals: Commercialism and Conflict in Big-Time College Sports*. Princeton, NJ: Princeton University Press, 1999.
7  As I was writing this, I came across an interview of the well-known cultural and literary critic, Terry Eagleton, who remains steadfast in his devotion to Marxist theory. When pressed for details, however, about what political advice he would offer to contemporary citizens of the rich Atlantic democracies, the best he could come up with is, "Get out of NATO. Get rid of capitalism. Put the economy back into public ownership." Don't hold your breath, and think smaller, but not less critically, would be my response to this wish list. See Dinitia Smith's, "Cultural Theorists, Start Your Epitaphs." *The New York Times*, January 3, 2004, p. A15.
8  Charles Taylor. *Multiculturalism and the Politics of Recognition*. Princeton, NJ: Princeton University Press, 1992.
9  Andrew Delbanco. *The Real American Dream: A Meditation on Hope*. Cambridge, MA: Harvard University Press, 1999, p. 10.
10  Ibid., pp. 9–10.
11  Ibid., p. 10.
12  I underscore my criticism of the Left in this regard; it is meant only in the broadest of terms. That is, what I am criticizing here are some of the general tendencies and

consequences of their critical writing, much of which, for reasons already stated, I greatly admire and respect. So, there are certainly critics in both these groups whose work has not altogether forsaken hope in the name of pessimism and, therefore, for whom my criticisms are not relevant.

13  Rorty, *Achieving Our Country*, p. 127.

14  Max Barry. *Jennifer Government*. New York: Doubleday, 2003; Richard Greenberg. *Take Me Out*. New York: Faber and Faber, 2003.

15  Strictly speaking, most of the action in the book takes place in what is called "The Australian Territories of the USA." However, as on the author's futuristic world map America encompasses most of the world with the exception of the member countries of the European Union, the Middle East, and most of the African continent, it is crystal clear what country is the target of his satirical novel. To remove any further doubt about this point, Barry has one of his main characters refer to Australia as "the new California." *Jennifer Government*, p. 49.

16  Ibid., p. 5

17  Ibid., p. 7.

18  Interestingly enough, if someone happens to steal or harm someone else in spite of the government's best efforts, punishing the perpetrators is not something the government has any money to pursue. Indeed, precisely because the government has no budget to punish those who steal from or harm others, Nike's plug-a-customer campaign singled out poor people as its victims. For it knew full well that these people would be hard pressed to pay the government to pursue the murderers of their kids, although one of the families in the book is able to do so but only after putting their house up for sale. Ibid., 64.

19  Ibid., p. 7.

20  Ibid., p. 140.

21  Ibid., p. 221.

22  Greenberg, *Take Me Out*, p. 5.

23  Ibid., p. 9.

24  Ibid., p. 15.

25  Ibid., p. 17.

26  Ibid., p. 45.

27  Ibid., p. 93.

28  Ibid., p. 62.

29  Ibid., p. 63.

30  Ibid., p. 9.

31  This is the title of an interview Heidegger gave to Der Spiegel, which he agreed to give on the condition that it be published after his death. See Rudiger Safranski. *Martin Heidegger: Beyond Good and Evil*. Cambridge, MA: Harvard University Press, 1998, p. 420.

32  It is precisely for this adoption of spectatorship over activism that Rorty, rightly to my mind, excoriates the American Left in his *Achieving Our Country* and which I have been arguing is apropos of much of the Left's criticism of contemporary sports. What makes the Left's self-imposed timidity in this regard all the worse is that the Right vigorously pursued an activist agenda during this same period in their effort to transform America and sports into things many of us would scarcely recognize, let alone prize.

33  Greenberg, *Take Me Out*, p. 35.

34  Ibid., p. 38.

35  Ibid., p. 66.

36  Ibid., p. 72.

37  The quote from Fitzgerald comes from the famous literary and American critic Alfred Kazin, in *Alfred Kazin's America*. Edited by Ted Solotaroff. New York: Harper Collins, 2003, p. 54. The reference to Marx comes from his *The Eighteenth Brumaire of Louis Bonaparte* and to his following famous quip, "Hegel remarks somewhere that all facts and

personages of great importance in world history occur … twice. He forgot to add: the first time as tragedy, the second as farce." See the *Karl Marx-Frederick Engels Collected Works: Volume 11, 1851–1853*. New York: International Publishers, 1979, p. 103.

# 1 The state of play

1 Bernard Williams. *Truth and Truthfulness*. Princeton, NJ: Princeton University Press, 2002, p. 20. My discussion of genealogy is heavily indebted to Chapter 2 of this book.

2 Friedrich Nietzsche. *On the Genealogy of Morals and Ecce Homo*. New York: Vintage Books, 1989, p. 19. The emphasis here is that of the author. I should say at the outset that all emphases in the text are those of the authors cited unless indicated otherwise.

3 Ibid., p. 21.

4 Paul Rabinov (ed.). *The Foucault Reader*. New York: Pantheon Books, 1984, p. 82.

5 As quoted by Foucault in *The Foucault Reader*, p. 79.

6 On this point, see Alaisdair MacIntyre. *Three Rival Versions of Moral Enquiry*. Notre Dame, IN: University of Notre Dame Press, 1990, p. 49.

7 Henry Aiken (ed.). *Hume's Moral and Political Philosophy*. Darien, CT: Hafner Publishing Co., 1970, p. 58.

8 Ibid., p. 59.

9 Robert Nozick. *Anarchy, State, and Utopia*. New York: Basic Books, 1974.

10 Williams, *Truth and Truthfulness*, p. 33.

11 Nozick, *Anarchy, State, and Utopia*, p. 7.

12 Williams, *Truth and Truthfulness*, p. 34.

13 Kenneth L. Schmitz. "Sport and Play: Suspension of the Ordinary." In William J. Morgan and Klaus V. Meier (eds). *Philosophic Inquiry in Sport*. Champaign, IL: Human Kinetic Publishers, 1988, p. 29. While I am at it, I should also point out that my state of play, as remarked, is restricted to a moral account of sport. For a larger fictional account of how sport itself may well have developed as a sophisticated social practice from a state of nature of sorts, I recommend Eleanor Metheny's excellent discussion in her important but, alas, largely forgotten, book, *Movement and Meaning*. New York: McGraw Hill, 1968.

14 For an interesting account that tries to explain the emergence of the political state from a state-of-nature story premised on sport, see J. Ortega y Gasset, "The Sportive Origin of the State." In Morgan and Meier (eds). *Philosophic Inquiry in Sport*.

15 Williams, *Truth and Truthfulness*, p. 24.

16 That does not mean that it would be conceptually ill-advised or not morally desirous to do so in certain circumstances for certain reasons; only that it would be wrong to presume that that is my present intention.

17 It might be objected that in describing the state of mind appropriate to the state of play as a single-minded, passionate one, I have just emptied most of the forms and levels of sports I previously included in this space. However, I think that is a misnomer. True, it does disgorge the casual, care-free recreational players and the sports they take up in this insouciant way, but that still leaves room for a great many players in youth sports, recreational sports, and folk games, who play sports in purposive, disciplined, and – yes – passionate ways. Of course, the range, duration, and intensity of those passions vary considerably.

18 Annette Baier. *The Commons of the Mind*. Chicago, IL: Open Court, 1997, p. 26–27.

19 Bill Bradley. *Values of the Game*. New York: Broadway Books, 1998, p. 5.

20 I should note that my invocation of the body here implicates a further feature of Foucault's conception of genealogy, namely, that genealogy necessarily "attaches itself to the body," which he claims is "the inscribed surface of events." *The Foucault Reader*, p. 83.

21 The phrase "commons of the mind" I borrow from Baier's aforementioned book of the same title, *The Commons of the Mind*. I should also say here that in an interesting

article by Malcom Gladwell in The New Yorker dealing with what he calls "physical" genius (he lumps highly accomplished surgeons, musicians, and athletes under this label), he touches on some of the themes I am discussing here. In particular, he remarks how gifted athletes have a special kinesthetic feel for the game, in the way in which surgeons have for surgery and musicians for playing music, which allows the entire game to come alive to them in ways unavailable to mere mortals. In particular, he cites professional hockey player Wayne Gretzky's uncanny ability to deliver the puck seemingly magically to his fellow teammates in congested areas with difficult angles. Of course, that does not imply that the state of mind appropriate to the state of play requires the possession of physical genius, only that these "felt" qualities are capable, in the right hands, of the most exquisite expression.

22 As quoted in Baier, *Commons of the Mind*, p. 50.
23 Bradley, *Values of the Game*, p. 5. It should also be said that being paid to play sports, especially being paid well, may not even be "compromising" if it provides people the financial security, not to mention a feeling of self-worth, to pursue sports as their central passion in life. Of course, there is a tipping point here at which the financial rewards become so great that people in and outside of sports willingly – and often unapologetically – prostitute themselves.

## 2 The moral case against contemporary American sports

1 Bernard Williams. *Shame and Necessity*. Berkeley, CA: University of California Press, 1994, p. 77.
2 At the same time, however, it goes without saying that they are too large and influential a target simply to ignore.
3 Nicholas Dixon. "On Winning and Athletic Superiority." In W. J. Morgan, K. Meier, A. Schneider (eds). *Ethics in Sport*. Urbana, IL: Human Kinetics, 2001, p. 62.
4 Ibid., p. 64.
5 Ibid., p. 65.
6 To the extent that intercollegiate sports likewise rely on an intraleague playoff system, they too are inculpated by Dixon's powerful arguments. However, Dixon offers an important caveat here and one that we need to keep in mind. To the extent that it is impractical if not logistically impossible for teams to play each other regularly over the course of the season, as is the case with the Olympics, World Cup, and (in collegiate sports) national championships, a playoff system is no longer a choice but a necessity. In these special circumstances, then, playoffs are not second best to season records as measures of athletic excellence but the only available method, however imperfect, to assess excellence. This does not, however, lessen the force of Dixon's central arguments, as it still remains the case that overall season records are the most accurate way in which to determine athletic success and that when they are an option they are clearly superior to playoffs. Lastly, collegiate sports are especially guilty of privileging money over excellence when highly talented teams pay relatively lucrative sums to much less talented teams to entice them to play their games in the former's home stadiums. These seldom make for good matchups, but they do enable the host teams both to pad their winning records and to play an extra home game, both of which affect the bottom line. This is a serious problem today because it has become of late a standard practice.
7 I owe this point and the background documentation to Merrell Noden's, "A New Record – By a Mile." *Sports Illustrated*, 91, No. 3 (July 19, 1999), p. 34.
8 See Mike Wise, "As the Stars in the NBA Rise, The League's Level of Play Falls." *New York Times* (February 8, 1998), pp. 1, 18.
9 Wilfred Sheed, "Why Sports Matter." *Wilson Quarterly* (Winter, 1995), p. 22.
10 I am indebted for the points raised in this paragraph to Christopher Lasch's interesting account of sports in his widely celebrated and read book, *The Culture of Narcissism*. New York: Warner Books, 1979, pp. 100–24.

11   On this point, see Walter LaFeber, *Michael Jordan and the New Global Capitalism*. New York: W.W. Norton, 1999, p. 145.

12   Susan Fauldi. "Sold Out: From Team Booster to TV Backdrop: The Demise of the True Fan." *Utne Reader* No. 97 (January–February, 2000), p. 54.

13   Sheed, "Why Sports Matter," p. 21.

14   Wise, "As the Stars in the NBA Rise, The League's Level of Play Falls," p. 18.

15   Robert Wright. "Boycott Nike and Reebok: Not Because They Oppress Asian Sweatshop Workers, But Because They Oppress Black Teenagers." *Slate* (posted May 22, 1997), p. 3.

16   See David Anderson, "Agents and Perks and Harmful Effects." *New York Times* (November 19, 2000), p. 41.

17   Sheed, "Why Sports Matter," p. 65.

18   I owe the point about Pat Riley to George Vescey's article, "Don't Worry: Sportsmanship Won't Be Catching." *New York Times* (February 21, 1999), p. 39.

19   Given my own extensive reliance in this chapter on journalists, especially from the New York Times and other magazines that pride themselves as much on their reporting prowess as on their ability to attract commercial advertising, I must exempt newspapers and magazines such as these and those that emulate them from the present critique.

20   Criminal action that crosses the border of acceptable moral action as well is the notable exception for sports pundits. However, the reportage of such athletic misconduct is almost always dominated by speculations as to the declining market value of the fallen hero, for which so-called public relations and management experts are called on en masse for their counsel.

21   Players, and especially their union representatives, have failed miserably on this score. To cite just one instance: when senator Arlen Specter from Pennsylvania introduced legislation requiring the National Football League to set aside 10 percent of its considerable television revenues for the building and renovating of stadiums, the players and their unions opposed the measure in lockstep with NFL management. Whereas the commissioner of the NFL, Paul Tagliabue, at least tried to offer some justification for his opposition by appealing speciously to the interests of local communities (which in this case was code not for the communities themselves but for the individual owners of sports teams), Gene Upshaw, the executive director of the NFL Players Association, based his opposition to Specter's bill squarely on the negative impact it would have on players' salaries. See Mike Freeman's piece, "Owners of NFL Teams Are Nervously Watching the Estate Tax Bill." *New York Times* (July 30, 2000), p. 26.

22   I lifted this joke from Steve Rushin's essay, "Who Stole the Show?" *Sports Illustrated* 84, No. 22 (June 3, 1996), pp. 26–27.

23   Fauldi, "Sold Out: From Team Booster to TV Backdrop," pp. 53–55.

24   Ibid., p. 53.

25   I gleaned my account of NASCAR from Chris Jenkins's expose "Wanted: Salesman, Must Drive." *USA Today* (July 12–14, 2002), pp. 1A–2A.

26   Two further points: first, this class of sports, in fact, encompasses three subclasses of sports, namely, Divisions I, II, and III. Moreover, Division I has three further subclasses: I A, which includes colleges that have big-time football programs; I AA, which includes colleges with second-tier football programs; and I AAA, which includes colleges with no football programs. Though Division III is actually the largest subcategory of intercollegiate sports, it is politically and economically the weakest in its ability to influence policy and bring in money. Though Division II and III sports are supposed to have athletic missions different from those of Division I (e.g., there are no athletic scholarships awarded to athletes from Division III), the facts suggest that those differences are for the most part nominal. For these reasons, most of my analysis is directed to Division I A sports, because it is clearly the most politically

influential and economically powerful subcategory, one that dominates the governing structure of the National Collegiate Athletic Association (hereafter, NCAA), which is the main regulatory agency of intercollegiate sports. The second point is that my effort to highlight the moral side of these sports and not their educational side is problematic to some extent because at times they clearly overlap. That is, the educational justification of sports in liberal arts colleges and universities includes its supposed inculcation of such distinctly moral values as service to and tolerance of others. Where they are clearly intertwined, then, I shall have to talk about both, but where they are not I will, as stated, steer clear of academic matters.

27  On this and other points, see Andrew Zimbalist's path-breaking work, *Unpaid Professionals: Commercialism and Conflict in Big-Time College Sports*. Princeton, NJ: Princeton University Press, 1999. In my estimation, Zimbalist has written the definitive book on college sports, one that anyone interested in the economically convoluted world of college sports would be well advised to read.

28  Alan Wertheimer. *Exploitation*. Princeton, NJ: Princeton University Press, 1999.

29  Sheed, "Why Sports Matter," p. 24.

30  Zimbalist, *Unpaid Professionals*, p. 137.

31  Dan Wetzel, Don Yaeger. *Sole Influence: Basketball, Corporate Greed, and the Corruption of America's Youth*. New York: Warner Books, 2000, p. 25

32  LaFeber, *Michael Jordan and the New Global Capitalism*, p. 92.

33  Zimbalist, *Unpaid Professionals*, p. 11.

34  For a compelling argument why, see Welch Suggs's important essay, "Colleges Make Slight Progress Toward Gender Equity in Sports." *The Chronicle of Higher Education* (July 25, 2003), pp. A30–A32.

35  Zimbalist, *Unpaid Professionals*, p. 153.

36  Ibid., p. 150.

37  Ibid., p. 153.

38  Ibid,. p. 150.

39  Ibid., p. 155.

40  To document the ripple effect of top-level, Division I A college sports on other men's and women's sports, all the empirical trends suggest that these latter programs are following in the footsteps of the elite athletic programs. Save a small enclave of schools at the Division III level, which want to deprofessionalize sports by, among other things, restricting the length of seasons, eliminating off-season practices, and abolishing national championships, there is very little discrepancy in outlook and practice among these divisions. Academic underperformance, which used to be the bane only of big-time football and basketball sports, is now a common feature of all college sports and all levels of men's and women's competition. For the first point, see Bill Pennington, "Play to Win, or Just to Play." *New York Times* (May 25, 2003), p. 24; for the second, see James Shulman and William Bowen, "How the Playing Field is Encroaching Upon the Admissions Office," *The Chronicle of Higher Education* (January 26, 2001), p. B8.

41  As quoted in Welch Suggs's article, "Players off the Field," *The Chronicle of Higher Education* (May 24, 2000), p. A61.

42  On this point, see William H. Honan, "Do Big-Money Sports Belong in College?" *New York Times* (January 7, 2001) Section 4A, p. 20.

43  Welch Suggs, "Conference Soap Opera Is Driven by Cash, But Cachet Matters Too," *The Chronicle of Higher Education* (May 30, 2003), p. 37.

44  Zimbalist, *Unpaid Professionals*, p. 106.

45  Mike Freeman, "On College Football." *New York Times* (August 25, 2002), p. 11; Welch Suggs, "Players Off the Field," p. 61.

46  I owe this line of thought and the facts that back it up to Zimbalist, *Unpaid Professionals*, p. 112.

47  Ibid., p. 37.

48 Ibid., pp. 173, 174.

49 For more on this point, see George Vescey, "Don't Worry: Sportsmanship Won't Be Catching.", p. 39. To be fair, I should say that Vescey's focus here is on professional sports. Of course, if my analysis is sound, this is a difference that does not make a difference.

50 Louis Menand. "Sporting Chances: The Cost of College Athletics." *The New Yorker* (January 22, 2001), p. 85.

51 It is not just that liberal arts institutions seem to emphasize values different from their athletic counterparts but that those values sometimes conflict, and not in trivial ways. For example, the principle of free speech is an important precondition of a reflective life. However, when college athletic entities sign endorsement deals with such shoe companies as Nike, contractually obligating players not to tape over the Nike Swoosh as a gesture of social protest against the wages and working conditions of their workers, they clearly undermine one of the pivotal goals of a college and university education. On this point, see Zimbalist, *Unpaid Professionals*, pp. 50–1.

52 For the first point, see Menand, "Sporting Chances: The Cost of College Athletics," p. 88; for the second, see Zimbalist, *Unpaid Professionals*, p. 51.

53 Ibid., p. 87.

54 Zimbalist, *Unpaid Professionals*, p. 48.

55 Ibid., p. 12.

56 Welch Suggs, "Sports as the University's 'Front Porch'. The Public is Skeptical." *The Chronicle of Higher Education* (May 2, 2003), p. A17.

57 William Honan, "Do Big-Time Sports Belong in College?" p. 21.

58 Jere Longman, "In a Class by Themselves." *New York Times* (May 29, 2003), p. C15.

59 Ibid., p. C15.

60 Alexander Wolff, George Dohrman, "A School for Scandal." 94, No. 9. *Sports Illustrated* (February 26, 2001), pp. 74–84.

61 George Dohrmann, "Sweat Shopping." 94, No. 26. *Sports Illustrated* (June 25, 2001), pp. 61–66.

62 Zimbalist, *Unpaid Professionals*, pp. 138–40,

63 Robert Lipsyte, "The Olympic Moment Isn't What It Used to Be." *New York Times*, p. 29.

64 E. M. Swift, "Made in the USA." *Sports Illustrated* (July 22, 1996), p. 24.

65 Roger Cohen and Jere Longman, "Many Sides of the Olympic Chief." *New York Times* (February 7, 1999), p. 24.

66 Torbjorn Tannsjo. "Is Our Admiration for Sports Heroes Fascistoid?" In W. J. Morgan, K. Meier, A. Schneider (eds). *Ethics in Sport*. Urbana, IL: Human Kinetics, p. 407.

67 It is precisely because so much is at stake in how we are to understand and interpret already existing sports (and therefore of my critique of them) that I do not regard this foray into the historical past as a scholastic exercise in the least.

## 3 Taking the longer moral measure of sports

1 Alan Schwartz, "Baseball in Crisis? Nah. It's Déjà vu All Over Again." *New York Times* (July 14, 2002), p. 16.

2 Elliot Gorn and Warren Goldstein. *A Brief History of American Sports*. New York: Hill and Wang, pp. 185, 246.

3 As quoted in Eric Dunning. *Sport Matters*. New York: Routledge, 1999, p. 166.

4 Andrew Zimbalist. *Unpaid Professionals: Commercialism and Conflict in Big-Time College Sports*. Princeton, NJ: Princeton University Press, 1999.

5 Gorn and Goldstein, *A Brief History of American Sports*, p. 231.

6 Zimbalist, *Unpaid Professionals*, p. 7.

7 Gorn and Goldstein, *A Brief History of American Sports*, p. 232.

8 Zimbalist, *Unpaid Professionals*, p. 9.

9  Steve Pope. *Patriotic Games: Sporting Traditions in the American Imagination, 1876–1926.* New York: Oxford University Press, 1997, p. 19.

10  Ibid., p. IX.

11  Allen Guttmann, "The Belated Birth and Threatened Death of Fair Play." *Yale Review* 74 (1985), p. 532.

12  Pope, *Patriotic Games*, p. IX.

13  Friedrich Nietzsche. "The Gay Science." In Walter Kaufmann (Ed. and Trans.). *The Portable Nietzsche.* New York: Viking Press, 1968, p. 95.

14  Jonathon Glover, in his important book, *Humanity: A Moral History of the Twentieth Century.* New Haven, CT: Yale University Press, 1999 argues persuasively that the last century was the most violent in human history, in which millions of people were murdered and butchered by the likes of Hitler, Stalin, Pol Pot, and Idi Amin.

15  In this regard, see Christopher Hitchen's thoughtful and interesting exegesis of Orwell's work in his book, *Why Orwell Matters.* New York: Basic Books, 2002.

16  David Grann, "Baseball Without Metaphor." *The New York Times Magazine* (September 1, 2002), p. 38.

17  Steve Pope, *Patriotic Games*, p. 16. I should say that the prose that Pope uses to state this claim is slightly more understated than mine, although the thesis he advances is every bit as sweeping as I have depicted it, and that he links amateur sport not just to Progressive nationalist forces but to military ones as well (with which I am presently not concerned).

18  Ibid., p. X.

19  Ibid., p. X.

20  David Zang. *Sports Wars: Athletes in the Age of Aquarius.* Fayetteville, AK: University of Arkansas Press, 2001, p. 88.

21  When it became a pernicious influence is open to question and one I address later when I narrate the alternative story of sports that I find more telling. Suffice to say for now that it obviously was a gradual process and that other social and political developments in American society had something to do with its transformation from a private good accorded certain players to a public force that threatened the core values of sports.

22  Melvin Adelman. *A Sporting Time: New York City and the Rise of Modern Athletics.* Urbana, IL: University of Illinois Press, 1986, p. 244.

23  Gorn and Goldstein, *A Brief History of American Sports*, p. 236. For the same reason that it has become unthinkable, because uneconomical, for colleges to pull out of conference play for a year or two, it has become unthinkable, because uneconomical, for the NCAA to levy costly penalties against colleges who break the rules, no matter the moral and legal severity of such rule infractions. This is why, despite the steady increase in major infractions in football and basketball the last three or four decades or so, the suspension of teams from postseason play and television appearances, two of the most serious penalties, has rapidly declined in this same period. This is also true of the so-called death penalty, which suspends offending teams for a year or more and which was last applied to Southern Methodist University in 1987. On these points, see Zimbalist, *Unpaid Professionals*, pp. 178, 179. It goes without saying, of course, that this weakening of rule enforcement in collegiate sports provides further evidence of the larger point at issue here: a shift in the way in which contemporary sports are financed and marketed.

24  William J. Baker. *Sports in the Western World.* Totowa, NJ: Roman & Littlefield, 1982, p. 311.

25  For a slightly different take on the moral perversity of such purity of heart, see Richard Rorty. *Philosophy and Social Hope.* New York: Penguin Books, 1991, p. 13.

26  This point confirms the obvious: that not only is such purity of purpose unattainable and incoherent in sports but outside them as well.

27 At this point, I suppose our fans would grow indignant, as it is their critics who not only get things wrong here but presume, rather arrogantly, the opposite.
28 My rendering of Wittgenstein's point is heavily indebted to Charles Taylor's critique of traditional epistemology. See his *Philosophical Arguments*. Cambridge, MA: Harvard University Press, 1995.
29 Jay Weiner, "Sports Centered," *Utne Reader* 97 (January–February, 2000), p. 49.
30 Gorn and Goldstein, *A Brief History of American Sports*, p. 254.
31 Allen Guttmann, "The Belated Birth and Threatened Death of Fair Play," p. 529. Two further points about Guttmann's important essay are in order. First, he takes pains to show that like the notion of amateurism itself, the ideal of fair play was also a product of the upper and upper-middle classes. Any charge of elitism here, however, would be misdirected, as fair play, unlike amateurism, works to the benefit of the lower classes as well. However, if it is claimed that what is morally objectionable about fair play is the very fact that it was a top-down initiative, one would be hard pressed to justify many, if not most, progressive reforms in or outside of this country. With specific regard to the progressive American scene, Rorty's following point is worth emphasizing: "The history of Leftist politics in America is a story of how top-down initiatives and bottom-up initiatives have interlocked." Richard Rorty. *Achieving our Country*. Cambridge, MA: Harvard University Press, 1998, p. 53. Second, Guttmann makes a good case that the ills of contemporary sports, and particularly the precarious hold the ethos of fair play has on these sports, is owed not to the excessive influence of money but to what he calls representational sports: the fact that for whatever reason, millions of people see themselves as personally represented by athletic heroes and teams. There is much to be said for this thesis, but one thing that cannot be said for it is that it explains the increasingly unfair character of modern athletic conduct itself. For the facts that professional athletes switch teams frequently to fetch a higher price and that so-called amateur athletes switch countries at an increasing rate to compete in the Olympics and world championships for the same monetary reason, seem to undercut any claim that these athletes break rules and use illicit substances because of the psychological pressures of representing so many people. Perhaps the most bizarre case of country switching occurred in the recent 2003 world track and field championship and involved the winner of the 3,000-meter steeplechase, Saif Saeed Shaheen of Qatar. What is odd about this case is that until two weeks before this event, he was known as Stephen Cherono of Kenya.
32 In this regard, see Mark Dyerson. *Making the American Team: Sport, Culture, and the Olympic Experience*. Urbana, IL: University of Illinois Press, 1998. I borrow liberally from Dyerson's book in recounting what I have been calling the alternative historical story of American sports.

# 4 Moral inquiry in sports

1 Bernard Williams. "Internal and External Reasons." In *Moral Luck*. New York: Cambridge University Press, 1981, p. 105. I should note here that Williams's account of internalism in no way supposes that the elements of a person's motivational set have to be egoistic. This is an important caveat because it speaks to the point that Dewey and others have made regarding the elastic boundaries of the self. For it may well be the case that one or more elements of a person's motivational set include concern for the welfare of others. In such instances, therefore, it is impossible to distinguish self-regarding interests from other-regarding ones, a fact that Dewey used to underscore why we should not distinguish too sharply between self-interest and morality. It would, of course, be foolish to deny Dewey's point if only because most of us know people and, if we are really fortunate, know a number of people, for whom the welfare of others is the abiding concern of their lives. However, it would be

equally foolish, at least from a sociological standpoint, to assume that a society such as ours is rife with such people and that it is structured and ordered in such a way as to turn out people of this altruistic ilk. Indeed, if my analysis is on the right track, ours is a society that encourages just the opposite in people.

2 Jurgen Habermas. *Justification and Application*. Cambridge, MA: MIT Press, 1993, p. 5.

3 Thomas Nagel. *The Possibility of Altruism*. Oxford: Clarendon Press, 1970, p. 90.

4 Another way of saying this is that the sort of egoism at work in our pragmatic interactions with one another is a bald one rather than an ethical one. That is to say, there is no Humean or otherwise ethical pretension apparent here in which some effort is made to square a self-interested life with an ethical life, to show that a life devoted to private interests is congruent with an ethical life. In short, the ethical does not figure here at all.

5 The word *wanton* is a term of art I lifted from Christine Korsgaard's important book, *The Sources of Normativity*. Cambridge, MA: Cambridge University Press, 1996.

6 Jurgen Habermas. *The Theory of Communicative Action: Volume Two*. Boston, MA: Beacon Press, 1987, p. 301.

7 Charles Taylor. *Sources of the Self*. Cambridge: Cambridge University Press, 1992, p. 14.

8 Williams, *Moral Luck*, p. 102.

9 However, to be dissatisfied with what one gets after having reflectively secured what one's basic desires and interests come to and after having correctly chosen the best means to realize them is another matter (and, I should add, decidedly not a pragmatic matter). For such ennui is sometimes what prompts people to fashion an altogether new life for themselves, one in which the ethical often plays an important part.

10 Annette Baier. *Postures of the Mind*. Minneapolis, MN: University of Minnesota Press, 1985, p. 293; Richard Rorty. *Contingency, Irony, and Solidarity*. Cambridge: Cambridge University Press, 1989, p. 59; Christine Korsgaard. *Creating The Kingdom of Ends*. Cambridge, MA: Harvard University Press, 1996, p. 275.

11 This explains, for instance, why Baier thinks that a child's trust in her mother is where all of our moral ladders begin. As cited in Rorty, "Idealizations, Foundations, and Social Practices." In S. Benhabib. *Democracy and Difference: Contesting the Boundaries of the Political*. Princeton, NJ: Princeton University Press, 1996, p. 335.

12 In this regard, see Samuel Scheffler, "Relationships and Responsibilities." *Philosophy and Public Affairs*, 26 (1997), p. 202.

13 This claim that our special ethical relationships with others are the source of our special responsibilities to others is also subject to a distributive objection, the claim that this unfairly privileges the subjects of these social relationships, who already enjoy the advantage of standing in such a relationship, in terms of extra opportunities and resources denied to others who don't stand in these relationships. A full response to this objection would take me too far afield. So, I just confine my response to the simple and obvious point that standing in special relationships to others does not in any way mitigate my more general ethical responsibilities to people who are not a party to these relationships.

14 As quoted in Richard Rorty, *Contingency, Irony and Solidarity*, p. 58.

15 Christine Korsgaard. *The Sources of Normativity*, p. 139.

16 Ibid., pp. 140–1.

17 Eduardo P. Archetti. *Masculinities: Football, Polo and the Tango in Argentina*. New York: Berg, 1999.

18 Alaisdair MacIntyre. *Dependent Rational Animals*. Chicago and La Salle, IL: Open Court, 1999, p. 87.

19 For more along these lines, see Alaisdair MacIntyre, "Politics, Philosophy and the Common Good." In Kevin Knight (ed.). *The MacIntyre Reader*. Notre Dame, IN: University of Notre Dame Press, 1998, p. 240.

20 Korsgaard, *Creating the Kingdom of Ends*, p. 288. This part of my analysis is heavily indebted to Korsgaard's discussion.
21 Charles Taylor. *Sources of the Self*, Ch. 2.
22 For more on the distinction between overcoming and silencing, see John McDowell. *Mind, Value, and Reality*. Cambridge, MA: Harvard University Press, 1998, pp. 91–2. As McDowell further notes, this notion of silencing "involves a high degree of idealization" but one that, he counsels, we should neither avoid nor apologize for.
23 Jurgen Habermas. *Moral Consciousness and Communicative Action*. Cambridge, MA: MIT Press, 1990, pp. 108-9.
24 Bernard Williams. *Ethics and the Limits of Philosophy*. Cambridge, MA: Harvard University Press, 1985, p. 113.
25 John Rawls. *A Theory of Justice*. Cambridge, MA: Harvard University Press, 1971, pp. 48–51.
26 John Rawls. "Kantian Constructivism in Moral Theory." In S. Freeman (ed.). *John Rawls: Collected Papers*. Cambridge, MA: Harvard University Press, 1999, pp. 306–7.
27 Korsgaard, *Sources of Normativity*, p. 91.
28 Habermas, *Justification and Application*, pp. 126–7.
29 That is not to say that there are never any borderline cases in which this is in dispute (i.e., in which we think we have been wronged or treated too harshly by our peers) and we try to make the case for our reinstatement. However, given the intersubjective character of ethical recognition, such cases would be few and far between, at least in a well-ordered ethical community.
30 Korsgaard, *Sources of Normativity*, p. 18.
31 David Wiggins, "Deliberation and Practical Reason." In A. Rorty. *Essays on Aristotle's Ethics*. Berkeley, CA: University of California Press, 1980, p. 225.
32 That means that our universal ethical responsibilities to others beyond our membership in particular ethical communities can best be rendered and achieved in ethical rather than moral terms. For ethical considerations are not averse to universalist-tending ones if by the latter we mean what Rawls calls universal "in reach" as opposed to universal "in authority" principles. Ethical considerations are not incompatible with universal "in reach" ones, as in our ethical encounters with others, both we and they may, potentially at any rate, hit on ethical views that all of us find persuasive and that, therefore, all of us are happy to endorse reflectively. However, ethical considerations are incompatible with universal "in authority" principles, as such principles require that we adopt them at the beginning rather than at the end of inquiry, and as they are held to "apply to all reasonable beings everywhere" even if they had no say in their formulation or do not find them especially authoritative. See John Rawls, *The Laws of Peoples*. Cambridge, MA: Harvard University Press, 1999, pp. 86–7. I should also say that the ethical incompatibility of these universal authoritative moral principles is only one count against them and not even the most damning one. For, as I argue in the next section, the principal problem here is that there are no such wide-ranging and abstract moral principles to be found.
33 Williams, *Ethics and the Limits of Philosophy*, pp. 14–15.
34 Thomas Nagel. *The Last Word*. New York: Oxford University Press, 1997, p. 122.
35 Habermas, *Moral Consciousness and Communicative Action*, p. 210.
36 Nagel, "Universality and the Reflective Self." In Korsgaard, *Sources of Normativity*, pp. 202–3.
37 Habermas, *Justification and Application*, p. 151.
38 Nagel, *The Last Word*, pp. 117–18.
39 Habermas, *Moral Consciousness and Communicative Action*, p. 207.
40 Ibid., p. 67.
41 Habermas, *The Philosophical Discourse of Modernity*. Cambridge, MA: MIT Press 1987, pp. 322–3.

42  Richard Rorty. "Feminism and Pragmatism." In *Truth and Progress: Philosophical Papers, Volume 3.* Cambridge: Cambridge University Press, 1998, p. 203.
43  As quoted in John McDowell, *Mind, Value, and Reality*, p. 118. The emphasis here is mine.
44  I should add that while moral philosophers of this universalist ilk regard their chief job to be certifying the (absolute) validity of moral norms, they are not unaware that the application conditions that tell us when it is appropriate to apply these norms deserve their considered attention as well. For example, Habermas supplements his discourse of justification with what he calls a *discourse of application* in which the principle of appropriateness (*angemessenheit*) is given primary consideration. Oddly enough, however, he argues that both of these principles of moral discourse are "purely" cognitive procedures notwithstanding the sensitivity to context demanded by the discourse of application. See his *Justification and Application*, p. 172.
45  Ibid., p. 177.
46  Nagel, *The Last Word*, p. 111.
47  Nagel, *The View from Nowhere*.New York: Oxford University Press, 1997, pp. 105–6.
48  Ibid., p. 146.
49  Ibid., pp. 146–7.
50  Nagel, *The Last Word*, pp. 114–15.
51  Habermas, *Justification and Application*, p. 154.
52  Nagel, *The View from Nowhere*, p. 11.
53  In John McDowell, *Mind, Value, and Reality*, p. 118.
54  I have borrowed this phrase from Rorty in his essay, "Daniel Dennett on Intrinsicality." In *Truth and Progress: Philosophical Papers, Volume 3.* Cambridge: Cambridge University Press, 1998, p. 105.
55  Nagel, *The View from Nowhere*, p. 11.
56  Alasdair MacIntyre. *Dependent Rational Animals*, p. 119.
57  I am indebted here to Charles Taylor's discussion in his book, *Ethics of Authenticity.* Cambridge, MA: Harvard University Press, 1992, pp. 2–3.
58  Alaisdair MacIntyre. *After Virtue.* Notre Dame, IN: University of Notre Dame Press, 1984, p. 228.
59  Ibid., p. 229.
60  My discussion here draws heavily on MacIntyre, *After Virtue*, Chapter 6.
61  This argument has been made forcibly by G. A. Cohen, "Reason, Humanity, and the Moral Law." In C. Korsgaard, *The Sources of Normativity*, pp. 167–8.
62  The latter argument comes from Gary Gutting. *Pragmatic Liberalism and the Critique of Modernity.* Cambridge: Cambridge University Press, 1999, p. 72.
63  The alert reader will already note my interchangeable use of the concepts ethical and moral in this and the immediately preceding paragraphs. My doing so is neither accidental nor incidental for, as I hope to show shortly, if we drop the abstract notion of the moral realm championed by such theorists as Nagel, there is no good reason of which I am aware to treat them as separate concepts.
64  Williams, *Ethics and the Limits of Philosophy*, p. 58.
65  On the distinction between the meaning and use of moral utterances see MacInytre, *After Virtue*, pp. 12–13.
66  Nagel, "Universality and the Reflective Self," p. 206.
67  He offers this argumentative promissory note in *The View from Nowhere*, p. 144.
68  Simon Blackburn. *Spreading the Word.* Oxford: Clarendon Press, 1984, p. 236.
69  John Searle. *Speech Acts.* Cambridge: Cambridge University Press, 1969, p. 52.
70  Ralph Feezell. "Sport and the View form Nowhere." *Journal of the Philosophy of Sport.* XXVIII, 2001, p. 9.
71  Williams, *Moral Luck*, p. 14.

72 Michael Walzer. *Thick and Thin: Moral Argument at Home and Abroad.* Notre Dame, IN: University of Notre Dame Press, 1994, p. 8.
73 Richard Rorty. "Letter 4." In A. Balslev, *Cultural Otherness: Correspondence with Richard Rorty.* Atlanta, GA: Scholars Press, 1991, p. 73.

## 5 A short moral history of America

1 Jonathan Glover. *Humanity: A Moral History of the Twentieth Century.* New Haven: Yale University Press, 1999. To get some idea of the scale of Glover's moral indictment, he asks us to focus on just the number of people killed in wars from 1900 to 1989. Though that number represents a small fraction of the world's population during this period and constitutes a relatively small number of the total number of people who died from hunger and treatable diseases, it still amounts to a staggering 86 million people. If one were to spread those deaths over this entire period, that would come out to 100 people killed every hour, around the clock, for 90 years.
2 As periodizations go, my previous caveat notwithstanding, this is a fairly uncontroversial one. That is why, no doubt, it matches up well with Delbanco's, Gitlin's, and Rorty's historical partitioning of contemporary America. See Andrew Delbanco, *The Real American Dream: A Meditation on Hope,* Cambridge, MA: Harvard University Press, 1999; Todd Gitlin. *The Twilight of Common Dreams.* New York: Henry Holt Co., 1996; and Richard Rorty. *Achieving Our Country.* Cambridge, MA: Harvard University Press, 1998.
3 Of course, the social and moral plight of gays and lesbians was not even on the radar screen of most Americans at this stage.
4 As quoted in Rorty, *Achieving Our Country,* p. 13.
5 Christopher Lasch. *The Culture of Narcissism.* New York: Warner Books, 1979; Alasdair MacIntyre. *After Virtue.* Notre Dame, IN: University of Nortre Dame Press, 1984.
6 See p. 224, note 32, Chapter 4.
7 I will have much more to say about this kind of Leftist theorizing and politics in my ensuing analysis.
8 My account here is heavily indebted not only to the writings of Delbanco, *The Real American Dream*; Gitlin, *The Twilight of Common Dreams*; and Rorty, *Achieving Our Country*, cited above, but as well to the following books: Eric Foner, *The Story of American Freedom,* New York: W. W. Norton, 1998; Peter Levine, *The New Progressive Era,* New York: Roman & Littlefield Co., 2000; Godfrey Hodgson, *More Equal Than Others,* Princeton, NJ: Princeton University Press, 2004; and Robert D. Putnam, *Bowling Alone,* New York: Simon & Schuster, 2000.
9 Putnam, *Bowling Alone,* p. 370.
10 Rorty, *Achieving our Country,* p. 101
11 Alexis de Tocqueville. *Democracy in America.* New York: Vintage Books, 1945, p. 32.
12 Delbanco, *The Real American Dream,* p. 66.
13 As quoted in Putnam, *Bowling Alone,* p. 372.
14 Levine, *The New Progressive Era,* p. 4.
15 Foner, *The Story of American Freedom,* p. 144.
16 de Tocqueville, *Democracy in America,* pp. 114, 118.
17 As Putnam noted, Progressives were quite concerned over the professionalization of politics, religion, art, and sport, which had the effect of turning ordinary folks into spectators rather than agents. See Putnam, *Bowling Alone,* p. 377.
18 As quoted in Jean Grondin, *Hans-Georg Gadamer: A Biography.* New Haven, CT: Yale University Press, 2003, p. 250.

19 This nicely anticipates Rawls's conception of the "reasonable," which means, in particular, that when parties deliberate with one another regarding matters of justice, they should venture only views that would be acceptable to and justifiable by all concerned, and, more generally, that they should always consider the likely effect their actions will have on the well-being of others. See John Rawls, *Political Liberalism*. New York: Columbia University Press, 1993, p. 49.

20 Levine, *The New Progressive Era*, pp. 25-7.

21 As quoted in Putnam, *Bowling Alone*, p. 396.

22 Ibid., p. 396.

23 Putnam quotes an observer of one of these community center debates who gives a vivid sense of the class and educational mixing that occurred in them, "the topic being the commission form of government, a Polish washwoman and the president of the WCTU [Women's Christian Temperance Union] were opposed by a day cleaner and a college professor." *Bowling Alone*, p. 397.

24 Ibid., pp. 378–95; Levine, *The New Progressive Era*, pp. 16, 21; and Foner, *The Story of American Freedom*, p. 159.

25 Robert Reich. *I'll Be Short: Essentials for a Decent Working Society*. Boston, MA: Beacon Press, 2002, p. 11.

26 This is also probably just as appropriate a point as any at which to stress that my own distinction between the pragmatic and moral spheres in Chapter 4 (which it will be remembered is not to be confused with the subsystem of morality that I tried to discredit in that same chapter) is not pure either. That means that in moral inquiry, instrumental considerations may play a role as long as it is a limited and clearly subordinate one. For example, when there is more than one morally good end that an agent has reason to pursue, that agent clearly has a compelling reason not to pursue all of them at the same time, because that would preclude his achieving any of them. On this point, see T. M. Scanlon. "Reasons: A Puzzling Duality?" In R. Wallace *et al.* (eds). *Reason and Value: Themes from the Moral Philosophy of Joseph Raz*. Oxford: Clarendon Press, 2004, p. 239.

27 Hodgson, *More Equal Than Others*, p. 9.

28 Delbanco, *The Real American Dream*, pp. 89–90.

29 According to Putnam, social trust in America rose precipitously between the mid-1940s and the mid-1960s. *Bowling Alone*, p. 139.

30 Gitlin, *Twilight of Common Dreams*, p. 135.

31 Allan Wolfe. *Moral Freedom: The Search for Virtue in a World of Choice*. New York: W. W. Norton, 2001, p. 210.

32 In this regard, see Paul Krugman's brilliant essay, " For Richer." *New York Times Magazine* (October 20, 2002). It should also be said, once again, that the usual suspects (mainly women and African-Americans) experienced not only very few gains in this period but some definite setbacks. In addition, there were some new victims to be added to the list of the morally victimized, to wit, those in the interment of Japanese-Americans during the Second World War.

33 Krugman, "For Richer," p. 62.

34 Putnam, *Bowling Alone*, p. 18.

35 Don DeLillo. *Pafko at the Wall*. New York: Scribner, 1997, p. 69.

36 Delbanco, *The Real American Dream*, pp. 83–4.

37 Gitlin, *Twilight of Common Dreams*, pp. 67–73; Rorty, *Achieving Our Country*, pp. 65–68.

38 Hodgson, *More Equal Than Others*, pp. 2, 16.

39 Delbanco, *The Real American Dream*, pp. 96–7; 106.

40 Reich, *I'll Be Short*, pp. 37–8.

41 Robert D. Kaplan. *An Empire Wilderness: Travels into America's Future*. New York: Random House, 1998, p. 60.

42 Delbanco, *The Real American Dream*, pp. 4, 107.

43  Hodgson, *More Equal Than Others*, p. 240
44  Ibid., pp. 91–2.
45  Ibid., p. 92.
46  Reich, *I'll Be Short*, p. 60.
47  Krugman, "For Richer," p. 64.
48  Barbara Ehrenreich. *Nickel and Dimed: On (Not) Getting By in America*. New York: Henry Holt, 2001, pp. 202–3; Reich, *I'll Be Short*, p. 16.
49  Krugman, "For Richer," p. 65.
50  Hodgson, *More Equal Than Others*, p. 244.
51  Here, too, current tax policy is skewed to the disadvantage of workers, as it gives to businesses tax breaks for moving their operations overseas as well as tariff protection for what it produces there (goods that originate from the United States can be reimported without duty if they are fabricated or put together overseas). A further point on outsourcing: at present, outsourcing is responsible for the elimination of only about one of every 50 jobs lost. That is a relatively benign number, but it could easily and quickly become a malignant one for two reasons. First, outsourcing is a rather new phenomenon and one that is quickly picking up steam in the global market. That is because there are a number of good-paying jobs that require only minimal computer skills and training, which means that many of these jobs will likely be outsourced in the near future (e.g., Cassidy cites a recent consulting firm report that forecasts that as many as three million jobs could go overseas in the next year alone). Second, the threat of cheap labor in such markets as China and India is much greater that it was, for instance, in the 1970s, when Japanese manufacturers started to compete seriously with American manufacturers. Though the wages of Japanese workers were about one-half of that of Americans, the wages of workers in India and China are respectively about one-fifth and one-tenth of their American counterparts. Finally, even though outsourcing is not as yet a major source of job loss in America, those who are laid off because of it and are lucky enough to find employment (and I do mean lucky, as many of their colleagues remain unemployed) in the mostly service sector make on average 13 percent less than they did in their old manufacturing jobs. On these and other related points, see John Cassidy. "Winners and Losers," *The New Yorker* (August 2, 2004), pp. 26–30.
52  Ibid., pp. 18, 89.
53  Rorty, *Achieving Our Country*, p. 84.
54  Reich, *I'll Be Short*, p. 20.
55  Kaplan's quote of a political activist from Omaha commenting on the political apathy of his rich neighbors in a nearby suburb is instructive in this regard. The activist complains that "they are too hooked on tennis, health clubs, [and] cyberspace" to care about politics. He then adds, "There is only one political issue that grabs their attention, and that is petition drives against taxes." This sends the clear message, the activist continues, "that people in poor neighborhoods such as North Omaha [will not] get substantial help from anyone other than themselves." Kaplan, *An Empire Wilderness*, p. 74.
56  Krugman, "For Richer," p. 65.
57  Hodgson, *More Equal Than Others*, p. 94.
58  Michael Walzer. "Multiculturalism and Individualism." *Dissent* (Spring, 1994), p. 187.
59  My discussion is heavily indebted here to Hodgson, *More Equal Than Others*, pp. 205–13. I should also say here that the claim suburbanization leads to privatization is in one important sense a misnomer. For though suburbs are mainly the creations of private businesses, a whole slew of them in fact, the financing for these communities was and is often furnished, as we shall shortly see, by local, state, and federal government agencies.

60 Kaplan, *An Empire Wilderness*, p. 63. The insular, homogeneous character of certain planned suburban communities tend to be rather extreme. In this regard, Kaplan mentions the planned California community of Westlake, which excluded not just people of color but old people as well. A British writer wrote of this community that its inhabitants "did not want, any longer, their ambience to be interesting or stimulating: they wanted it perfect: a safe and beautiful rest-home, cut out from the pain of the world, for healthy people." Ibid., p. 34.

61 Alan Wolfe, *Moral Freedom*, pp. 12–13.

62 Ibid., p. 203.

63 My entire discussion in this paragraph is indebted to Putnam's book, *Bowling Alone*, pp. 104–38.

64 Ibid., p. 117.

65 Putnam further attributes this diminution of social capital to the greatly expanded hours that Americans spend watching television, to two-career families, and to generational changes. See *Bowling Alone*, p. 367.

66 Michael Walzer, "On Involuntary Association." In *Freedom of Association*, A. Gutmann (ed.). Princeton, NJ: Princeton University Press, 1998, p. 70. I come back to this idea in the next chapter and argue that it is such practices as sport that provide the social cement needed to bind the republic together. My argument will be that if we are to strengthen the civic spirit of America, to enact a Progressive-inspired revitalization of our social and political infrastructure, it would be wise to start with social practices such as these, to build off of the social capital that they are still able, rather remarkably considering everything that has been said so far, to generate.

67 de Tocqueville, *Democracy in America*, p. 336 (emphasis mine).

68 Ehrenreich, *Nickel and Dimed*, p. 217.

69 Rorty thinks that one likely outcome of such exploitation, especially among the poor, is a new outbreak of a particularly virulent form of sadism in which the overt humiliation of women, people of color, and gays and lesbians will come back in fashion. For when the income-deprived poor realize that their "betters" have no intention of helping them out of their immiserated condition, they are not apt to take kindly to "having their manners dictated to them by college graduates." *Achieving our Country*, p. 90.

70 Reich, *I'll Be Short*, p. 19.

71 Taylor thinks America's inability to combine a sensible government-based "industrial policy" to harness private economic forces is one of the chief shortcomings of its politics of fragmentation. With respect to the rule of law, he also notes how the politics of judicial review, in which violation of individual rights are routed through and resolved by the courts and whose decisions are typically "winner take all; either you win or you lose," are further problematic in this regard. That is because they block public debate and sometimes more satisfactory political compromises. On this and the points made in the main body of the text see his *Ethics of Authenticity*, pp. 12–17.

72 Hodgson, *More Equal Than Others*, p. 52; Gitlin, *Twilight of Common Dreams*, p. 234.

73 Gitlin, *Twilight of Common Dreams*, p. 76.

74 Hodgson, *More Equal Than Others*, p. 215.

75 As Rorty avers, "To take pride in being black or gay is an entirely reasonable response to the sadistic humiliation to which one has been subjected. But insofar as this pride prevents someone from also taking pride in being an American citizen, or from being able to join with straights or whites in reformist initiatives, it is a political disaster." *Achieving Our Country*, p. 100.

76 Richard Rorty. "Who Are We? Moral Universalism and Economic Triage." *Diogenes* 173 (Spring, 1996), p. 13.

77 David Brooks. "The Organization Kid." *The Atlantic Monthly* (April, 2001), pp. 41, 49–50.

78  Putnam, *Bowling Alone*, p. 138.
79  This shows that the link between achievement and reward no longer holds for most of the rich as well but this time in reverse, as these lucky folks often receive great rewards for things we would be hard pressed to regard as genuine achievements. Celebrities are just one obvious example; the obscene perks and wages of CEOs are another.
80  Andrew Delbanco. "Are You Happy Yet?" *New York Times Magazine* (May 7, 2000), p. 46.
81  That is not to say that all their private slings missed the mark (e.g., we do know that welfare programs that are run the wrong way breed dependence on the government rather than genuine self-determination and that when such ditzy celebrities as Britney Spears get married while in a drunken state and then have their so-called marriages annulled the next day, they deserve whatever ridicule comes their way (surprisingly, or perhaps not surprisingly, most conservative commentators ignored this latter unseemly event probably because at the time they were more interested in derailing the hopes of gays to enter into committed, monogamous relationships recognized by the state as legitimate marriages than to criticize heterosexual marriages that were neither monogamous nor committed ones). Rather, the issue is that by privatizing their notion of morality, the great public vices that eat away at our society in an especially pernicious way, which I have been trying to document in this chapter, are given practically no notice at all – so much so, that it seems a mockery to refer to these conservative talking-heads as social critics let alone moral ones.
82  Of course, this does not get conservative moralists completely off the hook because of their capacious conception of markets (i.e., their constant insistence that practically everything we humans do could be substantially improved by treating them as if they, too, were markets). However, as my aim here is not to explain away the contradictions of conservative moral theory, which in any event I do not believe can be explained away, but only to highlight their commitment to a morality of negative freedom, I leave this matter to others.
83  There is no denying that conservatives do not speak for Americans on such moral issues as abortion, same-sex marriage, and the like, which still divide Americans far more than they unite them. At the same time, it does seem clear that conservative moralists do speak for most Americans when they talk about moral freedom in the highly individualistic way in which they do, especially in the case, as noted in the text, of the market, the associations that make up civil society, and the role of government.
84  When morality goes, the rule of law becomes that much more important in contemporary society, to include, of course, the importance of lawyers. For when no one trusts anyone, it becomes especially important to get everything down in writing, more specifically, to codify it in a formal, binding contract that is, of course, the bailiwick of lawyers. This explains in part, as Putnam notes, the explosion in the number of lawyers in contemporary America, the actual numbers of whom today exceed by some 150 percent what Americans estimated in the 1970s would be needed at this present juncture in our history. *Bowling Alone*, p. 146.
85  Michael Walzer. "Liberalism and the Art of Separation." *Political Theory* 12 (August, 1984), p. 325.
86  Charles Taylor. *The Ethics of Authenticity*. Cambridge, MA: Harvard University Press, 1992, p. 36 . My discussion on this point is wholly indebted to Taylor's illuminating analysis in Chapter IV of this important book.
87  Rorty, *Achieving Our Country*, p. 76.
88  Lasch, *Culture of Narcissism*, pp. 268–9.
89  As quoted in Robert Westbrook, *John Dewey and American Democracy*. Ithaca, NY: Cornell University Press, 1991, p. 185.

90 For a fair and balanced accounting of the pros and cons of the Progressive movement, see Putnam, *Bowling Alone*, and Levine, *The New Progressive Era*.

91 Rorty effectively notes in this regard that if the TV journalists and newspaper reporters were not present to document the beatings of union members by goons hired by their corporate bosses or the unleashing of police attack dogs by Southern sheriffs to stop civil rights marchers in their tracks and if sensitive viewers or readers did not respond to their reports, these heroic acts might well have gone unnoticed or described by their perpetrators as peaceful efforts to prevent "senseless violence" as opposed to acts of justified civil disobedience. *Achieving Our Country*, pp. 53–4.

92 It might be thought that this Leftist remedy works only or perhaps best with closeted gays and lesbians (i.e., those who try to escape the humiliation directed their way by denying or otherwise keeping their gayness secret). Racial humiliation, or so the argument goes, is another matter entirely, as the source of exploitation (which is bound up in one way or another with the color of one's skin) cannot be hidden, which means that what is being targeted here is one's undeniable membership in this racial group. The inference that supposedly follows is that racial exploitation does not result, as it seemingly does in the case of gays and lesbians, in the atomization of its members, their sense that they are alone and so must fend for themselves. However, I think the inference drawn here is mistaken, as racial exploitation such as that of gays similarly divides and separates those on whom it sets its sights (i.e., induces them to dissociate from or variously deny their racial group identity by drawing subtle invidious contrasts between darker- and lighter-skinned blacks or other no less invidious contrasts with respect to the stereotypes that are elicited by such exploitation). In short, what makes sadism of this sort so insidious is the inexorable internalization of the humiliation by its victims, which prompts not their solidarity with the group in question but opposite efforts to secede from the group, to extricate oneself from the identity conferred by it.

93 I should say here that this Left-inspired championing of difference, and so of local groups and identities over more expansive, cosmopolitan ones, marks a remarkable reversal of Marx's insistence that "workers have no country" because the only group or community that matters is the one that is inclusive of the whole of humanity. For an interesting argument along these lines, see Mitchell Cohen's essay, "Rooted Cosmopolitanism." In N. Mills (ed.). *Legacy of Dissent*. New York: Simon and Schuster, 1994, pp. 131–40.

94 A point Gitlin forcefully presses in claiming that "the politics of identity is silent on the deepest sources of social misery," chief among which, he insists, is the very same "sickening inequality between rich and poor" that I have identified as the main causal force behind the dismantling of the Progressive-liberal legacy. *Twilight of Common Dreams*, p. 236.

95 I do not mean to denigrate the cultural Left's very real achievements in reversing sadism in this regard. Rather, I mean to suggest only that appeal to one's national identity, to what we share in common instead of what differentiates us from one another, provides just as robust a defense of the rights of gay men and women, straight women, and people of color and at the same time avoids the tunnel vision one often finds in the politics of identity camp. So, in suggesting that it is high time we start thinking more about our larger national identity, I am not in any way suggesting that we should abandon the struggle against sadism but rather that we wage that struggle on a different, more expansive turf. On this point, see Gitlin, *The Twilight of Common Dreams*, p. 228.

96 I have borrowed this notion from Scott McLemee, "Freedom Philosophers." *The New York Times Book Review* (October 24, 2004), p. 22.

97 Matthew Arnold. *Culture and Anarchy*. New Haven, CT: Yale University Press, 1994, p. 5.

98 Michael Walzer, "Multiculturalism and Individualism," p. 186.

99  As Wolfe makes crystal clear in his survey of contemporary religious life in America, a large majority of Americans condemn the fear and shame approaches to morality characteristic, for example, of Victorian morality, not to mention theological doctrines that insist on the natural depravity of humankind. See his *Moral Freedom*, p. 183.

100 As Walzer notes in this regard, "Social democracy depends upon the validity of associational life. But the associations that we value most highly are rarely economically efficient." "Pluralism and Social Democracy," p. 53. Walzer's main point here is that market societies simply will not bankroll such social practices because most of them are not economically profitable, and those that can be made profitable, as he claims further, often are made so at the expense of the moral ideals and values on which their democratic validity depends. Either way, he concludes, market societies kill the very moral practices that they require to rein them in.

101 Gitlin, *The Twilight of Common Dreams*, p. 231.

102 Thomas Frank. *What's the Matter with Kansas?* New York: Metropolitan Books, 2004, as cited in Keith Gessen. "Winning Hearts, Losing Souls." *Dissent* (Fall, 2004), p. 105.

103 This is why Franks thinks that anti-intellectualism, precisely of the sort that Bush wears on his sleeves, is a "grand unifying theme of the backlash" among poor whites. He also notes in this connection that this backlash is not entirely racist, as least in the Midwest, as antiabortion crusaders are fond of quoting abolitionist Kansan John Brown. However, it is occasionally antiSemitic, which further explains the anti-intellectualism of less-well-off whites. As quoted in Gessen, *Dissent*, p. 106.

104 Wolfe, *Moral Freedom*, p. 18.

105 Hodgson, *More Equal Than Others*, pp. 292–3.

106 Putnam, *Bowling Alone*, p. 25.

107 Ehrenreich, *Nickel and Dimed*, pp. 52, 220.

108 David Miller, *Principles of Social Justice*, pp. 84–5.

109 Ehrenreich, *Nickel and Dimed*, p. 38.

110 Wolfe, *Moral Freedom*, p. 74.

111 Taylor, *Ethics of Authenticity*, p. 22.

# 6 A short moral history of American sports

1  My account of the Progressive conception of sport is heavily indebted to Dyerson's and Mrozek's fine books on this topic. Mark Dyreson. *Making the American Team: Sport, Culture, and the Olympic Experience*. Urbana and Chicago, IL: University of Illinois Press, 1998; Donald J. Mrozek. *Sport and American Mentality 1880–1910*. Knoxville, TN: University of Tennessee Press, 1983.

2  Mrozek, *Sport and American Mentality*, p. xiv.

3  The "Jacksonian emphasis on free will and competition" that fueled this tomfoolery was, therefore, not only to be tolerated but fully embraced and celebrated. On this point, see John Dizikes. *Sportsmen & Gamesmen*. Columbia, MO: University of Missouri Press, 2002, p. 124, pp. 134–139.

4  Wilfred Sheed. "Why Sports Matter." *Wilson Quarterly* (Winter, 1995), p. 11.

5  Mrozek, *Sport and American Mentality*, p. 27.

6  Ibid., p. 20.

7  Ibid., p. 30.

8  Dyreson, *Making the American Team*, p. 207.

9  As quoted in Richard Rorty, "Anticlericalism and Atheism." In S. Zabala (ed.). *The Future of Religion*. New York: Columbia University Press, 2005, p. 30.

10 Mrozek, *Sport and American Mentality*, p. xiv; Dyreson, *Making the American Team*, p. 18.

11  Dyreson, *Making the American Team*, pp. 20–1.
12  Ibid., p. 18.
13  Ibid., p. 27.
14  Mrozek, *Sport and American Mentality*, p. 233.
15  Ibid., p. 230.
16  Ibid., p. 235.
17  As quoted in Dyreson, *Making the American Team*, p. 11.
18  Ibid., p. 11.
19  Lasch goes on to say that more often than not what passes for such novelty and shock is an artwork's "sheer ugliness and banality." See Christopher Lasch. *The Culture of Narcissism*. New York: Warner Books, 1979, p. 190. As Lyotard further opines, this stress on novelty not only means that "anything goes" as far as the aesthetic standards used to judge works of art are concerned but inevitably leads to the assessment of them by money. In his own words, "this realism of the 'anything goes' is in fact money; in the absence of aesthetic criteria [which is what the "anything goes" amounts to], it remains possible and useful to assess the value of works of art according to the profits they yield." Jean-Francois Lyotard. *The Postmodern Condition: A Report on Knowledge*. Manchester: University of Manchester Press, 1986, p. 76.
20  Bernard Suits. *The Grasshopper: Games, Life and Utopia*. Toronto: University of Toronto Press, 1978. Suits's contemporary account of games spells out James's implicit point here regarding the unique rationality of sports more powerfully and comprehensively than any other account, contemporary or otherwise, with which I am familiar.
21  Ibid., pp. 37–8.
22  Price Collier. "Sport's Place in the Nation's Well-Being." *Outing* (July, 1998), p. 384.
23  My use of the metaphor "mirror" here to underscore the critical potential of sport, of course, has nothing in common with its more common use, one that I have already explicitly disavowed, which speciously suggests sport is simply a passive reflection of larger society.
24  Walt Whitman. *The Gathering of the Forces*. New York: G.P. Putnam's Sons, 1920, p. 207.
25  Besides the already noted success of Progressives in institutionalizing their reform efforts documented in Chapter 5, they also racked up impressive achievements in the sports realm. As Dyreson notes, as early as 1904 Progressives had managed to elect one of their own as president, Theodore Roosevelt, a well-known devotee of the "strenuous life" and of sports, sports were soaring in popularity and becoming an integral part of educational institutions, and a national playground movement was starting to make significant inroads in American's lives. See Dyreson, *Making the American Team*, pp. 98–9.
26  Bill Brown. "The Meaning of Baseball." *Public Culture* (Fall, 1991), p. 54.
27  William James. "The Moral Equivalent of War." In B. Wilshire (ed.). *William James: The Essential Readings*. New York: Harper and Row, 1971.
28  Ibid., p. 356.
29  Ibid., p. 358.
30  This idea that such practices as sports teach us the important things that we can accomplish by working in concert with one another is also what Progressives thought rightly casts suspicion on the rationality of the market, which by turning us essentially into rational egoists makes us, in this sense at any rate, rationally challenged agents. On this point, see Mrozek, *Sport and American Mentality*, p. 33. By turning us into rational egoists, this instrumental form of reason at work in the market and in certain other spheres was also thought to be a grave threat to morality itself. This is what Rousseau had in mind when he argued in the *Discourse on Inequality* that "Reason is what engenders egocentrism and reflection strengthens it. Reason is what turns man in

upon himself. Reason is what separates him and moves him to say in secret, at the sight of a suffering man, 'Perish if you will; I am safe and sound.'" As quoted in Annette Baier. *The Commons of the Mind*. Chicago and La Salle: Open Court, 1997, p. 48.

31  John Rawls. "Justice as Reciprocity." In S. Freeman (ed.). *John Rawls: Collected Papers*. Cambridge, MA: Harvard University Press, 1999, p. 210.

32  James, "The Moral Equivalent of War," p. 360.

33  I owe the substance of my claim here to Mrozek's excellent discussion of this matter. See Mrozek, *Sport and American Mentality*, p. 108.

34  The power of these connections, of course, is what gives them both their moral salience and, less happily, their potentially social and political divisive effects.

35  James, "Moral Equivalent of War," p. 358.

36  This notion that national and individual moral character are not immutable, as Mrozek astutely observes, is itself a part of the changing moral landscape of America in the late nineteenth century. See his *Sport and American Mentality*, p. 226.

37  For more along this line, see Dyreson, *Making the American Team*, pp. 125–6.

38  This is why Progressives, although in general supporters of amateurism, were scared off by the social class implications that the rich attributed to the amateur code, which simply excluded anyone who received financial remuneration for playing sports or instructing others interested in pursuing sports. By contrast, Progressive adherents of amateurism were more interested in instilling in athletes and spectators alike a more balanced, less winning focused, view of sports, one that was confused and confusing when it came to assessing the payment of money for athletic services. A prominent example of the confused and confusing Progressive defense of amateurism was the recruitment of a rowing coach by Harvard alumni in 1903–4 to bolster the fortunes of the crew team, in which the coach was paid for any loss of income that resulted from leaving his previous coaching position and for any other expenses incurred in the transition. They were able to justify such payment without running afoul of their high regard for the amateur code by reasoning that, strictly speaking, they were not technically paying their new coach for carrying out his new coaching duties. An ingenuous defense, no doubt, but an entirely specious one all the same. On this point, see Mrozek, *Sport and American Mentality*, pp. 130–2.

39  George Hibbard. "The Sporting Spirit: Ancient and Modern." *Outing* 36 (September, 1900), p. 600.

40  As quoted in Dyreson, *Making the American Team*, pp. 27–8.

41  Mrozek, *Sport and American Mentality*, p. 45.

42  Wilfred Sheed. "Why Sports Matter." *Wilson Quarterly* (Winter, 1995), p. 11.

43  Dyreson, *Making the American Team*, p. 12.

44  Mark Dyreson. "Maybe It's Better to Bowl Alone: Sport, Community and Democracy in American Thought." *Culture, Sport, Society*, Vol. 4, No. 1 (Spring, 2001), p. 21.

45  For an extended political discussion of the importance of such dispersals of power, see Michael Walzer, *Politics and Passion: Toward a More Egalitarian Liberalism*. New Haven, CT: Yale University Press, 2004.

46  As quoted in Allen Guttmann, "The Belated Birth and Threatened Death of Fair Play." *The Yale Review* 94 (1985), pp. 531–2.

47  The practicality of this combination, of course, was necessitated by the fact that solidarity could not reasonably be expected to do its job alone as long as the egoistic urges fueled by the market were still rife, which was still very much the case at the turn of the century and, of course, throughout much of the twentieth century.

48  John Rawls, "Justice as Reciprocity," p. 209.

49  Dyreson, *Making the American Team*, pp. 112–18.

50  Mrozek, *Sport and American Mentality*, p. 137.

51  Dyreson, *Making the American Team*, p. 105.

52  Ibid., p. 105.

53  Ibid., p. 105.

54  Mrozek, *Sport and American Mentality*, pp. 158–9.
55  Ibid., pp. 150–1.
56  Collier, "Sport's Place in the Nation's Well-Being," pp. 729–30.
57  Thorstein Veblen. *The Theory of the Leisure Class*. New York: Mentor Books, 1953, p. 174. It should be said, however, that although Veblen concurred with Collier's diagnosis of the ills of this period, he vigorously dissented from his recommendation of sports as a curative. For Veblen was not much enamored by sports and regarded them as "an addiction to … an archaic spiritual constitution," one marked by "an arrested development of … man's moral nature." *The Theory of the Leisure Class*, p. 170.
58  Robert Lipsyte. "Why Sports Don't Matter." *New York Times Magazine* (April 2, 1995), p. 54.
59  Dyreson, *Making the American Team*, p. 112.
60  Ibid., p. 111.
61  Mrozek, *Sport and American Mentality*, p. 232.
62  Sheed, "Why Sports Matter," p. 12.
63  Mrozek, *Sport and American Mentality*, p. 232.
64  Ibid., p. 89.
65  Mrozek, *Sport and American Mentality*, p. 102.
66  This might explain as well their occasional tendency to adapt traditional sports in rather exotic ways (e.g., fox hunting in cars). Ibid., p. 106.
67  Dyreson, *Making the American Team*, p. 103.
68  Ibid., p. 191. Of course, sporting Progressives such as Spaulding also got rich by catering to the private whims of sports consumers.
69  Ibid., p. 103.
70  Elliot Gorn and Warren Goldstein. *A Brief History of American Sports*. New York: Hill & Wang, 1993, pp. 195–6.
71  David W. Zang. *SportsWars: Athletes in the Age of Aquarius*. Fayetteville, AK: University of Arkansas Press, 2001, p. 12.
72  Ibid., p. 246.
73  Lipsyte, "Why Sports Don't Matter," pp. 51–2.
74  Zang, *SportsWars*, XI.
75  Mrozek, *Sport and American Mentality*, pp. 134–5.
76  *SportsWars*, p. 25.
77  These new physical cultural experts have created their own moral problems in sports. For their use of science to bolster performance in sports has rubbed off on athletes who, in addition to the help that they receive in the form of better training techniques and diets from these sports specialists, have also turned to pharmaceutical aids (steroids, human growth hormone, etc.) to enhance their performance. A significant part of this scientific community takes a very dim view of athletes who use such drugs (a minority, however, have assisted athletes in their quest to push the limits of human performance), but it is hard to understand their moral pique given their own unmistakable amoral regard for the scientific work they do. Moreover, this turn to excellence through chemistry, which promises to grow even more sinister with advances in genetic engineering, raises an entirely new issue with regard to fairness, which has broad implications not just for sports but for meritocratic societies such as our own. Such societies pride themselves on rewarding people for the effort that they expend in excelling at what they do. However, meritocratic faith of this sort seldom bothers to consider the role that natural talents play in the production of such excellence. As the saying goes, "Hard work beats talent that doesn't work hard" but not always, and almost never when the talented expend significant effort to hone their genetic advantage. Who among us seriously believes that we could defeat Michael Jordan at basketball no matter how well trained and conditioned we are? Those who do believe such are, of course, delusional. However, in the case of

drug and genetic enhancement, there is no doubt that what is being rewarded is not just effort alone. The rub is why the advantage that just winning the genetic lottery confers, without the use of drugs and genetic engineering, does not also offend our sense of fairness. For a provocative treatment of this issue, see Michael Sandel, "The Case Against Perfection." *The Atlantic Monthly* (April, 2004), pp. 51–62.

78  Dyerson, *Making the American Team*, p. 199.
79  Stanley Weintraub. *Silent Night: The Story of the World War I Christmas Truce*. New York: The Free Press, 2001, p. 105.
80  Richard Rorty. *Contingency, Irony, and Solidarity*. New York: Cambridge University Press, 1989, p. 53.
81  Bernard Yack. *The Longing for Total Revolution*. Princeton, NJ: Princeton University Press, 1986.
82  Of course, not everyone on the Left endorsed theories of this sort, not even members of the so-called Frankfurt School, who are most often accused of harboring such theoretical outlooks. Adorno, one of the leading members of this school, is a case in point in which one can find remarks such as the following scattered throughout his writings: "Sport is ambiguous, it can have an anti-barbarian and anti-sadistic effect by means of fair play, a spirit of chivalry, and consideration for the weak. On the other hand, in many of its varieties and practices it can promote aggression, brutality, and sadism." Theodor Adorno. *Critical Models, Interventions, and Catchwords*. New York: Columbia University Press, 1999, pp. 196–7. As Walzer further notes, the right has its own version of this "interactionist" theory, which treats society, predictably, as a market writ large. Michael Walzer, *Thick and Thin: Moral Argument at Home and Abroad*. Notre Dame, IN: University of Notre Dame Press, 1994, p. 35.
83  It is also little wonder why, then, this same New Left regarded its predecessors as not Leftists at all, as for them what it means to be a Leftist is defined by the desire to overthrow capitalism itself. On this point, see Richard Rorty, *Achieving Our Country*. Cambridge, MA: Harvard University Press, 1999, p. 42.
84  Zang's treatment of the New Left critique of sport in his book *SportsWars*, is one of the best I have seen, and one from which I liberally draw here.
85  Zang, *SportsWars*, pp. 65–6.
86  Ibid., p. 85.
87  Ibid., p. 24.
88  David Guterson. "Moneyball." *Harper's Magazine* (September, 1994), p. 45.
89  Zang, *SportsWars*, XXI.
90  I am simply paraphrasing here what Rorty claimed of liberalism with regard to Western social and political thought, namely, that it was "the last *conceptual* revolution" it needed. *Contingency, Irony, and Solidarity*, p. 63.

# 7  Progressive sport and progressive America

1  Thomas Frank, in his best selling and smartly written and argued book, *What's The Matter With Kansas?* New York: Henry Holt and Company, 2004, does a better job that anyone I have read thus far in untying this knotty problem by persuasively making the case that it has a lot to do with a certain "backlash" mentality that has gripped America's heartland. This backlash, he opines, was a long time in coming but it has done most of its damage in the last decade or so.
2  Charles Taylor. *Modern Social Imaginaries*. Durham, NC: Duke University Press, 2004, p. 23.
3  Ibid., p. 25.
4  Charles Taylor. *Hegel*. New York: Cambridge University Press, 1975, p. 382.
5  Vincent Descombes. "Is There an Objective Spirit?" In J. Tully (ed.). *Philosophy in an Age of Pluralism*. New York: Cambridge University Press, 1994, p. 106.

6  The phrase "social repertory" comes directly from Taylor. See his essay, "Reply and Re-Articulation." In J. Tully (ed.). *Philosophy in an Age of Pluralism*. New York: Cambridge University Press, 1994, p. 238.

7  For the moral importance of such adaptations as this one, see Bernard William's interesting and incisive discussion, "Professional Morality and its Dispositions." In Chapter 16, *Making Sense of Humanity*. New York: Cambridge University Press, 1995, pp. 192–202.

8  By and large, Progressive reformers were, interestingly enough, enthusiasts of boxing but were careful to distinguish it from bare-knuckle prizefighting, which they disdained. It should also be said, however, that their enthusiasm for boxing did not match their enthusiasm for such team sports as baseball. With regard for their views on boxing, see Mark Dyerson, *Making the American Team*. Urbana and Chicago, IL: University of Illinois Press, 1998, p. 19.

9  Richard Rorty. "The Continuity Between the Enlightenment and 'Postmodernism'." In K. Baker and P. Reill (eds). *What's Left of Enlightenment*, Palo Alto, CA: Stanford University Press, 2001, p.19.

10  Ibid., p. 19.

11  Ibid., p. 19.

12  Besides, I have already weighed in on the historicist side of this debate in Chapter 4.

13  I owe this point to Christopher Hitchen's new and insightful study of Jefferson. See his *Thomas Jefferson: Author of America*. New York: Harper and Collins, 1005, p. 18.

14  Because, however, Hegel was very much a metaphysician, in the sense noted here, when it came to Reason, he qualified his otherwise noteworthy endorsement of sport as an "organ of spirit" by ending this sentence with the following words: "even though in these contests [man] has not advanced to the highest grade of serious thought." G. W. F. Hegel. "The Philosophy of History." In C. J. Friedrich (ed.). *The Philosophy of Hegel*. New York: The Modern Library, 1954, p. 55.

15  Karl Marx. *Das Kapital: Volume Three*. New York: International Publishers, 1977, p. 820.

16  Marx makes this very point but suggests further that labor can cast its human spell over the "external natural urgencies" that give rise to labor in the first place by transforming them into human wants. As he writes, "certainly labour obtains its measure from the outside, through the aim to be attained and the obstacles to be overcome in attaining it. But this overcoming of obstacles is itself a liberating activity – and that, further the external natural urgencies become stripped of the semblance of merely external natural urgencies, and become posited as aims which the individual himself posits – hence as self-realization … real freedom whose action is, precisely, labour." *Grundrisse*. New York: Vintage Books, 1973, p. 611. Hegel and Marx may well disagree here, but if they do, it is irrelevant, or so I argue, to the point that both make here. Hegel could easily argue, for instance, that as these newly minted human wants take their measure and must do so from what were formerly "external natural urgencies," they are deficient in freedom in just the sense at issue: namely, those ends are not wholly human ones. I am not entirely sure what Marx might say in response, but given that even these human wants require that human agents treat them in an instrumental manner, they could not be regarded as ends-in-themselves, which in Marx's argument would itself be reason enough to exclude them from the realm of freedom.

17  My understanding of the role that Spirit plays in Hegel's immensely complicated philosophical system owes much to Terry Pinkard's magisterial book, *Hegel's Phenomenology: The Sociality of Reason*. New York: Cambridge University Press, 1996.

18  The inability to see or appreciate the point of this distinction between instrumental and game rationality is, of course, precisely the rational and normative bind in which

sports and the entire ensemble of cultural practices that fall under the realm of freedom find themselves today. That bind is not a simple Kantian one, an incoherence owed to an individual's failure to apply properly a moral law, but a pervasive social breakdown in our practical and normative reasoning owing to contradictions that reside in the social practice itself and the larger society in which it is situated. For an insightful discussion of the character of such breakdowns, see Terry Pinkard's excellent essay, "MacIntyre's Critique of Modernity." In M. Murphy (ed.). *Alasdair MacIntyre*. New York: Cambridge University, 2003.

19 G. W. F. Hegel. *Phenomenology of Spirit*. Translated by A. V. Miller. Oxford: Clarendon Press, 1977, p. 110.

20 The quote from Spinoza comes from Baier, which is referenced in the same part of the text I quote immediately after from Baier. For both references then, see Annette Baier, *Postures of the Mind*. Minneapolis. MN: University of Minnesota Press, 1985, p. 107.

21 That some things have the same value and meaning for people and that some others have not just the same meaning and value for people but further this sameness is acknowledged between them in public space is how Charles Taylor distinguishes between what he calls "convergent" and "common" matters. See his *Philosophical Arguments*. Cambridge, MA: Harvard University Press, 1995, pp. 139–40.

22 This is just one of the reasons why the taking of spectators to task for not being participants themselves, a constant refrain, or so it seems, in the history of sports, is so fundamentally misguided.

23 John Rawls. *A Theory of Justice*. Cambridge, MA: Harvard University Press, 1971, p. 525.

24 Ibid., p. 526.

25 Bernard Suits. *The Grasshopper: Games, Life and Utopia*. Toronto: University of Toronto Press, 1978, Chapter 3.

26 I should acknowledge that in the case of nondefective athletic games (i.e., games properly socially constructed such that the outcome is decided predominantly by skillful play rather than by chance) and in athletic games in good social working order (i.e., free of taints that might encourage, say, lopsided contests or drawing invidious contrasts between winners and losers), an authentically mutual commitment to the lusory goals of sports can scarcely be distinguished from a mutual commitment to a good game.

27 George Fletcher. "The Case for Linguistic Self-Defense." In R. McKim and J. McMahan (eds). *The Morality of Nationalism*. New York: Oxford University Press, 1997, p. 332. Partial confirmation of Fletcher's point is offered by Pieper's observation that "In the German-speaking world, fairness does not seem to be a philosophical concept, much less an ethico-philosophical concept." As quoted in Claudia Pawlenka. "The Idea of Fairness: A General Ethical Concept or One Particular to Sports Ethics." *Journal of the Philosophy of Sport*. XXXII (2005), p. 58.

28 John Stuart Mill. *On Liberty*. New York: Prometheus Books, 1986, p. 19.

29 My entire discussion here is heavily indebted to Walzer's account of a career open to talents in his book, *Thick and Thin: Moral Argument at Home and Abroad*. Notre Dame, IN: University of Notre Dame Press, 1994, pp. 22–5.

30 G. A. Cohen. *History, Labour, and Freedom*. Oxford: Clarendon Press, 1988, pp. 207–8.

31 Marx, *Grundrisse*, p. 611.

32 Walzer, *Thick and Thin*, p. 23.

33 Cohen, *History, Labour, and Freedom*, p. 208.

34 Ibid., p. 208.

35 That rowers have little if any chance of turning their craft into a money-making venture is the main reason why David Halberstam's book chronicling some of America's best Olympic oarsmen is titled, *The Amateurs: The Story of Four Young*

*Men and Their Quest for an Olympic Gold Medal.* New York: William and Morrow Co., 1985.

36  Karl Marx. *Das Kapital: Volume One.* New York: International Publishers, 1967, p. 41.

37  Wilfred Sheed, "Why Sports Matter." *Wilson Quarterly* (Winter, 1995), p. 65. See also Chapter 2 of the text, p. 58.

38  Ibid., p. 22.

39  Bernard Suits, *The Grasshopper: Games, Life and Utopia,* p. 172.

40  Charles Taylor. *The Ethics of Authenticity.* Cambridge, MA: Harvard University Press, 1992, p. 37.

41  Richard Rorty. *Contingency, Irony, and Solidarity.* New York: Cambridge University Press, 1989, p. 24. In fairness to Rorty, his own account of the strong poet is balanced against his equally robust defense of a public, political domain, one of the jobs of which is to ensure that this poetic self-overcoming does not get out of hand. Many of Rorty's epigones are not as careful as he is in this regard and as a result too frequently throw caution to the wind in singing the praises of the strong poet.

42  Terry Roberts, "Sport and Strong Poetry." *Journal of the Philosophy of Sport* (1995), Vol. XXII, p. 103.

43  Taylor, *The Ethics of Authenticity,* p. 36. I used Taylor's same argument, but not the same example, to press a similar point in Chapter 5, p. 201.

44  Ibid., p. 36.

45  Charles Taylor. "The Politics of Recognition." In A. Gutmann (ed.). *Multiculturalism and 'The Politics of Recognition.'* Princeton, NJ: Princeton University Press, 1992, p. 51.

46  David Miller. *Principles of Social Justice.* Cambridge, MA: Harvard University Press, 1999, p. 120, and Simon Keller, "Patriotism as Bad Faith." *Ethics* (April, 2005), Vol. 115, No. 3, pp. 578–9. The optional status of sports is also commonly alleged to follow from their place in the hallowed realm of freedom, a more than ironic claim as it leaves unexplained why sports are singled out here and such things as music or painting, established members of this same august domain, are not.

47  Keller, "Patriotism as Bad Faith," p. 579.

48  Ibid., p. 578.

49  That others are not intentionally deceived in both cases doesn't mean no deception is involved. Clearly, there is deception, but it is not directed at the other, as it is in lying, but in fact at the one presenting the case. But it is misleading to say the deception is aimed at the authors, for intentionality doesn't really play a role in these instances. What is going on in both cases is, as Keller notes, a case of what Sartre called "bad faith," in which, to quote Keller's quote of Sartre, "'I must know in my capacity as deceiver the truth which is hidden from me in my capacity as the one deceived." Keller, "Patriotism as Bad Faith," p.579

50  Miller, *Principles of Social Justice,* p. 120.

51  Annette Baier, *Postures of the Mind,* p. 93.

52  Ibid., p. 93.

53  This essay appears in a collection of his essays that bears the same title. Harry G. Frankfurt, *The Importance of What We Care About.* Cambridge: Cambridge University Press, 1995. My treatment of caring here borrows heavily from Frankfurt's important essay.

54  Ibid., p. 84.

55  Ibid., p. 84.

56  See our discussion of a "wanton" in Chapter 4 and to the citation to Korsgaard from which it is drawn.

57  Ibid., p. 84.

58  Frankfurt, *The Importance of What We Care About,* p. 93.

59  Taylor, *Ethics of Authenticity,* p. 40.

60  As just said, of course, that does not mean that settled traditions cannot be revisited and debated and argued about, nor does it entail that traditions cannot change the normative standards in which they once had confidence but no longer do. Nor does it cut off intercultural debate as to whose standards are normatively superior in certain circumstances. What it does preclude, however, is that we can decide any of these normative matters either individually or from some extracultural standpoint, because such issues are not at bottom either wholly subjective or wholly objective ones. The full arguments for these somewhat controversial claims can be found in my discussion of the ethical realm in Chapter 4.

61  Frankfurt also thinks that his sidewalk-averse walker is deluded but for a different reason. His charge that this person is deluded is not owed to the error that what he cares about is not important, as he does think that if he cares about it, it does very much matter to him. Rather, Frankfurt thinks that the walker is deluded because what he cares about is not "*worth* caring about" (my emphasis, p. 93), such that he should not have cared about it in the first place. So, for Frankfurt, the error is an evaluative one. However, this difference is not as large as it may at first seem, because Taylor's claim is also an evaluative one but one that he thinks, unlike Frankfurt, is embedded in the caring and importance connection itself, rather than the two-step process Frankfurt makes it out to be. Whereas, then, Taylor thinks that caring makes something important only if it passes evaluative muster by obtaining the concurrence of significant others, Frankfurt evidently holds that, first, we care about things and by virtue of doing so make them matter and then we evaluate whether what we regard as important by virtue of our caring about them really warrants such caring. Either way, both reject any purely subjective account of importance.

62  Joseph Raz. *The Practice of Value.* Oxford: Clarendon Press, 2003, p. 22.

63  Joseph Raz. *Value, Respect, and Attachment.* Cambridge: Cambridge University Press, 2001, pp. 161–3.

64  For an especially compelling argument that the notion of moral obligation has been given too much play in philosophical ethics, see Bernard Williams, *Ethics and the Limits of Philosophy.* Cambridge, MA: Harvard University Press, 1985.

65  As Raz notes in this regard, reasons of respect are in one sense more basic than reasons of engagement when it comes to value, as "there is a general reason to preserve what is of value." That means, for example, that though "Not everyone has much time for Picasso's paintings ... no one should destroy them, or treat them in ways inconsistent with the fact that they are aesthetically valuable." *Value, Respect, and Attachment*, pp. 162–164. The same, of course, would go for sports in a culture such as ours, where they are highly valued by many.

66  Christine M. Korsgaard. *The Sources of Normativity.* Cambridge: Cambridge University Press, 1996, p. 101.

67  Frankfurt, *The Importance of What We Care About*, p. 86.

68  Ibid., p. 86.

69  Korsgaard, *Sources of Normativity*, p. 18. I had occasion to speak of this in Chapter 4 as well, when a person's peers make one, in effect, an outcast, not one of us, owing to ethical misdeeds on our part.

70  Nicholas Dixon, "The Ethics of Supporting Sports Teams," *Journal of Applied Philosophy* (2001), Vol. 18, No. 2, pp. 151–2.

71  Thomas Scanlon. "Contractualism and Utilitarianism." In A. Sen and B. Williams (eds). *Utilitarianism and Beyond.* Cambridge: Cambridge University Press, 1982, p. 104.

72  Gerald Graff, "Hidden Intellectualism," *Pedagogy: Critical Approaches to Teaching Literature, Language, Composition, and Culture*, Vol. 1, No. 1 (2001), p. 27. It will be remembered as well, I trust, that Mason Marzac, the unlikely fictional hero of Greenberg's satirical text *Take Me Out* that I discussed in the Introduction, was similarly motivated "to engage in a learned debate" with his mates over last night's

game. See my Introduction, p. 12, and Greenberg, *Take Me Out*. New York: Faber & Faber, 2003, p. 140.

73 To see just how badly and wrong they can go, see Suits, *The Grasshopper: Games, Life and Utopia*, pp. 27–8.

74 Ibid., p. 166.

75 Allen Guttmann, "The Belated Birth and Threatened Death of Fair Play." *The Yale Review* (1985), 94, pp. 531–2.

76 Ibid., pp. 532, 535. Walzer points out here that any strong emotional commitment was considered a threat to the social stability and political order needed for the exercise of the gentlemanly virtues. Michael Walzer, *Politics and Passion*. New Haven, CT: Yale University Press, 2004, p. 116.

77 Guttmann, "The Belated Birth and Threatened Death of Fair Play," p. 526. For an alternative account of fairness in Greek sports see Matthew Dickie, "Fair and Foul in the Funeral Games in the Iliad." *Journal of Sport History* (Summer, 1984), Vol. 11, No. 2.

78 Matthew 20:1–16.

79 Of course, the central precepts of Christianity were by and large contemptuous of such bodily practices as sports, as they were of people's concern for their public reputations, of seeking the good opinion of others in public settings. Seeking such a reputation is, of course, crucial to modern sports but for many Christians is regarded as a sin of pride.

80 Charles Taylor, "Comment on Jürgen Habermas 'From Kant to Hegel and Back.'" *European Journal of Philosophy* (1999), Vol. 7, No. 2, pp. 161–3.

81 Ibid., p. 162.

82 This is a slightly misleading way of putting it, as it is slightly simplistic. For many people agree on such basic concepts as gender equality and nondiscrimination in the workplace but disagree widely on their differing conceptions of these notions (i.e., on how to remedy them). This would explain the otherwise curious fact of how people who all say that they favor gender equality seem to disagree so strongly on their varying conceptions of how to achieve it. However, this point does not, I believe, cause problems for Taylor's main claim here.

83 Ibid., p. 162. That does not mean that some will not try to turn back the clock, as continues to happen with Title IX, or even that some of these efforts at reversal will not succeed, but it does mean they will not be able to rely on the old, defeated arguments to do so. That means that here will always be reason to be vigilant as the losers of these important arguments search for ingenious ways to reverse their losses, which is why if what the *New York Times* and other newspapers of similar rank are presently reporting is accurate, we need to keep a close eye on the more recent and more clever proponents of so-termed "creationism."

# Index